CHANGE AND TRADITION

Revolutionary Europe and Colonial Nigeria

Global and Historical Studies Program,
Butler University

Learning Solutions

New York   Boston   San Francisco
London   Toronto   Sydney   Tokyo   Singapore   Madrid
Mexico City   Munich   Paris   Cape Town   Hong Kong   Montreal

Cover Art:
Heading of the Abiku Children, by Twins Seven Seven (Taiwo Olaniyi Oyewale), 1973, courtesy of the Indianapolis Museum of Art.

Liberty Leading the People, by Eugene Delacroix, 1830, courtesy of Erich Lessing/Art Resource, NY.

All readings have been selected by the Butler University Change and Tradition faculty. Editorial decisions were made by Faculty Coordinator David Mason and Program Coordinator Elizabeth Barrett. Introductions written by Change and Tradition staff members are followed by the writers' names. Introductions without attribution are taken from the publications in which the selections originally appeared.

Pearson Learning Solutions, 501 Boylston Street, Suite 900, Boston, MA 02116
A Pearson Education Company
www.pearsoned.com

Printed in the United States of America

23 2020

2009440034

LB/JR

ISBN 10: 0-558-56483-6
ISBN 13: 978-0-558-56483-4

CONTENTS

Revolutionary Europe, 1789–1989

John Locke

1632–1704

▣ *John Locke was an English Enlightenment philosopher who advocated government by consent of the people and mankind's "natural rights" of life, liberty and property. His most influential works were his two treatises* On Civil Government, *published just after the "Glorious Revolution" of 1688–89 in Britain. During this bloodless revolt, Parliament forced the resignation of King James II, and installed William and Mary on the throne, accompanied by a "Bill of Rights" that sharply circumscribed monarchical powers. In his* Second Treatise, *excerpted here, Locke asserts his beliefs in popular government, equality, natural rights and private property.*

David Mason

From The Second Treatise of Civil Government, 1690

John Locke

Preface

Reader, thou hast here the beginning and end of a discourse concerning government; what fate has otherwise disposed of the papers that should have filled up the middle, and were more than all the rest, it is not worth while to tell thee. These, which remain, I hope are sufficient to establish the throne of our great restorer, our present King William; to make good his title, in the consent of the people, which being the only one of all lawful governments, he has more fully and clearly, than any prince in Christendom; and to justify to the world the people of England, whose love of their just

Reprinted from *The Second Treatise of John Locke,* (1690).

and natural rights, with their resolution to preserve them, saved the nation when it was on the very brink of slavery and ruin. If these papers have that evidence, I flatter myself is to be found in them, there will be no great miss of those which are lost, and my reader may be satisfied without them: for I imagine, I shall have neither the time, nor inclination to repeat my pains, and fill up the wanting part of my answer, by tracing Sir Robert again, through all the windings and obscurities, which are to be met with in the several branches of his wonderful system. The king, and body of the nation, have since so thoroughly confuted his Hypothesis, that I suppose no body hereafter will have either the confidence to appear against our common safety, and be again an advocate for slavery; or the weakness to be deceived with contradictions dressed up in a popular stile, and well-turned periods: for if any one will be at the pains, himself, in those parts, which are here untouched, to strip Sir Robert's discourses of the flourish of doubtful expressions, and endeavour to reduce his words to direct, positive, intelligible propositions, and then compare them one with another, he will quickly be satisfied, there was never so much glib nonsense put together in well-sounding English. If he think it not worth while to examine his works all thro', let him make an experiment in that part, where he treats of usurpation; and let him try, whether he can, with all his skill, make Sir Robert intelligible, and consistent with himself, or common sense. I should not speak so plainly of a gentleman, long since past answering, had not the pulpit, of late years, publicly owned his doctrine, and made it the current divinity of the times. It is necessary those men, who taking on them to be teachers, have so dangerously misled others, should be openly shewed of what authority this their Patriarch is, whom they have so blindly followed, that so they may either retract what upon so ill grounds they have vented, and cannot be maintained; or else justify those principles which they preached up for gospel; though they had no better an author than an English courtier: for I should not have writ against Sir Robert, or taken the pains to shew his mistakes, inconsistencies, and want of (what he so much boasts of, and pretends wholly to build on) scripture-proofs, were there not men amongst us, who, by crying up his books, and espousing his doctrine, save me from the reproach of writing against a dead adversary. They have been so zealous in this point, that, if I have done him any wrong, I cannot hope they should spare me. I wish, where they have done the truth and the public wrong, they would be as ready to redress it, and allow its just weight to this reflection, viz. that there cannot be done a greater mischief to prince and people, than the propagating wrong notions concerning government; that so at last all times might not have reason to complain of the Drum Ecclesiastic. If any one, concerned really for truth, undertake the confutation of my Hypothesis, I promise him either to recant my mistake, upon fair conviction; or to answer his difficulties. But he must remember two things.

First, That cavilling here and there, at some expression, or little incident of my discourse, is not an answer to my book.

Secondly, That I shall not take railing for arguments, nor think either of these worth my notice, though I shall always look on myself as bound to give satisfaction to any one, who shall appear to be conscientiously scrupulous in the point, and shall shew any just grounds for his scruples.

I have nothing more, but to advertise the reader, that Observations stands for Observations on Hobbs, Milton, &c. and that a bare quotation of pages always means pages of his Patriarcha, Edition 1680.

Of Civil-Government
Book II

Chap. I.

Sec. 1. It having been shewn in the foregoing discourse,

1. That Adam had not, either by natural right of fatherhood, or by positive donation from God, any such authority over his children, or dominion over the world, as is pretended:

2. That if he had, his heirs, yet, had no right to it:

3. That if his heirs had, there being no law of nature nor positive law of God that determines which is the right heir in all cases that may arise, the right of succession, and consequently of bearing rule, could not have been certainly determined:

4. That if even that had been determined, yet the knowledge of which is the eldest line of Adam's posterity, being so long since utterly lost, that in the races of mankind and families of the world, there remains not to one above another, the least pretence to be the eldest house, and to have the right of inheritance:

All these premises having, as I think, been clearly made out, it is impossible that the rulers now on earth should make any benefit, or derive any the least shadow of authority from that, which is held to be the fountain of all power, Adam's private dominion and paternal jurisdiction; so that he that will not give just occasion to think that all government in the world is the product only of force and violence, and that men live together by no other rules but that of beasts, where the strongest carries it, and so lay a foundation for perpetual disorder and mischief, tumult, sedition and rebellion, (things that the followers of that hypothesis so loudly cry out against) must of necessity find out another rise of government, another original of political power, and another way of designing and knowing the persons that have it, than what Sir Robert Filmer hath taught us.

Sec. 2. To this purpose, I think it may not be amiss, to set down what I take to be political power; that the power of a magistrate over a subject may be distinguished from that of a father over his children, a master over his servant, a husband over his wife, and a lord over his slave. All which distinct powers happening sometimes together in the same man, if he be considered under these different relations, it may help us to distinguish these powers one from wealth, a father of a family, and a captain of a galley.

Sec. 3. Political power, then, I take to be a right of making laws with penalties of death, and consequently all less penalties, for the regulating and preserving of property, and of employing the force of the community, in the execution of such laws, and in the defence of the common-wealth from foreign injury; and all this only for the public good.

Chap. II.

Of the State of Nature.

Sec. 4. To understand political power right, and derive it from its original, we must consider, what state all men are naturally in, and that is, a state of perfect freedom to order their actions, and dispose of their possessions and persons, as they think fit, within the bounds of the law of nature, without asking leave, or depending upon the will of any other man.

A state also of equality, wherein all the power and jurisdiction is reciprocal, no one having more than another; there being nothing more evident, than that creatures of the same species and rank, promiscuously born to all the same advantages of nature, and the use of the same faculties, should also be equal one amongst another without subordination or subjection, unless the lord and master of them all should, by any manifest declaration of his will, set one above another, and confer on him, by an evident and clear appointment, an undoubted right to dominion and sovereignty.

Sec. 5. This equality of men by nature, the judicious Hooker looks upon as so evident in itself, and beyond all question, that he makes it the foundation of that obligation to mutual love amongst men, on which he builds the duties they owe one another, and from whence he derives the great maxims of justice and charity. His words are,

"The like natural inducement hath brought men to know that it is no less their duty, to love others than themselves; for seeing those things which are equal, must needs all have one measure; if I cannot but wish to receive good, even as much at every man's hands, as any man can wish unto his own soul, how should I look to have any part of my desire herein satisfied, unless myself be careful to satisfy the like desire, which is undoubtedly in other men, being of one and the same nature? To have any thing offered them repugnant to this desire, must needs in all respects grieve them as much as me; so that if I do harm, I must look to suffer, there being no reason that others should shew greater measure of love to me, than they have by me shewed unto them: my desire therefore to be loved of my equals in nature as much as possible may be, imposeth upon me a natural duty of bearing to themward fully the like affection; from which relation of equality between ourselves and them that are as ourselves, what several rules and canons natural reason hath drawn, for direction of life, no man is ignorant, Eccl. Pol. Lib. 1 ."

Sec. 6. But though this be a state of liberty, yet it is not a state of licence: though man in that state have an uncontroulable liberty to dispose of his person or possessions, yet he has not liberty to destroy himself, or so much as any creature in his possession, but where some nobler use than its bare preservation calls for it. The state of nature has a law of nature to govern it, which obliges every one: and reason, which is that law, teaches all mankind, who will but consult it, that being all equal and independent, no one ought to harm another in his life, health, liberty, or possessions: for men being all the workmanship of one omnipotent, and infinitely wise maker; all the servants of one sovereign master, sent into the world by his order, and about his business; they are his property, whose workmanship they are, made to last during his, not one another's pleasure: and being furnished with like faculties, sharing all in one community of nature, there cannot be supposed any such subordination among us, that may authorize us to destroy one another, as if we were made for one another's uses, as the inferior ranks of creatures are for our's. Every one, as he is bound to preserve himself, and not to quit his station wilfully, so by the like reason, when his own preservation comes not in competition, ought he, as much as he can, to preserve the rest of mankind, and may not, unless it be to do justice on an offender, take away, or impair the life, or what tends to the preservation of the life, the liberty, health, limb, or goods of another.

Sec. 7. And that all men may be restrained from invading others rights, and from doing hurt to one another, and the law of nature be observed, which willeth the peace and preservation of all mankind, the execution of the law of nature is, in that state, put into every man's hands, whereby every one has a right to punish the transgressors of that law to such a degree, as may hinder its violation: for the law of nature would, as all other laws that concern men in this world be in vain, if there were no body that in the state of nature had a power to execute that law, and thereby preserve the innocent and restrain offenders. And if any one in the state of nature may punish another for any evil he has done, every one may do so: for in that state of perfect equality, where naturally there is no superiority or jurisdiction of one over another, what any may do in prosecution of that law, every one must needs have a right to do.

Sec. 8. And thus, in the state of nature, one man comes by a power over another; but yet no absolute or arbitrary power, to use a criminal, when he has got him in his hands, according to the passionate heats, or boundless extravagancy of his own will; but only to retribute to him, so far as calm reason and conscience dictate, what is proportionate to his transgression, which is so much as may serve for reparation and restraint: for these two are the only reasons, why one man may lawfully do harm to another, which is that we call punishment. In transgressing the law of nature, the offender declares himself to live by another rule than that of reason and common equity, which is that measure God has set to the actions of men, for their mutual security; and so he becomes dangerous to mankind, the tye, which is to secure them from injury and violence, being slighted and broken by him. Which being a trespass against the whole species, and the peace and safety of it, provided for by the law of nature, every man upon this score, by the right he hath to preserve mankind in general, may restrain, or where it is necessary, destroy things noxious to them, and so may bring such evil on any one, who hath transgressed that law, as may make him repent the doing of it, and thereby deter him, and by his example others, from doing the like mischief. And in the case, and upon this ground, every man hath a right to punish the offender, and be executioner of the law of nature.

Sec. 9. I doubt not but this will seem a very strange doctrine to some men: but before they condemn it, I desire them to resolve me, by what right any prince or state can put to death, or punish an alien, for any crime he commits in their country. It is certain their laws, by virtue of any sanction they receive from the promulgated will of the legislative, reach not a stranger: they speak not to him, nor, if they did, is he bound to hearken to them. The legislative authority, by which they are in force over the subjects of that commonwealth, hath no power over him. Those who have the supreme power of making laws in England, France or Holland, are to an Indian, but like the rest of the world, men without authority: and therefore, if by the law of nature every man hath not a power to punish offences against it, as he soberly judges the case to require, I see not how the magistrates of any community can punish an alien of another country; since, in reference to him, they can have no more power than what every man naturally may have over another.

Sec. 10. Besides the crime which consists in violating the law, and varying from the right rule of reason, whereby a man so far becomes degenerate, and declares himself to quit the principles of human nature, and to be a noxious creature, there is commonly injury done to some person or other, and some other man receives damage by his transgression: in which case he who hath received any damage, has, besides the right of punishment common to him with other men, a particular right to seek reparation from him that has done it: and any other person, who finds it just, may also join with him that is injured, and assist him in recovering from the offender so much as may make satisfaction for the harm he has suffered.

Sec. 11. From these two distinct rights, the one of punishing the crime for restraint, and preventing the like offence, which right of punishing is in every body; the other of taking reparation, which belongs only to the injured party, comes it to pass that the magistrate, who by being magistrate hath the common right of punishing put into his hands, can often, where the public good demands not the execution of the law, remit the punishment of criminal offences by his own authority, but yet cannot remit the satisfaction due to any private man for the damage he has received. That, he who has suffered the damage has a right to demand in his own name, and he alone can remit: the damnified person has this power of appropriating to himself the goods or service of the offender, by right of self-preservation, as every man has a power to punish the crime, to prevent its being committed again, by the right he has of preserving all mankind, and doing all reasonable things he can in order to that end: and thus it is, that every man, in the state of nature, has a power to kill a murderer, both to deter others from doing the like injury, which no reparation can compensate, by the example of the punishment that attends it from every body, and also to secure men from the attempts of a criminal, who having renounced reason, the common rule and measure God hath given to mankind, hath, by the unjust violence and slaughter he hath committed upon one, declared war against all mankind, and therefore may be destroyed as a lion or a tyger, one of those wild savage beasts, with whom men can have no society nor security: and upon this is grounded that great law of nature, Whoso sheddeth man's blood, by man shall his blood be shed. And Cain was so fully convinced, that every one had a right to destroy such a criminal, that after the murder of his brother, he cries out, Every one that findeth me, shall slay me; so plain was it writ in the hearts of all mankind.

Sec. 12. By the same reason may a man in the state of nature punish the lesser breaches of that law. It will perhaps be demanded, with death? I answer, each transgression may be punished to that degree, and with so much severity, as will suffice to make it an ill bargain to the offender, give him cause to repent, and terrify others from doing the like. Every offence, that can be committed in the state of nature, may in the state of nature be also punished equally, and as far forth as it may, in a commonwealth: for though it would be besides my present purpose, to enter here into the particulars of the law of nature, or its measures of punishment; yet, it is certain there is such a law, and that too, as intelligible and plain to a rational creature, and a studier of that law, as the positive laws of commonwealths; nay, possibly plainer; as much as reason is easier to be understood, than the fancies and intricate contrivances of men, following contrary and hidden interests put into words; for so truly are a great part of the municipal laws of countries, which are only so far right, as they are founded on the law of nature, by which they are to be regulated and interpreted.

Sec. 13. To this strange doctrine, viz. That in the state of nature every one has the executive power of the law of nature, I doubt not but it will be objected, that it is unreasonable for men to be judges in their own cases, that selflove will make men partial to themselves and their friends: and on the other side, that ill nature, passion and revenge will carry them too far in punishing others; and hence nothing but confusion and disorder will follow, and that therefore God hath certainly appointed government to restrain the partiality and violence of men. I easily grant, that civil government is the proper remedy for the inconveniencies of the state of nature, which must certainly be great, where men may be judges in their own case, since it is easy to be imagined, that he who was so unjust as to do his brother an injury, will scarce be so just as to condemn himself for it: but I shall desire those who make this objection, to remember, that absolute monarchs are but men; and if government is to be the remedy of those evils, which necessarily follow from men's being judges in their own cases, and the state of nature is therefore not to how much better it is than the state of nature, where one man, commanding a multitude, has the liberty to be judge in his own case, and may do to all his subjects whatever he pleases, without the least liberty to any one to question or controul those who execute his pleasure and in whatsoever he cloth, whether led by reason, mistake or passion, must be submitted to much better it is in the state of nature, wherein men are not bound to submit to the unjust will of another: and if he that judges, judges amiss in his own, or any other case, he is answerable for it to the rest of mankind.

Sec. 14. It is often asked as a mighty objection, where are, or ever were there any men in such a state of nature? To which it may suffice as an answer at present, that since all princes and rulers of independent governments all through the world, are in a state of nature, it is plain the world never was, nor ever will be, without numbers of men in that state. I have named all governors of independent communities, whether they are, or are not, in league with others: for it is not every compact that puts an end to the state of nature between men, but only this one of agreeing together mutually to enter into one community, and make one body politic; other promises, and compacts, men may make one with another, and yet still be in the state of nature. The promises and bargains for truck, &c. between the two men in the desert island, mentioned by Garcilasso de la Vega, in his history of Peru; or between a Swiss and an Indian, in the woods of America, are binding to them, though they are perfectly in a state of nature, in reference to one another: for truth and keeping of faith belongs to men, as men, and not as members of society.

Sec. 15. To those that say, there were never any men in the state of nature, I will not only oppose the authority of the judicious Hooker, Eccl. Pol. lib. i. sect. 10, where he says, The laws which have been hitherto mentioned, i.e. the laws of nature, do bind men absolutely, even as they are men, although they have never any settled fellowship, never any solemn agreement amongst themselves what to do, or not to do: but forasmuch as we are not by ourselves sufficient to furnish ourselves with competent store of things, needful for such a life as our nature doth desire, a life fit for the dignity of man; therefore to supply those defects and imperfections which are in us, as living single and solely by ourselves, we are naturally induced to seek communion and fellowship with others: this was the cause of men's uniting themselves at first in politic societies. But I moreover affirm, that all men are naturally in that state, and remain so, till by their own consents they make themselves members of some politic society; and I doubt not in the sequel of this discourse, to make it very clear.

Chap. III.

Of the State of War.

Sec. 16. The state of war is a state of enmity and destruction: and therefore declaring by word or action, not a passionate and hasty, but a sedate settled design upon another man's life, puts him in a state of war with him against whom he has declared such an intention, and so has exposed his life to the other's power to be taken away by him, or any one that joins with him in his defence, and espouses his quarrel; it being reasonable and just, I should have a right to destroy that which threatens me with destruction: for, by the fundamental law of nature, man being to be preserved as much as possible, when all cannot be preserved, the safety of the innocent is to be preferred: and one may destroy a man who makes war upon him, or has discovered an enmity to his being, for the same reason that he may kill a wolf or a lion; because such men are not under the ties of the commonlaw of reason, have no other rule, but that of force and violence, and so may be treated as beasts of prey, those dangerous and noxious creatures, that will be sure to destroy him whenever he falls into their power.

Sec. 17. And hence it is, that he who attempts to get another man into his absolute power, does thereby put himself into a state of war with him; it being to be understood as a declaration of a design upon his life: for I have reason to conclude, that he who would get me into his power without my consent, would use me as he pleased when he had got me there, and destroy me too when he had a fancy to it; for no body can desire to have me in his absolute power, unless it be to compel me by force to that which is against the right of my freedom, i.e. make me a slave. To be free from such force is the only security of my preservation; and reason bids me look on him, as an enemy to my preservation, who would take away that freedom which is the fence to it; so that he who makes an attempt to enslave me, thereby puts himself into a state of war with me. He that, in the state of nature, would take away the freedom that belongs to any one in that state, must necessarily be supposed to have a design to take away everything else, that freedom being the foundation of all the rest; as he that in the state of society would take away the freedom belonging to those of that society or commonwealth, must be supposed to design to take away from them every thing else, and so be looked on as in a state of war.

Sec. 18. This makes it lawful for a man to kill a thief, who has not in the least hurt him, nor declared any design upon his life, any farther than, by the use of force, so to get him in his power, as to take away his money, or what he pleases, from him; because using force, where he has no right, to get me into his power, let his pretence be what it will, I have no reason to suppose, that he, who would take away my liberty, would not, when he had me in his power, take away every thing else. And therefore it is lawful for me to treat him as one who has put himself into a state of war with me, i.e. kill him if I can; for to that hazard does he justly expose himself, whoever introduces a state of war, and is aggressor in it.

Sec. 19. And here we have the plain difference between the state of nature and the state of war, which however some men have confounded, are as far distant, as a state of peace, good will, mutual assistance and preservation, and a state of enmity, malice, violence and mutual destruction, are one from another. Men living together according to reason, without a common superior on earth, with authority to judge between them, is properly the state of nature. But force, or a declared design of force, upon the person of another, where there is no common superior on earth to appeal to for relief, is the state of war: and it is the want of such an appeal gives a man the right of war even against an aggressor, tho' he be in society and a fellow subject. Thus a thief, whom I cannot harm, but by appeal to the law, for having stolen all that I am worth, I may kill, when he sets on me to rob me but of my horse or coat; because the law, which was made for my preservation, where it cannot interpose to secure my life from present force, which, if lost, is capable of no reparation, permits me my own defence, and the right of war, a liberty to kill the aggressor, because the aggressor allows not time to appeal to our common judge, nor the decision of the law, for remedy in a case where the mischief may be irreparable. Want of a common judge with authority, puts all men in a state of nature: force without right, upon a man's person, makes a state of war, both where there is, and is not, a common judge.

Sec. 20. But when the actual force is over, the state of war ceases between those that are in society, and are equally on both sides subjected to the fair determination of the law; because then there lies open the remedy of appeal for the past injury, and to prevent future harm: but where no such appeal is, as in the state of nature, for want of positive laws, and judges with authority to appeal to, the state of war once begun, continues, with a right to the innocent party to destroy the other whenever he can, until the aggressor offers peace, and desires reconciliation on such terms as may repair any wrongs he has already done, and secure the innocent for the future; nay, where an appeal to the law, and constituted judges, lies open, but the remedy is denied by a manifest perverting of justice, and a barefaced wresting of the laws to protect or indemnify the violence or injuries of some men, or party of men, there it is hard to imagine any thing but a state of war: for wherever violence is used, and injury done, though by hands appointed to administer justice, it is still violence and injury, however coloured with the name, pretences, or forms of law, the end whereof being to protect and redress the innocent, by an unbiassed application of it, to all who are under it; wherever that is not bona fide done, war is made upon the sufferers, who having no appeal on earth to right them, they are left to the only remedy in such cases, an appeal to heaven.

Sec. 21. To avoid this state of war (wherein there is no appeal but to heaven, and wherein every the least difference is apt to end, where there is no authority to decide between the contenders) is one great reason of men's putting themselves into society, and quitting the state of nature: for where there is an authority, a power on earth, from which relief can be had by appeal, there the continuance of the state of war is excluded, and the controversy is decided by that power. Had there been any such court, any superior jurisdiction on earth, to determine the right between Jephtha and the Ammonites, they had never come to a state of war: but we see he was forced to appeal to heaven. The Lord the Judge (says he) be judge this day between the children of Israel and the children of Ammon, Judg. xi. 27. and then prosecuting, and relying on his appeal, he leads out his army to battle: and therefore in such controversies, where the question is put, who shall be judge? It cannot be meant, who shall decide the controversy; every one knows what Jephtha here tells us, that the Lord the Judge shall judge. Where there is no judge on earth, the appeal lies to God in heaven. That question then cannot mean, who shall judge, whether another hath put himself in a state of war with me, and whether I may, as Jephtha did, appeal to heaven in it? of that I myself can only be judge in my own conscience, as I will answer it, at the great day, to the supreme judge of all men.

Chap. IV.

Of Slavery.

Sec. 22. The natural liberty of man is to be free from any superior power on earth, and not to be under the will or legislative authority of man, but to have only the law of nature for his rule. The liberty of man, in society, is to be under no other legislative power, but that established, by consent, in the commonwealth; nor under the dominion of any will, or restraint of any law, but what that legislative shall enact, according to the trust put in it. Freedom then is not what Sir Robert Filmer tells us, Observations, A. 55. a liberty for every one to do what he lists, to live as he pleases, and not to be tied by any laws: but freedom of men under government is, to have a standing rule to live by, common to every one of that society, and made by the legislative power erected in it; a liberty to follow my own will in all things, where the rule prescribes not; and not to be subject to the inconstant, uncertain, unknown, arbitrary will of another man: as freedom of nature is, to be under no other restraint but the law of nature.

Sec. 23. This freedom from absolute, arbitrary power, is so necessary to, and closely joined with a man's preservation, that he cannot part with it, but by what forfeits his preservation and life together: for a man, not having the power of his own life, cannot, by compact, or his own consent, enslave himself to any one, nor put himself under the absolute, arbitrary power of another, to take away his life, when he pleases. No body can give more power than he has himself; and he that cannot take away his own life, cannot give another power over it. Indeed, having by his fault forfeited his own life, by some act that deserves death; he, to whom he has forfeited it, may (when he has him in his power) delay to take it, and make use of him to his own service, and he does him no injury by it: for, whenever he finds the hardship of his slavery outweigh the value of his life, it is in his power, by resisting the will of his master, to draw on himself the death he desires.

Sec. 24. This is the perfect condition of slavery, which is nothing else, but the state of war continued, between a lawful conqueror and a captive: for, if once compact enter between them, and make an agreement for a limited power on the one side, and obedience on the other, the state of war and slavery ceases, as long as the compact endures: for, as has been said, no man can, by agreement, pass over to another that which he hath not in himself, a power over his own life.

I confess, we find among the Jews, as well as other nations, that men did sell themselves; but, it is plain, this was only to drudgery, not to slavery: for, it is evident, the person sold was not under an absolute, arbitrary, despotical power: for the master could not have power to kill him, at any time, whom, at a certain time, he was obliged to let go free out of his service; and the master of such a servant was so far from having an arbitrary power over his life, that he could not, at pleasure, so much as maim him, but the loss of an eye, or tooth, set him free, Exod. xxi.

Chap. V.

Of Property.

Sec. 25. Whether we consider natural reason, which tells us, that men, being once born, have a right to their preservation, and consequently to meat and drink, and such other things as nature affords for their subsistence: or revelation, which gives us an account of those grants God made of the world to Adam, and to Noah, and his sons, it is very clear, that God, as king David says, Psal. cxv. 16. has given the earth to the children of men; given it to mankind in common. But this being supposed, it seems to some a very great difficulty, how any one should ever come to have a property in any thing: I will not content myself to answer, that if it be difficult to make out property, upon a supposition that God gave the world to Adam, and his posterity in common, it is impossible that any man, but one universal monarch, should have any property upon a supposition, that God gave the world to Adam, and his heirs in succession, exclusive of all the rest of his posterity. But I shall endeavour to shew, how men might come to have a property in several parts of that which God gave to mankind in common, and that without any express compact of all the commoners.

Sec. 26. God, who hath given the world to men in common, hath also given them reason to make use of it to the best advantage of life, and convenience. The earth, and all that is therein, is given to men for the support and comfort of their being. And tho' all the fruits it naturally produces, and beasts it feeds, belong to mankind in common, as they are produced by the spontaneous hand of nature; and no body has originally a private dominion, exclusive of the rest of mankind, in any of them, as they are thus in their natural state: yet being given for the use of men, there must of necessity be a means to appropriate them some way or other, before they can be of any use, or at all beneficial to any particular man. The fruit, or venison, which nourishes the wild Indian, who knows no enclosure, and is still a tenant in common, must be his, and so his, i.e. a part of him, that another can no longer have any right to it, before it can do him any good for the support of his life.

Sec. 27. Though the earth, and all inferior creatures, be common to all men, yet every man has a property in his own person: this no body has any right to but himself. The labour of his body, and the work of his hands, we may say, are properly his. Whatsoever then he removes out of the state that nature hath provided, and left it in, he hath mixed his labour with, and joined to it something that is his own, and thereby makes it his property. It being by him removed from the common state nature hath placed it in, it hath by this labour something annexed to it, that excludes the common right of other men: for this labour being the unquestionable property of the labourer, no man but he can have a right to what that is once joined to, at least where there is enough, and as good, left in common for others.

Sec. 28. He that is nourished by the acorns he picked up under an oak, or the apples he gathered from the trees in the wood, has certainly appropriated them to himself. No body can deny but the nourishment is his. I ask then, when did they begin to be his? when he digested? or when he eat? or when he boiled? or when he brought them home? or when he picked them up? and it is plain, if the first gathering made them not his, nothing else could. That labour put a distinction between them and common: that added something to them more than nature, the common mother of all, had done; and so they became his private right. And will any one say, he had no right to those acorns or apples, he thus appropriated, because he had not the consent of all mankind to make them his? Was it a robbery thus to assume to himself what belonged to all in common? If such a consent as that was necessary, man had starved, notwithstanding the plenty God had given him. We see in commons, which remain so by compact, that it is the taking any part of what is common, and removing it out of the state nature leaves it in, which begins the property; without which the common is of no use. And the taking of this or that part, does not depend on the express consent of all the commoners. Thus the grass my horse has bit; the turfs my servant has cut; and the ore I have digged in any place, where I have a right to them in common with others, become my property, without the assignation or consent of any body. The labour that was mine, removing them out of that common state they were in, hath fixed my property in them.

Sec. 29. By making an explicit consent of every commoner, necessary to any one's appropriating to himself any part of what is given in common, children or servants could not cut the meat, which their father or master had provided for them in common, without assigning to every one his peculiar part. Though the water running in the fountain be every one's, yet who can doubt, but that in the pitcher is his only who drew it out? His labour hath taken it out of the hands of nature, where it was common, and belonged equally to all her children, and hath thereby appropriated it to himself.

Sec. 30. Thus this law of reason makes the deer that Indian's who hath killed it; it is allowed to be his goods, who hath bestowed his labour upon it, though before it was the common right of every one. And amongst those who are counted the civilized part of mankind, who have made and multiplied positive laws to determine property, this original law of nature, for the beginning of property, in what was before common, still takes place; and by virtue thereof, what fish any one catches in the ocean, that great and still remaining common of mankind; or what ambergrise any one takes up here, is by the labour that removes it out of that common state nature left it in, made his property, who takes that pains about it. And even amongst us, the hare that any one is hunting, is thought his who pursues her during the chase: for being a beast that is still looked upon as common, and no man's private possession; whoever has employed so much labour about any of that kind, as to find and pursue her, has thereby removed her from the state of nature, wherein she was common, and hath begun a property.

Sec. 31. It will perhaps be objected to this, that if gathering the acorns, or other fruits of the earth, &c. makes a right to them, then any one may ingross as much as he will. To which I answer, Not so. The same law of nature, that does by this means give us property, does also bound that property too. God has given us all things richly, 1 Tim. vi. 12. is the voice of reason confirmed by inspiration. But how far has he given it us? To enjoy. As much as any one can make use of to any advantage of life before it spoils, so much he may by his Labour fix a property in: whatever is beyond this, is more than his share, and belongs to others. Nothing was made by God for man to spoil or destroy. And thus, considering the plenty of natural provisions there was a long time in the world, and the few spenders; and to how small a part of that provision the industry of one man could extend itself, and ingross it to the prejudice of others; especially keeping within the bounds, set by reason, of what might serve for his use; there could be then little room for quarrels or contentions about property so established.

Sec. 32. But the chief matter of property being now not the fruits of the earth, and the beasts that subsist on it, but the earth itself; as that which takes in and carries with it all the rest; I think it is plain, that property in that too is acquired as the former. As much land as a man tills, plants, improves, cultivates, and can use the product of, so much is his property. He by his labour does, as it were, inclose it from the common. Nor will it invalidate his right, to say every body else has an equal title to it; and therefore he cannot appropriate, he cannot inclose, without the consent of all his fellow-commoners, all mankind. God, when he gave the world in common to all mankind, commanded man also to labour, and the penury of his condition required it of him. God and his reason commanded him to subdue the earth, i.e. improve it for the benefit of life, and therein lay out something upon it that was his own, his labour. He that in obedience to this command of God, subdued, tilled and sowed any part of it, thereby annexed to it something that was his property, which another had no title to, nor could without injury take from him.

Sec. 33. Nor was this appropriation of any parcel of land, by improving it, any prejudice to any other man, since there was still enough, and as good left; and more than the yet unprovided could use. So that, in effect, there was never the less left for others because of his enclosure for himself: for he that leaves as much as another can make use of, does as good as take nothing at all. No body could think himself injured by the drinking of another man, though he took a good draught, who had a whole river of the same water left him to quench his thirst: and the case of land and water, where there is enough of both, is perfectly the same.

Sec. 34. God gave the world to men in common; but since he gave it them for their benefit, and the greatest conveniencies of life they were capable to draw from it, it cannot be supposed he meant it should always remain common and uncultivated. He gave it to the use of the industrious and rational, (and labour was to be his title to it;) not to the fancy or covetousness of the quarrelsome and contentious. He that had as good left for his improvement, as was already taken up, needed not complain, ought not to meddle with what was already improved by another's labour: if he did, it is plain he desired the benefit of another's pains, which he had no right to, and not the ground which God had given him in common with others to labour on, and whereof there was as good left, as that already possessed, and more than he knew what to do with, or his industry could reach to.

Sec. 35. It is true, in land that is common in England, or any other country, where there is plenty of people under government, who have money and commerce, no one can inclose or appropriate any part, without the consent of all his fellowcommoners; because this is left common by compact, i.e. by the law of the land, which is not to be violated. And though it be common, in respect of some men, it is not so to all mankind; but is the joint property of this country, or this parish. Besides, the remainder, after such enclosure, would not be as good to the rest of the commoners, as the whole was when they could all make use of the whole; whereas in the beginning and first peopling of the great common of the world, it was quite otherwise. The law man was under, was rather for appropriating. God commanded, and his wants forced him to labour. That was his property which could not be taken from him where-ever he had fixed it. And hence subduing or cultivating the earth, and having dominion, we see are joined together. The one gave title to the other. So that God, by commanding to subdue, gave authority so far to appropriate: and the condition of human life, which requires labour and materials to work on, necessarily introduces private possessions.

Sec. 36. The measure of property nature has well set by the extent of men's labour and the conveniencies of life: no man's labour could subdue, or appropriate all; nor could his enjoyment consume more than a small part; so that it was impossible for any man, this way, to intrench upon the right of another, or acquire to himself a property, to the prejudice of his neighbour, who would still have room for as good, and as large a possession (after the other had taken out his) as before it was appropriated. This measure did confine every man's possession to a very moderate proportion, and such as he might appropriate to himself, without injury to any body, in the first ages of the world, when men were more in danger to be lost, by wandering from their company, in the then vast wilderness of the earth, than to be straitened for want of room to plant in. And the same measure may be allowed still without prejudice to any body, as full as the world seems: for supposing a man, or family, in the state they were at first peopling of the world by the children of Adam, or Noah; let him plant in some inland, vacant places of America, we shall find that the possessions he could make himself, upon the measures we have given, would not be very large, nor, even to this day, prejudice the rest of mankind, or give them reason to complain, or think themselves injured by this man's incroachment, though the race of men have now spread themselves to all the corners of the world, and do infinitely exceed the small number was at the beginning. Nay, the extent of ground is of so little value, without labour, that I have heard it affirmed, that in Spain itself a man may be permitted to plough, sow and reap, without being disturbed, upon land he has no other title to, but only his making use of it. But, on the contrary, the inhabitants think themselves beholden to him, who, by his industry on neglected, and consequently waste land, has increased the stock of corn, which they wanted. But be this as it will, which I lay no stress on; this I dare boldly affirm, that the same rule of propriety, (viz.) that every man should have as much as he could make use of, would hold still in the world, without straitening any body; since there is land enough in the world to suffice double the inhabitants, had not the invention of money, and the tacit agreement of men to put a value on it, introduced (by consent) larger possessions, and a right to them; which, how it has done, I shall by and by shew more at large.

Sec. 37. This is certain, that in the beginning, before the desire of having more than man needed had altered the intrinsic value of things, which depends only on their usefulness to the life of man; or had agreed, that a little piece of yellow metal, which would keep without wasting or decay, should be worth a great piece of flesh, or a whole heap of corn; though men had a right to appropriate, by their labour, each one of himself, as much of the things of nature, as he could use: yet this could not be much, nor to the prejudice of others, where the same plenty was still left to those who would use the same industry. To which let me add, that he who appropriates land to himself by his labour, does not lessen, but increase the common stock of mankind: for the provisions serving to the support of human life, produced by one acre of inclosed and cultivated land, are (to speak much within compass) ten times more than those which are yielded by an acre of land of an equal richness lying waste in common. And therefore he that incloses land, and has a greater plenty of the conveniencies of life from ten acres, than he could have from an hundred left to nature, may truly be said to give ninety acres to mankind: for his labour now supplies him with provisions out of ten acres, which were but the product of an hundred lying in common. I have here rated the improved land very low, in making its product but as ten to one, when it is much nearer an hundred to one: for I ask, whether in the wild woods and uncultivated waste of America, left to nature, without any improvement, tillage or husbandry, a thousand acres yield the needy and wretched inhabitants as many conveniencies of life, as ten acres of equally fertile land do in Devonshire, where they are well cultivated?

Before the appropriation of land, he who gathered as much of the wild fruit, killed, caught, or tamed, as many of the beasts, as he could; he that so imployed his pains about any of the spontaneous products of nature, as any way to alter them from the state which nature put them in, by placing any of his labour on them, did thereby acquire a propriety in them: but if they perished, in his possession, without their due use; if the fruits rotted, or the venison putrified, before he could spend it, he offended against the common law of nature, and was liable to be punished; he invaded his neighbour's share, for he had no right, farther than his use called for any of them, and they might serve to afford him conveniencies of life.

Sec. 38. The same measures governed the possession of land too: whatsoever he tilled and reaped, laid up and made use of, before it spoiled, that was his peculiar right; whatsoever he enclosed, and could feed, and make use of, the cattle and product was also his. But if either the grass of his enclosure rotted on the ground, or the fruit of his planting perished without gathering, and laying up, this part of the earth, notwithstanding his enclosure, was still to be looked on as waste, and might be the possession of any other. Thus, at the beginning, Cain might take as much ground as he could till, and make it his own land, and yet leave enough to Abel's sheep to feed on; a few acres would serve for both their possessions. But as families increased, and industry inlarged their stocks, their possessions inlarged with the need of them; but yet it was commonly without any fixed property in the ground they made use of, till they incorporated, settled themselves together, and built cities; and then, by consent, they came in time, to set out the bounds of their distinct territories, and agree on limits between them and their neighbours;

and by laws within themselves, settled the properties of those of the same society: for we see, that in that part of the world which was first inhabited, and therefore like to be best peopled, even as low down as Abraham's time, they wandered with their flocks, and their herds, which was their substance, freely up and down; and this Abraham did, in a country where he was a stranger. Whence it is plain, that at least a great part of the land lay in common; that the inhabitants valued it not, nor claimed property in any more than they made use of. But when there was not room enough in the same place, for their herds to feed together, they by consent, as Abraham and Lot did, Gen. xiii. 5. separated and inlarged their pasture, where it best liked them. And for the same reason Esau went from his father, and his brother, and planted in mount Seir, Gen. xxxvi. 6.

Sec. 39. And thus, without supposing any private dominion, and property in Adam, over all the world, exclusive of all other men, which can no way be proved, nor any one's property be made out from it; but supposing the world given, as it was, to the children of men in common, we see how labour could make men distinct titles to several parcels of it, for their private uses; wherein there could be no doubt of right, no room for quarrel.

Sec. 40. Nor is it so strange, as perhaps before consideration it may appear, that the property of labour should be able to over-balance the community of land: for it is labour indeed that puts the difference of value on every thing; and let any one consider what the difference is between an acre of land planted with tobacco or sugar, sown with wheat or barley, and an acre of the same land lying in common, without any husbandry upon it, and he will find, that the improvement of labour makes the far greater part of the value. I think it will be but a very modest computation to say, that of the products of the earth useful to the life of man nine tenths are the effects of labour: nay, if we will rightly estimate things as they come to our use, and cast up the several expences about them, what in them is purely owing to nature, and what to labour, we shall find, that in most of them ninety-nine hundredths are wholly to be put on the account of labour.

Sec. 41. There cannot be a clearer demonstration of any thing, than several nations of the Americans are of this, who are rich in land, and poor in all the comforts of life; whom nature having furnished as liberally as any other people, with the materials of plenty, i.e. a fruitful soil, apt to produce in abundance, what might serve for food, raiment, and delight; yet for want of improving it by labour, have not one hundredth part of the conveniencies we enjoy: and a king of a large and fruitful territory there, feeds, lodges, and is clad worse than a day-labourer in England.

Sec. 42. To make this a little clearer, let us but trace some of the ordinary provisions of life, through their several progresses, before they come to our use, and see how much they receive of their value from human industry. Bread, wine and cloth, are things of daily use, and great plenty; yet notwithstanding, acorns, water and leaves, or skins, must be our bread, drink and cloathing, did not labour furnish us with these more useful commodities: for whatever bread is more worth than acorns, wine than water, and cloth or silk, than leaves, skins or moss, that is wholly owing to labour and industry; the one of these being the food and raiment which unassisted nature furnishes us with; the other, provisions which our industry and pains prepare for us, which how much they exceed the other in value, when any one hath computed, he will then see how much labour makes the far greatest part of the value of things we enjoy in this world: and the ground which produces the materials, is scarce to be reckoned in, as any, or at most, but a very small part of it; so little, that even amongst us, land that is left wholly to nature, that hath no improvement of pasturage, tillage, or planting, is called, as indeed it is, waste; and we shall find the benefit of it amount to little more than nothing.

This shews how much numbers of men are to be preferred to largeness of dominions; and that the increase of lands, and the right employing of them, is the great art of government: and that prince, who shall be so wise and godlike, as by established laws of liberty to secure protection and encouragement to the honest industry of mankind, against the oppression of power and narrowness of party,

---

will quickly be too hard for his neighbours: but this by the by. To return to the argument in hand,

Sec. 43. An acre of land, that bears here twenty bushels of wheat, and another in America, which, with the same husbandry, would do the like, are, without doubt, of the same natural intrinsic value: but yet the benefit mankind receives from the one in a year, is worth 5 pounds and from the other possibly not worth a penny, if all the profit an Indian received from it were to be valued, and sold here; at least, I may truly say, not one thousandth. It is labour then which puts the greatest part of value upon land, without which it would scarcely be worth any thing: it is to that we owe the greatest part of all its useful products; for all that the straw, bran, bread, of that acre of wheat, is more worth than the product of an acre of as good land, which lies waste, is all the effect of labour: for it is not barely the plough-man's pains, the reaper's and thresher's toil, and the baker's sweat, is to be counted into the bread we eat; the labour of those who broke the oxen, who digged and wrought the iron and stones, who felled and framed the timber employed about the plough, mill, oven, or any other utensils, which are a vast number, requisite to this corn, from its being feed to be sown to its being made bread, must all be charged on the account of labour, and received as an effect of that: nature and the earth furnished only the almost worthless materials, as in themselves. It would be a strange catalogue of things, that industry provided and made use of, about every loaf of bread, before it came to our use, if we could trace them; iron, wood, leather, bark, timber, stone, bricks, coals, lime, cloth, dying drugs, pitch, tar, masts, ropes, and all the materials made use of in the ship, that brought any of the commodities made use of by any of the workmen, to any part of the work; all which it would be almost impossible, at least too long, to reckon up.

Sec. 44. From all which it is evident, that though the things of nature are given in common, yet man, by being master of himself, and proprietor of his own person, and the actions or labour of it, had still in himself the great foundation of property; and that, which made up the great part of what he applied to the support or comfort of his being, when invention and arts had improved the conveniencies of life, was perfectly his own, and did not belong in common to others.

Sec. 45. Thus labour, in the beginning, gave a right of property, wherever any one was pleased to employ it upon what was common, which remained a long while the far greater part, and is yet more than mankind makes use of. Men, at first, for the most part, contented themselves with what unassisted nature offered to their necessities: and though afterwards, in some parts of the world, (where the increase of people and stock, with the use of money, had made land scarce, and so of some value) the several communities settled the bounds of their distinct territories, and by laws within themselves regulated the properties of the private men of their society, and so, by compact and agreement, settled the property which labour and industry began; and the leagues that have been made between several states and kingdoms, either expresly or tacitly disowning all claim and right to the land in the others possession, have, by common consent, given up their pretences to their natural common right, which originally they had to those countries, and so have, by positive agreement, settled a property amongst themselves, in distinct parts and parcels of the earth; yet there are still great tracts of ground to be found, which (the inhabitants thereof not having joined with the rest of mankind, in the consent of the use of their common money) lie waste, and are more than the people who dwell on it do, or can make use of, and so still lie in common; tho' this can scarce happen amongst that part of mankind that have consented to the use of money.

Sec. 46. The greatest part of things really useful to the life of man, and such as the necessity of subsisting made the first commoners of the world look after, as it doth the Americans now, are generally things of short duration; such as, if they are not consumed by use, will decay and perish of themselves: gold, silver and diamonds, are things that fancy or agreement hath put the value on, more than real use, and the necessary support of life. Now of those good things which nature hath provided in common, every one had a right (as hath been said) to as much as he could use, and property in all that he could effect with his labour; all that his industry could extend to, to alter from the state nature had put it in, was his. He that gathered a hundred bushels of acorns or apples, had thereby a property in them, they were his goods as soon as gathered. He was only to look, that he used them before they spoiled, else he took more than his share, and robbed others. And indeed it was a foolish thing, as well as dishonest, to hoard up more than he could make use of. If he gave away a part to any body else, so that it perished not uselesly in his possession, these he also made use of. And if he also bartered away plums, that would have rotted in a week, for nuts that would last good for his eating a whole year, he did no injury; he wasted not the common stock; destroyed no part of the portion of goods that belonged to others, so long as nothing perished uselesly in his hands. Again, if he would give his nuts for a piece of metal, pleased with its colour; or exchange his sheep for shells, or wool for a sparkling pebble or a diamond, and keep those by him all his life he invaded not the right of others, he might heap up as much of these durable things as he pleased; the exceeding of the bounds of his just property not lying in the largeness of his possession, but the perishing of any thing uselesly in it.

Sec. 47. And thus came in the use of money, some lasting thing that men might keep without spoiling, and that by mutual consent men would take in exchange for the truly useful, but perishable supports of life.

Sec. 48. And as different degrees of industry were apt to give men possessions in different proportions, so this invention of money gave them the opportunity to continue and enlarge them: for supposing an island, separate from all possible commerce with the rest of the world, wherein there were but an hundred families, but there were sheep, horses and cows, with other useful animals, wholesome fruits, and land enough for corn for a hundred thousand times as many, but nothing in the island, either because of its commonness, or perishableness, fit to supply the place of money; what reason could any one have there to enlarge his possessions beyond the use of his family, and a plentiful supply to its consumption, either in what their own industry produced, or they could barter for like perishable, useful commodities, with others? Where there is not some thing, both lasting and scarce, and so valuable to be hoarded up, there men will not be apt to enlarge their possessions of land, were it never so rich, never so free for them to take: for I ask, what would a man value ten thousand, or an hundred thousand acres of excellent land, ready cultivated, and well stocked too with cattle, in the middle of the inland parts of America, where he had no hopes of commerce with other parts of the world, to draw money to him by the sale of the product? It would not be worth the enclosing, and we should see him give up again to the wild common of nature, whatever was more than would supply the conveniencies of life to be had there for him and his family.

Sec. 49. Thus in the beginning all the world was America, and more so than that is now; for no such thing as money was any where known. Find out something that hath the use and value of money amongst his neighbours, you shall see the same man will begin presently to enlarge his possessions.

Sec. 50. But since gold and silver, being little useful to the life of man in proportion to food, raiment, and carriage, has its value only from the consent of men, whereof labour yet makes, in great part, the measure, it is plain, that men have agreed to a dispropor-tionate and unequal possession of the earth, they having, by a tacit and voluntary consent, found out, a way how a man may fairly pos-sess more land than he himself can use the product of, by receiving in exchange for the overplus gold and silver, which may be hoarded up without injury to any one; these metals not spoiling or decaying in the hands of the possessor. This partage of things in an inequality of private possessions, men have made practicable out of the bounds of society, and without compact, only by putting a value on gold and silver, and tacitly agreeing in the use of money: for in governments, the laws regulate the right of property, and the possession of land is determined by positive constitutions.

Sec. 51. And thus, I think, it is very easy to conceive, without any difficulty, how labour could at first begin a title of property in the common things of nature, and how the spending it upon our uses bounded it. So that there could then be no reason of quarrelling about title, nor any doubt about the largeness of possession it gave.

Right and conveniency went together; for as a man had a right to all he could employ his labour upon, so he had no temptation to labour for more than he could make use of. This left no room for controversy about the title, nor for encroachment on the right of others; what portion a man carved to himself, was easily seen; and it was useless, as well as dishonest, to carve himself too much, or take more than he needed.

Immanuel Kant

1724–1804

■ *Kant was a Prussian philosopher, the last major philosopher of the Enlightenment period and one of the most influential thinkers in world history. His most
widely read and important work was* Critique of Pure Reason *(1781), where
he develops his philosophy of "transcendental idealism." His essay* Was ist
Aufklärung?, *in translation below, is the most influential philosophical definition
of Enlightenment.*

David Mason

An Answer to the Question:
"What Is Enlightenment?"

Immanuel Kant

Enlightenment is man's emergence from his self-incurred immaturity. Immaturity is the inability to use one's own understanding without the guidance of another. This immaturity is self-incurred if its
cause is not lack of understanding, but lack of resolution and courage
to use it without the guidance of another. The motto of enlightenment is therefore: Sapere aude! Have courage to use your own understanding!

Laziness and cowardice are the reasons why such a large proportion of men, even when nature has long emancipated them from
alien guidance (naturaliter maiorennes), nevertheless gladly remain
immature for life. For the same reasons, it is all too easy for others
to set themselves up as their guardians. It is so convenient to be
immature! If I have a book to have understanding in place of me, a
spiritual adviser to have a conscience for me, a doctor to judge my

Reprinted from *An Answer to the Question: "What is Enlightenment?"*, (September
30, 1784), Konigsberg in Prussia.

diet for me, and so on, I need not make any efforts at all. I need not think, so long as I can pay; others will soon enough take the tiresome job over for me. The guardians who have kindly taken upon themselves the work of supervision will soon see to it that by far the largest part of mankind (including the entire fair sex) should consider the step forward to maturity not only as difficult but also as highly dangerous. Having first infatuated their domesticated animals, and carefully prevented the docile creatures from daring to take a single step without the leading-strings to which they are tied, they next show them the danger which threatens them if they try to walk unaided. Now this danger is not in fact so very great, for they would certainly learn to walk eventually after a few falls. But an example of this kind is intimidating, and usually frightens them off from further attempts.

Thus it is difficult for each separate individual to work his way out of the immaturity which has become almost second nature to him. He has even grown fond of it and is really incapable for the time being of using his own understanding, because he was never allowed to make the attempt. Dogmas and formulas, those mechanical instruments for rational use (or rather misuse) of his natural endowments, are the ball and chain of his permanent immaturity. And if anyone did throw them off, he would still be uncertain about jumping over even the narrowest of trenches, for he would be unaccustomed to free movement of this kind. Thus only a few, by cultivating their own minds, have succeeded in freeing themselves from immaturity and in continuing boldly on their way.

There is more chance of an entire public enlightening itself. This is indeed almost inevitable, if only the public concerned is left in freedom. For there will always be a few who think for themselves, even among those appointed as guardians of the common mass. Such guardians, once they have themselves thrown off the yoke of immaturity, will disseminate the spirit of rational respect for personal value and for the duty of all men to think for themselves. The remarkable thing about this is that if the public, which was previously put under this yoke by the guardians, is suitably stirred up by some of the latter who are incapable of enlightenment, it may subsequently compel the guardians themselves to remain under the yoke. For it is very harmful to propagate prejudices, because they finally avenge themselves on the very people who first encouraged them (or whose predecessors did so). Thus a public can only achieve enlightenment slowly. A revolution may well put an end to autocratic despotism and to rapacious or power-seeking oppression, but it will never produce a true reform in ways of thinking. Instead, new prejudices, like the ones they replaced, will serve as a leash to control the great unthinking mass.

For enlightenment of this kind, all that is needed is freedom. And the freedom in question is the most innocuous form of all—freedom to make public use of one's reason in all matters. But I hear on all sides the cry: Don't argue! The officer says: Don't argue, get on parade! The tax-official: Don't argue, pay! The clergyman: Don't argue, believe! (Only one ruler in the world says: Argue as much as you like and about whatever you like, but obey!). All this means restrictions on freedom everywhere. But which sort of restriction prevents enlightenment, and which, instead of hindering it, can actually promote it? I reply: The public use of man's reason must always be free, and it alone can bring about enlightenment among men; the private use of reason may quite often be very narrowly restricted, however, without undue hindrance to the progress of enlightenment. But by the public use of one's own reason I mean that use which anyone may make of it as a man of learning addressing the entire reading public. What I term the private use of reason is that which a person may make of it in a particular civil post or office with which he is entrusted.

Now in some affairs which affect the interests of the commonwealth, we require a certain mechanism whereby some members of the commonwealth must behave purely passively, so that they may, by an artificial common agreement, be employed by the government for public ends (or at least deterred from vitiating them). It is, of course, impermissible to argue in such cases; obedience is imperative. But in so far as this or that individual who acts as part of the machine also considers himself as a member of a complete commonwealth or even of cosmopolitan society, and thence as a man of learning who may through his writings address a public in the truest sense of the word, he may indeed argue without harming the affairs in which he is employed for some of the time in a passive capacity. Thus it would be very harmful if an officer receiving an order from his superiors were to quibble openly, while on duty, about the appropriateness or usefulness of the order in question. He must simply obey. But he cannot reasonably be banned from making observations as a man of learning on the errors in the military service, and from submitting these to his public for judgement. The citizen cannot refuse to pay the taxes imposed upon him; presumptuous criticisms of such taxes, where someone is called upon to pay them, may be punished as an outrage which could lead to general insubordination. Nonetheless, the same citizen does not contravene his civil obligations if, as a learned individual, he publicly voices his thoughts on the impropriety or even injustice of such fiscal measures. In the same way, a clergyman is bound to instruct his pupils and his congregation in accordance with the doctrines of the church he serves, for he was employed by it on that condition. But as a scholar, he is completely free as well as obliged to impart to the public all his carefully considered, well-intentioned thoughts on the mistaken aspects of those doctrines, and to offer suggestions for a better arrangement of religious and ecclesiastical affairs. And there is nothing in this which need trouble the conscience. What he teaches in pursuit of his duties as an active servant of the church is presented by him as something which he is not empowered to teach at his own discretion, but which he is employed to expound in a prescribed manner and in someone else's name. He will say: Our church teaches this or that, and these are the arguments it uses. He then extracts as much practical value as possible for his congregation from precepts to which he would not himself subscribe with full conviction, but which he can nevertheless undertake to expound, since it is not in fact wholly impossible that they may contain truth. At all events, nothing opposed to the essence of religion is present in such doctrines. For if the clergyman thought he could find anything of this sort in them, he would not be able to carry out his official duties in good conscience, and would have to resign. Thus the use which someone employed as a teacher makes of his reason in the presence of his congregation is purely private, since a congregation, however large it is, is never any more than a domestic gathering. In view of this, he is not and cannot be free as a priest, since he is acting on a commission imposed from outside. Conversely, as a scholar addressing the real public (i.e. the world at large) through his writings, the clergyman making public use of his reason enjoys unlimited freedom to use his own reason and to speak in his own person. For to maintain that the guardians of the people in spiritual matters should themselves be immature, is an absurdity which amounts to making absurdities permanent.

But should not a society of clergymen, for example an ecclesiastical synod or a venerable presbytery (as the Dutch call it), be entitled to commit itself by oath to a certain unalterable set of doctrines, in order to secure for all time a constant guardianship over each of its members, and through them over the people? I reply that this is quite impossible. A contract of this kind, concluded with a view to preventing all further enlightenment of mankind for ever, is absolutely null and void, even if it is ratified by the supreme power, by Imperial Diets and the most solemn peace treaties. One age cannot enter into an alliance on oath to put the next age in a position where it would be impossible for it to extend and correct its knowledge, particularly on such important matters, or to make any progress whatsoever in enlightenment. This would be a crime against human nature, whose original destiny lies precisely in such progress. Later generations are thus perfectly entitled to dismiss these agreements as unauthorised and criminal. To test whether any particular measure can be agreed upon as a law for a people, we need only ask whether a people could well impose such a law upon itself. This might well be possible for a specified short period as a means of introducing a certain order, pending, as it were, a better solution. This would also mean that each citizen, particularly the clergyman, would be given a free hand as a scholar to comment publicly, i.e. in his writings, on the inadequacies of current institutions. Meanwhile, the newly established order would continue to exist, until public insight into the nature of such matters had progressed and proved itself to the point where, by general consent (if not unanimously), a proposal could be submitted to the crown. This would seek to protect the congregations who had, for instance, agreed to alter their religious establishment in accordance with their own notions of what higher insight is, but it would not try to obstruct those who wanted to let things remain as before. But it is absolutely impermissible to agree, even for a single lifetime, to a permanent religious constitution which no one might publicly question. For this would virtually nullify a phase in man's upward progress, thus making it fruitless and even detrimental to subsequent generations. A man may for his own person, and even then only for a limited period, postpone enlightening himself in matters he ought to know about. But to renounce such enlightenment completely, whether for his own person or even more so for later generations, means violating and trampling underfoot the sacred rights of mankind. But something which a people may not even impose upon itself can still less be imposed upon it by a monarch; for his legislative authority depends precisely upon his uniting the collective will of the people in his own. So long as he sees to it that all true or imagined improvements are compatible with the civil order, he can otherwise leave his subjects to do whatever they find necessary for their salvation, which is none of his business. But it is his business to stop anyone forcibly hindering others from working as best they can to define and promote their salvation. It indeed detracts from his majesty if he interferes in these affairs by subjecting the writings in which his subjects attempt to clarify their religious ideas to governmental supervision. This applies if he does so acting upon his own exalted opinions—in which case he exposes himself to the reproach: Caesar non est supra Grammaticos—but much more so if he demeans his high authority so far as to support the spiritual despotism of a few tyrants within his state against the rest of his subjects.

If it is now asked whether we at present live in an enlightened age, the answer is: No, but we do live in an age of enlightenment. As things are at present, we still have a long way to go before men as a whole can be in a position (or can ever be put into a position) of using their own understanding confidently and well in religious matters, without outside guidance. But we do have distinct indications that the way is now being cleared for them to work freely in this direction, and that the obstacles to universal enlightenment, to man's emergence from his self-incurred immaturity, are gradually becoming fewer. In this respect our age is the age of enlightenment, the century of Frederick.

A prince who does not regard it as beneath him to say that he considers it his duty, in religious matters, not to prescribe anything to his people, but to allow them complete freedom, a prince who thus even declines to accept the presumptuous title of tolerant, is himself enlightened. He deserves to be praised by a grateful present and posterity as the man who first liberated mankind from immaturity (as far as government is concerned), and who left all men free to use their own reason in all matters of conscience. Under his rule, ecclesiastical dignitaries, notwithstanding their official duties, may in their capacity as scholars freely and publicly submit to the judgement of the world their verdicts and opinions, even if these deviate here and there from orthodox doctrine. This applies even more to all others who are not restricted by any official duties. This spirit of freedom is also spreading abroad, even where it has to struggle with outward obstacles imposed by governments which misunderstand their own function. For such governments can now witness a shining example of how freedom may exist without in the least jeopardising public concord and the unity of the commonwealth. Men will of their own accord gradually work their way out of barbarism so long as artificial measures are not deliberately adopted to keep them in it.

I have portrayed matters of religion as the focal point of enlightenment, i.e. of man's emergence from his self-incurred immaturity. This is firstly because our rulers have no interest in assuming the role of guardians over their subjects so far as the arts and sciences are concerned, and secondly, because religious immaturity is the most pernicious and dishonourable variety of all. But the attitude of mind of a head of state who favours freedom in the arts and sciences extends even further, for he realises that there is no danger even to his legislation if he allows his subjects to make public use of their own reason and to put before the public their thoughts on better ways of drawing up laws, even if this entails forthright criticism of the current legislation. We have before us a brilliant example of this kind, in which no monarch has yet surpassed the one to whom we now pay tribute.

But only a ruler who is himself enlightened and has no fear of phantoms, yet who likewise has at hand a well-disciplined and numerous army to guarantee public security, may say what no republic would dare to say: Argue as much as you like and about whatever you like, but obey! This reveals to us a strange and unexpected pattern in human affairs (such as we shall always find if we consider them in the widest sense, in which nearly everything is paradoxical). A high degree of civil freedom seems advantageous to a people's intellectual freedom, yet it also sets up insuperable barriers to it. Conversely, a lesser degree of civil freedom gives intellectual freedom enough room to expand to its fullest extent. Thus once the germ on which nature has lavished most care—man's inclination and vocation to think freely—has developed within this hard shell, it gradually reacts upon the mentality of the people, who thus gradually become increasingly able to act freely. Eventually, it even influences the principles of governments, which find that they can themselves profit by treating man, who is more than a machine, in a manner appropriate to his dignity.

BEAUMARCHAIS

1732–1799

Most people know The Marriage of Figaro *only as a delightful comic opera by Wolfgang Amadeus Mozart. But the opera was based on a highly successful and controversial play written in 1778 by Pierre-Augustin Caron de Beaumarchais, who was at various times a musician, courtier, financier, diplomat, merchant, publisher and secret agent. Beaumarchais was a typical Enlightenment intellectual, a member of the nobility who satirized privilege and high society, and an advocate of reform, but not of revolution (at least in France). At the time of the American Revolution, he urged the French King Louis XIV to support the revolutionaries against the British, and himself raised money to send military equipment to the rebellious colonists.*

In The Marriage of Figaro, *Beaumarchais pokes fun at numerous institutions of the old regime, including social hierarchy, inherited privilege, incompetent officials, censorship and the courts. When the play was first written, Louis XVI was so appalled by its impertinence that he mandated it could never be performed. However, after numerous changes to the play by the author (including changing the setting of the play from France to Spain) and by the censors, the play was finally approved and performed in Paris by the* Comedie Francaise *in 1784. Despite its four-hour length, it was enormously popular, ran for 68 successive performances, and became the greatest success of 18ᵗʰ century theater in France.*

DAVID MASON

THE MARRIAGE OF FIGARO

or

The Follies of a Day

CHARACTERS

COUNT ALMAVIVA, Governor of Andalusia
THE COUNTESS, his wife
FIGARO, his valet and major-domo
SUZANNE, maid to the Countess, betrothed to Figaro
MARCELINE, housekeeper
ANTONIO, gardener of the castle, uncle of Suzanne, and father of Fanchette
FANCHETTE, Antonio's daughter
CHÉRUBIN, a page
BARTHOLO, a doctor from Seville
BAZILE, music master to the Countess
Don GUZMAN BRID'OISON, a judge
DOUBLEMAIN, his clerk
GRIPE-SOLEIL, a shepherd lad
PEDRILLO, the Count's huntsman
An usher
A shepherdess
An alguazil
A magistrate
Servants, valets, peasants, and huntsmen

SCENE: *The castle of Aguas-Frescas, three leagues from Seville.*

Reprinted from *The Barber of Seville; The Marriage of Figaro*, translated by John Wood, (1964), by permission of Penguin Books, Ltd.

ACT ONE

SCENE: *A bedroom partly stripped of furniture; a large high-backed chair in the middle.*

> [FIGARO *with a six-foot rule is measuring the floor.* SUZANNE *is trying on a wreath of orange blossom in front of the glass.*]

FIGARO: Nineteen feet by twenty-six.

SUZANNE: Look, Figaro. My wreath of orange blossom. Do you like it better so?

FIGARO: [*taking her hands*]: Splendid, my darling! Oh! How precious in an adoring bridegroom's eyes is the charming virginal wreath that adorns the head of his beloved on her wedding morning.

SUZANNE: And what are you measuring there, my dear?

FIGARO: I'm just thinking about this fine bed which His Lordship is giving us. The question is—will it go here?

SUZANNE: In this room?

FIGARO: This is the one he's letting us have.

SUZANNE: Well *I* don't want it.

FIGARO: Why?

SUZANNE: I just don't.

FIGARO: But why not?

SUZANNE: I don't like it.

FIGARO: You might give a reason?

SUZANNE: Suppose I don't want to?

FIGARO: Ay! Once they are sure of us . . .

SUZANNE: Giving a reason for being right amounts to admitting I could be wrong. Are you my humble servitor or aren't you?

FIGARO: Why take a prejudice against the room? It's the most convenient one in the castle, and it's in between the two suites of rooms. Suppose My Lady wants something in the night—she rings from her side—Hey presto! A couple of steps and you are in her room. On the other hand, should His Lordship want anything he need only give a tinkle and lo and behold! A hop and a skip and I'm there.

SUZANNE: Very nice too! But suppose he has given a tinkle in the morning and sent you off on some lengthy task—Hey presto! A couple of steps and he's at my door. Then lo and behold! A hop and a skip . . .

FIGARO: Whatever *are* you talking about?

SUZANNE: Why don't you listen?

FIGARO: But good Lord! What is it all about?

SUZANNE: This is what it's about, my dear boy—My Lord the Count, tired of cultivating rustic beauties, has a mind to return to the castle but not to his wife: it's yours he has cast his eye on, understand, and he thinks that this room might well prove quite convenient; so the ever-loyal Bazile, faithful agent of his master's pleasures and my esteemed singing teacher, daily suggests to me as he gives me my lesson.

FIGARO: Ah! Friend Bazile! If a good stout cudgel properly applied to anyone's back and shoulders could . . .

SUZANNE: You didn't think, silly boy, that this dowry I am to receive was a tribute to your own outstanding merits?

FIGARO: I have done sufficient to hope so.

SUZANNE: How stupid clever men can be!

FIGARO: So they say.

SUZANNE: Yes, but some people are unwilling to believe it.

FIGARO: That's where you are wrong.

SUZANNE: Let me tell you—he means to use it some time when he gets me alone for a few minutes to exact an ancient *Droit de Seigneur* . . . you know what that means.

FIGARO: So much so that if His Lordship hadn't abolished the infamous privilege when he got married himself I would never have married you within his domains.

SUZANNE: Very well! He may have abolished it, but now he wishes he hadn't and it's with your bride-to-be that he means to revive it today.

FIGARO: [*rubbing his forehead*]: I'm quite dizzy with the shock—and my forehead is sprouting . . . already . . .

SUZANNE: Don't rub it then.

FIGARO: There's no danger, is there?

SUZANNE: If there were to be the slightest little swelling . . . superstitious people . . .

FIGARO: You are laughing at me, you witch! Ah! If only there were some means of catching out this arch-deceiver, of leading him into a trap and pocketing his money.

SUZANNE: Intrigue and money—you are in your element now.

FIGARO: It isn't any sense of shame that restrains me.

SUZANNE: What is it, then, fear?

FIGARO: There's nothing in taking risks, but to take risks and at the same time turn them to your advantage—that's something! To enter some fellow's house at night, do him down with his wife, and to get a good hiding for your pains—nothing easier: a thousand blundering boobies have done it but . . .

[*Bell within.*]

SUZANNE: That means Her Ladyship is awake. She asked me to be the first person to speak to her on my wedding morning.

FIGARO: Has that some significance as well?

SUZANNE: There's an old saying that it brings luck to neglected wives. Good-bye, dear Fi-Fi-Figaro! Think about our little problem.

FIGARO: What about a kiss to encourage me?

SUZANNE: From my lover of today? I should think not! What will my husband say about it tomorrow?

[FIGARO *kisses her.*]

SUZANNE: There! There!

FIGARO: You just have no idea how I love you.

SUZANNE: [*disengaging herself*]: When are you going to give up telling me so from morning to night, stupid?

FIGARO: When I can prove it from night until morning.

[*A second ring.*]

SUZANNE: [*finger-tips to her lips*]: There's your kiss back, Sir. I want nothing more of you now.

FIGARO: [*running after her*]: But you didn't say that when I gave it to you.

[*Exit* SUZANNE.]

FIGARO: Dear charming girl! For ever laughing, blooming, full of gaiety and wit, loving and wholly delightful! And yet prudent. [*Walks up and down rubbing his forehead.*] And so, Your Lordship, you would do me down, would you! I wondered why, having put me in charge of the household, he wanted to take me with him on his embassy and make me his courier. I have got the idea, Your Highness! It's a triple promotion! You—Minister Plenipotentiary, me—the breakneck postilion, Suzie—lady of the back stairs and pocket ambassadress! And then, off you go, courier! While I'm galloping in one direction you'll be progressing nicely in another—with my little wife! I shall be fighting my way through rain and mud for the greater glory of your family while you are condescending to cooperate in the increase of mine. A pretty sort of reciprocity! But it's going too far, My Lord! To be doing both your master's job and your valet's at the same time, representing the King—and myself—at a foreign court is overdoing it. It's too much by half! As for you, Bazile, you dirty old dog, I'll teach you to run with the hounds, I'll—no, we shall have to dissimulate if we are to use one against the other. Look to the day's work, Master Figaro! First bring forward the hour of your wedding to make sure of the ceremony taking place, head off Marceline who's so deucedly fond of you, pocket the money and the presents, thwart His Lordship's little game, give Master Bazile a good thrashing, and . . .

[*Enter* MARCELINE *and* BARTHOLO.]

Ha! Ha! Here comes the portly doctor; now the party will be complete! Hello! Good day to you, my dear doctor. Is it my marriage with Suzanne that brings you to the castle?

BARTHOLO [*disdainful*]: Not at all, my good sir, not at all.

FIGARO: That would be very generous on your part.

BARTHOLO: It would indeed—too absurd for anything.

FIGARO: I having had the misfortune to thwart your own marriage.

BARTHOLO: Have you anything else to say?

FIGARO: Are they taking care of your mule?

BARTHOLO [*enraged*]: Incorrigible babbler! Leave us!

FIGARO: You are not annoyed, Doctor, are you? Men in your position are very hard—no pity for poor animals, no more than if they were men! Good day to you, Marceline! Are you still anxious to put me in court?

'Because one loves not—must one loathe oneself?'

I leave it to the doctor.

BARTHOLO: What's that?

FIGARO: She'll tell you about it—and a lot more.

[*Exit* FIGARO.]

BARTHOLO [*watching him go*]: Just the same scoundrel as ever! If he escapes the gallows I predict that he'll end up as the most insolent, outrageous . . .

MARCELINE [*turns him about*]: There you are! The everlasting Doctor! Always so grave and formal that one might die waiting for your help just as a certain person once got married in spite of all your precautions.

BARTHOLO: Nasty-minded and spiteful as ever! Anyhow, why is my presence required at the castle? Has My Lord the Count had some mishap?

MARCELINE: No, Doctor.

BARTHOLO: Rosine, his deceitful Countess, is perhaps unwell, Heaven be praised!

MARCELINE: She's listless, languishing, pining away.

BARTHOLO: What's wrong with her?

MARCELINE: Her husband neglects her.

BARTHOLO [*with satisfaction*]: Ah! Noble husband! He avenges me.

MARCELINE: One doesn't know just how to describe the Count. He's both dissolute and jealous.

BARTHOLO: Dissolute from boredom. Jealous from vanity. That goes without saying.

MARCELINE: Today, for example, he's giving our Suzanne in marriage to his man Figaro. The union is a method of showing his favour.

BARTHOLO: A union which His Excellency has made necessary?

MARCELINE: Not entirely, but one His Excellency would like a share in celebrating with the bride.

BARTHOLO: Of Master Figaro? No doubt an arrangement could be made.

MARCELINE: Bazile says not.

BARTHOLO: Is that scoundrel here too? It's a den of thieves. What's he doing here?

MARCELINE: All the mischief he can. The worst thing from my point of view is the tiresome fancy he's so long had for me.

BARTHOLO: You could easily get rid of his attentions.

MARCELINE: How?

BARTHOLO: By marrying him.

MARCELINE: Cruel mocker! Why didn't you get rid of mine in the same way? Wasn't that what you ought to have done? Have you no memory for your obligations? What became of our little Emmanuel, fruit of a forgotten passion that should have led us to the altar?

BARTHOLO [*taking off his hat*]: Did you have me come from Seville to listen to this sort of nonsense? If you are so full of enthusiasm for marriage . . .

MARCELINE: All right. We'll say no more about it. But since nothing could induce you to do the right thing and marry me, at least help me to marry someone else.

BARTHOLO: By all means! Let us discuss it. But what mortal, abandoned of gods and women, could . . . it be?

MARCELINE: Why! Who else could it be but the gay, handsome Figaro?

BARTHOLO: That worthless scoundrel!

MARCELINE: Never angry, always good-humoured, living for the pleasure of the moment, worrying as little about the future as the past, carefree and . . . generous . . . generous as . . .

BARTHOLO: As a thief!

MARCELINE: As a lord! He's utterly charming! Yet he's a cruel monster.

BARTHOLO: And his Suzanne?

MARCELINE: She shall never have him, cunning little thing though she is, if you'll help me, Doctor, to enforce an obligation he has to me.

BARTHOLO: What! On his wedding day?

MARCELINE: It's never too late to break 'em off. If it weren't for giving away feminine secrets . . .

BARTHOLO: Do women have any secrets from their doctors?

MARCELINE: Ah! You know that I have none from you! Our sex is ardent but timid. However much we are attracted to pleasure, the most venturesome of women hears a voice within her say, 'Be fair if you can, wise if you will, but be circumspect you must.' So,

since one must at least be circumspect as every woman real-
izes—let us first frighten Suzanne about any possible disclosure
of the offers which are being made to her.

BARTHOLO: Where does that lead us to?

MARCELINE: Shame will drive her to persist in saying 'no' to the
Count, who in revenge will throw his weight against the marriage: and so mine will be assured.

BARTHOLO: By Jove, she's right! It would be a good stroke to marry
off my old governess to the rascal who helped to rob me of my
young mistress.

MARCELINE: And hoped to add to his own pleasure by disappoint-
ing me.

BARTHOLO: And once robbed me of a hundred crowns, as I still
haven't forgotten.

MARCELINE: Ah, what a satisfaction it will be!

BARTHOLO: To punish a scoundrel.

MARCELINE: To marry him, Doctor! To marry him!

[Enter SUZANNE, carrying a hat with a wide ribbon and a dress on
her arm.]

SUZANNE: 'To marry him! To marry him!' Who? My Figaro?

MARCELINE [bitterly]: Why not? You are for marrying him, aren't you?

BARTHOLO [laughing]: Now for a fine slanging-match between two
angry women! We were saying, my dear Suzie, how fortunate he'll
be in possessing a girl such as you.

MARCELINE: Not to mention my Lord the Count!

SUZANNE [curtseying]: Your servant, Madam! There's always something nasty about your remarks.

MARCELINE [curtseying]: And I, yours! What is there nasty in that, may
I ask? Isn't it right and proper that so liberal a nobleman should
have a share in the happiness he procures for his servants?

SUZANNE: Procures?

MARCELINE: That was the word I used.

SUZANNE: Fortunately your jealousy is as notorious as your claims
on Figaro are slight.

MARCELINE: I might have strengthened them had I cared to cement
them by the same methods as yours.

SUZANNE: Oh! The methods are well known to ladies of your learning and experience.

MARCELINE: And you have no experience? Innocent as sin, eh?

BARTHOLO [*drawing Marceline away*]: Good-bye, sweetheart of Master Figaro.

MARCELINE [*curtseying*]: And object of My Lord's secret understanding.

SUZANNE [*curtseying*]: Who holds you in the highest esteem.

MARCELINE [*curtseying*]: Will she not do me the honour of adding a
measure of affection?

SUZANNE [*curtseying*]: You may be sure that I leave you nothing to
desire in that respect, Madam.

MARCELINE [*curtseying*]: Such a pretty young lady!

SUZANNE [*curtseying*]: Sufficiently so to spoil your satisfaction—

MARCELINE [*curtseying*]: And above all so careful of her reputation—

SUZANNE [*curtseying*]: Reputation one leaves to duennas.

MARCELINE [*outraged*]: Duennas! To duennas!

BARTHOLO [*checking her*]: Marceline!

MARCELINE: Let us go, Doctor. Or I shan't be able to control myself.
Good day to you, Madam. [*Curtseys.*]

[*Exeunt* MARCELINE *and* BARTHOLO.]

SUZANNE: Be off! Be off, you pedantic old hag! Little I care for you
or your insults. The old witch! Because she has had some education and made her Ladyship miserable when she was young she
wants to domineer over the whole castle. [*Throws dress on chair.*]
I don't remember what I came in for.

CHÉRUBIN: [*running in*]: Ah, Suzie, I've been waiting this last hour
for a chance to catch you alone. Alas, you are getting married and
I'm going away!

SUZANNE: What has my marriage to do with the departure of His
Lordship's favourite page?

CHÉRUBIN [*pitifully*]: Suzanne, he's sending me away.

SUZANNE [*imitating him*]: Chérubin, have you done something silly
again?

CHÉRUBIN: He caught me with your cousin Fanchette yesterday
evening. I was putting her through her part for tonight. He was

furious when he saw me. 'Get out,' he said, 'you little—'I daren't repeat the rude word he used to a lady. 'Get out—you . . . You shan't sleep another night in the castle!' It's all up, Suzanne, unless Her Ladyship, my dear godmother, can get him to relent. I shall never, never see you any more.

SUZANNE: See me? So it's my turn now, is it? It's no longer the Mistress you are secretly sighing for?

CHÉRUBIN: Ah, Suzie! She's noble and beautiful, but how unapproachable!

SUZANNE: You mean that I'm not, and with me you dare hope. . . .

CHÉRUBIN: You know only too well, you naughty thing, that I daren't hope for anything at all! But how lucky you are! To see her all the time, to talk to her, to dress her in the morning and undress her at night—one pin after another—Ah, Suzie! I'd give . . . What's that you have there?

SUZANNE [teasing him]: Alas! the fortunate night-cap and the equally fortunate ribbon that does up your fair godmother's hair for the night.

CHÉRUBIN: Her ribbon! Give it me, sweetheart!

SUZANNE: Oh, no, you don't! Sweetheart forsooth! How familiar he's getting! If only he weren't just a snotty little good-for-nothing! Ah! [As CHÉRUBIN snatches it] The ribbon!

CHÉRUBIN [dodging round the large chair]: You can say that it got torn, dirty, lost, anything you like.

SUZANNE [chasing him]: Oh, what a worthless scamp you'll be when you are a year or two older! Give me the ribbon! [Tries to get it.]

CHÉRUBIN [taking a sheet of music from his pocket]: Leave go! Ah! Let me go, Suzie! I'll give you my ballad, and when the memory of your beautiful mistress saddens my days thoughts of you will be my one consolation.

SUZANNE: Your one consolation, you young scamp! Do you think you are talking to that Fanchette of yours? You are caught with her yet you'll sigh for your Mistress. Now on top of all that you are trying it on with me.

CHÉRUBIN [exalted]: Upon my word it's quite true! I don't know what's coming over me. For some time I have had such a strange feeling within me. My pulse quickens at the very sight of a woman. The word love makes my heart go pit-a-pat. In fact, I feel such a need to say 'I love you' to someone that I catch myself saying it to myself walking in the park, to your Mistress, to you, to the trees, to the clouds, to the wind which wafts them away with my fleeting words. Yesterday I met Marceline. . . .

SUZANNE [*laughing*]: Ha ha ha!

CHÉRUBIN: Why not? She's a woman. Woman—girl—maiden! How thrilling the words are!

SUZANNE: He's going dippy!

CHÉRUBIN: Fanchette is kind. She does listen to me! You aren't kind at all.

SUZANNE: A pity, isn't it? Now listen, young man! [*She tries to snatch the ribbon.*]

CHÉRUBIN [*dodges away*]: Ah, would you! Only over my dead body! If that's not enough shall we say . . . plus a thousand kisses? [*He chases her now.*]

SUZANNE [*dodges him*]: Plus a thousand slaps if you come near me. I shall complain to the Mistress. So far from interceding for you I'll say to his Lordship, 'You did well, my Lord! Send him away— the little thief! Send him home to his family, the nasty little thing! He has the audacity to be in love with his Mistress and yet wants to be kissing me too.'

[CHÉRUBIN, *seeing the* COUNT *enter, throws himself behind the chair in terror.*]

CHÉRUBIN: I'm done for!

SUZANNE [*not seeing the Count*]: What's frightening him? [*Seeing the Count*] Oh! [*Goes to the chair to hide Chérubin.*]

THE COUNT: You are excited, Suzie! Talking to yourself and your little heart going pit-a-pat . . . very understandable of course on such a day. . . .

SUZANNE [*in concern*]: What do you want of me, My Lord? Suppose anyone found you here with me. . . .

THE COUNT: I should be very sorry indeed if they did. But you know what an interest I take in you. Bazile must have let you know of my love for you. I have only a moment to explain what I have in mind. Listen. [*Sits on chair.*]

SUZANNE: I won't listen!

THE COUNT [*takes her hand*]: You know that the King has appointed me his ambassador in London. I'm taking Figaro with me. I'm giving him an excellent job, and as a wife's duty is to follow her husband . . .

SUZANNE: Ah! If only I dare speak!

THE COUNT [*drawing her to him*]: Speak. Speak, my dear! Take advantage here and now of your influence over me, an influence that will endure. . . .

SUZANNE [*alarmed*]: I wish for none, Sir. I wish for none! Leave me, I beseech you!

THE COUNT: But tell me first. . . .

SUZANNE [*angrily*]: I don't remember what I was saying. . . .

THE COUNT: We were talking of wifely duty. . . .

SUZANNE: Very well. Since your Lordship rescued your own wife from the Doctor and married her for love—since you abolished at her instance a certain horrible privilege . . .

THE COUNT [*gaily*]: To the great disappointment of the girls! Ah, Suzie! A charming custom! If only you would come and talk about it with me this evening in the garden I would make the favour so worth while that . . .

BAZILE [*off-stage*]: He's not at home, Sir.

THE COUNT [*rising*]: Whose voice was that?

SUZANNE: Ah, unhappy me!

THE COUNT: Go, in case anyone comes in.

SUZANNE [*worried*]: And leave you here?

BAZILE: His Lordship was with My Lady. He's out—I'll go and inquire.

THE COUNT: Nowhere to hide. Ah, behind the armchair! That's not much good. Send him away quickly.

[SUZANNE *bars his way. He pushes her gently. She recoils but still puts herself between him and the page. As the* COUNT *crouches down* CHÉRUBIN *turns and throws himself into the chair in a kneeling position and hides his head in terror.* SUZANNE *takes the dress she is carrying, covers him up, and stands in front of the chair.*

Enter BAZILE.]

BAZILE: Haven't you seen His Lordship, Miss?

SUZANNE [*sharply*]: Why should I have seen him? Get out.

BAZILE [*still coming forward*]: If only you were more reasonable you would see that there's nothing surprising in my question. It's Figaro who's looking for him.

SUZANNE: Then he's looking for the man who next after you wishes him most harm.

THE COUNT [*aside*]: We shall see now what sort of servant I have.

BAZILE: So—to wish a woman well is to wish her husband harm?

SUZANNE: Not according to your horrible ideas—agent of corruption that you are!

BAZILE: What is being asked of you that you aren't going to lavish on another? Thanks to one little ceremony, what is forbidden you today will be required of you tomorrow.

SUZANNE: Shame!

BAZILE: Considering what a farce it is to take marriage so seriously, I had in mind . . .

SUZANNE: Horrible things, no doubt! Anyhow who gives you permission to come in here?

BAZILE: There, there, Spitfire! May Heaven teach you patience! You shall have it your own way; but don't think that I regard Master Figaro as any obstacle in My Lord's way. As for that little page . . .

SUZANNE [*timidly*]: What, Master Chérubin?

BAZILE [*imitating her*]: *Cherubino di amore,* that dear little cherub who's always hanging round you and only this morning was prowling about here waiting to get in when I left you—that's true, isn't it?

SUZANNE: What a tale! Go away, horrid man!

BAZILE: Because I don't go about with my eyes shut I'm a horrid man. Wasn't this ballad he makes such a fuss about intended for you?

SUZANNE [*annoyed*]: Oh, of course! For me, indeed!

BAZILE: Always assuming he didn't write it for Her Ladyship. They say he can't keep his eyes off her when he's serving at table. My goodness! Don't let him play any tricks in that quarter! His Lordship has no mercy on that sort of thing.

SUZANNE [*outraged*]: Are you knave enough to go spreading gossip to ruin an unfortunate lad who's already in disgrace with his master!

BAZILE: Did I invent it? I'm only repeating what everybody's saying.

THE COUNT [*springing to his feet*]: And what *is* everybody saying?

SUZANNE: Oh heavens!

BAZILE: Ha! Ha!

THE COUNT: Off you go, Bazile. Have him turned out at once.

BAZILE: Ah! How I wish I hadn't come in!

SUZANNE [*thoroughly alarmed*]: Oh, my goodness!

THE COUNT [*to Bazile*]: She's fainting. Sit her down in the chair.

SUZANNE [*pushing him away vigorously*]: I don't want to sit down. Fancy his coming in like that! It's disgusting!

THE COUNT: There are two of us here, my dear. There's not the slightest danger now.

BAZILE: I'm sorry I made a joke about the page, since you could hear me: I only did it to find out what she really thought. At bottom . . .

THE COUNT: Give him fifty crowns and a horse, and send him home to his family.

BAZILE: But My Lord—all because of a joke?

THE COUNT: The little reprobate! I've already surprised him once today with the gardener's daughter.

BAZILE: With Fanchette?

THE COUNT: In her bedroom, at that!

SUZANNE [*scandalized*]: Where My Lord no doubt had business as well!

THE COUNT [*gaily*]: I like that!

BAZILE: It's a good augury!

THE COUNT [*gaily*]: No. I went there to look for your uncle Antonio, my drunkard of a gardener, to give him his instructions. I knock. It's some time before the door is opened: your cousin looks a bit embarrassed and I become suspicious. Still carrying on the conversation I take a look round. There's a sort of curtain behind the door—a wardrobe of some sort. Slowly and stealthily I lift the curtain [*showing how by lifting the dress from the chair*] and what do I see? [*Perceives the page.*] Ah!

BAZILE: Ha! Ha!

THE COUNT: Just like the last time!

BAZILE: Better!

THE COUNT [*to Suzanne*]: Very nice, too! Not even married yet and already up to all the tricks! You wanted to be alone so that you could receive my page, eh? As for you, Sir, your behaviour's all of a piece. You have so little respect for your mistress as to address your attentions to her maid, to the wife of your friend. But I won't allow Figaro, a man I love and esteem, to be a victim of such deception. Was he with you, Bazile?

SUZANNE [*furious*]: There was no deception and no victim. He was there all the time you were talking to me.

THE COUNT [*equally furious in his turn*]: How can you tell such an untruth? His worst enemy wouldn't wish him such a misfortune.

SUZANNE: He was asking me to get Her Ladyship to intervene on his behalf. He was so frightened by your arrival that he hid behind the chair.

THE COUNT: What a diabolical fib! I sat in it when I came in.

CHÉRUBIN: Alas, My Lord! I was shivering behind it.

THE COUNT: Another fabrication! I have just been behind it myself.

CHÉRUBIN: Pardon me, but it was then that I hid myself in it.

THE COUNT [*more enraged than ever*]: Then the little snake overheard all we said!

CHÉRUBIN: On the contrary, My Lord, I did my best not to hear anything.

THE COUNT: Oh, the perfidy! [*To Suzanne*] You shan't marry Figaro, now.

BAZILE: Hush! There's somebody coming.

THE COUNT [*picking Chérubin up and setting him on his feet*]: He shall stand there for all the world to see.

[*Enter the* COUNTESS, FIGARO, FANCHETTE, *and peasants all in white.*]

FIGARO [*carrying a woman's headress trimmed with white feathers and ribbons—addressing the Countess*]: No one but Your Ladyship can obtain this favour for us.

THE COUNTESS: You see what they are, My Lord—they credit me with an influence which I do not enjoy. But since what they ask is not unreasonable . . .

THE COUNT [*embarrassed*]: It would have to be very much so before . . .

FIGARO [*aside to Suzanne*]: Back me up!

SUZANNE [*aside to Figaro*]: No use!

FIGARO [*as before*]: Try, all the same.

THE COUNT [*to Figaro*]: Well? What do you want?

FIGARO: My Lord! Your vassals, gratified by the abolition of a certain objectionable privilege which you, in your affection for My Lady . . .

THE COUNT: Very well! The privilege is abolished. What do you want to say?

FIGARO [*slyly*]: That it is high time that the virtues of so good a Master were publicly acclaimed. Since I derive such signal benefit from it today, I would like my marriage to be the first celebration of it.

THE COUNT [*more embarrassed still*]: You are mistaken, my friend. The abolition of a shameful custom is no more than an acknowledgement of what is due to common decency. A Spaniard may aspire to achieve the conquest of beauty by his own assiduities, but to exact the first, the most precious enjoyment of it as a servile requirement—that's the tyranny of a vandal, not the privilege of a noble Castilian.

FIGARO [*taking Suzanne by the hand*]: Permit, then, that this young lady, whose honour your wisdom has preserved, may publicly receive at your hands, as a symbol of the purity of your intentions, this virginal toque adorned with white feathers and ribbons: accept this ceremony for all future marriages, and may these verses which we sing in chorus for ever preserve the memory . . .

THE COUNT [*embarrassed*]: If I didn't know that lover, poet, and musician are the three titles of indulgence for every sort of folly and . . .

FIGARO: Join with me, friends!

ALL: His Lordship! His Lordship!

SUZANNE [*to the Count*]: Why seek to avoid a tribute you have so well deserved?

THE COUNT [*aside*]: Perfidious creature!

FIGARO: Look at her, My Lord! No fairer bride will ever exemplify the magnitude of your sacrifice.

SUZANNE: Stop talking about me and concentrate on praising his virtue.

THE COUNT [*aside*]: What a game!

THE COUNTESS: My Lord, I join my plea to theirs. I shall always cherish the memory of a ceremony which has its origins in the love you once bore me.

THE COUNT: And still do, Madam, and to that consideration I yield.

ALL: [*Vivat!*]

THE COUNT [*aside*]: I'm caught! [*Aloud*] I would only suggest that the ceremony may be postponed until later in order that it may be more effectively known. [*Aside to Bazile*] Quick—get them to find Marceline.

FIGARO [*to Chérubin*]: Hey, you scamp! Why aren't you applauding?

SUZANNE: He's in despair. His Lordship has banished him.

THE COUNTESS: Ah, Sir! I ask your clemency on his behalf.

THE COUNT: He doesn't deserve it.

THE COUNTESS: Alas! He's so young.

THE COUNT: Not so young as you think.

CHÉRUBIN [*trembling*]: The right to pardon generously was not the one you renounced when you married Her Ladyship.

SUZANNE: If the right to pardon were the one His Lordship had renounced it would surely be the first one he would wish to resume.

THE COUNT [*embarrassed*]: Of course!

THE COUNTESS: Then what need to resume it?

CHÉRUBIN [*to the Count*]: It's true, My Lord, that I acted unwisely, but I never talked indiscreetly.

THE COUNT: All right—that's enough.

FIGARO: What does he mean?

THE COUNT: Enough, enough! Everybody wants him forgiven. I agree and I'll go further. I'll give him a company in my own regiment.

ALL: [*Vivat!*]

THE COUNT: On condition that he leaves for Catalonia to join it immediately.

FIGARO: Ah, My Lord! Tomorrow!

THE COUNT: Immediately—that is my decision.

CHÉRUBIN: I obey.

THE COUNT: Say farewell to your godmother and ask her to pray for your protection.

[CHÉRUBIN *goes on one knee before the Countess, but cannot find words to speak.*]

THE COUNTESS [*moved*]: Go, young man, since we may not keep you even for today. Destiny calls: go and fill it worthily. Do credit to your benefactor. Remember this house where your youth has found such indulgence. Be obedient, honourable, and brave; we shall rejoice in your successes.

[CHÉRUBIN *rises and returns to his place.*]

THE COUNT: Your Ladyship is greatly moved.

THE COUNTESS: I don't deny it. Who knows what may be the fate of a boy thrown into a career of such danger. He is my kinsman and, what is more, my godchild.

THE COUNT [*aside*]: I see that Bazile was right. [*To Chérubin*] Young man, salute Suzanne for the last time.

FIGARO: But why the last time, Your Highness? He'll come here during his winter leave. . . . Kiss me too, Captain! [*He embraces him.*] Good-bye, my dear Chérubin. You are going to a very different life. By Jove, yes! No more running round all day with the girls, no more cream buns and custard tarts; no more 'tig' and blind-man's-buff. Soldiers of the Queen, by Gad! Just think of 'em, weather-beaten and ragged arsed, weighed down with their muskets, right turn, left wheel, forward march! On to the field

of glory and no flinching on the way—unless a round of shot
. . .

SUZANNE: Oh! For goodness' sake!

THE COUNTESS: What a prospect!

THE COUNT: Where is Marceline? It's very strange that she's not with you people.

FANCHETTE: She's gone into the town by the little path by the farm.

THE COUNT: When will she be back?

BAZILE: In God's good time.

FIGARO: If only he'd keep her away for good!

FANCHETTE: The Doctor was with her.

THE COUNT [sharply]: The Doctor is here, is he?

FANCHETTE: She button-holed him as soon as he arrived.

THE COUNT [aside]: He couldn't have come at a better time.

FANCHETTE: She seemed to be very annoyed about something. She was talking loudly as they went along and then she stopped and did like this—with open arms, and the doctor did like this—trying to calm her down: she seemed to be terribly angry and kept mentioning cousin Figaro.

THE COUNT [chin on hand]: Cousin—future husband—

FANCHETTE [pointing to Chérubin]: My Lord! Have you forgiven us for yesterday?

THE COUNT [interrupting]: That's all right, that's all right, my dear!

FIGARO: She's brooding on her confounded affection for me! She wanted to upset our wedding. . . .

THE COUNT [aside]: She'll upset it yet, I promise you. . . . [Aloud] Let us go in, Madam. Bazile, I shall want you.

SUZANNE [to Figaro]: Are you coming back to see me?

FIGARO [whispers]: Have you got him on the hook?

SUZANNE: Silly boy!

[All go out. As they are going FIGARO stops Chérubin and Bazile and brings them back.]

FIGARO: Now, you two. One stage of the ceremony over, my celebrations follow this evening. Let's run over our plans; don't let us be like some actors who never perform so badly as the day when the critics are all there in force. There's no chance of doing this better another time. Let us know our parts properly today.

BAZILE [*significantly*]: Mine's more difficult than you would think.

FIGARO [*making a gesture of hitting him without his seeing it*]: Ah! But you little know what reward it will bring you.

CHÉRUBIN: But, my dear Figaro, you forget that I'm leaving.

FIGARO: And you would rather stay?

CHÉRUBIN: Ah! If only I could!

FIGARO: We must dissemble. Not a word of complaint about having to go. Put your travelling coat over your arm, do all your packing: let your horse be seen at the gate, gallop as far as the farm, return on foot the back way. His Lordship will think you are gone: just take care to keep out of his sight and leave it to me to pacify him after the celebrations.

CHÉRUBIN: But Fanchette doesn't know her part.

BAZILE: Then what the deuce have you been teaching her the last week? You've been with her all the time!

FIGARO: You've nothing to do today: give her an additional lesson.

BAZILE: Be careful, young man! Be careful! Her father isn't pleased: the girl's had her ears boxed: it's not study she's been doing with you. Oh, Chérubin! You'll get yourself into trouble one of these days. The pitcher can go to the well, you know. . . .

FIGARO: Listen to the old fool and his proverbs. All right, you old pedant, what does the wisdom of the ages say? The pitcher can go to the well—and what happens?

BAZILE: It gets filled.

FIGARO [*going*]: Not too bad! Not too bad!

ACT TWO

SCENE: *A bedroom furnished with great splendour; a bed in a recess; a dais downstage of it; a door upstage right; door to a small closet downstage left; door upstage to the maid's quarters; window at the other side.*

[SUZANNE *and the* COUNTESS *enter from the right.*]

THE COUNTESS [*throwing herself into an easy-chair*]: Close the door, Suzanne, and tell me exactly what happened.

SUZANNE: I have withheld nothing from you, Madam.

THE COUNTESS: You really mean to say, Suzie, that he was endeavouring to seduce you?

SUZANNE: Not at all! His Lordship doesn't put himself to so much trouble as that with a servant: he merely wanted a financial arrangement.

THE COUNTESS: And the page was there all the time?

SUZANNE: Behind the armchair in fact. He had come to ask me to persuade you to intercede for him.

THE COUNTESS: Why didn't he come to me? Should I have refused him, Suzie?

SUZANNE: That's what I told him: but he was so distressed at leaving and particularly at parting from Your Ladyship . . . 'Ah! Suzie! How noble and beautiful she is! But how unapproachable!'

THE COUNTESS: Do I really seem like that, Suzie? I, who have always been his protector.

SUZANNE: He no sooner saw your ribbon which I had in my hand than he fairly leapt at it.

THE COUNTESS [*smiling*]: My ribbon! What childishness!

SUZANNE: I tried to get it back from him. He fought like a lion, Your Ladyship. His eyes flashed. 'Over my dead body!' he said in his shrill high-pitched voice.

THE COUNTESS [*lost in thought*]: And then, Suzie?

SUZANNE: And then, Madam? What can you do with such a young demon? On the one hand, respect for his godmother, on the other —'If only I could —' And because he daren't even venture to kiss the hem of Your Ladyship's gown he wanted to embrace me, if you please!

THE COUNTESS [*still dreaming*]: A truce to these foolish things. So, my dear Suzanne, my husband ended by telling you —

SUZANNE: That if I wouldn't listen to him he would support Marceline. . . .

THE COUNTESS [*rising and walking up and down fanning herself*]: He no longer loves me.

SUZANNE: Then why is he so jealous?

THE COUNTESS: Like all husbands, my dear—from pride—nothing more. Ah, I have loved him too dearly! I have wearied him with my solicitude and tired him with my love. That's the only offence I have been guilty of: but I don't intend to let you suffer for having rebuffed him: you shall marry your Figaro. He's the one person who can help us. Is he coming back?

SUZANNE: When he's seen the hunt move off.

THE COUNTESS [*fanning herself*]: Open the window a little. It's hot in here.

SUZANNE: Your Ladyship takes so much out of herself. [*Opens window upstage.*]

THE COUNTESS [*dreaming*]: Men are all the same. . . . Were it not for his persistence in avoiding me . . .

SUZANNE: Ah, there goes His Lordship riding across the park with Pedrillo and two, three—four greyhounds.

THE COUNTESS: Then we have time still. [*Sits down.*] Was that someone knocking, Suzie?

SUZANNE [*running to open the door, saying*]: Ah! It's my Figaro! My Figaro! Do come in, my dear! Her Ladyship is anxious to see you.

FIGARO: And how about you, my dear Suzanne? There's no need for Her Ladyship to worry. What, in fact, does it amount to? A mere nothing! His Lordship finds a young woman attractive: he would like to make her his mistress. It's all very natural.

SUZANNE: Natural?

FIGARO: So he appoints me his courier and Suzie Counsellor to the Embassy. . . . Not a bad idea at all, is it?

SUZANNE: Oh, do give up!

FIGARO: And now because Suzanne, my fiancée, doesn't accept the honour he confers on her, he proposes to take up the cause of

Marceline. What could be simpler? Somebody thwarts one's plans so one gets one's own back by upsetting theirs. Everybody does it—and it's what we are going to do too. That's all there is to it.

THE COUNTESS: Figaro! How can you treat so lightly a scheme which threatens the happiness of every one of us?

FIGARO: Who says I do so, Your Ladyship?

SUZANNE: Instead of taking our troubles to heart . . .

FIGARO: Isn't it sufficient that I take them in hand? No, if we are to go about things as methodically as he does, let us discourage his ardour for what is ours by giving him cause for concern for what is his.

THE COUNTESS: All very well. But how?

FIGARO: It's already done, Your Ladyship—a false report about you . . . a trifling scandal . . .

THE COUNTESS: About me? Are you out of your mind?

FIGARO: *He* must be!

THE COUNTESS: A man so jealous as . . .

FIGARO: So much the better: if you are to cope with such people what you need to do is to get them annoyed. How well women understand that! Once you get a man thoroughly enraged, a little manoeuvring and you can do what you like with him—lead him into the Guadalquivir if you want to. I have arranged for Bazile to receive a letter from an unseen hand warning His Lordship that a young man intends to meet you tonight at the ball.

THE COUNTESS: You'll play tricks with truth which involve a virtuous woman . . .

FIGARO: There are few, Madam, with whom I would have dared take the risk—lest it might prove to be true.

THE COUNTESS: I suppose I'm to be thankful for that!

FIGARO: But don't you think it's considerate of me to have arranged his little day for him so that he'll spend his time rushing round and cursing his own wife when he meant to be ingratiating himself with mine? He's already quite beside himself. He's galloping here, searching there, and worried to death! Look! There he goes—charging across country after a poor helpess hare. The time for the wedding will soon be here and he'll have done nothing to prevent it and won't dare to in Your Ladyship's presence.

SUZANNE: No, but that old blue stocking, Marceline, will.

FIGARO: Pah! A lot that worries me! You must send word to His Lordship that you'll meet him at dusk in the garden.

SUZANNE: You are still relying on that idea?

FIGARO: Oh, confound it, listen to me! Folk who won't try never get anywhere. That's my opinion.

SUZANNE: And very nice too!

THE COUNTESS: Are you going to let her go?

FIGARO: Of course not! I'll dress somebody else in Suzanne's clothes: when we surprise him at the rendezvous, how will he be able to get out of it?

SUZANNE: And who are you dressing up in my clothes?

FIGARO: Chérubin.

THE COUNTESS: He's gone.

FIGARO: Not if I know anything. Will you leave it to me?

SUZANNE: Since it's a question of intrigue we can.

FIGARO: Two, three, four threads at once—tangled and crossed into the bargain! I'm a courtier born. . . .

SUZANNE: They say it's a difficult trade.

FIGARO: Receive, take, ask again—that's the secret in so many words.

THE COUNTESS: He has so much confidence he ends by inspiring me with it!

FIGARO: That's the intention.

SUZANNE: You were saying –

FIGARO: That while His Lordship is away I'll send Chérubin to you. You arrange his hair and dress him up. I'll get hold of him and teach him his part and then—dance, Your Lordship! [*Exit* FIGARO.]

THE COUNTESS [*powder-box in hand*]: Heavens, Suzie, what a sight I am! This young man who's coming in . . .

SUZANNE: Your Ladyship doesn't mean to let him off?

THE COUNTESS [*lost in thought before her glass*]: I? You see how I'll scold him. . . .

SUZANNE: Let's make him sing his ballad. [*Puts it on the Countess's knee.*]

THE COUNTESS: My hair really is in a most dreadful state. . . .

SUZANNE: We only have two curls to do again. Your Ladyship will scold him all the better—

THE COUNTESS [*dreaming*]: What's that you say?

[*Enter* CHÉRUBIN *with a disconsolate air.*]

SUZANNE: Come in, gallant officer! The ladies are at home.

CHÉRUBIN [*coming forward hesitatingly*]: Oh! How that word hurts me! It reminds me that I have to go away and leave a godmother who was so kind . . .

SUZANNE: And so beautiful!

CHÉRUBIN [*with a sigh*]: Yes, of course!

SUZANNE [*imitating him*]: Yes, of course! Poor little man with his sly downcast eyes! Come on, pretty one, sing Her Ladyship your ballad.

THE COUNTESS [*opening it*]: About whom is it . . . may one ask?

SUZANNE: Look! How he blushes!

CHÉRUBIN: Is it wrong to . . . to be in love?

SUZANNE [*putting her fist under his nose*]: I'll tell everything, you wretch!

THE COUNTESS: There now—can he sing?

CHÉRUBIN: Ah, Madam! I'm so nervous. . . .

SUZANNE [*laughing*]: There, there, diddums then! As soon as Her Ladyship wants to hear it, we go all modest and shy. I'll accompany you.

THE COUNTESS: Take my guitar.

[*She sits holding the manuscript to follow the music.* SUZANNE *is behind the chair and reads the accompaniment over her Mistress's shoulder. The page faces them, eyes downcast as in the print after Vanloo called 'Conversation Espagnole'.*]

CHÉRUBIN [*to the tune* 'Marlbrough s'en va t'en Guerre']:

> My steed was weary and slow
> (Alas, but my heart is in pain)
> Our heads alike hanging low
> As we wandered over the plain.

As we wandered over the plain
(Alas, but my heart is in pain)
My tears I strove to restrain
As I rode with a loose-hanging rein.

As I rode with a loose-hanging rein
(Alas, but my heart is in pain)
The Queen passing by said, 'Pray tell me why
You ride with a tear in your eye.'

Why you ride with a tear in your eye
(Alas, but my heart is in pain)
I shall ne'er see my true love again
I shall ne'er see my true love again.

THE COUNTESS: Very artless and—quite moving . . . in its way. . . .

SUZANNE [*putting the guitar on a chair*]: Oh, yes, when it comes to sentiment this young man is . . . but have they told you, gallant Sir, how we mean to enliven the evening. We want to see first whether you can get my dress on. . . .

THE COUNTESS: I fear not.

SUZANNE [*measuring herself against him*]: He's about my height. Let's have the coat off first. [*Takes it off.*]

THE COUNTESS: Suppose someone were to come.

SUZANNE: We are doing nothing wrong. I'll go and shut the door. I want to see what we can do about his hair first. . . .

THE COUNTESS: There's a bonnet of mine on the table.

[SUZANNE *goes into closet off-stage.*]

Until the very moment the ball begins the Count won't know you are still at the castle. We'll explain to him afterwards that it was having to wait for your commission to be made out that suggested the idea to us. . . .

CHÉRUBIN [*showing it*]: Alas, Your Ladyship—I already have it here. Bazile handed it to me.

THE COUNTESS: So soon! They didn't mean to lose any time. [*She reads it.*] They were in such a hurry they forgot to put the seal on. [*She hands it back to him.*]

SUZANNE [*coming in with a large bonnet*]: What seal on what?

THE COUNTESS: On his commission.

SUZANNE: Already?

THE COUNTESS: That was what I said. Is that my bonnet?

SUZANNE [*sitting beside the Countess*]: It's the nicest one you have. [*Singing with pins in her mouth*]

> Turn and face me
>
> Dearest love . . .

[CHÉRUBIN *kneels down and she does his hair*.]

Madam—he looks charming.

THE COUNTESS: Make it look more girlish at the neck.

SUZANNE [*adjusting it*]: There! Just look at the little brat! Doesn't he make a pretty girl? I'm really quite jealous. [*Takes him by the chin.*] Wouldn't you like to be pretty like this?

THE COUNTESS: Silly! Tuck up the sleeve so that the under-sleeve shows better. [*She pushes it up.*] What's this on his wrist, a ribbon?

SUZANNE: And one of yours! I'm very pleased Your Ladyship has seen it. I told him I'd tell you. I'd have got it back if His Lordship hadn't come in when he did. I'm nearly as strong as he is.

THE COUNTESS: There's blood on it. [*She takes off the ribbon.*]

CHÉRUBIN [*ashamed*]: It happened this morning. Thinking I was leaving . . . I was arranging my horse's bit—he tossed his head and the point of the curb cut my wrist.

THE COUNTESS: But one would never use a ribbon to bandage . . .

SUZANNE: Particularly a stolen one . . . what is all this about curbs and bits and studs, anyway! I don't understand a word of it. . . . Oh! Look how white his arm is—like a girl's! It's whiter than mine. Just look, Your Ladyship!

[*The* COUNTESS *compares them.*]

THE COUNTESS [*crossly*]: You would do better to get me the sticking-plaster from my room.

[*The* COUNTESS *does not speak for a moment—her eyes are on the ribbon while* CHÉRUBIN'S *eyes devour her.*]

As to the ribbon, Sir—the colour particularly suits me and I should have been very sorry to have lost it.

SUZANNE [*returning*]: How are you going to tie it up? [*Gives the Countess sticking-plaster and scissors.*]

THE COUNTESS: While you are looking for clothes for him take the ribbon out of another bonnet.

[SUZANNE *goes out off-stage, taking with her Chérubin's cloak.*]

CHÉRUBIN [*eyes on ground, still kneeling*]: The one I had would soon have made it better.

THE COUNTESS: How? [*Offers the sticking-plaster.*] This will do more good.

CHÉRUBIN [*shyly*]: When a ribbon has been used to bind the hair or touched the skin of someone—some person . . .

THE COUNTESS [*sharply*]: Unknown—it acquires healing properties, eh? I wasn't aware of it! I'll keep the one which bound your arm just to try it. The first time one of my women cuts herself—we'll see what happens.

CHÉRUBIN [*sadly*]: You will keep it. And I shall go away.

THE COUNTESS: Not for ever.

CHÉRUBIN: I'm so unhappy.

THE COUNTESS [*moved*]: He's crying. It's all because of what that wicked Figaro said about soldiers.

CHÉRUBIN: Ah, would it were the moment he foretold! Were I but sure of dying here and now perchance my lips would venture . . .

THE COUNTESS [*interrupting him and drying his eyes with her handkerchief*]: There, there, child! What nonsense you do talk!

[*Knock on door.*]

Who's that knocking?

THE COUNT [*outside*]: Why are you locked in?

THE COUNTESS: Heavens! My husband! [*To Chérubin*] You without your coat, your neck and arms all bare, alone here with me! Everything in disorder—and he'll have had the letter—Oh! and he so jealous!

THE COUNT: Are you not going to open?

THE COUNTESS: I'm . . . I'm alone.

THE COUNT: Alone—then to whom are you talking?

THE COUNTESS [*desperately*]: You, of course.

CHÉRUBIN [*aside*]: After what happened yesterday and this morning he'll kill me on the spot.

[*He runs to the dressing-closet and pulls the door to behind him. The* COUNTESS *takes the key out and runs to open the door to the Count.*]

THE COUNTESS: Oh! How could we be so foolish!

THE COUNT [*a little severely*]: You don't usually lock yourself in.

THE COUNTESS [*ill at ease*]: I was sewing. Yes, I was doing some sewing with Suzanne. She's just gone through to her room, as I told you.

THE COUNT: You look worried.

THE COUNTESS: It's not surprising—not in the least—we were just talking about you, and, as I said, she's just gone. . . .

THE COUNT: Talking about me, were you? I came back because I'm concerned about a letter that was put into my hands just as I was about to mount my horse. I don't believe a word of it but—all the same—I'm . . . concerned.

THE COUNTESS: Why? What letter?

THE COUNT: The fact is, Madam, there are some pretty disreputable people about. I have been warned that someone might be endeavouring to see you today . . . unknown to me.

THE COUNTESS: Then he'll have to get in here, whoever he may be. I don't intend to leave my room today.

THE COUNT: Even though Suzanne is getting married this evening?

THE COUNTESS: Not on any account. I'm not well.

THE COUNT: Fortunately the Doctor is here.

[*The* PAGE *knocks a chair over in the closet.*]

What's that noise?

THE COUNTESS: *What* noise?

THE COUNT: Someone knocked something over.

THE COUNTESS: I didn't hear anything.

THE COUNT: You must be terribly preoccupied.

THE COUNTESS: Preoccupied—with what?

THE COUNT: There is someone in that room, Madam.

THE COUNTESS: And—whom do you imagine it could be?

THE COUNT: That's what I'm asking you. I have only just come.

THE COUNTESS: It must be Suzanne—apparently she's looking for something.

THE COUNT: You said she'd gone to her room.

THE COUNTESS: She went out somewhere—in there or somewhere else. I don't know just where.

THE COUNT: If it's Suzanne why are you so concerned?

THE COUNTESS: Concerned about my maid?

THE COUNT: I don't know about your maid, but you are certainly concerned.

THE COUNTESS: What is certain, Sir, is that you are concerned about her—much more than I am.

THE COUNT: I'm so far concerned, Madam, that I want to see her immediately.

THE COUNTESS: I believe you often do so—but there's nothing in your suspicions.

[*Enter* SUZANNE *upstage with dresses.*]

THE COUNT: Then they'll be the more easily disposed of. [*He looks towards the dressing-room and calls to Suzanne*] Come out, Suzie, come out!

[SUZANNE *stops near the door to the alcove upstage.*]

THE COUNTESS: She's practically undressed. Do you really have to come disturbing us women like this? She was trying on some dresses I was giving her as a wedding present. She ran out when she heard you coming.

THE COUNT: If she doesn't want to be seen—she can at least make herself heard. [*Indicating the dressing-room*] Answer, Suzie, are you there?

[SUZANNE *upstage, goes into alcove and hides.*]

THE COUNTESS [*hurrying towards the dressing-room*]: Suzie, I forbid you to reply. [*To the Count*] Whoever heard of such outrageous behaviour!

THE COUNT [*moving towards the dressing-room*]: All right! If she won't answer I'll see her—dressed or undressed.

THE COUNTESS [*standing in front of him*]: I may not be able to prevent it elsewhere, but I should hope that here in my own room . . .

THE COUNT: I'll know who this mysterious Suzanne is. I suppose it's no use asking you for the key, but there's no difficulty in breaking the door in. Hello, there!

THE COUNTESS: Go on! Call your servants! Cause a public scandal! Make us the talk of the castle!

THE COUNT: Very well, Madam. I can manage myself—I'll just go and get what I need. [*He makes to go out and turns back.*] But so that everything remains as it is will you be good enough to come with me and avoid the scandal and gossip which you find so displeasing? You won't refuse me so simple a request?

THE COUNTESS [*troubled*]: Ah, Sir, who would think of refusing you anything?

THE COUNT: Ah, I was forgetting the door to the maid's quarters. I must lock that as well in order that you may be fully justified. [*He goes to the door upstage and takes the key.*]

THE COUNTESS [*aside*]: Heavens—what dreadful obstinacy!

THE COUNT [*rejoining her*]: Now that the room is secured may I offer you my arm? [*Raising his voice*] And as for Suzanne in the dressing-room, she must be good enough to wait for me: should any harm come to her before my return—

THE COUNTESS: Really, Sir! This is too horrible!

[*The* COUNT *leads her off and locks the door behind him.*]

SUZANNE [*running out from the alcove to the door of the dressing-room*]: Open, Chérubin, open at once—it's Suzanne—open and come out!

CHÉRUBIN [*coming out*]: Ah, Suzie! What a dreadful business!

SUZANNE: Out you go! You haven't a moment to lose!

CHÉRUBIN: But how?

SUZANNE: I don't know, but you must.

CHÉRUBIN: Supposing there *isn*'t a way out?

SUZANNE: After what's just happened he'd murder you and it would be the end of all of us. Run and tell Figaro what's happened.

CHÉRUBIN: Perhaps it's not too big a drop into the garden. [*Runs to the window.*]

SUZANNE [*frightened*]: It's a whole storey. Impossible! Oh, my poor mistress! And my wedding! Oh Heavens!

CHÉRUBIN: It's over the kitchen garden—I might get away at the price of spoiling a few of his flower-beds.

SUZANNE [*holding him back*]: He'll kill himself!

CHÉRUBIN [*exalted*]: Into the flaming pit itself, Suzie, rather than any harm should come to her—a kiss for luck! [*He kisses her, runs to the window, and jumps out.*]

SUZANNE [*uttering a cry of fright*]: Ah! [*Falls into a chair: goes miserably to the window and looks out.*] Oh, he's already quite a distance away! The young scamp! As nimble as he's pretty! If he ever wants for women . . . I'd better take his place at once. [*Going into the dressing-room*] Now, Your Highness, you can break the lock if you want to; Devil a word will I answer. [*Goes in.*]

THE COUNT [*entering, pincers in hand*]: Everything as I left it! Before you oblige me to break open the door, consider the consequences. Once again, will you open it?

THE COUNTESS: Ah, Sir! Whatever can induce you to destroy our relationship? Were it love that drove you to such fury I could excuse your immoderation. I could perhaps forget—if that were the reason—how offensive was your method of showing it. But can mere vanity drive a man of honour to such excesses?

THE COUNT: Love or vanity, you shall open the door or I'll . . .

THE COUNTESS: Do stop, Sir, if you please! Do you really believe I can be so wanting in self-respect?

THE COUNT: I'll believe anything you like, Madam, but I mean to see who's in the dressing-room.

THE COUNTESS [*alarmed*]: Very well, Sir. You *shall* see. Only listen a moment—

THE COUNT: Then it isn't Suzie?

THE COUNTESS [*timidly*]: At least it is someone—whom you can't be mistrustful of. . . . We were preparing a joke—an entirely innocent joke for this evening, and I assure you—

THE COUNT: Of what do you assure me?

THE COUNTESS: That we had no intention of offending you—he or I.

THE COUNT: So it is a man!

THE COUNTESS: A boy, Sir!

THE COUNT: Ha! And who is it?

THE COUNTESS: I hardly dare mention his name.

THE COUNT [*furious*]: I'll kill him.

THE COUNTESS: Great heavens!

THE COUNT: Speak then!

THE COUNTESS: Young——Chérubin——

THE COUNT: Chérubin! The impudent scoundrel! All my suspicions——in the letter——are justified.

THE COUNTESS [*joining her hands*]: Ah, Sir——please don't think——

THE COUNT [*stamping his foot——aside*]: This confounded page, I run across him everywhere. Come, Madam, open! You could have spared your emotion when you took leave of him this morning: had he gone when I commanded him you wouldn't have needed to resort to such deceit in your story about Suzanne: and he wouldn't have been so carefully concealed if there had been nothing wrong in it.

THE COUNTESS: He was afraid you would be angry if you saw him.

[*The* COUNT, *beside himself, hurries towards the dressing-room.*]

THE COUNT: Come out, you little wretch!

THE COUNTESS [*pushing him away*]: Ah, Sir, your anger gives me concern for his safety. Don't, please don't harbour unjust suspicions——don't let his disordered dress——

THE COUNT: His disordered dress!

THE COUNTESS: Alas, Sir! He was getting ready to dress as a woman——my bonnet on his head . . . in his shirt without his coat—— neck open——arms bare . . . he was going to try on . . .

THE COUNT: And you were going to keep to your room——unworthy wife! Ay, you *shall* keep to it, and for a long time too! But first I'll punish the impudent scoundrel so that I shall never come across him anywhere any more!

THE COUNTESS [*throwing herself on her knees*]: Oh, My Lord! Spare the boy! I shall never forgive myself for having caused . . .

THE COUNT: Your concern for him aggravates his offence.

THE COUNTESS: He's not to blame——he was going away. It was I who recalled him. . . .

THE COUNT [*furious*]: Get up and begone! How dare you plead for him!

THE COUNTESS: All right, I will go, Sir. I *will* get up. I even give you the key of the room. But in the name of your love—for me—

THE COUNT: My love for you! Perfidious creature!

THE COUNTESS [*handing him the key*]: Promise that you will let the boy go unharmed. Then you may vent all your fury on me if I cannot convince you . . .

THE COUNT [*taking the key*]: I'll hear no more!

THE COUNTESS [*throwing herself on to couch*]: Heavens! It's the end of him!

THE COUNT [*opening door*]: Suzanne!

SUZANNE [*comes out laughing*]: 'I'll kill him! I'll kill him!' Kill him then, the wretched page!

THE COUNT [*aside*]: Ah! What a sell! [*Looking at the Countess, who is petrified with astonishment*] And you too—pretending to be astonished! But perhaps she's not alone. . . . [*Goes in.*]

SUZANNE [*running to her mistress*]: Pull yourself together, Mistress. He's far enough away. He jumped out.

THE COUNTESS: Ah, Suzie! I shall never survive it!

[*The* COUNT *comes out of the dressing-room bewildered. After a short silence*]

THE COUNT: There's nobody there. I was entirely wrong. Madam, you are quite an actress.

SUZANNE [*gaily*]: And I, My Lord?

[*The* COUNTESS, *her handkerchief to her mouth while she recovers her composure, says nothing.*]

THE COUNT: So you were pleased to joke, Madam!

THE COUNTESS [*recovering a little*]: And why not, Sir?

THE COUNT: A pretty dreadful sort of joke! What's the point of it, I ask you?

THE COUNTESS: Do your follies deserve any sympathy?

THE COUNT: Follies you call them—where my honour is involved?

THE COUNTESS [*gradually becoming more assured*]: Did I marry you to be delivered over to perpetual neglect and jealousy—such as only you dare justify—

THE COUNT: Ah, Madam! It was not intentional.

SUZANNE: Her ladyship need only have let you call the servants—

THE COUNT: True. I have indeed reason to be ashamed. Forgive me, I'm not quite myself. . . .

SUZANNE: You must admit, My Lord, that you did deserve it—a little.

THE COUNT: But why didn't you come out when I called—you wretch!

SUZANNE: I was getting dressed, pinning myself together again, and besides, Her Ladyship had told me not to—and she did quite right.

THE COUNT: Why don't you help me to gain her forgiveness instead of harping on my errors.

THE COUNTESS: No, Sir! An outrage of this kind cannot be passed over. . . . I shall retire into a convent. I can see that it is more than time that I did so.

THE COUNT: And could you do so—without some regrets?

SUZANNE: It *would* be a sad day for everyone, I'm sure.

THE COUNTESS: Ah, would it were so, Suzie! Better regrets than the humiliation of forgiving him. He has offended me too deeply.

THE COUNT: Rosine!

THE COUNTESS: I'm no longer the Rosine whom you once wooed so assiduously. I'm the Countess Almaviva, the sad and neglected wife whom you no longer love.

SUZANNE: Madam!

THE COUNT [*in supplication*]: For pity's sake . . .

THE COUNTESS: You had none for me.

THE COUNT: It was the letter that made my blood boil.

THE COUNTESS: I wasn't responsible for that.

THE COUNT: But you knew of it?

THE COUNTESS: It was that stupid Figaro.

THE COUNT: *He* was in it?

THE COUNTESS: He handed it to Bazile.

THE COUNT: Who said he had it from a peasant. Oh, treacherous music master! You shall pay for the whole lot!

THE COUNTESS: You ask forgiveness for yourself, but you deny it to others. That's men exactly! Supposing I *were* to grant my for-

giveness on the grounds that you were provoked by the letter—
it would have to be a general pardon.

THE COUNT: With all my heart—but however can I make amends
for so heinous a fault?

THE COUNTESS: The fault was on both sides.

THE COUNT: Ah, no! Say it was mine only! What's beyond my com-
prehension is how women can so quickly and convincingly assume
the air and tone that the circumstances require. You blushed; you
wept; you seemed embarrassed. Upon my word, you still do!

THE COUNTESS [forcing herself to smile]: I blushed—from resentment
at your suspicions. But men are not sufficiently sensitive to distinguish between righteous indignation—and guilty embarrassment.

THE COUNT [smiling]: And the page in a state of disorder—
undressed—almost naked?

THE COUNTESS: Is before you now. Aren't you pleased that you have
found her rather than the person you expected to find? You don't
usually show any objection to meeting her!

THE COUNT [laughing]: And the entreaties and feigned tears?

THE COUNTESS: You make me laugh, but it's no laughing matter.

THE COUNT: We men think we know something about dissimulation,
but we are only children. It's you, you, Madam, whom the King
should be sending as his Ambassador to London. How women
must study the art of controlling their demeanour to succeed in
such a degree!

THE COUNTESS: You men drive us to it.

SUZANNE: Regard us as prisoners on parole and you'll see whether
we can be trusted.

THE COUNTESS: Let us leave it at that! I may have gone too far, but
my forbearance under such grave provocation ought at least to
ensure me yours.

THE COUNT: But will you confirm that you forgive me?

THE COUNTESS: Did I ever say that I would, Suzie?

SUZANNE: I didn't hear it, Your Ladyship.

THE COUNT: Ah, then—won't you say it now?

THE COUNTESS: Do you deserve it, ungrateful man?

THE COUNT: Has my repentance not earned it?

SUZANNE: Imagining there was a man in Her Ladyship's dressing-room!

THE COUNT: She has punished me severely!

SUZANNE: Not believing her when she said it was her maid!

THE COUNT: Are you really implacable, Rosine?

THE COUNTESS: Ah, Suzie! How weak I am! What an example I set you. [*Giving the Count her hand*] No one will believe in a woman's resentment any more.

SUZANNE: Well! Don't we always have to come to this with them in the end?

[*The COUNT kisses his wife's hand ardently. Enter FIGARO out of breath.*]

FIGARO: I heard Your Ladyship was unwell. . . . I came as quickly as I could. I'm delighted to see it was nothing.

THE COUNT [*harshly*]: You are very attentive!

FIGARO: It's my duty, Sir. But, since apparently there's nothing in it, may I say, Sir, that all the young men and women in your service are below with violins and pipes and waiting to accompany me—as soon as you will permit me—to conduct my bride to . . .

THE COUNT: And who will stay and look after the Countess at the castle?

FIGARO: Stay and look after her? She isn't ill?

THE COUNT: No, but what about the man who is coming to visit her?

FIGARO: What man?

THE COUNT: The man in the letter you gave to Bazile!

FIGARO: Who said I did?

THE COUNT: If no one else had told me, you dog, your own face would accuse you and prove you a liar.

FIGARO: In that case my face must be lying. I'm not.

SUZANNE: My poor, dear Figaro, don't waste words in denying. We have told everything.

FIGARO: And what have you told? What do you take me for? A Bazile?

SUZANNE: We told how you wrote the letter so that when His Lordship came in he would believe that the page was in the dressing-room where I was hiding.

THE COUNT: And what do you say to that?

THE COUNTESS: There's nothing to hide now, Figaro, the joke's over.

FIGARO [*trying to make it out*]: The joke . . . is over?

THE COUNT: Yes—all over. What do you say to that, eh?

FIGARO: What do I say? That I wish I could say the same for my marriage, and if you will give your command . . .

THE COUNT: You admit then about the letter. . . .

FIGARO: Since Her Ladyship wants it that way and it's what Suzie wants and what you want yourself, then I suppose it must be what I want too. But if I were in your place, My Lord, I really wouldn't believe a word of it.

THE COUNT: You still go on lying in the teeth of the evidence. I shall end by getting annoyed.

THE COUNTESS [*laughing*]: Poor man! Must you really insist that he tells the truth for once?

FIGARO [*aside to Suzanne*]: I warned him of his danger. I couldn't be expected to do otherwise?

SUZANNE [*aside*]: Did you see the page?

FIGARO [*aside*]: Still a bit shaken.

SUZANNE [*aside*]: Oh! Poor boy!

THE COUNTESS: Come, My Lord, they are longing to be united: their impatience is natural: let us go down to the ceremony.

THE COUNT [*aside*]: And Marceline . . . Marceline . . . [*to the others*] I would just like to change for the occasion.

THE COUNTESS: For our own servants? I haven't.

[*Enter* ANTONIO *with a broken wallflower pot.*]

ANTONIO: My Lord! My Lord!

THE COUNT: Well, Antonio, what do you want?

ANTONIO: I want bars on the windows that open on to my flower-beds. They chuck all sorts of things down. They've just thrown a man out.

THE COUNT: Out of these windows?

ANTONIO: Look what they've done to my wallflowers!

SUZANNE [*aside*]: Look out, Figaro! Look out!

FIGARO: My Lord! He's been drunk all the morning.

ANTONIO: That's where you are wrong! It's a hangover from yesterday. See how they jump to erroneous conclusions!

THE COUNT [*fiercely*]: Where is this man? Where is he?

ANTONIO: Where is he?

THE COUNT: Yes.

ANTONIO: That's just what I want to know. It's what I have been trying to find out. I'm Your Lordship's servant—the only fellow that cares anything about your garden: a man comes tumbling into it . . . and you understand . . . my reputation's involved. . . .

SUZANNE [*low, to Figaro*]: Get him off the subject. . . .

FIGARO: So you *will* keep on drinking?

ANTONIO: I should go mad if I didn't.

THE COUNTESS: But why drink so much?

ANTONIO: That's all that distinguishes us from the beasts, Madam— drinking when we aren't thirsty and making love whenever we feel like it. . . .

THE COUNT: Give me an answer, now, or I shall turn you away.

ANTONIO: And do you think I should go?

THE COUNT: What do you mean?

ANTONIO [*touching his forehead*]: If you haven't enough up here to know when to keep a good servant, I'm not so soft as to get rid of a good master.

THE COUNT [*shaking him*]: You said someone had thrown a man out of this window.

ANTONIO: That's it, Your Excellency. Just now, in a white shirt he was, and he ran off, egad, like . . .

THE COUNT [*impatiently*]: And then?

ANTONIO: I would have run after him, but I had given myself such a clout against the gate that I couldn't lift a finger. . . .

THE COUNT: Anyway you'd recognize the fellow?

ANTONIO: Ay, that I would—if I had had a good look at him.

SUZANNE [*whispering to Figaro*]: He didn't see who it was.

FIGARO: What a fuss about a plant pot. How much do you want for your wallflower, you old misery? There's no point in looking for him, My Lord. I was the man who jumped out.

THE COUNT: You?

ANTONIO: 'How much do you want, you old misery!' You've grown a bit since then. You looked a deal shorter and slimmer to me.

FIGARO: Of course—one crouches in jumping.

ANTONIO: I would have said it was more like . . . that whippersnapper of a page.

THE COUNT: Chérubin, you mean?

FIGARO: Yes, with his horse as well, I suppose—come back from the gates of Seville on purpose to do it.

ANTONIO: No, no. I didn't say that. I didn't see no horses jump out, or I'd have said so.

THE COUNT: Heaven grant me patience!

FIGARO: I was in the bedroom—in a white shirt. . . . It was so hot. I was waiting for Suzie when I heard Your Lordship's voice—and a great to-do . . . and, I don't quite know why—but I took fright because of the letter—I must admit I was foolish. I jumped down into the flower-bed. I twisted my ankle a bit. [*Rubs it.*]

ANTONIO: Well if it were you, then I ought to give you this bit of paper that dropped out of your jacket as you fell.

THE COUNT [*snatching it*]: Give it me. [*Opens it and rolls it up again.*]

FIGARO [*aside*]: Caught!

THE COUNT: I suppose the fright won't have made you forget what's in the letter or how it came to be in your pocket?

FIGARO [*embarrassed, feeling in his pockets*]: Of course not . . . but I have so many—they are all to reply to . . . [*Looks at one piece of paper.*] What's this, for example? Ah, a letter from Marceline—four pages of it: very nice too—and what's this? Could it be the petition from that unfortunate poacher who's in jail? No, that's here. I had the inventory of the palace furniture in the other pocket. . . .

[*The* COUNT *again opens the paper he is holding.*]

THE COUNTESS [*whispers to Suzanne*]: Heavens, Suzie! It's his officer's warrant.

SUZANNE [*to Figaro*]: All's lost—it's the warrant for his commission.

THE COUNT [*refolding the paper*]: Can't you guess—and you a man of so many resources?

ANTONIO [*approaching Figaro*]: His Lordship says can't you guess?

FIGARO: Don't come shoving into me, you clown!

THE COUNT: You don't recall what it is, then?

FIGARO: Oh! Goodness me! It will be the commission of that unfortunate boy. He gave it to me, and I forgot to let him have it back! Oh dear! How stupid of me! What will he do without it? I must run and . . .

THE COUNT: And why should he have given it to you?

FIGARO [*in difficulties*]: He wanted me to do . . . something with it . . .

THE COUNT [*looking at it*]: There's nothing omitted.

THE COUNTESS [*low to Suzanne*]: The seal—

SUZANNE [*low to Figaro*]: The seal's missing.

THE COUNT [*to Figaro*]: You don't reply.

FIGARO: It was . . . the fact is . . . there was something missing—he said it was the custom . . . to . . .

THE COUNT: Custom? What custom? The custom to what?

FIGARO: To seal it with your seal . . . Of course it may not have been worth the trouble. . . .

THE COUNT [*opening the scroll again and crumpling it up angrily*]: All right! It's evident I'm to know nothing! [*Aside*] This fellow Figaro is at the bottom of everything. If only I could get my own back! [*Makes to go.*]

FIGARO [*interrupting*]: Are you going without giving the authority for my marriage?

[*Enter* MARCELINE, BAZILE, *servants, and tenants.*]

MARCELINE: Don't give the authority, My Lord! Before you show him any favours you must do justice between us. He has obligations to me.

THE COUNT [*aside*]: Here's my chance of revenge!

FIGARO: Obligations! What sort of obligations? Explain yourself.

MARCELINE: I'll explain myself, you scoundrel!

[*The* COUNTESS *sits down.* SUZANNE *stands behind her.*]

THE COUNT: What is it all about, Marceline?

MARCELINE: A promise of marriage.

FIGARO: A receipt for money lent, nothing more.

MARCELINE: On condition that he marries me. You are a great nobleman . . . Chief Justice of the province . . .

THE COUNT: Present yourself before the Court . . . there I do justice to each and all.

BAZILE [*pointing to Marceline*]: In that case will Your Highness permit me to establish my claims on Marceline?

THE COUNT [*aside*]: Ah! There's my rascally friend of the letter.

FIGARO: Another fool of the same sort.

THE COUNT [*to Bazile—annoyed*]: Your claims! Your claims! You do well to talk of your claims before me, you blockhead of blockheads!

ANTONIO [*clapping his hands*]: Got him first time! That's him to a T.

THE COUNT: Marceline. Everything must be held up pending examination of your claims. It will be held publicly in the Great Hall. My good Bazile, trusty and reliable agent that you are, you can go into the town and find the members of the Bench.

BAZILE: For *his* case?

THE COUNT: And you can also bring along the peasant who gave you the letter.

BAZILE: How do I know him?

THE COUNT: Do you refuse?

BAZILE: I didn't come to the castle to run errands.

THE COUNT: Then what did you come for?

BAZILE: As village organist, teacher of the harpsichord to Her Ladyship, of singing to her ladies, and of the mandoline to the pages. Apart from that my major responsibility is to entertain Your Lordship's guests with my guitar whenever it pleases Your Highness to ask for it.

GRIPE-SOLEIL [*stepping forward*]: I'll go, My Lord, as it please you.

THE COUNT: Who are you and what is your job?

GRIPE-SOLEIL: Gripe-Soleil, Your Lordship. I be the herd boy for the goats and I be here for the fireworks today. I be on holiday from the herd and I know where all that made legal lot do hang out.

THE COUNT: Your zeal pleases me. Off you go! As for you—[*to Bazile*] accompany the gentleman and play the guitar to him on the way. He's one of my guests.

GRIPE-SOLEIL [*delighted*]: What, I be one?

[SUZANNE *restrains him, indicating that the Countess is present.*]

BAZILE [*amazed*]: I am to go with Gripe-Soleil and play . . .

THE COUNT: It's what you are here for. Off you go or I sack you. [*He goes out.*]

BAZILE [*to himself*]: I'm not going to quarrel with the kettle—since I'm only . . .

FIGARO: A mug!

BAZILE [*aside*]: I'll go and make sure of my own marriage with Marceline instead of helping at theirs. [*To Figaro*] Take my advice—don't settle anything until I come back. [*Picks up the guitar from the armchair upstage.*]

FIGARO [*following him*]: 'Don't settle anything!' Be off! I'm not worried—not even if you *never* come back. You don't seem to be singing. Shall I start you off? Come on! Cheer up! We'll have a song for the bride.

[*He leads the procession off in a* seguidilla; BAZILE *accompanies him and everyone joins in.*]

Rather than riches
I choose goodness—which is
Whose?
Why Sue—Sue—Suzie's
Suzie's
Suzie's . . .

[*They go off dancing and the sound of their singing dies away.*]

THE COUNTESS: Well, Suzanne, you see what a mess that foolish man of yours has got me into with his letter.

SUZANNE: Ah, Madam, if you could have seen your own face when I slipped out of the dressing-room! First it went white as a sheet, but it was only a passing moment, and then how you blushed! How you blushed!

THE COUNTESS: And he really jumped out of the window?

SUZANNE: Without hesitation, the dear boy! As light as a feather. . . .

THE COUNTESS: And that fatal gardener! I thought I should have died! I couldn't think of a thing.

SUZANNE: On the contrary, Madam—it was then that I saw how moving in high society teaches a lady to tell fibs without showing it at all.

THE COUNTESS: And do you think the Count was taken in? Suppose he were to find the boy was still at the castle.

SUZANNE: I'll tell him to keep so well hidden that . . .

THE COUNTESS: He must go. After what has just happened, you'll understand that I'm not anxious to send him to the rendezvous in the garden in place of you.

SUZANNE: And I'm certainly not going either. Now my marriage is again . . .

THE COUNTESS [rising]: Wait . . . instead of sending you or someone else—suppose I went myself.

SUZANNE: You, Madam?

THE COUNTESS: No one else need run any risk . . . the Count wouldn't be able to deny it . . . having punished his jealousy and proved his unfaithfulness it would be . . . Come, we have been lucky once—I'm tempted to try again. Let him know at once that you'll be in the garden. But above all, let no one else know.

SUZANNE: What about Figaro—

THE COUNTESS: No, he would want to put his own oar in. . . . My mask and my cane and I'll go on to the terrace and think about it.

[SUZANNE goes into dressing-room.]

It's quite audacious—my little scheme. [Turning round.] Oh, my ribbon, my dear little ribbon! I had forgotten you! [She rolls it up.] I won't part with you, shall remind me of the incident when the poor child—Ah, My Lord the Count! What have you done? And what am I doing now?

[Enter SUZANNE The COUNTESS slips the ribbon into her bosom.]

SUZANNE: Here's the cane and your mask.

THE COUNTESS: Remember. I forbid you to say a word to Figaro.

SUZANNE: Madam, it's a delightful scheme. I've just been thinking about it. It fits everything together, rounds it all off, and brings everything to a conclusion—and whatever happens my marriage is certain now.

[She kisses the Countess's hand and they go out.]

*

During the Interval attendants arrange the Great Hall: they bring in benches for the lawyers which are placed to either side but leaving free passage behind.

Mid-stage they put a platform with two steps and set the Count's chair on it. Downstage they set a table for the clerk and his stool beside it and seats for Brid'oison and the other judges on either side of the Count.

ACT THREE

SCENE: *A room in the castle known as the Throne Room, which serves as an audience chamber: on one side a canopy over a portrait of the King.*

> [*Enter the* COUNT *and* PEDRILLO *in riding attire holding a sealed packet.*]

THE COUNT [*sharply*]: You understand?

PEDRILLO: Yes, Your Excellency. [*Goes out.*]

THE COUNT: Pedrillo!

PEDRILLO [*returning*]: Excellency?

THE COUNT: No one has seen you?

PEDRILLO: Not a soul.

THE COUNT: Take the Arab.

PEDRILLO: He's at the gate, saddled and ready.

THE COUNT: Right! Straight to Seville, then.

PEDRILLO: Only three leagues and a good road.

THE COUNT: When you get there find if the page has arrived.

PEDRILLO: At the house.

THE COUNT: Yes—and what's more, find out how long he's been there!

PEDRILLO: I understand.

THE COUNT: Deliver him his commission and come back at once.

PEDRILLO: And if he's not there?

THE COUNT: Come back all the quicker–and let me know. Off you go!

> [*Exit* PEDRILLO.]

THE COUNT: I made a mistake in sending Bazile away. Temper is no help at all. The note sent by him warning me of a plot against the Countess—the maid shut in the dressing-room when I arrived—her Mistress in a state of alarm—real or feigned—a man jumping out of the window and the other fellow admitting—or pretending it was he. . . . I don't get the thread of it all . . . there's something not clear somewhere . . . the liberties some of my people are taking—not that it matters unduly among such people—but the Countess? Suppose some fellow were to attempt . . . what am I talking about . . . ? The truth is that when one lets one's temper run away with one even the best-regulated imagination may become disordered. She was just having a joke . . . the suppressed laughter, the joy she could hardly repress—after all she knows what is due to herself! Then there's my honour—how the Deuce does that stand? On the other hand, where am I myself getting to? Has that chit Suzanne given me away? She's not married to him yet. How do I come to be involved in this preposterous entanglement? A score of times I've wanted to give it up. . . . It just shows where not knowing one's own mind leads one . . . If it were just a straightforward question I should-n't have anything like the desire for her that I have. This fellow Figaro always keeps one waiting. I must sound him carefully . . . [FIGARO *appears upstage—he stops*] . . . and find out by some means whether or not he knows what I feel about Suzanne.

FIGARO [*aside*]: Now for it!

THE COUNT [*aside*]: If she's said a single word to him—

FIGARO [*aside*]: I'm under suspicion.

THE COUNT [*aside*]: I'll make him marry the old woman.

FIGARO [*aside*]: Master Bazile's fancy, eh?

THE COUNT [*aside*]: And then we'll see what can be done with the girl.

FIGARO [*aside*]: My wife, if you don't mind.

THE COUNT [*turning round*]: Ah, what's that?

FIGARO: Me—you sent for me.

THE COUNT: And what were you saying?

FIGARO: I said nothing.

THE COUNT: 'My wife, if you don't mind.'

FIGARO: It was the end of a sentence. I was saying to someone else, 'Go tell my wife, if you don't mind.'

THE COUNT [*walking up and down*]: His *wife*! And may I inquire what business could be detaining you, Sir, when I had summoned you here?

FIGARO [*pretending to dust his clothes*]: I got myself dirty when I fell into those flower-beds. I've been changing.

THE COUNT: Does that take an hour?

FIGARO: It takes a while.

THE COUNT: The servants in this house take longer to dress than their masters.

FIGARO: Because they have no servants to assist them.

THE COUNT: I still don't understand what made you take such a foolish risk as to throw yourself—

FIGARO: Risk! Anyone might think I'd been buried alive!

THE COUNT: Don't try to prevaricate with me, Sir! You understand perfectly well that I'm not interested in the risk that you took but in your reason for taking it.

FIGARO: You arrive in a state of fury as a result of false information— raging like a torrent in the Sierra Morena—you are looking for a man, and a man you mean to have, or you'll force the lock or break down the doors. I just happened to be there and who was to know, in the state you were in, what . . .

THE COUNT: You could have escaped down the stairs.

FIGARO: And let you catch me in the passage?

THE COUNT [*furious*]: In the passage? [*Aside*] I'm losing my self-control. . . . I shan't get the information I want.

FIGARO [*aside*]: Careful! We must play our cards cautiously.

THE COUNT [*recovering himself*]: That wasn't what I wanted to talk about. We'll leave it. I was thinking—yes—I had some idea of taking you with me to London as my courier but—on reflection . . .

FIGARO: Your Lordship has changed his mind.

THE COUNT: In the first place you don't know any English.

FIGARO: I can say 'God damn!'

THE COUNT: I don't understand.

FIGARO: I said I can say 'God damn!'

THE COUNT: Well? And what about it?

FIGARO: Why! English is a devilish fine language. You can get along with so little of it. If you can say 'God damn!' you needn't want for anything anywhere in England. Suppose you fancy a nice chicken, you go into a tavern and just do like this to the waiter [*imitating a spit*].'God damn!' They bring you a round of salt beef and no bread. It's amazing! You feel like a bottle of good burgundy or claret, then you just do so [*gesture of drawing a cork*].'God damn!' In they come with a foaming tankard of beer. It's marvellous! Perhaps you meet some pretty wench coming mincing along, eyes on the ground, elbows well back, hips lightly swinging—you give her a friendly chuck under the chin.'God damn!' She lands you one that makes you wonder what hit you! Which shows that she understands perfectly well. It's true that the English put in a few other words here and there in conversation but obviously'God damn!' is the basis of the language. So, if Your Highness has no other reason for leaving me in Spain –

THE COUNT [*aside*]: He wants to come to London. She hasn't said anything.

FIGARO [*aside*]: He thinks I know nothing. I'll play him at his own game for a while.

THE COUNT: What made the Countess play such a trick on me?

FIGARO: Upon my word, you know better than I do, My Lord.

THE COUNT: I anticipate her every wish. I heap gifts upon her.

FIGARO: You give her presents, but you are unfaithful to her. Are we ever grateful for superfluities from those who deprive us of necessities?

THE COUNT: There was a time—when you told me everything. . . .

FIGARO: I'm hiding nothing from you now.

THE COUNT: How much has the Countess given you for your support in this pretty business?

FIGARO: How much did you give me for getting her out of the hands of the Doctor? Come, Your Excellency, don't let us humiliate a man who does us good service for fear of making him a bad valet.

THE COUNT: Why has there always to be some ambiguity in your behaviour?

FIGARO: Because you are always on the look-out for it.

THE COUNT: A detestable reputation!

FIGARO: And suppose I were better than my reputation? Are there many noblemen who could say as much?

THE COUNT: How many times have I seen you on the road to fortune and yet never getting there?

FIGARO: Think of the mob there is in these days all intent on setting the pace, hurrying, pushing, elbowing, trampling each other down, every man for himself and the Devil take the hindmost! That's how it is and for my part I've given it up.

THE COUNT: Given up your ambitions? [*Aside*] That's something new.

FIGARO [*aside*]: My turn now. [*To the Count*] Your Excellency was good enough to bestow on me the stewardship of the castle and a very pleasant existence it is. It's true that I miss the satisfactions of the bringer of exciting news, but, on the other hand, I shall dwell happily with my wife in the heart of Andalusia.

THE COUNT: What's to stop you taking her with you to London?

FIGARO: I should have to leave her so often I might find it tiresome.

THE COUNT: But with your brains and character you could hope for advancement in the service.

FIGARO: Brains a means to advancement! Your Highness is pleased to make fun of me. Mediocrity and subservience—those are the qualities one needs. Given them a man can get anywhere.

THE COUNT: You only need to study the art of politics a little under my direction.

FIGARO: I know it already.

THE COUNT: Like English, eh? . . . the basis of the language?

FIGARO: Yes—if it's anything to be proud of. To pretend not to know what one does know and know what one doesn't, to hear what one doesn't understand and not hear what one does, above all to promise beyond one's abilities; to make a great secret of hiding what isn't there; to withdraw to one's privacy and employ it in sharpening pens, appearing profound when one is really empty and dull, to play a part well or badly, to encourage spies and reward traitors, to tamper with seals, intercept letters, and endeavour to compensate for poverty of means by exaggerating the importance of one's ends—that's all there is in politics or I'm sadly mistaken.

THE COUNT: Oh, but what you are defining is intrigue.

FIGARO: Policy, intrigue—as you will! To my mind they are pretty much of a muchness. Let them meddle with them who want to. 'For I prefer my dearie oh!' as the old song says.

THE COUNT [*aside*]: He means to stay at home! I understand. Suzanne has given me away.

FIGARO [*aside*]: I'm paying him back in his own coin. Let him make what he can of that one!

THE COUNT: And so you hope to win your case against Marceline?

FIGARO: Will you make it a crime for me to refuse an old maid when Your Excellency permits himself to do us out of the young ones?

THE COUNT [*laughingly*]: On the Bench a magistrate puts his own interest aside and looks only to the provisions of the statute.

FIGARO: Indulgent to the strong, severe on the weak!

THE COUNT: Do you think I'm joking?

FIGARO: Ah! Who knows, My Lord! *Tempo e galant' uomo* as they say in Italian: time will show in the end who means harm and who doesn't.

THE COUNT [*aside*]: I see that he's heard everything. He shall marry the duenna.

FIGARO [*aside*]: He's been trying me out. What does he know?

[*Enter lackey.*]

LACKEY [*announcing*]: Don Guzman Brid' oison.

THE COUNT: Brid' oison?

FIGARO: Oh! Of course. The judge, your colleague and assessor.

[*For a moment* FIGARO *watches the Count, who is lost in thought.*]

THE COUNT: Send him in.

[*Exit lackey.*]

FIGARO: Is that all Your Excellency requires?

THE COUNT: What? Oh, yes. Arrange the room for the hearing.

FIGARO: What more is needed? The big armchair is for you, the others for your colleagues on the Bench, stool for the clerk, benches for the lawyers, the front of the hall for the gentry, and the rabble behind. I'll go and send away the cleaners. [*Exit.*]

THE COUNT: The rascal embarrasses me. Give him half a chance in discussion, he gets you in his grip and you are helpless. Scoundrels both of them! In league to take advantage of me! You can be friends—lovers—what you like to each other, I don't mind, but husband and wife –

[*Enter* SUZANNE, *out of breath.*]

SUZANNE: My Lord—Oh, beg pardon!

THE COUNT [*ironically*]: What is it, young lady?

SUZANNE: You are angry!

THE COUNT: You were wanting something, apparently.

SUZANNE [*shyly*]: The Mistress has the vapours. I was coming to ask you to lend us your smelling-salts. I'll return them immediately.

THE COUNT [*handing her the phial*]: Keep them for yourself. No doubt you'll soon find them useful.

SUZANNE: Do you imagine that women of my class have the vapours? It's a genteel malady. They only catch it in drawing-rooms.

THE COUNT: A loving bride and she's losing her young man. . . .

SUZANNE: But by paying Marceline with the dowry that you promised. . . .

THE COUNT: *I* promised?

SUZANNE [*lowering her gaze*]: My Lord, I thought I heard so.

THE COUNT: Ay!—if only you *would* hear me. . . .

SUZANNE [*eyes on the ground*]: Is it not my duty to listen to Your Lordship?

THE COUNT: Then why, cruel child, didn't you say so before?

SUZANNE: Is it ever too late for the truth?

THE COUNT: Will you be in the garden this evening?

SUZANNE: Don't I walk there every evening?

THE COUNT: Why were you so obstinate this morning?

SUZANNE: This morning—with the page behind the chair?

THE COUNT: She's quite right. I had forgotten. But why this persistent refusal when Bazile, on my behalf . . .

SUZANNE: What need of a Bazile?

THE COUNT: She's right again. But there's a certain Figaro to whom I fear you may have told things?

SUZANNE: Why, of course! I tell him everything—except what he ought not to know.

THE COUNT: Charming! And you promise me? If you go back on your word, let us be clear, my dear: no rendezvous no dowry—no dowry no marriage.

SUZANNE [*curtseying*]: But no marriage also means no *Droit de Seigneur*, My Lord!

THE COUNT: Where does she pick it all up? Upon my word I shall dote on her! But your Mistress is waiting for the phial. . . .

SUZANNE [*laughing and handing it back*]: I had to have some excuse to talk to you. . . .

THE COUNT [*trying to kiss her*]: Delicious creature!

SUZANNE [*evading him*]: Someone is coming.

THE COUNT [*aside*]: She's mine. [*Goes off.*]

SUZANNE: I must go and tell Her Ladyship.

[*Enter* FIGARO.]

FIGARO: Suzanne. Where are you running off to . . . after parting from His Lordship?

SUZANNE: Go to Court now if you wish. You have just won your case. . . .

FIGARO [*following*]: Ah but . . . tell me . . . [*Exit.*]

[*Enter the* COUNT.]

THE COUNT: 'You have just won your case!' What a beautiful trap I was walking into there! I'll punish you both for that, my imprudent friends! A just verdict . . . very just. . . . But suppose he *were* to pay the duenna—but what could he pay with? If he were to pay . . . Ah ha! Haven't I the proud Antonio whose lofty pride scorns the nonentity of a Figaro for his niece—I'll encourage that idea and—why not? In the vast field of intrigue one must contrive to cultivate everything, even the vanity of an old fool. [*He calls*] Antonio! [*Goes off.*]

[*Enter* BRID'OISON, MARCELINE, *and* BARTHOLO.]

MARCELINE: Sir, please listen to my case.

BRID'OISON [*wearing his gown, stammering slightly*]: Very well, let's hear what you have to say.

BARTHOLO: It's a question of a promise of marriage . . .

MARCELINE: Along with a loan of money . . .

BRID'OISON: I follow—the usual consequences *et cetera*.

MARCELINE: No, Sir. No consequences—no *et cetera*.

BRID'OISON: I follow—have you got the money?

MARCELINE: No, Sir, I was the lender. . . .

BRID'OISON: I follow—you are wanting your money back.

MARCELINE: No, Sir, I want him to marry me.

BRID'OISON: Ah! Now I do follow—and does *he* want to marry you?

MARCELINE: No, Sir. That's what the case is about.

BRID'OISON: Do you think I don't f-follow that?

MARCELINE: No, Sir. [*To Bartholo*] Where are we? [*To Brid'oison*] What! Are you going to try the case?

BRID'OISON: What do you think I purchased the office for?

MARCELINE [*sighing*]: It's a great abuse—the sale of offices.

BRID'OISON: Yes, it would be better if we could get them for nothing. Whom are you suing?

[*Enter* FIGARO *rubbing his hands.*]

MARCELINE [*pointing to him*]: This wicked man, Sir.

FIGARO [*gaily to Marceline*]: I'm embarrassing you perhaps? [*To Brid'oison*] His Lordship will be here in a moment, Sir.

BRID'OISON: I've seen this fellow somewhere before.

FIGARO: In Seville, Sir. I was in your wife's service.

BRID'OISON: When was th-that?

FIGARO: Rather less than a year before the birth of your son, Sir. The younger one, and a very handsome child too, if I may say so. . . .

BRID'OISON: He's the best looking one of the family. I understand you are up to your tricks again. . . .

FIGARO: You are too kind, Sir . . . it's a trifling matter.

BRID'OISON: A promise of marriage. Ah—poor simpleton!

FIGARO: Sir . . .

BRID'OISON: Has the young man seen my clerk?

FIGARO: You mean Doublemain? . . . the clerk of the Court?

BRID'OISON: Yes, he's got a finger in every pie.

FIGARO: Finger. Both hands if I know anything! Oh, yes, I've seen him about the depositions and the supplementary pleadings—all the usual procedure.

BRID'OISON: We have to comply with the forms. . . .

FIGARO: Oh, of course! Cases begin with the litigants but we all
    it's the forms that enable lawyers to live.

BRID'OISON: This young man isn't as green as I thought. Al
    friend, since you know a thing or two about the job we
    after your interests.

FIGARO: Sir, I rely on your integrity even though you are one ᴏⅰ ᴜ—
    judges.

BRID'OISON: What's that? Oh, yes, I'm a judge. But if you owe money
    and won't pay . . .

FIGARO: Then you see, Sir, it's just as if it never was owing.

BRID'OISON: Quite! Hey! What's that he said?

    [Enter Usher preceding Court.]

USHER: Gentlemen—His Lordship!

THE COUNT: Fully robed, Master Brid'oison! This is only a domes-
    tic matter. Ordinary dress would have been good enough here.

BRID'OISON: You are too good, Your Lordship, but I never go with-
    out it—you see it's a part of the forms. A man may laugh at a
    judge in a short gown who would tremble before a mere deputy
    magistrate in full robes. We must comply with the forms.

THE COUNT: Let the public in.

USHER [opening the door]: Court!

    [Enter ANTONIO, servants, peasants. The COUNT sits in his great chair,
    BRID'OISON beside him, the Clerk on his stool behind his table—
    magistrates and lawyers on side-benches, MARCELINE with BARTHOLO
    at her side, FIGARO on the other bench. Peasants standing behind.]

BRID'OISON: Doublemain, call the case list.

DOUBLEMAIN [reading a document]: The noble, the most noble, most
    infinitely noble Don Pedro George, Hidalgo, Baron de los Altos,
    Y Montes Fieros, Y otros Montes: against Alonzo Calderon, drama-
    tist. It's a case of a play—stillborn, which each disavows and attrib-
    utes to the other.

THE COUNT: Very sensible of both of them! Verdict—to ensure some
    degree of success should they collaborate in another work, let the
    Nobleman give his name, the writer his talent!

DOUBLEMAIN [reading again]: Andre Petruchio, labourer, against the
    Provincial Treasurer—a case of arbitrary enforcement. . . .

THE COUNT: It's outside my competence. I shall serve my vassals better by interceding for them with the Crown. Next.

[DOUBLEMAIN, *picks up a third document.* BARTHOLO *and* FIGARO *rise.*]

DOUBLEMAIN: Barbe—Agar—Raab—Madeleine—Nicole—Marceline de Verte-Allure, spinster

[MARCELINE *rises and curtseys.*]

against Figaro—baptismal name not given.

FIGARO: Anonymous.

BRID'OISON: A-a-anonymous. Which patron saint is that?

FIGARO: Mine.

DOUBLEMAIN: Against Anonymous Figaro. Description?

FIGARO: Gentleman.

THE COUNT *You* a gentleman?

[*The Clerk is writing it down.*]

FIGARO: Had Heaven so willed I should have been the son of a princely house.

THE COUNT [*to the Clerk*]: Get on with it.

USHER [*barks*]: Silence, Gentlemen!

DOUBLEMAIN [*reading again*]: In the matter of an objection lodged against the marriage of the said Figaro by the afore-said Verte-Allure, Dr Bartholo representing the plaintiff and the aforesaid Figaro pleading on his own behalf, if the Court will so permit, contrary though it be to the use and custom of the bar –

FIGARO: Use, Master Doublemain, is often an abuse. A client with any knowledge at all understands his case better than a lawyer starting from scratch and bawling at the top of his voice knowing everything except his brief and equally unconcerned about ruining his client, putting the justices to sleep, and boring everybody in Court. Such fellows are more puffed up than if they had composed one of Cicero's Orations. For my own part I shall put the facts in a few words. . . . Gentlemen . . .

DOUBLEMAIN: This is all beside the point. You aren't the plaintiff. Your job is to defend yourself. Come forward, Doctor, and read the promise of marriage.

FIGARO: Ay, let's have the promise.

BARTHOLO [*putting on spectacles*]: It is in precise terms.

BRID'OISON: We must have it produced.

DOUBLEMAIN: Silence then, Gentlemen!

USHER [*barks*]: Silence!

BARTHOLO [*reads*]: I the undersigned acknowledge having received from the aforesaid Miss . . . etc. Marceline de Verte-Allure the sum of two thousand milled-edge piastres—which sum I will repay on demand at the Castle and in consideration of which I will marry her—etc. etc. Signed Figaro—plain Figaro. The claim is for repayment of the money and execution of the undertaking with costs. A more interesting case, Gentlemen, was never submitted to the jurisdiction of the Court. Since the day when Alexander the Great made a promise of marriage to the fair Thalestris . . .

THE COUNT: Before we proceed any further, is there agreement on the validity of the document?

BRID'OISON: Have you anything to say against the document as read?

FIGARO: I contend that there was malice, error, or deliberate misrepresentation in the reading of the document, the words, as written, being not 'which sum I will repay her *and* I will marry her' but 'which sum I will repay her *or* I will marry her'.

THE COUNT: Is the word in the document 'and' or 'or'?

BARTHOLO: It's 'and'

FIGARO: 'Or'.

BRID'OISON: D-Doublemain, read it yourself.

DOUBLEMAIN: It's always safer: parties to the case often misrepresent in reading. [*Reads*]'M,'m,'m, . . . Miss'm,'m,'m, Verte-Allure . . . repay upon demand at the castle and . . . or, and—or . . . the word's badly written . . . and there's a blot. . . .

BRID'OISON: A b-b-blot? I know these blots.

BARTHOLO: My case is that it is the coordinating conjunction 'and' linking the coordinate clauses 'I will pay the lady' *and* 'I will marry her'.

FIGARO: And I maintain that it is the alternating conjunction *or* which separates the two clauses—I pay the damsel *or* I espouse her. As for this pedant, I'll out-pedant him; if he's for talking Latin I'll talk Greek and wipe the floor with him

THE COUNT: How is one to decide such a question?

BARTHOLO: To cut the matter short, Gentlemen, and not to quibble about a single word—we'll concede that it was 'or'.

FIGARO: I want that recorded.

BARTHOLO: Agreed. The guilty won't escape by resorting to a miserable get-out like that. Let us examine the document in another sense—[*Reads*] 'Which sum I will repay to her at the Castle where I will marry her.' Just as one might say, Gentlemen, 'You'll be bled in this bed *where* you'll stay and keep warm.' That is to say '*in which*'. 'You shall take two grains of rhubarb wherein you shall mix a pinch of tamarind' —'in which you shall mix'. So 'the Castle *Where* I will marry her' —'the Castle *in which—wherein—*'

FIGARO: Not a bit of it! The passage is intended to be read in this sense —'Either the malady will kill you *or* the doctor will'—*or else* the doctor will, it's beyond question. Another example— 'Either you'll write nothing readable *or* fools will run down your work'—' or fools'—The sense is clear, for in this case either fools or knaves, you may be sure, are the governing substantives. Does Master Bartholo think I have forgotten my grammar? 'I will repay her at the Castle—comma—*or* I will marry her.'*

BARTHOLO [*sharply*]: No comma.

FIGARO: Oh, yes, there *is* a comma, Gentlemen. 'Comma, or else I will marry her.'

BARTHOLO [*glancing quickly at the paper*]: No comma, Gentlemen.

FIGARO [*quickly*]: It *was* there, Gentlemen. Besides, if a man marries can he be held to repay his spouse?

BARTHOLO: Yes, We marry but keep separate properties.

FIGARO: *We* keep separate persons if marriage doesn't make us quits.

[*The judges rise to discuss this in whispers.*]

BARTHOLO: That's a fine way of acquitting yourself.

DOUBLEMAIN: Silence, Gentlemen!

USHER [*barks*]: Silence!

---

* The play on the meaning of '*où*' = 'where' and '*ou*' = 'or' is untranslatable. In performance in English it is well to cut from Bartholo's speech 'To cut the matter short, Gentleman' to the stage direction *The judges rise to discuss this in whispers* below.

BARTHOLO: And the scoundrel calls that paying his debts!

FIGARO: Are you pleading your case, Sir, or aren't you?

BARTHOLO: I'm defending this lady.

FIGARO: Then keep on talking nonsense but cut out the insults. When the Courts, fearing that litigants might be carried away by their feelings, allowed so-called third parties to plead for them, they never intended that these disinterested advocates should come to enjoy the privilege of being impudent with impunity—it's degrading a noble institution.

[*The judges continue their discussion in whispers.*]

ANTONIO [*to Marceline, indicating the judges*]: What are they jabbering about?

MARCELINE: Someone has got at the presiding judge and now he's getting at the others—result—I'm losing my case.

BARTHOLO [*gloomily*]: I fear so.

FIGARO [*gaily*]: Courage, Marceline!

DOUBLEMAIN [*getting up and addressing Marceline*]: That's going too far! I denounce you! I demand in the interests of the honour of the Court that a judgement be given on this matter before proceeding to the other offences.

THE COUNT [*sitting down*]: No, my dear Clerk, I shall pass no opinion on the personal reflection. A Spanish judge need not blush for excesses more fitly attributable to Asiatic tribunals. There are sufficient other abuses! I mean to correct a second one by giving you the justification of my decision: any judge who declines to do so is an enemy of the laws. What can the plaintiff legitimately demand? Marriage in default of payment. The two together would be incompatible.

DOUBLEMAIN: Silence, Gentlemen.

USHER [*barks*]: Silence!

THE COUNT: What reply does the defendant make? If he wishes to retain his freedom he may do so.

FIGARO [*joyfully*]: I've won!

THE COUNT: But since the document says 'which sum I will pay immediately upon demand or I will marry,' etc., the Court condemns the defendant to pay two thousand piastres to the plaintiff or to marry her *today*. [*He rises.*]

FIGARO [*stupefied*]: I've lost!

ANTONIO [*joyfully*]: A splendid judgement!

FIGARO: What's splendid about it?

ANTONIO: Splendid that you aren't going to be my nephew. Thank you very much, My Lord!

USHER [*barks*]: Pass along, Gentlemen.

[*People go out.*]

ANTONIO: I must go tell my niece all this. [*Exit.*]

MARCELINE [*sitting down*]: Ah! I breathe again.

FIGARO: And I'm stifling!

THE COUNT [*aside*]: At least I have got my own back. That's some satisfaction!

FIGARO [*aside*]: And that fellow Bazile who was to have put in an objection to Marceline's marriage, where's he got to? [*To the Count, who is going out*] You are leaving us, My Lord?

THE COUNT: The judgement is given.

FIGARO [*to Brid'oison*]: It's this great windbag of a counsellor. . . .

BRID'OISON: A windbag, me?

FIGARO: Yes. And I shan't marry her. *I'll* play the gentleman for once.

[*The Count stops.*]

BARTHOLO: You'll marry her.

FIGARO: Without the permission of my noble parents?

BARTHOLO: Where are they? Show us them.

FIGARO: Give me a little time. I'm pretty near to finding them. I've been seeking them fifteen years.

BARTHOLO: The foolish braggart! He's some foundling or other.

FIGARO: Not found but lost, Doctor, or possibly stolen.

THE COUNT: Lost or stolen, where's your proof? Or will he say that's an insult?

FIGARO: My Lord! If the lace shawls, embroidered wrappings, and jewels the brigands found on me did not indicate high birth, the precautions someone had taken to give me marks of distinction would be sufficient testimony that I was a child someone valued: this mysterious letter on my arm. [*Rolls up his sleeve.*]

MARCELINE [*jumping up quickly*]: A spatula on your right arm!

FIGARO: How do you know it?

MARCELINE: Heavens, 'tis he!

FIGARO: It's me all right!

BARTHOLO: And who is he?

MARCELINE: Emmanuel!

BARTHOLO: You were stolen by gipsies?

FIGARO [*excited*]: Near a castle. Good Doctor, if you restore me to my noble house put your own price upon the service: mountains of money wouldn't deter my illustrious parents.

BARTHOLO [*pointing to Marceline*]: Behold your mother!

FIGARO: Foster mother?

BARTHOLO: Your own mother!

THE COUNT: His *mother*!

FIGARO: Explain yourself.

MARCELINE [*pointing to Bartholo*]: Behold your father!

FIGARO [*desolated*]: Oh, oh, oh! Have pity on me!

MARCELINE: Has nature not told you so a thousand times?

FIGARO: Never!

THE COUNT [*aside*]: His *mother*!

BRID'OISON: He won't marry her. That's clear.

(BARTHOLO: Nor I either!*

MARCELINE: Nor you! And what about your son? Did you not swear to me . . .

BARTHOLO: I was a fool. If such old associations were binding, there's no saying who one would have to marry.

BRID'OISON: And if we looked at it carefully enough, no one would marry anybody.

BARTHOLO: Faults so notorious. A deplorable youth –

MARCELINE [*warming to it by degrees*]: Ay! Deplorable! More so than you think! I won't attempt to deny my faults—they have been fully exposed today! But it's hard to have to expiate them after thirty years of decent living. I was by nature good and so remained

---

*The passage in brackets was omitted in the original production at the instance of the actors but Beaumarchais restored the cuts in the printed version of the play.

as long as I was allowed to do so, but just at the age when we are beset by illusions, inexperience, and necessity, when seducers besiege us and want stabs us in the back, what can a young girl do against the serried ranks of her enemies? The very man who judges us so severely now has probably compassed the ruin of a dozen such unfortunates himself!

FIGARO: Those who are most blameworthy are the least generous themselves. That's always the way!

MARCELINE: You men, lost to all sense of obligation, who stigmatize with your contempt the playthings of your passions—your unfortunate victims! It's you who ought to be punished for the errors of our youth—you and your magistrates so vain of their right to judge us, you who by your culpable negligence allow us to be deprived of all honest means of existence. What is there for these unhappy girls to do? They had a natural right to make all feminine apparel and yet they let thousands of men be trained to it.

FIGARO [*furiously*]: They even set soldiers to embroidery!

MARCELINE [*carried away by her own eloquence*]: Even in the more exalted walks of life you accord us women no more than a derisory consideration. In a state of servitude behind the alluring pretences of respect, treated as children where our possessions are concerned we are punished as responsible adults where our faults are in question! Ah! Whatever way one looks at it your conduct towards us must provoke horror or compassion!

FIGARO: She's right!

THE COUNT [*aside*]: All too much so.

BRID'OISON: My God! How right she is!

MARCELINE: But what if an unjust man denies us justice, my son? Think no more about whence you came but whither you are bound. That is all that matters to any of us. Within a few months your financée will be her own mistress: she'll accept you: that I'll answer for. Live, then, henceforward in company of a loving wife and mother who will be rivals only in affection for you. Be indulgent towards them and rejoice in your happiness, my son; be gay, free, openhearted with all the world: your mother will seek no other happiness.

FIGARO: You speak wonderfully persuasively, Mother, but I hold to my own opinion. What fools we are indeed! Here the world's been turning for thousands and thousands of years, and in face of that ocean of time, from which I've chanced to snatch some miserable thirty years or so that will never come again, I'm tormenting myself over the question of whom I owe them to. So much the worse for those who bother about such things! Spending one's life on such trivial worries means pulling against the collar with never a break, like the miserable horses on the tow-paths of our rivers: even when they come to a halt they still keep on pulling. We'll take what comes to us.)

THE COUNT: This nonsensical business is spoiling my plans.

BRID'OISON [to Figaro]: And the noble birth and the castle you talked of? You were trying to impose upon justice.

FIGARO: And a fine trick Justice was going to make me do. After all the times I've refrained from breaking this gentleman's neck because of his cursed hundred crowns—he now turns out to be my father! However, since Heaven has prevented me from committing a crime, accept my apologies, Father. And you, Mother, embrace me—as maternally as you can.

[As MARCELINE embraces him, SUZANNE runs in with a purse in her hand, followed by ANTONIO.]

SUZANNE: Stop them, My Lord! Don't let them marry. My Mistress has given me the money to pay her!

THE COUNT: The Devil take her mistress! It seems they are all in conspiracy together! [He goes out.]

ANTONIO [seeing FIGARO embracing his mother]: Hey! Wait a bit, lass, before you start paying.

SUZANNE: I have seen enough: come along, Uncle.

FIGARO [stopping her]: No, you don't! What have you seen?

SUZANNE: My own folly and your baseness.

FIGARO: Neither the one nor the other.

SUZANNE [angrily]: You can jolly well marry her, since you show such affection for her.

FIGARO [*gaily*]: Affectionate we are, but there's no question of marrying.

[SUZANNE *makes to go but* FIGARO *detains her.*]

SUZANNE [*giving him a slap*]: And you have the audacity to try to keep me here!

FIGARO [*to the company*]: I ask you! That's not very loving, is it? [*To Suzanne*] Before you leave us I ask you to take a look at this lady.

SUZANNE: I *am* looking at her.

FIGARO: And what do you think of her?

SUZANNE: She's horrible!

FIGARO: Jealousy! Jealousy! One can always rely on it!

MARCELINE: Come and embrace your mother-to-be, my dear Suzanne. This naughty man who is teasing you so is my very own son.

SUZANNE [*running to her*]: You are his mother?

[*They embrace.*]

ANTONIO: Has it just happened?

FIGARO: So far as I know.

MARCELINE: No, my heart was drawn to him. Only in my motive was I mistaken. It was blood calling to blood.

FIGARO: In my case my own good sense served me for instinct when I refused you. It wasn't that I ever disliked you. After all, I borrowed your money.

MARCELINE: It's yours now. Take your agreement. It can be your wedding gift.

SUZANNE [*giving him the purse*]: And take this too.

FIGARO: Thank you very much.

MARCELINE: Unhappy as a girl, I was about to become the most miserable of wives, and here I am now the most fortunate of mothers: embrace me, my children. In you all my affections unite. My happiness is complete. Ah! My children, how I shall love you!

FIGARO [*touched himself*]: Go easy, mother! Would you have me drown my eyes with the first tears I have ever known? At any rate they are tears of joy. But how stupid of me. I was almost ashamed of them. I felt them trickling between my fingers and tried to restrain them: away with pride! I'll laugh and cry at the same time: one doesn't have such an experience twice. [*Embraces his mother and Suzanne—one on either side of him.*]

MARCELINE: Oh, my dear boy!

SUZANNE: Oh, my dear boy!

BRID'OISON [*wiping his eyes with his handkerchief*]: Ay well! Can it be that I'm getting silly too?

FIGARO [*exalted*]: Misfortune! Now I can defy you! Touch me now if you can with these two dear women to protect me!

ANTONIO [*to Figaro*]: Less of your blarney if you don't mind! When it comes to marrying into a family it's well that the parents should be married first. You understand? Have yours joined hands yet?

BARTHOLO: Have I given my hand? May it wither and drop off before I give it to the mother of such a fool.

ANTONIO: Then you are no father at all! [*To Figaro*] In that case, my lad, there's no more to be said.

SUZANNE: Oh, Uncle!

ANTONIO: Am I going to give my own sister's daughter to a fellow who's nobody's child?

BRID'OISON: How can that be, you fool? We are all somebody's children.

ANTONIO: Fiddle-de-dee! He shan't have her—never! [*Goes out.*]

BARTHOLO [*to Figaro*]: Go and find someone else to adopt you!

[*He is about to go, but* MARCELINE *throws her arms about him and brings him back.*]

MARCELINE: Stay, Doctor! Don't go!

FIGARO [*aside*]: Ay! It seems that all the fools in Andalusia are out to hinder my marriage.

SUZANNE [*to Bartholo*]: Dear father, he's your son!

MARCELINE [*to Bartholo*]: In ability, in brains, and in looks!

FIGARO [*to Bartholo*]: And he hasn't cost you a farthing.

BARTHOLO: What about the hundred crowns that he robbed me of?

MARCELINE [*stroking him*]: We shall take such care of you, papa!

SUZANNE [*likewise—other side*]: We shall all be so proud of you, daddy dear!

BARTHOLO [*weakening*]: Father, papa, daddy dear! It seems that I'm even sillier than this gentleman here [*indicating Brid'oison*].

I'm giving way like a child. [MARCELINE *and* SUZANNE *kiss him.*] No, no! I haven't said yes. [*Turning away*] What's happened to His Lordship?

FIGARO: Let's go to him and make him give the final word! If he's allowed to start any more trickery we shall be back where we started.

ALL: Come along. Hurry!

[*They drag Bartholo with them.*]

BRID'OISON [*alone*]: Sillier than this gentleman here! There are things one can say to oneself . . . they really are a rude lot round here!

ACT FOUR

SCENE: *A gallery with candelabra, hung with flowers and garlands all ready for a fête. Downstage left a writing-table with an armchair behind it.*

FIGARO [*his arm about Suzanne*]: Well, my love, are you content? This silver-tongued mother of mine has converted her Doctor. Little as he likes it, he's going to marry her and your scoundrelly uncle will be silenced: the only one who's still annoyed is His Lordship, for our marriage now becomes the price of theirs. Do laugh at this happy ending!

SUZANNE: Was anything ever so strange?

FIGARO: Or so amusing! We only planned to extract a dowry from His Excellency: we already have two which owe nothing to him. You had a desperate rival; I was tormented by a fury; instead we now have the kindest of mothers. Yesterday I was—as it were—alone in the world; now I have both my parents—not so grand, it's true, as I had imagined them but good enough for us—who lack the vanity of the wealthy.

SUZANNE: All the same, my boy, not one of the things you had planned, and we were expecting, has come true.

FIGARO: Chance has done better than any of us could, my dear. That's the way things are: one works, one schemes, one arranges things in one way: fortune determines them otherwise: from the insatiable conqueror who would gobble up the whole earth to the poor harmless blind creature who lets himself be led by his dog, we are all at the mercy of fortune's caprices: what's more, the blind man with his dog is often better guided, less deceived in his purposes than the other blind man with his train of dependants. As for the blind god whom we call Love . . . [*He takes her tenderly in his arms.*]

SUZANNE: He's the only one who interests me!

FIGARO: Allow me then—to pursue the foolish metaphor—to be your faithful dog that brings love to your pretty little door—and there we are installed for life!

SUZANNE: Love and you?

FIGARO: Me and love.

SUZANNE: And you'll not seek any other abode?

FIGARO: If you ever catch me I'm willing that a thousand million lovers . . .

SUZANNE: You are beginning to exaggerate! Stick to the truth.

FIGARO: My truth is *the* truth.

SUZANNE: Fie! You rascal! Is there more than one sort?

FIGARO: Why yes! Of course! Ever since someone first noticed that in the course of time old follies become wisdom and little seeds of falsehood blossom from modest beginnings into great truths there have been a thousand varieties. There are the truths one knows but dare not divulge—for not all truths can be spoken; those one subscribes to without really believing—for not all truths are acceptable; lovers' vows, mothers' threats, statements made in drink, promises of men in high position, the final word of our merchants—there's no end to them. There's only one truth worth relying on—that's my love for Suzie.

SUZANNE: I love to hear you talk nonsense. It shows how happy you are. But now let's talk about my rendezvous with the Count.

FIGARO: Or rather let's never mention it! It nearly cost me my Suzanne.

SUZANNE: Don't you want it to take place then?

FIGARO: If you love me, Suzie—promise me faithfully to let him go and shiver there alone and serve him right!

SUZANNE: It was much more difficult to say yes to him than it will be to say no. That's decided then.

FIGARO: The truth—you really mean that?

SUZANNE: I'm not like you clever ones—I only know one sort of truth.

FIGARO: And you'll love me a little?

SUZANNE: Lots and lots!

FIGARO: That's not much!

SUZANNE: What d'you mean?

FIGARO: When it comes to love, you know, even too much isn't enough.

SUZANNE: I don't follow these subtleties, but I shall love none but my husband.

FIGARO: Stick to that and you'll be a wonderful exception to the rule. [*He endeavours to kiss her as the* COUNTESS *enters.*]

THE COUNTESS: Ah! I was quite right! Wherever they are, I said, they'll be together. Come, Figaro, it's anticipating the future to be having your *tête-à-tête* now. Your master is wanting you.

FIGARO: True, Madam, I'm forgetting myself. I'll take my excuse with me. [*Endeavours to take Suzanne.*]

THE COUNTESS [*detaining her*]: She shall follow you. [*To Suzanne*] Have you arranged for our change of clothes?

SUZANNE: It won't be needed. The rendezvous is off.

THE COUNTESS: Ah! So you have changed your mind?

SUZANNE: It's Figaro.

THE COUNTESS: You are deceiving me.

SUZANNE: Heavens, no!

THE COUNTESS: Figaro isn't the man to let a dowry slip.

SUZANNE: Ah, Madam, what do you mean?

THE COUNTESS: You have come to an understanding with the Count, so you now regret that you told me his plans. I can see through you. Leave me. [*She makes to go out.*]

SUZANNE [*kneeling before her*]: In Heaven's name and as I hope for salvation, you don't know, Madam, how much you wrong me. After all your goodness and the dowry you have given me . . .

THE COUNTESS [*raising her*]: Alas . . . I don't know what I'm saying! Let me take your place in the garden—so, you'll avoid going yourself, keep faith with your husband, and help me to bring mine back to me.

SUZANNE: But how you have hurt me!

THE COUNTESS: I was just being stupid! [*She kisses her forehead.*] Where is your rendezvous?

SUZANNE: The garden is all I remember.

THE COUNTESS [*pointing to the table*]: Take this pen and let us arrange a place.

SUZANNE: Write to *him*?

THE COUNTESS: You must.

SUZANNE: But Your Ladyship, surely it's you who should . . .

THE COUNTESS: I'll take the responsibility.

[SUZANNE *sits down and the* COUNTESS *dictates.*]

The latest song—the tune 'May it be fine tonight beneath the chestnut trees—may it be fine—tonight'.

SUZANNE [*writing*]: ' . . . beneath the chestnut trees', and then?

THE COUNTESS: Do you think he'll not understand?

SUZANNE [*reading it again*]: It's all right. [*Folds the note.*] How are we to seal it?

THE COUNTESS: Pin it. Quick! It will serve for the reply. Write on the outside, 'Send back the seal.'

SUZANNE [*writes laughing*]: Ah! The seal. This is even more amusing than . . . the affair of the warrant.

THE COUNTESS [*sadly*]: Ah!

SUZANNE [*searching*]: I haven't a pin.

THE COUNTESS [*opening her dress*]: Take this one. [*The ribbon falls to the ground.*] Ah, my ribbon!

SUZANNE [*picking it up*]: It's that little robber's. How could you be so cruel!

THE COUNTESS: Could I let him keep it on his arm? That would have been a nice thing. Give it to me!

SUZANNE: Your Ladyship isn't going to keep it—all stained with that young man's blood?

THE COUNTESS: It will do for Fanchette. The first time she brings me a nosegay . . .

[*Enter* CHÉRUBIN *dressed as a shepherdess*, FANCHETTE *and other girls carrying bouquets.*]

FANCHETTE: Your Ladyship. Here are the village girls bringing flowers for you.

THE COUNTESS [*quickly putting away the ribbon*]: Charming! I'm sorry that I don't know you all. [*Points to Chérubin.*] Who is this charming child who has so modest an air?

A SHEPHERDESS: She's a cousin of mine, Madam. Just here for the wedding.

THE COUNTESS: She's charming. Since I can't hold twenty bouquets we'll do honour to the stranger. [*Takes Chérubin's bouquet and kisses 'her' forehead.*] She's blushing! [*To Suzanne*] Suzanne, don't you think she's like someone . . .

SUZANNE: Yes—almost to the life!

CHÉRUBIN [*aside, bands on his heart*]: Ah! How I've longed for that kiss!

[*Enter the* COUNT *and* ANTONIO.]

ANTONIO: I tell you he's here, My Lord: they changed his clothes in my daughter's room—all his own things are there still and here's his soldier's cap—I picked it up.

[*He goes up to the girls—looks along the line, recognizes Chérubin, and plucks off his woman's bonnet so that his hair falls down straight to his shoulders. He puts the military cap on Chérubin's head.*]

Ay! By Gad! There's our officer!

THE COUNTESS [*recoils*]: Heavens!

SUZANNE: The scamp!

ANTONIO: Didn't I say he was here!

THE COUNT [*angrily*]: Well, Madam!

THE COUNTESS: Well, Sir! I'm more surprised than you are—and no less annoyed.

THE COUNT: Yes, but what do you say now about what happened this morning?

THE COUNTESS: I mustn't keep up the deception any further. He had come down to my room—we started the joke which these young people here have continued. You took us by surprise while we were dressing him. Your first reaction was so violent that he took to flight: I was upset—and the fright we were all in did the rest.

THE COUNT [*angrily to Chérubin*]: Why didn't you go?

CHÉRUBIN [*snatching off his cap*]: My Lord, I . . .

THE COUNT: I shall punish your disobedience.

FANCHETTE [*thoughtlessly*]: Oh, Your Lordship! Listen to me! Whenever you come wanting to kiss me, you always say, 'I'll give you anything you like if only you'll love me, my little Fanchette!'

THE COUNT [*blushing*]: *I* say that?

FANCHETTE: Yes, Your Lordship! So instead of punishing Chérubin let me marry him and I'll love you to distraction.

THE COUNT [*aside*]: To be bewitched by a page!

THE COUNTESS: Well, Sir, it's your turn now. This child's confession, as naïve as my own, confirms a double truth. Any cause for disquiet I may give you is always unintentional, but you do everything possible to justify mine.

ANTONIO: You as well, My Lord! Egad! I shall have to straighten her up as I did her mother. . . . It's not that it matters now, but as Her Ladyship knows very well, little girls when they grow up . . .

THE COUNT [*aside, disconcerted*]: Some evil genius here turns everything to my disadvantage.

[*Enter* FIGARO.]

FIGARO: My Lord, if you are going to detain our young ladies we shan't be able to start either the fête or the dancing.

THE COUNT: Dancing? *You* dance? What are you thinking about? After falling this morning and spraining your ankle!

FIGARO [*shaking his foot*]: I still feel it a little, but it's nothing. [*To the girls*] Come along, my beauties. Come along.

THE COUNT [*detaining him*]: You were lucky that the flower-beds were so soft to fall on.

FIGARO: Very lucky! Otherwise . . .

ANTONIO: [*detaining him*]: But then he curled himself up as he jumped!

FIGARO: I suppose a better jumper would have remained in midair, eh? Come along, ladies!

ANTONIO [*detaining him*]: And all the time the page was on his horse and galloping towards Seville, eh?

FIGARO: Galloping or cantering . . .

THE COUNT: And you with his warrant in your pocket.

FIGARO [*a little surprised*]: Of course! Why all this questioning? Come along, girls.

ANTONIO [*catching Chérubin by the waist*]: There's one here can prove my future nephew a liar.

FIGARO: Chérubin! [*Aside*] Confound the little fool!

ANTONIO: You get it now, eh?

FIGARO [*thinking rapidly*]: Yes, I get it. I get it. What tale is *he* telling?

THE COUNT: His tale is that he did the jumping into the wall-flowers.

FIGARO: Well—it could be—if he says so. I don't dispute what I know nothing about.

THE COUNT: So you and he both . . .

FIGARO: Why not? Jumping can be infectious. Remember Panurge's sheep. And when Your Lordship is in a temper most people would prefer to risk . . .

THE COUNT: What, two at a time?

FIGARO: Two dozen at a time. But what does it matter since no one was hurt? [*To the girls*] Are you coming or not?

THE COUNT [*annoyed*]: Is this a play we are acting? [*Fanfare off.*]

FIGARO: That's the signal for the procession. To your positions ladies! Come, Suzanne, give me your arm.

[*All run off, leaving Chérubin behind. He hangs his head.*]

THE COUNT [*watching Figaro go*]: The audacity! As for you, Master Sly-boots—who pretend to be ashamed of yourself now—go and get dressed at once and don't let me set eyes on you at tonight's entertainment.

THE COUNTESS: He's going to be terribly bored.

CHÉRUBIN [*thoughtlessly*]: Bored? A certain imprint on my forehead would compensate for a hundred years' confinement. [*Puts his cap on and runs off.*]

THE COUNT: What imprint has he on his forehead that he's so pleased about?

THE COUNTESS [*embarrassed*]: Of his—first soldier's cap. Everything's a toy for children his age. [*She is going out.*]

THE COUNT: Are you not staying?

THE COUNTESS: You know I'm not feeling well.

THE COUNT: Stay awhile for the sake of your protégée, or I shall believe you are annoyed.

THE COUNTESS: Here come the wedding parties. Let us sit and receive them.

THE COUNT: Weddings! I suppose one must put up with what one cannot prevent.

[*They sit down at one side of the stage. Enter the bridal parties to the tune of* Les Folies d'Espagne. *First huntsmen with shouldered guns. The alguazil, the magistrate, and* BRID'OISON, *peasants in holiday costume, girls carrying the bridal crown, some with the veil, some with gloves and bouquet.* ANTONIO *gives his hand to Suzanne as the one who is to give her away: other young girls carry another set of bridal regalia for Marceline.* FIGARO *gives his hand to Marceline, he being the one who will give her away (to the* DOCTOR, *who brings up the rear with a great bouquet). The peasants, having taken up positions on opposite sides of the stage, dance the fandango. While the refrain is being played* ANTONIO *brings Suzanne forward to the Count and she kneels before him. While the* COUNT *presents her with the bridal toque, the veil, and the bouquet, two girls sing:*]

Young wife about to be sing the glory and the praise
Of a Lord who is renouncing a right of former days!
Forgoing his own pleasure your honour he prefers
And on a happy husband a virgin bride confers!

SUZANNE *is kneeling, and during the last words of the verse she pulls at the Count's coat and shows him the note which she is holding: then she brings the hand nearest the audience in which she holds the letter up to her head and as the* COUNT *makes as if to adjust her toque she gives it to him. He puts it inside his breast pocket; the singing finishes;* SUZANNE *rises and makes a deep curtsey.* FIGARO *receives her from the Count and returns with her to the opposite side of the stage near to Marceline while the fandango is danced again. The* COUNT *seeks an opportunity to read the letter and withdraws towards the wings, but as he draws it from his coat he makes the gesture of a man pricked by a pin. He shakes his finger, presses it, sucks it, and looks at the paper.*]

THE COUNT: Confound the way women stick pins everywhere.

FIGARO [*who has seen everything, to his mother and Suzanne*]: It's a love-letter from some young woman. The pin has had the audacity to prick him.

[*During the foregoing speeches the orchestra plays* pianissimo. *The dance is resumed. The* COUNT *has read the letter, turned it over, and seen the invitation to return the pin. He looks for it on the ground, picks it up, and sticks it in his sleeve.*]

FIGARO: Everything is precious that belongs to the loved one. See how he picks up the pin! Ah, what a fellow he is!

[*Meanwhile* SUZANNE *exchanges signs with the* COUNTESS, *the dance finishes, and the chorus begins again.* FIGARO *brings up Marceline and the* COUNT *is about to take the crown when there is an interruption.*]

USHER [*at the door*]: Stop, gentlemen! You can't all come in! Help me, guards!

[*Guards move to the door.*]

THE COUNT: What is it?

USHER: My Lord, it's Don Bazile. The whole village is following him. He's still singing as he goes.

THE COUNT: Let him come in, alone!

THE COUNTESS: Permit me to retire.

THE COUNT: I appreciate your forbearance.

THE COUNTESS: Suzanne! She'll come back. [*Aside to Suzanne*] Come along and let us change clothes.

[*They go out together.*]

MARCELINE: He always comes at the wrong time.

FIGARO: I'll make him sing small.

[*Enter* BAZILE *with his guitar and* GRIPE-SOLEIL.]

BAZILE [*singing*]:

> Let those whose love is firm and true
> Despise the love that's fleeting.
> What harm if I should cast an eye
> On every girl I'm meeting?
> If love is not to fly away

> Then what has Cupid wings for, pray?
> If love is not to fly away
> Then what has Cupid wings for, pray?

FIGARO [*advancing to meet him*]: Ay! We all know what his wings are for! But tell me, friend, what's all this noise about?

BAZILE [*pointing to Gripe-Soleil*]: So that, having proved my loyalty to His Lordship by diverting this gentleman who is His Lordship's guest, I may in my turn demand justice of him.

GRIPE-SOLEIL: Bah! My Lord! He ain't diverted me in the least. All them old fag-ends of tunes . . .

THE COUNT: Well, then, what do you want of me, Bazile?

BAZILE: What belongs to me. The hand of Marceline—and I'm here to oppose . . .

FIGARO: How long is it since you looked a fool in the face, Sir?

BAZILE: I am doing now.

FIGARO: Since my eyes make so good a mirror, take good note of my prediction. If you so much as show the slightest sign of coming near the lady . . .

BARTHOLO [*laughing*]: Why not? Let's hear what he has to say.

BRID'OISON [*coming between them*]: Why should two friends . . .

FIGARO: Friends! Us!

BAZILE: What an idea!

FIGARO: Just because he writes stupid music for church?

BAZILE: Because he scribbles his piffling verses?

FIGARO: A taproom warbler!

BAZILE: A newspaper hack!

FIGARO: An oratorio blockhead!

BAZILE: A diplomat jockey!

THE COUNT [*seated*]: They are equally insolent.

BAZILE: He never shows me any respect.

FIGARO: True! But how could I?

BAZILE: Goes about calling me a fool everywhere.

FIGARO: So you think I'm an echo?

BAZILE: Whereas there's never a singer I don't set on the road to success.

FIGARO: Set off bawling, you mean!

BAZILE: There he goes again!

FIGARO: And why not, if it's the truth? Are you a prince of the blood that one has to flatter you? Since there's nothing to be got from lying to you, you must put up with the truth, you idiot. Anyhow, if you are frightened of our telling you the truth, why do you come interfering with our marriage?

BAZILE [*to Marceline*]: Did you—or did you not—promise me that if you weren't fixed up within four years you'd give me the chance?

MARCELINE: On what condition did I promise it?

BAZILE: That if you could find a certain lost child I should adopt him.

ALL: He's found!

BAZILE: He can't be!

ALL [*indicating Figaro*]: Here he is!

BAZILE [*recoiling*]: The Devil!

BRID'OISON: So . . . you renounce your claim to the mother?

BAZILE: Could anything be worse than to be thought the father of a scoundrel?

FIGARO: To be thought the son! Are you getting at me?

BAZILE [*pointing to Figaro*]: Since this gentleman is apparently somebody here, then let me be a nobody. [*He goes out.*]

BARTHOLO [*laughing*]: Ha ha ha!

FIGARO [*jumping with joy*]: So I'm to have my wife in the end!

THE COUNT [*aside*]: And I my mistress!

BRID'OISON [*to Marceline*]: So everybody's satisfied.

THE COUNT: Let the two contracts be prepared. I will sign them.

ALL: *Vivat!* [*They go out.*]

THE COUNT: I too need to retire a while. [*Makes as if to go.*]

GRIPE-SOLEIL: And I must see to fixing the fireworks under the big chestnut trees as instructed.

THE COUNT [*turning back*]: What fool has given such an instruction?

FIGARO: Why not?

THE COUNT [*sharply*]: The Countess is unwell! How is she going to see the display? It must be on the terrace in front of her apartments.

FIGARO: You hear, Gripe-Soleil? The terrace.

THE COUNT: Under the chestnuts! A fine idea! [*Aside as he goes*] They were going to light up my rendezvous! [*He goes.*]

FIGARO: He shows unusual consideration for his wife!

MARCELINE: A word with you, son. I want to make things straight with you. Mistaken impressions led me to do your wife an injustice: I thought she had an understanding with the Count, though Bazile always maintained that she kept him at a distance.

FIGARO: You don't understand your son if you think he can be upset by any aberrations of the female sex. I defy the cleverest of them to make a fool of me.

MARCELINE: There's no harm in thinking that, my son: jealousy . . .

FIGARO: Springs either from pride or from folly! I'm philosophic on that score—imperturbable! Should Suzanne ever deceive me, I pardon her beforehand. She'll have her work cut out!

[*Enter* FANCHETTE.]

Ah, my little cousin is eavesdropping!

FANCHETTE: No. No, I'm, not—they say it's naughty to listen.

FIGARO: True, but it's useful: people don't always realize that.

FANCHETTE: I was looking to see if there was anyone here.

FIGARO: One fib already, you scamp! You know that he couldn't be . . .

FANCHETTE: Who?

FIGARO: Chérubin.

FANCHETTE: I'm not looking for him. I know where he is. It's my cousin, Suzanne.

FIGARO: And what does my little cousin want with her?

FANCHETTE: I'll tell you since you are my cousin now—it's only a pin I have to give back to her.

FIGARO: A pin! A pin! From whom, you minx? So young and already plying your trade. . . . [*Recovers his self-control.*] You have done very well, Fanchette. It's very kind of my little cousin. . . .

FANCHETTE: Then what are you so annoyed about? I'm going.

FIGARO [*detaining her*]: No, no! I'm only joking; look, your little pin is the one His Lordship told you to give back to Suzanne: it was used to fasten up a note that he held in his hand. You see I know all about it.

FANCHETTE: Then if you know all this why do you ask about it?

FIGARO [*fishing*]: Because it would be amusing to know how His Lordship contrived to give you the pin.

FANCHETTE [*naïvely*]: Just as you said. 'Here, little Fanchette, give this pin to your fair cousin and just say that it's the seal for the big chestnut trees.'

FIGARO: The big —?

FANCHETTE: Chestnut trees. It's true that he added, 'Take care nobody sees you.'

FIGARO: And you must do as you were told, cousin. Fortunately nobody has seen you. So go do your job nicely and don't tell Suzanne anything but what His Lordship told you to do.

FANCHETTE: Why should I? He seems to take me for a fool, this new cousin of mine! [*Exit skipping.*]

FIGARO: Well, mother?

MARCELINE: Well, son?

FIGARO [*as if choking*]: Well it just shows—some things really are . . .

MARCELINE: What things?

FIGARO [*holding his chest*]: Something I've heard. It weighs as heavy as lead on my heart.

MARCELINE [*laughing*]: So all this assurance was nothing but an inflated balloon—one little pin deflates it.

FIGARO [*furious*]: But the pin was the one he picked up, mother!

MARCELINE [*recalling his words*]: Jealousy! Oh, 'I'm philosophic on that score! Should Suzanne ever deceive me I pardon her. . . .'

FIGARO: Oh mother! We talk as our feelings dictate. Put the coolest of judges to plead his own cause and see him expound the law! I see now why he was concerned about the fireworks! But as for the young lady with the pin, she isn't going to get away with it—she and her chestnuts! If I'm sufficiently married to give me the right to be angry—on the other hand, I'm not so much committed that I can't marry someone else and leave her to . . .

MARCELINE: A fine conclusion, I must say! Let's destroy ourselves on the merest suspicion! What proof have you, my boy, that she's deceiving you and not the Count? Have you some new insight into her character that you condemn her unheard? Are you sure that she'll go to the rendezvous? And why? Or what she'll say when she gets there? Or what she'll do when she does? I thought you had more sense!

FIGARO [*kissing her hand*]: My mother's right! She's right, right, always right! But let's allow something, mother, for human nature: we feel better for it afterwards. We'll look into it before accusing and taking action—I know the rendezvous. Good-bye, mother. [*Goes out.*]

MARCELINE: Good-bye. And I know as well. Having dealt with him, we'll see what Suzanne's up to, or rather we'll give her a warning: she's such a pretty creature. Ah! How we poor downtrodden women are drawn to run to each other's help against these proud and terrible simpletons—men—when personal interest doesn't set us against each other!

ACT FIVE

SCENE: *A chestnut grove in a park; pavilions, kiosks, or garden temples are on either side; upstage is a clearing between two hedges; a garden seat downstage. It is dark.*

[FANCHETTE *alone, holding in one hand two biscuits and an orange, in the other a paper lantern, lighted.*]

FANCHETTE: In the left-hand pavilion, he said. That's this one. Supposing he were not here yet my little partner—those horrid people in the kitchen didn't even want to give me an orange and a couple of biscuits. . . . 'Who wants them?' 'Oh, well, Sir, they're for someone. . . . 'Ah we know!' Well, what if they do know! Just because His Lordship can't bear the sight of him, does he have to perish of hunger? Even then it cost me a kiss! Who knows, perhaps he'll repay me!

[*She sees* FIGARO, *who comes and looks closely at her. She cries out: 'Ah!', then takes to her heels and runs across to the pavilion on her left.*]

FIGARO [*wearing a cloak and a hat with the wide brim turned down*]: It's Fanchette.

[*Enter* BARTHOLO, BAZILE, ANTONIO, BRID'OISON, GRIPE-SOLEIL, *valets, and workmen.*]

FIGARO [*fiercely, looking closely at each of the others as they arrive*]: Good evening, Gentlemen, good evening! Are you all here?

BAZILE: All whom you required to come.

FIGARO: About what time is it?

ANTONIO [*looking up*]: Moon should be up by now.

BARTHOLO: And what dark deeds are you up to now? He has a conspiratorial air!

FIGARO: I ask you! Didn't you come to the castle for a wedding?

BRID'OISON: Certainly.

ANTONIO: We were going down to the park to await the signal for the fête.

FIGARO: You won't need to go any farther, Gentlemen. It's here under the chestnuts that we are going to sing the praises of my worthy fiancée and the noble lord who has his own intentions in regard to her.

BAZILE [*recalling the day's events*]: Ah, yes, I know what it is! Take my advice and let's retire. It's a question of a rendezvous. I'll tell you all about it later.

BRID'OISON [*to Figaro*]: We—we'll c-come back!

FIGARO: Don't fail to come at once when I call. You can blame me if you don't see something interesting.

BARTHOLO: Remember that a wise man doesn't meddle with the affairs of the great.

FIGARO: I'll remember.

BARTHOLO: They are always one up on us because of their rank.

FIGARO: Apart from their ingenious little ways which you are forgetting about. But remember also that once a man is known to be faint-hearted he's at the mercy of every rascal that comes along.

BARTHOLO: Very true.

FIGARO: And that I bear on my mother's side the honoured name of Verte-Allure.

BARTHOLO: The Devil's in him!

BRID'OISON: He is, he—is, he is!

BAZILE [*aside*]: The Count and Suzanne have managed without me! So I don't mind what trick he plays.

FIGARO [to the servants]: As for you others, knaves that you are, do as I told you and get the whole area lighted up or, by that death I wish I was at grips with, if I get hold of any of you—[Seizes Gripe-Soleil by the arm.]

GRIPE-SOLEIL [goes off howling]: Ah, oh, ooh! You brute!

BAZILE [going]: Heaven send you joy, Mr Bridegroom!

[They all go out.]

FIGARO [gloomily walking up and down in the dark]: Oh, woman, woman, woman, feeble creature that you are! No living thing can fail to be true to its nature. Is it yours to deceive? After stubbornly refusing when I urged her to it in the presence of her mistress— at the very moment of her plighting her, word to me, in the very midst of the ceremony . . . and he smiled while he read it, the scoundrel! And I standing by like a blockhead! No, My Lord Count, you shan't have her, you shall not have her! Because you are a great nobleman you think you are a great genius. . . . Nobility, fortune, rank, position! How proud they make a man feel! What have *you* done to deserve such advantages? Put yourself to the trouble of being born—nothing more! For the rest— a very ordinary man! Whereas I, lost among the obscure crowd, have had to deploy more knowledge, more calculation and skill merely to survive than has sufficed to rule all the provinces of Spain for a century! Yet you would measure yourself against me. . . . Somebody's coming—it's she! No, it's nobody at all. The night's as dark as the very devil and here am I plying the stupid trade of husband though I'm still only half married. [Sits down.] Could anything be stranger than a fate like mine? Son of goodness knows whom, stolen by bandits, brought up to their way of life, I become disgusted with it and yearn for an honest profession—only to find myself repulsed everywhere. I study Chemistry, Pharmacy, Surgery, and all the prestige of a great nobleman can barely secure me the handling of a horse-doctor's probe! Weary of making sick animals worse and determined to do something different, I throw myself headlong into the theatre. Alas, I might as well have put a stone round my neck! I fudge up a play about the manners of the Seraglio: a Spanish author, I imag-

.ned, could attack Mahomet without scruple, but, immediately, some envoy from goodness-knows-where complains that some of my lines offend the Sublime Porte, Persia, some part or other of the East Indies, the whole of Egypt, and the Kingdoms of Cyrenaica, Tripoli, Tunis, Algiers, and Morocco. Behold my play scuppered to please a set of Mohammedan princes—not one of whom I believe can read—who habitually beat a tattoo on our shoulders to the tune of 'Down with the Christian dogs!' Unable to break my spirit they decided to take it out of my body. My cheeks grew furrowed: my time was out. I saw in the distance the approach of the fell sergeant, his quill stuck into his wig: trembling I summoned all my resources. Economic matters were under discussion. Since one can talk about things even though one doesn't possess them—and though in fact I hadn't a penny, I wrote a treatise on the Theory of Value and its relation to the net product of national wealth. Whereupon I found myself looking from the depths of a hired carriage at the drawbridge of a castle, lowered for my reception, and abandoned all hope of liberty. [*Rises.*] How I would like to have hold of one of those Jacks in office—so indifferent to the evils that they cause—when disaster had extinguished his pride! I'd tell him that stupidities that appear in print acquire importance only in so far as their circulation is restricted, that unless there is liberty to criticize, praise has no value, and that only trivial minds are apprehensive of trivial scribbling. [*He sits again.*] Tiring of housing an obscure pensioner, they put me into the street eventually, and, since a man must eat even though he isn't in jail, I sharpen my quill again, inquire how things are going, and am told that during my economic retreat there had been established in Madrid a system of free sale of commodities which extended even to the products of the press, and that, provided I made no reference in my articles to the authorities or to religion, or to politics, or to morals, or to high officials, or to influential organizations, or the Opera, or to any theatrical productions, or to anybody of any standing whatsoever, I could freely print anything I liked—subject to the approval of two or three censors! In order to profit from this very acceptable freedom I announce a new periodical which, not wishing to tread on anyone else's toes, I call the *Good for Nothing Journal*. Phew! A thousand miserable scribblers are immediately up in arms against me: my paper is suppressed and there I am out of work once again! I was on the point of giving up in despair when it occurred to someone to offer me a job. Unfortunately I had some qualification for it— it needed a knowledge of figures—but it was a dancer who got it! Nothing was left to me but stealing, so I set up as a banker at Faro. Now notice what happens! I dine out in style, and so-called fashionable people throw open their houses to me—keeping three-quarters of the profits for themselves. I could well have restored my fortunes: I even began to understand that in making money *savoir-faire* is more important than true knowledge. But since everybody was involved in some form of swindle and at the same time demanding honesty from me, I inevitably went under again. This time I renounced the world, and twenty fathoms of water might have divided me from it when a beneficent Providence recalled me to my original estate. I picked up my bundle and my leather strop and, leaving illusions to the fools who can live by them and my pride in the middle of the road as too heavy a burden for a pedestrian, I set out with my razor from town to town, and lived henceforward carefree. A great nobleman comes to Seville and he recognizes me. I get him safely married, and as a reward for my trouble in helping him to a wife he now wants to intercept mine! Intrigue! Plots—stormy interludes! I'm on the point of falling into an abyss and marrying my own mother when, lo and behold, my parents turn up one after the other! [*He rises.*] Debate and discussion. It's you, it's him, it's me, it's thee, no, it isn't any of us, no, who is it then? [*Falls into his seat again.*] Oh! Fantastic series of events! Why should they happen to me? Why these things and not others? Who made me responsible? Obliged to follow a road I set out on, all unknowing, and one I shall come to the end of, willy nilly, I have strewn it with such flowers as my high spirits have permitted: I say my high spirits without knowing whether they are any more mine than the rest or who is this 'me' that I'm worrying about: a formless aggregation of unidentified parts, then a puny stupid being, a frisky little animal, a young man ardent in the pursuits of pleasure with every taste for enjoyment, plying all sorts of trades in order to live—now master, now servant, as fortune pleases, ambitious from vanity, industrious from necessity, but lazy from inclination! Orator in emergency, poet for relaxation, musician when occasion demands, in love by mad fits and starts. I've seen everything, done everything, been everything. At last all illusions destroyed—disabused—all too much disabused—Oh, Suzie, Suzie, Suzie, what torture you put upon me! I hear some-one coming. This is the moment of decision!

[*Withdraws off-stage—right. Enter the* COUNTESS, *dressed as Suzanne,* SUZANNE, *dressed as the Countess, and* MARCELINE.]

SUZANNE [*to the Countess in a whisper*]: Yes, Marceline told me that Figaro would be here.

MARCELINE: So he is. Lower your voice.

SUZANNE: So—one listens and the other comes looking for me. Let us begin.

MARCELINE: I don't mean to lose a word. I'll hide in this pavilion.

[*Goes in where Fanchette is.*]

SUZANNE: Your Ladyship is trembling. Are you cold?

THE COUNTESS: The evening is damp. I'm going to go inside.

SUZANNE: If Your Ladyship doesn't need me I'll take the air a little under the trees.

THE COUNTESS: You'll get the dew on you.

SUZANNE: I'm prepared for it.

FIGARO [*aside*]: Oh, yes! For the dew!

[SUZANNE *retires towards the alley opposite where Figaro is. Enter* CHÉRUBIN *in uniform singing gaily the chorus of his ballad.*]

CHÉRUBIN:

> Alas! My heart is in pain
> I shall ne'er see my true love again. . . .

THE COUNTESS [*aside*]: The page!

CHÉRUBIN [*stops*]: There's someone about! Let me get to my hiding-place where little Fanchette . . . It's a woman!

THE COUNTESS [*overhearing*]: Heavens!

CHÉRUBIN [*bending down and peering through the darkness*]: Am I mistaken? From the headdress and features I can just make out in the dark it seems to be Suzie.

THE COUNTESS [*aside*]: Supposing the Count were to come. . . .

[*The* COUNT *appears upstage.*]

CHÉRUBIN [*approaching and taking the Countess's hand in spite of her attempts to avoid him*]: Yes, it's no other than our charming Suzie. Could I mistake this soft little hand and the way that it trembles—or the beating of my own heart?

[*The* COUNTESS *draws her hand away.*]

THE COUNTESS [*in a whisper*]: Go away!

CHÉRUBIN: If it is pity that has drawn you to the part of of the park where I'm hiding . . .

THE COUNTESS: Figaro is coming.

THE COUNT [*coming downstage—aside*]: Isn't it Suzanne I see?

CHÉRUBIN: I'm not frightened of Figaro. It isn't him you are waiting for.

THE COUNTESS: Who is it, then?

THE COUNT [*aside*]: There's someone with her.

CHÉRUBIN: It's His Lordship, you hussy! He asked for a rendezvous with you when I was behind the chair this morning.

THE COUNT [*aside, furious*]: It's that infernal page again.

FIGARO [*aside*]: And they say one shouldn't eavesdrop!

SUZANNE [*aside*]: The little chatterer.

THE COUNTESS [*to the page*]: Be good enough to go away.

CHÉRUBIN: Not until I've received the reward of obedience.

THE COUNTESS [*alarmed*]: You have the audacity . . .

CHÉRUBIN [*with enthusiasm*]: Twenty kisses for yourself and then a hundred for your fair Mistress.

THE COUNTESS: How dare you!

CHÉRUBIN: Oh, I dare all right! You take her place with the Count. I take his with you—the one most taken in is Figaro.

FIGARO [*aside*]: Scoundrel!

SUZANNE [*aside*]: Cheeky as only a page can be!

[CHÉRUBIN *attempts to kiss the Countess, the* COUNT *puts himself between them and receives the kiss.*]

THE COUNTESS [*slipping aside*]: Heavens!

FIGARO [*aside—hearing the kiss*]: A nice little girl I was marrying!

CHÉRUBIN [*feeling at the Count's clothes—aside*]: It's His Lordship! [*Runs into pavilion where Marceline and Fanchette are.*]

FIGARO [*coming towards him*]: I'm going to . . .

THE COUNT [*thinking he is talking to the page*]: Since you aren't repeating the kiss . . . [*Aims a blow at him.*]

FIGARO [*who receives it*]: Ah!

THE COUNT: That's one paid off.

FIGARO [*aside as he rubs his cheek*]: Eavesdropping isn't all fun.

SUZANNE [*laughing out loud from the other side of the stage*]: Ha, ha, ha!

THE COUNT [*to the Countess, whom he takes for Suzanne*]: What can one make of this page! He gets a slap like that and goes off laughing.

FIGARO [*aside*]: If he'd got the one that I got –

THE COUNT: I can't take a step without . . . but let's forget all this nonsense. He'll spoil all the pleasure of finding you here.

THE COUNTESS [*pretending to talk like Suzanne*]: Were you expecting to?

THE COUNT: After your clever message! [*Takes her hand.*] You are trembling.

THE COUNTESS: I was frightened!

THE COUNT: I didn't mean you to forgo a kiss because I got his.

THE COUNTESS: What liberties!

FIGARO [*aside*]: You hussy!

SUZANNE [*aside*]: Charming!

THE COUNT [*taking her hand*]: What a lovely skin! Would the Countess had such a hand!

THE COUNTESS [*aside*]: How little you know!

THE COUNT: Or an arm so firm and rounded! Or such pretty fingers!

THE COUNTESS [*counterfeiting Suzanne's voice*]: Is this how love . . .

THE COUNT: Love is no more than the story of one's heart; pleasure is the reality that brings me to your feet. . . .

THE COUNTESS: Don't you love her any more?

THE COUNT: Very much—but three years of marriage makes it seem so respectable.

THE COUNTESS: What did you seek in her?

THE COUNT: What I find in you, my beautiful one.

THE COUNTESS: Such as?

THE COUNT: I don't know. More variety perhaps . . . more liveliness of manner, some indefinable quality that constitutes charm: an occasional rebuff perhaps? How do I know? Our wives think they do all that is necessary in loving us. Once it's settled that they love us—they go on doing so. *How* they go on! (Assuming they do love us!) They are so complaint, so acquiescent—always and all the time, until one fine day one is surprised to find satiety where one looked for happiness.

THE COUNTESS [*aside*]: Ah! What a lesson!

THE COUNT: The truth is, Suzie, I have thought many a time that, if we husbands pursue elsewhere the pleasure which eludes us with our wives, it's because they don't give enough attention to the art of holding our interest, of renewing affection, and, so to speak, reviving the charm of possession with the spice of variety.

THE COUNTESS: So it all rests with them?

THE COUNT [*laughing*]: Certainly it doesn't rest with us! Can we change the order of nature? Our part is to win them—theirs –

THE COUNTESS: Theirs?

THE COUNT: Is to keep us. It's too often forgotten.

THE COUNTESS: *I* shan't forget it.

THE COUNT: Nor *I*!

FIGARO [*aside*]: Nor *I*!

SUZANNE [*aside*]: Nor *I*!

THE COUNT [*taking his wife's hand*]: There's an echo somewhere about. We mustn't speak so loud. You don't need to worry, you whom love has so endowed with life and with beauty. Just a dash of caprice and you would be the most provoking of mistresses. [*Kisses her forehead.*] My Suzanne—a Castilian's word is his bond. Here is the gold I promised for the re-purchase of the right I no longer enjoy to the delicious moment you are going to accord me. But, because the grace with which you accord it is beyond price, I add to it this brilliant to wear for love of me.

THE COUNTESS [*curtseying*]: Suzanne accepts all that you offer.

FIGARO [*aside*]: Could depravity go farther?

SUZANNE [aside]: So much more grist to the mill.

THE COUNT [aside]: She's mercenary. So much the better.

THE COUNTESS [looking upstage]: I see torches.

THE COUNT: It's the people preparing for your marriage celebrations. We'll go in one of these pavilions and let them pass by.

THE COUNTESS: Without a light?

THE COUNT: Why not? We aren't going to read!

FIGARO: Upon my word, she's going in! I might have known it!
    [Comes forward.]

THE COUNT [in a commanding tone]: Who goes there?

FIGARO: I'm not going. I'm coming.

THE COUNT: It's Figaro! [Flies.]

THE COUNTESS: I'll follow you.
    [She goes into the pavilion on the right, while the COUNT disappears among the trees.]

FIGARO [still thinking the Countess was Suzanne, trying to see where they have gone]: I hear nothing now. They've gone in and there it is! [In an altered voice] You foolish husbands who rely on hired investigators and spend months struggling with your suspicions and never arriving at any certainty—why don't you follow my example? From the very outset I follow my wife, I listen and immediately know all there is to know. Charming! No doubts, no suspicions! I know just where I stand. [Moving quickly] Fortunately I don't mind in the least, her trickery doesn't touch me at all. But now I have got them . . .

SUZANNE [coming forward in the dark—aside]: You shall pay for these suspicions. [Imitating the Countess] Who goes there?

FIGARO [wildly]: Who goes there! One who heartily wishes that he'd never been born!

SUZANNE [again as the Countess]: Why! It's Figaro!

FIGARO [peering at her]: Your Ladyship!

SUZANNE: Don't talk so loud.

FIGARO: Ah, Madam! Heaven brings you here at the right moment. Where do you think His Lordship is?

SUZANNE: What does he matter to me? Ungrateful that he is. . . .

FIGARO: And Suzanne—my bride-to-be—where do you think she is?

SUZANNE: Not so loud.

FIGARO: That Suzie whom I thought so virtuous, who pretended to be so modest . . . they are in there together. . . . I'm going to call . . .

SUZANNE [*putting her hand over her mouth and forgetting to disguise her voice*]: Don't!

FIGARO: It's Suzie. God damn!

SUZANNE [*in the Countess's voice*]: You seem distraught.

FIGARO [*aside*]: The traitress! She's trying to trick me.

SUZANNE: We must have our revenge, Figaro.

FIGARO: you really want it?

SUZANNE: I shouldn't be true to my sex if I didn't . . . but men have a hundred ways of . . .

FIGARO [*confidently*]: Madam. We need everyone here. The woman's way—is much the best.

SUZANNE [*aside*]: How I'll wallop him!

FIGARO [*aside*]: It would be a lark if before the marriage . . .

SUZANNE: But what sort of revenge is it that a little love won't add spice to?

FIGARO: Though love may not be visible, it may well be concealed under the cloak of deference.

SUZANNE [*hurt*]: I don't know whether you really think that but it's not nice of you to say it.

FIGARO [*with a comic pretence of emotion—on his knees*]: Ah, Madam, I adore you! Consider the time and the place and the circumstances—and may your resentment make up for any graces my supplications may lack!

SUZANNE [*aside*]: My hand is itching!

FIGARO [*aside*]: My heart is pounding.

SUZANNE: But, Sir, have you considered?

FIGARO: Yes, Madam, I have considered.

SUZANNE: That where anger and love are concerned . . .

FIGARO: He who hesitates is lost. Your hand, Madam?

SUZANNE [*in her natural voice—giving him a smack*]: There it is!

FIGARO: Oh *demonio!* What a clout!

SUZANNE: Then what about this one? [*Gives him another.*]

FIGARO: Oh! What's this? The devil! What do you think you are doing? Beating carpets?

SUZANNE [*hitting him at each phrase*]: 'Oh! What's this?' It's me—Suzanne. There's one for your suspicions and one for your revenge, and another for your treachery and your tricks and your insults and all that you were going to do! Is that the way you love me? How does it square with the way you talked this morning?

FIGARO: Ah! Santa Barbara! Yes—it's love all right! Oh happiness! Oh, a hundred times happy Figaro! Keep it up, my darling! Beat me to your heart's content. But when you've beaten me black and blue give a kind glance, Suzie, to the luckiest man who was ever beaten by the hand of a woman!

SUZANNE: The luckiest man! You scoundrel! And yet you didn't hesitate to try it on with the Countess and with such a farrago of specious nonsense that, forgetting who I was, it really was on her behalf that I yielded.

FIGARO: And do you think I could mistake your own lovely voice?

SUZANNE [*laughing*]: You recognized me? Oh! How I'll get my own back yet.

FIGARO: You give a fellow a hiding and yet bear malice; that's just like a woman! But do explain how I came to find you here, when I thought you were with him: why these clothes which misled me and now prove your innocence?

SUZANNE: Ah! You are the innocent! You walk straight into the trap laid for someone else. Is it our fault—if we try to muzzle one fox and catch two?

FIGARO: Well, who's caught the other fellow?

SUZANNE: His wife.

FIGARO: His wife?

SUZANNE: His wife!

FIGARO [*wildly*]: Ah Figaro! Go hang yourself! Fancy not twigging that! His wife? Oh! The cunning—the infinite cunning of women. And so the kisses I heard in this alley –

SUZANNE: Were bestowed on Her Ladyship.

FIGARO: And the page's?

SUZANNE: On His Lordship.

FIGARO: And earlier—behind the sofa.

SUZANNE: On nobody.

FIGARO: Are you sure?

SUZANNE [*laughing*]: You are asking for another smack, Figaro!

FIGARO [*kissing her hand*]: I treasure every single one. But the one the Count gave was in earnest.

SUZANNE: There you go again! On your knees!

FIGARO: I deserve it! On my knees! I crawl. I grovel! [*He does so.*]

SUZANNE [*laughing*]: Ah! The poor Count! What a lot of trouble he's gone to. . . .

FIGARO [*getting up*]: To achieve the conquest of his own wife.

[*The* COUNT *appears upstage.*]

THE COUNT [*to himself*]: I can't find her anywhere in the wood. Perhaps she's here.

SUZANNE [*whispering to Figaro*]: Here he comes!

THE COUNT [*opening the door to the pavilion*]: Suzie, are you there?

FIGARO [*whispering*]: He's looking for *her*—and I thought —

SUZANNE: He hasn't recognized her.

FIGARO: Shall we go through with it? [*Kisses her hand.*]

THE COUNT: A man on his knees to the Countess! Ah, and I'm without my sword. . . . [*Comes downstage.*]

FIGARO [*getting up and speaking in an assumed voice*]: Forgive me, Madam, I had not realized that our usual rendezvous was chosen for the wedding party. . . .

THE COUNT: The man in the dressing-room this morning! [*Strikes his forehead.*]

FIGARO [*as before*]: But let it not be said that such a stupid obstacle came between us and our pleasures.

THE COUNT [*aside*]: Hell! Death! Damnation!

FIGARO [*leading her towards the pavilion, whispering*]: He's blaspheming. [*Aloud*] Let us hurry, Madam, and make up for what we missed when I had to jump from the window.

THE COUNT [*aside*]: Ah! Now we know all!

SUZANNE [*near the left-hand pavilion*]: Before we go in make sure that we aren't followed. [*Kisses Figaro's forehead.*]

THE COUNT [*shouting*]: Vengeance!

[SUZANNE *runs into the pavilion where Fanchette, Marceline, and Chérubin are. The* COUNT *seizes Figaro's arm.*]

FIGARO [*with exaggerated alarm*]: The Master!

THE COUNT [*recognizing him*]: Ah! You dog, it's you, is it? Hello, there! Hello everybody!

[*Enter* PEDRILLO, *booted and spurred.*]

PEDRILLO: My Lord! I find you at last!

THE COUNT: Good. It's Pedrillo. Are you alone?

PEDRILLO: Just back post-haste from Seville.

THE COUNT: Come here! Shout as loudly as you can!

PEDRILLO [*bawling at the top of his voice*]: Not a sign of the page anywhere. Here's the packet.

THE COUNT [*pushing him away*]: Ah! You stupid fool!

PEDRILLO: Your Lordship told me to shout.

THE COUNT [*still hanging on to Figaro.*]: For help I meant! Hello there! Anyone who can hear me—come quickly!

PEDRILLO: There's already Figaro and me! How many more do you want?

[*Enter running* BRID'OISON, BAZILE, BARTHOLO, ANTONIO, GRIPESOLEIL, *all the wedding party with torches.*]

BARTHOLO [*to Figaro*]: You see—as soon as you gave us the the signal . . .

THE COUNT [*indicating the pavilion on his left*]: Pedrillo—guard that door. . . .

BAZILE [*whispering to Figaro*]: Did you catch him with Suzanne?

THE COUNT [*pointing to Figaro*]: You, my vassals—surround this man for me. You shall answer to me for his life!

BAZILE: Ha, ha!

THE COUNT [*furious*]: Silence! [*To Figaro in an icy tone*] Now, Sir, answer my questions!

FIGARO [*coolly*]: How could I do otherwise, My Lord! You command everything here—except yourself.

THE COUNT: Except myself!

ANTONIO: Now that's talking!

THE COUNT [*furious again*]: If anything could add to my fury it's this calm collected air of his.

FIGARO: Are we soldiers to kill or be killed for causes we know nothing of? For my part I like to know what I'm angry about.

THE COUNT [*beside himself*]: Outrageous! [*Controlling himself*] So you pretend you don't know, sir! Be good enough at any rate to say who is the lady you have brought to this pavilion?

FIGARO [*maliciously indicating the other one*]: That one?

THE COUNT [*sharply*]: This one!

FIGARO [*coldly*]: Oh, that's different. A lady who honours me with particular marks of her affection.

BAZILE [*astounded*]: Ha, ha!

THE COUNT: You hear him, Gentlemen?

BARTHOLO [*astounded*]: We hear him.

THE COUNT: And has the lady any other commitments that you are aware of?

FIGARO [*coldly*]: I know that a certain nobleman was interested in her once, but whether he has given her up or she prefers me to a man with greater advantages—she accords me the preference *now*.

THE COUNT [*sharply*]: The preference! [*Controlling himself*] At any rate he's open about it. He admits, gentlemen, what I assure you I have heard from the lips of his accomplice.

BRID'OISON [*stupefied*]: Ac-com-plice!

THE COUNT [*furious*]: When dishonour is flaunted openly the punishment must be similarly proclaimed. [*He goes into the pavilion.*]

ANTONIO: That's fair and proper.

BRID'OISON [*to Figaro*]: W-which has taken the other's wife?

FIGARO [*laughing*]: Neither has had that particular pleasure.

THE COUNT [*heard talking inside the pavilion and dragging someone out*]: All your efforts are in vain. You are lost, Madam! Your hour is come! [*He hasn't looked to see who it is.*] How fortunate that no pledge of so detestable union . . .

FIGARO [*crying out*]: Chérubin!

THE COUNT: My page!

BAZILE: Ha, ha!

THE COUNT [*aside, and beside himself*]: Always this confounded page! What were *you* doing in there?

CHÉRUBIN [*timidly*]: Keeping out of your sight as you told me to.

PEDRILLO: And I ruined a good horse!

THE COUNT: You go in, Antonio, and bring forth for judgement the infamous creature who has dishonoured me.

BRID'OISON: Is it Her La-Ladyship you are seeking?

ANTONIO: It would serve you right. You've done it yourself often enough.

THE COUNT [*furious*]: Get in!

[ANTONIO *goes in.*]

THE COUNT: You will see, gentlemen, that he wasn't alone.

CHÉRUBIN: My lot would have been unendurable had no kind-hearted person sweetened the bitterness for me. . . .

ANTONIO [*dragging someone out*]: Come on, Madam. No use begging to be left inside—everybody knows you went in.

FIGARO [*crying out*]: My little cousin!

THE COUNT: Fanchette!

ANTONIO: Ah! *Sacramento!* That *is* kind of His Lordship! Fancy choosing me to show that it was my own daughter that was causing the trouble.

THE COUNT [*outraged*]: Who was to know *she* was there!

[*Makes to go in himself.*]

BARTHOLO: Allow me, Your Excellency. This is all most bewildering. I'm less excitable. . . . [*He goes in.*]

BRID'OISON: Quite a complicated b-business.

BARTHOLO [*talking to someone as he brings her out*]: Fear nothing, Madam, I'll do you no harm, I promise you. . . . Marceline!

BAZILE: Ha, ha!

FIGARO: Ha! What a joke! My mother's in it as well!

ANTONIO: So much the worse.

THE COUNT: What do I care about her? The Countess . . .

[SUZANNE *comes out with her fan over her face.*]

Ah, here she comes! [*He seizes her violently by the arm.*] Gentlemen! What do you think should be done with this odious –

[SUZANNE *falls on her knees, still looking down.*]

THE COUNT: No, no!

[FIGARO *throws himself on his knees at the other side.*]

THE COUNT [*louder*]: No, no!

[*All fall on their knees, except Brid'oison.*]

THE COUNT: Not if there were a hundred of you!

[*The* COUNTESS *emerges from the other pavilion.*]

THE COUNTESS [*throwing herself on her knees*]: Allow me to join you.

THE COUNT [*looking from Suzanne to the Countess*]: Ah! Whatever is this?

BRID'OISON [*laughing*]: B-by Jove! It's Her Ladyship!

THE COUNT [*endeavouring to raise her*]: What! It was you, Countess?
[*In a supplicating voice*] Only your generous forgiveness . . .

THE COUNTESS [*laughing*]: You'd say, 'No, no!' if you were in my place. Whereas I for the third time today accord it unconditionally. [*She rises.*]

SUZANNE: And I too. [*Gets up.*]

MARCELINE: And I too. [*Gets up.*]

FIGARO: And I too. There's an echo somewhere about.
[*They all get up.*]

THE COUNT: An echo! I thought I was being clever and they've treated me like a child.

THE COUNTESS [*laughing*]: Don't regret it, My Lord!

FIGARO [*dashing his knees with his cap*]: A day's work like this is good practice for a diplomat.

THE COUNT [*to Suzanne*]: The message you fastened with a pin?

SUZANNE: Her Ladyship dictated it.

THE COUNT: Then the reply should be made to her. [*Kisses her hand.*]

THE COUNTESS: Everyone shall have his own. [*She gives the purse to Figaro and the diamond to Suzanne.*]

SUZANNE [*to Figaro*]: Another dowry.

FIGARO [*slapping the purse with his hand*]: And of the three this took most getting.

SUZANNE: Like our marriage.

GRIPE-SOLEIL: And the marriage garter—can I have it?

THE COUNTESS [*throws the ribbon which she has taken from her bodice*]: The garter. It was with her clothes. Here it is.

CHÉRUBIN [*who is quickest to pick it up*]: I defy anyone to get it from me!

THE COUNT [*laughing*]: How did you like the smack on the ear you got a little while ago?

CHÉRUBIN [*recoiling and half drawing his sword*]: I got?

FIGARO [*miming his discomfort*]: He got it on *my* ear! That's how great men dispense justice.

THE COUNT [*laughing*]: *You* got it? Ah! What do you say to that, my dear?

THE COUNTESS [*absorbed in her thoughts, but replying with fervour*]: Ah, yes, dear for ever and ever, I assure you.

THE COUNT [*slapping the judge on the shoulder*]: And you, Brid'oison— what's your opinion?

BRID'OISON: What's my opinion, Your Lordship? All I can say is— I don't know what to think!

ALL: A very sensible verdict!

FIGARO: I was poor and people despised me. I showed some evidence of ability and got myself disliked for it. Now, with a pretty wife and a fortune . . .

THE COUNT: Everyone will be your friend.

FIGARO: Can that really be?

BARTHOLO: I know them.

FIGARO [*to the audience*]: My wife and my fortune apart—You will, I am sure, do me honour. . . .

[*All join in singing and dancing.*]

BAZILE [*sings*]:

> Triple dowry, charming wife,
> What a start for married life.
> A noble Lord—a beardless boy!
> Such rivals only fools annoy.
> The clever man for all they say
> In the end will get his way.

FIGARO: I know. [*Sings*]

> Let those who are well born rejoice.

BAZILE: No. [*Sings*]

> Let those who are well found rejoice.

SUZANNE:

> Let a husband break his vows

It's just a joke the world allows —
But should a wife like freedom take
The world will punish her mistake.
The strong it is for all they say
Who in the end will have their way.

FIGARO:

Many a man who takes a wife
Thinks to lead a quiet life.
He keeps a watchdog—silly man
To guard his house—as if he can.
For woman's love—for all they say
Finds the means to fly away.

BRID'OISON [*sings*]:

G-gentlemen, you've seen our play
What it's worth you best can say.
In one respect it's true to life
All the fuss, the hubbub—strife,
In the end—for all they say
Are but follies of a day.

CURTAIN

Cahiers of Dourdan

When Louis XVI convoked the Estates-General in the fall of 1788, he also called upon his subjects to draft cahiers de doléances, or grievance lists, expressing their views about needed reforms in the kingdom. When the clergy, nobility, and commoners convened their separate electoral assemblies in the spring of 1789, they drafted their cahiers, most of which still exist in the French National Archives. These grievance lists tell us a great deal about what was on the minds of French men as the Old Regime teetered on the brink of revolution.

This extraordinary gesture of the king had two important impacts. First, it served to politicize the populace, heightening awareness about the problems confronting the country and giving people the sense that something could, and ought to, be done about them. Second, it raised expectations among the people, and when the deputies at Versailles failed to move swiftly on a program of reform the people grew impatient and restive.

Paul Hanson

Cahier of the Clergy of Dourdan
27 March, 1789

Although not as reactionary in tone as many of the cahiers of the clergy, this document indicates adequately the conservative point of view which characterized the first estate of France. . . .

When the King summons his subjects about him to consult them concerning the needs of the State, the ministers of religion are among the most eager to give him proof of their respectful gratitude. Their dual role as citizens and ecclesiastics entitles them to bring to the foot of the throne the most comprehensive wishes for the welfare of the monarchy and the maintenance of a religion that assures its tranquility. Accordingly, His Majesty shall be humbly supplicated:

Reprinted from *A Documentary Survey of the French Revolution*, edited by John Hall Stewart, (1951), by permission of Prentice-Hall, Inc.

Chapter I Religion

1. To preserve in its integrity the precious depository of the Catholic, Apostolic, and Roman religion, the most stable support of the fundamental laws of the State, to effect the enforcement of ordinances concerning the respect which is due churches, sanctification of feast days and Sundays, and, in general, whatever affects public worship.

2. To give consideration to the representations made by the last assembly of the clergy concerning the edict on non-Catholics[1] and not to permit any religion other than the Catholic to hold worship or give public instruction. . . .

5. Imbued with profound grief at the sight of the appalling deterioration of religion and the depravation of morals in the kingdom, we direct to His Majesty the most ardent and humble representations concerning the disastrous and widely acknowledged cause of this deplorable subversion of all principles. It obviously derives from the disgraceful excess of writings in which the spirit of libertinage, incredulity, and independence prevails, in which faith, modesty, reason, the throne, and the altar are attacked with equal audacity—impious and corrupting books circulated on all sides with the most revolting profusion and licence, to which the strongest resistance could not be too promptly opposed.

6. Since diversity of religious opinion in the schools for French youth is the greatest danger in the world, His Majesty shall be humbly supplicated also to order all necessary precautions lest there be admitted into any of the universities and academic societies of the kingdom any teacher or member who has not previously given proofs of the greatest ability and of his respectful devotion to the Catholic religion.

---

[1] Representation refers to the vigorous protests of the Catholic clergy on the occasion of the granting, by the second Assembly of Notables, of the famous Edict of Toleration of 1787. For the edict itself see Jourdan, *Recueil général des anciennes lois françaises* v. 28, pp. 472–482.

7. Since national education is degenerating daily, the King will be willing to take into consideration a matter so pertinent to morals and to the glory of the kingdom, and in his wisdom to provide resources for the talents of indigence by the endowment of the provincial colleges, almost all of which are insufficiently endowed, because a good education is the only means of assuring the State of good citizens, and religion of virtuous ministers. . . .

Chapter II Constitution

1. Since monarchical government is the steadfast constitution of the nation the most conducive to its internal tranquility and external security the most suitable for the extent of its provinces, and the most consistent with the character of its people, who always have distinguished themselves by their love for and devotion to their sovereigns, we will never countenance anything that would tend to alter this form of government. We are inviolably attached to it by the most sacred duties of obedience, by ties of oath and fidelity, by love and respect for our masters, and by the happiness of being subject thereto.

2. We desire that in matters brought under deliberation in the Estates General relative to all orders, voting be by head; but in those concerning more especially one of the three orders, we request that voting be by order. . . .

CAHIER OF THE NOBLES OF DOURDAN
29 MARCH, 1789

This cahier *represents a more enlightened attitude than is usually found in the requests made by the nobility. It is interesting to note that just as the clergy of Dourdan had criticisms to make of the nobles, so, in turn, the nobles saw faults in their privileged ecclesiastical contemporaries. The inclusion of a section dealing with commerce is suggestive of new interests on the part of the Second Estate. The last section of the document indicates that the "nobles of the sword" were not yet willing to give full recognition to "the nobles of the robe."*

Constitution

The citizens comprising the order of the nobility of the *bailliage* of Dourdan consider that, as soon as the Estates General is convened and the assembly constituted, an address should be voted to the King to thank him for the magnanimous act of justice he has just accorded the nation in restoring its rights, and to pledge to him, in the name of all Frenchmen, unlimited gratitude and love, inviolable submission and fidelity to his sacred person, his legitimate authority, and his august royal house. They would doubtless wish to use this liberty first in paying him new homage of their blood and fortune; but they wish more, they wish to contribute with all their power to the personal happiness of His Majesty, as well as to the general welfare of his people, by working in concert with him to bolster the tottering edifice of the French Constitution, by rendering his faithful commons happier through a just distribution of the taxes necessary to the State, by freeing him of the troubles and anxieties which extensive and absolute legislation necessarily entails; finally, by leaving to him only favors to grant and benefits to dispense throughout the free nation that he governs; thus the subjects of all orders, encompassing the Monarch with their liberty, their happiness, and their unlimited devotion, will render him, if possible, still more beloved throughout his realm, and assuredly more respected abroad.

Accordingly the noble citizens of the *bailliage* of Dourdan request:

That the legislative power reside collectively in the hands of the King and the united nation. . . .

Since the constitutional laws assure each and every one of his liberty, fortune, position, and property, the nobility requests:

That every arbitrary order prejudicial to the liberty of citizens be abolished entirely;

That individual liberty be assured and guaranteed, so that every citizen arrested may be placed in the prisons of the courts which are to take cognizance of his offence within twenty-four hours of the time of his arrest; that, immediately upon his detention, he be permitted to choose a counsel or advocate. . . .

That liberty of the press be granted, upon condition that author and printer are responsible; and the Estates General shall determine the most severe restrictions in order to prevent such liberty from degenerating into licence.

The nobility of the *bailliage* of Dourdan requests, likewise, that, according to the formal wish of His Majesty, no tax be established and no loan be made without the concurrence of the legislative power.

That the administrator of finances be not permitted to make any anticipation or assignment other than on the annual income, under penalty for *lése-patrie,* the lenders to forfeit all claim. . . .

That all property, whoever be the owner, be inviolable and sacred, property being whatever one owns on public faith and on the affirmation of the law; that no one be deprived thereof except for public interest, and that he then be compensated therefor without delay, and at the highest possible price.

Finally, that ministers henceforth be responsible and accountable to the Estates General. . . .

The order of nobility desires further that the distinction of three orders in the Estates General be strengthened and regarded as inherent in the Constitution of the French monarchy, and that opinions be given therein only by order.

That in the event, however, that vote by order be absolutely rejected by the Estates General, and the deputy of the *bailliage* of Dourdan see that further resistance to vote by head is useless, he then request that vote by head be taken in the separate chamber of every order and not in the assembly of the three orders united.

That vote by head never take place on matters of particular interest to one of the three orders alone. . . .

Justice

That venality of offices be generally abolished, and that the Estates General consider the wisest means of reimbursing officeholders, at the same time undertaking to fill the vacant offices by election . . . .

Finally, the nobility declares that, in order to evince its sentiments of esteem, natural equity, and affection for its fellow citizens of the third estate, it wishes to share with them, in proportion to the property and possessions of all orders, whatever imposts and taxes are approved by the nation; claiming to reserve only the sacred rights of property, the prerogatives of rank, honor, and dignity which must appertain to it according to the constitutional principles of the French monarchy.

CAHIER OF THE THIRD ESTATE OF DOURDAN
29 MARCH, 1789

The demands made in this cahier should be compared with Sieyes' attitude concerning the Third Estate. . . .

The order of the third estate of the City, *Bailliage,* and County of Dourdan, imbued with gratitude prompted by the paternal kindness of the King, who deigns to restore its former rights and its former constitution, forgets at this moment its misfortunes and impotence, to harken only to its foremost sentiment and its foremost duty, that of sacrificing everything to the glory of the *Patrie* and the service of His Majesty. It supplicates him to accept the grievances, complaints, and remonstrances which it is permitted to bring to the foot of the throne, and to see therein only the expression of its zeal and the homage of its obedience. It wishes:

1. That his subjects of the third estate, equal by such status to all other citizens, present themselves before the common father without other distinction which might degrade them.

2. That all the orders, already united by duty and a common desire to contribute equally to the needs of the State, also deliberate in common concerning its needs.

3. That no citizen lose his liberty except according to law; that, consequently, no one be arrested by virtue of special orders, or, if imperative circumstances necessitate such orders, that the prisoner be handed over to the regular courts of justice within forty-eight hours at the latest.

4. That no letters or writings intercepted in the post be the cause of the detention of any citizen, or be produced in court against him, except in case of conspiracy or undertaking against the State.

5. That the property of all citizens be inviolable, and that no one be required to make sacrifice thereof for the public welfare, except upon assurance of indemnification based upon the statement of freely selected appraisers. . . .

9. That the national debt be verified; that the payment of arrears of said debt be assured by such indirect taxes as may not be injurious to the husbandry, industry, commerce, liberty, or tranquility of the citizens.

10. That an annual reimbursement fund be established to liquidate the capital of the debt.

11. That as one part of the debt is liquidated, a corresponding part of the indirect tax also be liquidated.

12. That every tax, direct or indirect, be granted only for a limited time, and that every collection beyond such term be regarded as peculation, and punished as such. . . .

15. That every personal tax be abolished; that thus the *capitation* and the *taille* and its accessories be merged with the *vingtiémes* in a tax on land and real or nominal property.

16. That such tax be borne equally, without distinction, by all classes of citizens and by all kinds of property, even feudal and contingent rights.

Justice

3. That seigneurial courts of justice created by purely gratuitous right be suppressed. . . .

7. That venality of offices be suppressed by successive reimbursement in proportion to their disestablishment; that, accordingly, a fund be constituted forthwith to effect such reimbursement. . . .

9. That all exceptional jurisdictions, *élections, maîtrises,* salt stores, and financial bureaux be suppressed as useless and productive of lawsuits and jurisdictional conflicts; . . .

13. That military ordinances which restrict entrance to the service to those possessing nobility be reformed.

What Is the Third Estate?

Emmanuel-Joseph Sieyès

By February, 1789, the elections had begun. They took place, for the most part, in an atmosphere of turmoil intensified by the complex electoral technique and the continued economic distress. Of all the external forces affecting the elections one of the most vital was the growing intellectual ferment which had derived a powerful stimulus from the Order in Council of 5 July, 1788. One of the most significant aspects of this ferment was the appearance of numerous critical pamphlets. One of the most outstanding of these pamphlets was Abbé Sieyès' What is the Third Estate? . . .

This pamphlet appeared in January, 1789, and attracted a wide public. Sieyès' treatment of the already familiar gospel of the importance of the Third Estate imparted a new vitality to his theme. The sixth chapter of the pamphlet provided the basis of the plan eventually followed in transforming the Estates General into a National Constituent Assembly.

[FROM *A DOCUMENTARY SURVEY OF THE FRENCH REVOLUTION*, JOHN HALL STEWARD, EDITOR]

The plan of this pamphlet is very simple. We have three questions to ask:

1st. What is the third estate? Everything.

2nd. What has it been heretofore in the political order? Nothing.

3rd. What does it demand? To become something therein.

We shall see if the answers are correct. Then we shall examine the measures that have been tried and those which must be taken in order that the third estate may in fact become *something*. Thus we shall state:

4th. What the ministers have *attempted*, and what the privileged classes themselves propose in its favor.

Reprinted from *A Documentary Survey of the French Revolution*, edited by John Hall Stewart, (1951), by permission of Prentice-Hall, Inc.

5th. What *ought* to have been done.

6th. Finally, what remains to be done in order that the third estate may take its rightful place.

Chapter I
The Third Estate Is a Complete Nation

What are the essentials of national existence and prosperity? *Private* enterprise and *public* functions.

Private enterprise may be divided into four classes: 1st. Since earth and water furnish the raw material for man's needs, the first class will comprise all families engaged in agricultural pursuits. 2nd. Between the original sale of materials and their consumption or use, further workmanship more or less manifold, adds to these materials a second value, more or less compounded. Human industry thus succeeds in perfecting the benefits of nature and in increasing the gross produce twofold, tenfold, one hundred fold in value. Such is the work of the second class. 3rd. Between production and consumption, as well as among the different degrees of production, a group of intermediate agents useful to producers as well as to consumers, comes into being; these are the dealers and merchants. . . . 4th. In addition to these three classes of industrious and useful citizens concerned with goods for consumption and use, a society needs many private undertakings and endeavors which are *directly* useful or agreeable to the *individual*. This fourth class includes from the most distinguished scientific and liberal professions to the least esteemed domestic services. Such are the labors which sustain society. Who performs them? The third estate.

Public functions likewise under present circumstances may be classified under four well known headings: the Sword, the Robe, the Church, and the Administration. It is unnecessary to discuss them in detail in order to demonstrate that the third estate everywhere constitutes nineteen-twentieths of them, except that it is burdened with all that is really arduous, with all the tasks that the privileged order refuses to perform. Only the lucrative and honorary positions are held by members of the privileged order . . . nevertheless they have dared lay the order of the third estate under an interdict. They have said to it: "Whatever be your services, whatever your talents, you shall go thus far and no farther. It is not fitting that you be honored."

. . .

It suffices here to have revealed that the alleged utility of a privileged order to public service is only a chimera; that without it, all that is arduous in such service is performed by the third estate; that without it, the higher positions would be infinitely better filled; that they naturally ought to be the lot of and reward for talents and recognized services; and that if the privileged classes have succeeded in usurping all the lucrative and honorary positions, it is both an odious injustice to the majority of citizens and a treason to the commonwealth.

Who, then, would dare to say that the third estate has not within itself all that is necessary to constitute a complete nation? It is the strong and robust man whose one arm remains enchained. If the privileged order were abolished, the nation would be not something less but something more. Thus, what is the third estate? Everything; but an everything shackled and oppressed. What would it be without the privileged order? Everything; but an everything free and flourishing. Nothing can progress without it; everything would proceed infinitely better without the others. It is not sufficient to have demonstrated that the privileged classes, far from being useful to the nation, can only enfeeble and injure it; it is necessary, moreover, to prove that the nobility does not belong to the social organization at all; that, indeed, it may be a burden upon the nation, but that it would not know how to constitute a part thereof.[1]

What is a nation? a body of associates living under a common law and represented by the same legislature.

---

[1] In a footnote, Sieyès says that he does not include the clergy because he considers it not an order, but a potentially useful profession in the public service.

Is it not exceedingly clear that the noble order has privileges, exemptions, even rights separate from the rights of the majority of citizens? Thus it deviates from the common order, from the common law. Thus its civil rights already render it a people apart in a great nation. It is indeed *imperium in imperio*.

Also, it enjoys its political rights separately. It has its own representatives, who are by no means charged with representing the people. Its deputation sits apart; and when it is assembled in the same room with the deputies of ordinary citizens, it is equally true that its representation is essentially distinct and separate; it is foreign to the nation in principle, since its mandate does not emanate from the people, and in aim, since its purpose is to defend not the general but a special interest.

The third estate, then, comprises everything appertaining to the nation; and whatever is not the third estate may not be regarded as being of the nation. What is the third estate? Everything!

. . .

CHAPTER III WHAT DOES THE THIRD ESTATE DEMAND? TO BECOME SOMETHING

. . . The true petitions of this order may be appreciated only through the authentic claims directed to the government by the large municipalities of the kingdom. What is indicated therein? That the people wishes to be *something,* and, in truth, the very least that is possible. It wishes to have real representatives in the Estates General, that is to say, deputies *drawn from its order,* who are competent to be interpreters of its will and defenders of its interests. But what will it avail it to be present at the Estates General if the predominating interest there is contrary to its own! Its presence would only consecrate the oppression of which it would be the eternal victim. Thus, it is indeed certain that it cannot come to vote at the Estates General unless it is to have in that body *an influence at least equal to that of the privileged classes;* and it demands a number of representatives equal to that of the first two orders together.[2] Finally, this equality of representation would become completely illusory if every chamber voted separately. The third estate demands, then, that votes be taken *by head and not by order*. This is the essence of those claims so alarming to the privileged classes, because they believed that thereby the reform of abuses would become inevitable. The real intention of the third estate is to have an influence in the Estates General equal to that of the privileged classes. I repeat, can it ask less? And is it not clear that if its influence therein is less than equality, it cannot be expected to emerge from its political nullity and become *something*?

. . .

Chapter VI What Remains To Be Done. Development of Some Principles

The time is past when the three orders, thinking only of defending themselves from ministerial despotism, were ready to unite against the common enemy. . . .

. . .

The third estate awaits, to no purpose, the meeting of all classes, the restitution of its political rights, and the plenitude of its civil rights; the fear of seeing abuses reformed alarms the first two orders far more than the desire for liberty inspires them. Between liberty and some odious privileges, they have chosen the latter. Their soul is identified with the favors of servitude. Today they dread this Estates General which but lately they invoked so ardently. All is well with them; they no longer complain except of the spirit of innovation. They no longer lack anything; fear has given them a constitution.

The third estate must perceive in the trend of opinions and circumstances that it can hope for nothing except from its own enlightenment and courage. Reason and justice are in its favor; . . . there is no longer time to work for the conciliation of parties. What accord

---

[2] Sieyès has a footnote on the fact that this has been granted, but, in his opinion, it is meaningless.

can be anticipated between the energy of the oppressed and the rage of the oppressors?

They have dared pronounce the word secession. They have menaced the King and the people. Well! Good God! How fortunate for the nation if this so desirable secession might be made permanently! How easy it would be to dispense with the privileged classes! How difficult to induce them to be citizens!

. . .

In vain would they close their eyes to the revolution which time and force of circumstances have effected; it is none the less real. Formerly the third estate was serf, the noble order everything. Today the third estate is everything, the nobility but a word. . . .

In such a state of affairs, what must the third estate do if it wishes to gain possession of its political rights in a manner beneficial to the nation? There are two ways of attaining this objective. In following the first, the third estate must assemble apart: it will not meet with the nobility and the clergy at all; it will not remain with them, either by *order* or by *head*. I pray that they will keep in mind the enormous difference between the assembly of the third estate and that of the other two orders. The first represents 25,000,000 men, and deliberates concerning the interests of the nation. The two others, were they to unite, have the powers of only about 200,000 individuals, and think only of their privileges. The third estate alone, they say, cannot constitute the *Estates General*. Well! So much the better! It will form a *National Assembly*.

DECLARATION OF THE RIGHTS OF MAN AND CITIZEN ADOPTED AUGUST 26, 1789

This declaration was one of the first tasks undertaken by the Estates-General, now calling itself the National Assembly. Lafayette, Mirabeau, and Sieyès all had a hand in its drafting. Intended as a universal statement of human rights, it can also be read as an indictment of the failings of the Old Regime. One sees clearly the influence of Rousseau and Montesquieu, and also of John Locke. It is interesting to compare this document to the Declaration of Independence of the United States. It is also interesting to consider not only what this document says, but also what it very pointedly does not say.

PAUL HANSON

The representatives of the French people, constituted as a National Assembly, considering that ignorance, disregard or contempt of the rights of man are the sole causes of public misfortunes and governmental corruption, have resolved to set forth a solemn declaration of the natural, inalienable and sacred rights of man, in order that this declaration, by being constantly present to all members of the social body, may keep them at all times aware of their rights and duties; that the acts of both the legislative and executive powers, by being liable at every moment to comparison with the aim of all political institutions, may be the more fully respected; and that demands of the citizens, by being founded henceforward on simple and incontestable principles, may always redound to the maintenance of the constitution and the general welfare.

The Assembly consequently recognizes and declares, in the presence and under the auspices of the Supreme Being, the following rights of man and the citizen:

    I. Men are born and remain free and equal in rights. Social distinctions may be based only on common utility.

II. The aim of all political association is to preserve the natural and imprescriptible rights of man. These rights are liberty, property, security and resistance to oppression.

III. The principle of all sovereignty rests essentially in the nation. No body and no individual may exercise authority which does not emanate from the nation expressly.

IV. Liberty consists in the ability to do whatever does not harm another; hence the exercise of the natural rights of each man has no limits except those which assure to other members of society the enjoyment of the same rights. These limits can only be determined by law.

V. Law may rightfully prohibit only those actions which are injurious to society. No hindrance should be put in the way of anything not prohibited by law, nor may any man be forced to do what the law does not require.

VI. Law is the expression of the general will. All citizens have the right to take part, in person or by their representatives, in its formation. It must be the same for all whether it protects or penalizes. All citizens being equal in its eyes are equally admissible to all public dignities, offices and employments, according to their capacity, and with no other distinction than that of their virtues and talents.

VII. No man may be indicted, arrested or detained except in cases determined by law and according to the forms which it has prescribed. Those who instigate, expedite, execute or cause to be executed arbitrary orders should be punished; but any citizen summoned or seized by virtue of the law should obey instantly, and renders himself guilty by resistance.

VIII. Only strictly necessary punishments may be established by law, and no one may be punished except by virtue of a law established and promulgated before the time of the offence, and legally put into force.

IX. Every man being presumed innocent until judged guilty, if it is deemed indispensable to keep him under arrest, all rigor not necessary to secure his person should be severely repressed by law.

X. No one may be disturbed for his opinions, even in religion, provided that their manifestation does not trouble public order as established by law.

XI. Free communication of thought and opinion is one of the most precious of the rights of man. Every citizen may therefore speak, write and print freely, on his own responsibility for abuse of this liberty in cases determined by law.

XII. Preservation of the rights of man and the citizen requires the existence of public forces. These forces are therefore instituted for the advantage of all, not for the private benefit of those to whom they are entrusted.

XIII. For maintenance of public forces and for expenses of administration common taxation is necessary. It should be apportioned equally among all citizens according to their capacity to pay.

XIV. All citizens have the right, by themselves or through their representatives, to have demonstrated to them the necessity of public taxes, to consent to them freely, to follow the use made of the proceeds and to determine the shares to be paid, the means of assessment and collection and the duration.

XV. Society has the right to hold accountable every public agent of administration.

XVI. Any society in which the guarantee of rights is not assured or the separation of powers not determined has no constitution.

XVII. Property being an inviolable and sacred right, no one may be deprived of it except for an obvious requirement of public necessity, certified by law, and then on condition of a just compensation in advance.

THE DECLARATION OF THE RIGHTS OF WOMAN

OLYMPE DE GOUGES

De Gouges was a butcher's daughter from Montauban who wrote several plays and a number of pamphlets on the coming Estates General. In this work de Gouges states that the Declaration of the Rights of Man and Citizen is not being applied to women. She implies the vote for women, demands a national assembly of women, stresses that men must yield rights to women, and emphasizes women's education. She addresses Les Droits de la Femme to the Queen, trusting perhaps that the Queen could be converted to the cause of political rights for women and become principal spokeswoman for a feminist program. De Gouges' allegiances are complexly divided between royalty and the national legislature.

[FROM *WOMEN IN REVOLUTIONARY PARIS, 1789–1795*, EDITED BY DARLENE GAY, ET AL]

To the Queen: Madame,

Little suited to the language one holds to with kings, I will not use the adulation of courtiers to pay you homage with this singular production. My purpose, Madame, is to speak frankly to you; I have not awaited the epoch of liberty to thus explain myself; I bestirred myself as energetically in a time when the blindness of despots punished such noble audacity.

When the whole empire accused you and held you responsible for its calamities, I alone in a time of trouble and storm, I alone had the strength to take up your defense. I could never convince myself that a princess, raised in the midst of grandeur, had all the vices of baseness.

Reprinted from *Women in Revolutionary Paris, 1789–1795,* edited by Darlene Gay Levy, Harriet Branson Applewhite, and Mary Durham Johnson, (1979), University of Illinois Press.

Yes, Madame, when I saw the sword raised against you, I threw my observations between that sword and you, but today when I see who is observed near the crowd of useless hirelings, and [when I see] that she is restrained by fear of the laws, I will tell you, Madame, what I did not say then.

If the foreigner bears arms into France, you are no longer in my eyes this falsely accused Queen, this attractive Queen, but an implacable enemy of the French. Oh, Madame, bear in mind that you are mother and wife; employ all your credit for the return of the Princes. This credit, if wisely applied, strengthens the father's crown, saves it for the son, and reconciles you to the love of the French. This worthy negotiation is the true duty of a queen. Intrigue, cabals, bloody projects will precipitate your fall, if it is possible to suspect that you are capable of such plots.

Madame, may a nobler function characterize you, excite your ambition, and fix your attentions. Only one whom chance has elevated to an eminent position can assume the task of lending weight to the progress of the Rights of Woman and of hastening its success. If you were less well informed, Madame, I might fear that your individual interests would outweigh those of your sex. You love glory; think, Madame, the greatest crimes immortalize one as much as the greatest virtues, but what a different fame in the annals of history! The one is ceaselessly taken as an example, and the other is eternally the execration of the human race.

It will never be a crime for you to work for the restoration of customs, to give your sex all the firmness of which it is capable. This is not the work of one day, unfortunately for the new regime. This revolution will happen only when all women are aware of their deplorable fate, and of the rights they have lost in society. Madame, support such a beautiful cause; defend this unfortunate sex, and soon you will have half the realm on your side, and at least one-third of the other half.

Those, Madame, are the feats by which you should show and use your credit. Believe me, Madame, our life is a pretty small thing, especially for a Queen, when it is not embellished by people's affection and by the eternal delights of good deeds.

If it is true that the French arm all the powers against their own Fatherland, why? For frivolous prerogatives, for chimeras. Believe, Madame, if I judge by what I feel—the monarchical party will be destroyed by itself, it will abandon all tyrants, and all hearts will rally around the fatherland to defend it.

There are my principles, Madame. In speaking to you of my fatherland, I lose sight of the purpose of this dedication. Thus, any good citizen sacrifices his glory and his interests when he has none other than those of his country.

I am with the most profound respect, Madame,

Your most humble and most obedient servant,

de Gouges

THE RIGHTS OF WOMAN

Man, are you capable of being just? It is a woman who poses the question; you will not deprive her of that right at least. Tell me, what gives you sovereign empire to oppress my sex? Your strength? Your talents? Observe the Creator in his wisdom; survey in all her grandeur that nature with whom you seem to want to be in harmony, and give me, if you dare, an example of this tyrannical empire. Go back to animals, consult the elements, study plants, finally glance at all the modifications of organic matter, and surrender to the evidence when I offer you the means; search, probe, and distinguish, if you can, the sexes in the administration of nature. Everywhere you will find them mingled; everywhere they cooperate in harmonious togetherness in this immortal masterpiece.

Man alone has raised his exceptional circumstances to a principle. Bizarre, blind, bloated with science and degenerated—in a century of enlightenment and wisdom—into the crassest ignorance, he wants to command as a despot a sex which is in full possession of its intellectual faculties; he pretends to enjoy the Revolution and to claim his rights to equality in order to say nothing more about it.

Declaration of the Rights of Woman and the Female Citizen

For the National Assembly to decree in its last sessions, or in those of the next legislature:

Preamble

Mothers, daughters, sisters [and] representatives of the nation demand to be constituted into a national assembly. Believing that ignorance, omission, or scorn for the rights of woman are the only causes of public misfortunes and of the corruption of governments, [the women] have resolved to set forth in a solemn declaration the natural, inalienable, and sacred rights of woman in order that this declaration, constantly exposed before all the members of the society, will ceaselessly remind them of their rights and duties; in order that the authoritative acts of women and the authoritative acts of men may be at any moment compared with and respectful of the purpose of all political institutions; and in order that citizens' demands, henceforth based on simple and incontestable principles, will always support the constitution, good morals, and the happiness of all.

Consequently, the sex that is as superior in beauty as it is in courage during the sufferings of maternity recognizes and declares in the presence and under the auspices of the Supreme Being, the following Rights of Woman and of Female Citizens.

Article I

Woman is born free and lives equal to man in her rights. Social distinctions can be based only on the common utility.

Article II

The purpose of any political association is the conservation of the natural and imprescriptible rights of woman and man; these rights are liberty, property, security, and especially resistance to oppression.

Article III

The principle of all sovereignty rests essentially with the nation, which is nothing but the union of woman and man; no body and no individual can exercise any authority which does not come expressly from it [the nation].

Article IV

Liberty and justice consist of restoring all that belongs to others; thus, the only limits on the exercise of the natural rights of woman are perpetual male tyranny; these limits are to be reformed by the laws of nature and reason.

Article V

Laws of nature and reason proscribe all acts harmful to society; everything which is not prohibited by these wise and divine laws cannot be prevented, and no one can be constrained to do what they do not command.

Article VI

The law must be the expression of the general will; all female and male citizens must contribute either personally or through their representatives to its formation; it must be the same for all: male and female citizens, being equal in the eyes of the law, must be equally admitted to all honors, positions, and public employment according to their capacity and without other distinctions besides those of their virtues and talents.

Article VII

No woman is an exception; she is accused, arrested, and detained in cases determined by law. Women, like men, obey this rigorous law.

Article VIII

The law must establish only those penalties that are strictly and obviously necessary, and no one can be punished except by virtue of a law established and promulgated prior to the crime and legally applicable to women.

Article IX

Once any woman is declared guilty, complete rigor is [to be] exercised by the law.

Article X

No one is to be disquieted for his very basic opinions; woman has the right to mount the scaffold; she must equally have the right to mount the rostrum, provided that her demonstrations do not disturb the legally established public order.

Article XI

The free communication of thoughts and opinions is one of the most precious rights of woman, since that liberty assures the recognition of children by their fathers. Any female citizen thus may say freely, I am the mother of a child which belongs to you, without being forced by a barbarous prejudice to hide the truth; [an exception may be made] to respond to the abuse of this liberty in cases determined by the law.

Article XII

The guarantee of the rights of woman and the female citizen implies a major benefit; this guarantee must be instituted for the advantage of all, and not for the particular benefit of those to whom it is entrusted.

Article XIII

For the support of the public force and the expenses of administration, the contributions of woman and man are equal; she shares all the duties [*corvées*] and all the painful tasks; therefore, she must have the same share in the distribution of positions, employment, of offices, honors, and jobs [*industrie*].

Article XIV

Female and male citizens have the right to verify, either by themselves or through their representatives, the necessity of the public contribution. This can only apply to women if they are granted an equal share, not only of wealth, but also of public administration, and in the determination of the proportion, the base, the collection, and the duration of the tax.

Article XV

The collectivity of women, joined for tax purposes to the aggregate of men, has the right to demand an accounting of his administration from any public agent.

Article XVI

No society has a constitution without the guarantee of rights and the separation of powers; the constitution is null if the majority of individuals comprising the nation have not cooperated in drafting it.

Article XVII

Property belongs to both sexes whether united or separate; for each it is an inviolable and sacred right; no one can be deprived of it, since it is the true patrimony of nature, unless the legally determined public need obviously dictates it, and then only with a just and prior indemnity.

Postscript

Woman, wake up; the tocsin of reason is being heated throughout the whole universe; discover your rights. The powerful empire of nature is no longer surrounded by prejudice, fanaticism, superstition, and lies. The flame of truth has dispersed all the clouds of folly and usurpation. Enslaved man has multiplied his strength and needs recourse to yours to break his chains. Having become free, he has become unjust to his companion. Oh, women, women! When will you cease to be blind? What advantage have you received from the Revolution? A more pronounced scorn, a more marked disdain. In the centuries of corruption you ruled only over the weakness of men. The reclamation of your patrimony, based on the wise decrees of nature—what have you to dread from such a fine undertaking? The *bon mot* of the legislator of the marriage of Cana? Do you fear that our French legislators, correctors of that morality, long ensnared by political practices now out of date, will only say again to you: women, what is there in common between you and us? Everything, you will have to answer. If they persist in their weakness in putting this non sequitur in contradiction to their principles, courageously oppose the force of reason to the empty pretentions of superiority; unite yourselves beneath the standards of philosophy; deploy all the energy of your character, and you will soon see these haughty men, not groveling at your feet as servile adorers, but proud to share with you the treasures of the Supreme Being. Regardless of what barriers confront you, it is in your power to free yourselves; you have only to want to. Let us pass now to the shocking tableau of what you have been in society; and since national education is in question at this moment, let us see whether our wise legislators will think judiciously about the education of women.

Women have done more harm than good. Constraint and dissimulation have been their lot. What force had robbed them of, ruse returned to them; they had recourse to all the resources of their charms, and the most irreproachable person did not resist them. Poison and the sword were both subject to them; they commanded in crime as in fortune. The French government, especially, depended throughout the centuries on the nocturnal administration of women; the cabinet kept no secret from their indiscretion; ambassadorial post, command, ministry, presidency, pontificate, college of cardinals; finally, anything which characterizes the folly of men, profane and sacred, all have been subject to the cupidity and ambition of this sex, formerly contemptible and respected, and since the revolution, respectable and scorned.

In this sort of contradictory situation, what remarks could I not make! I have but a moment to make them, but this moment will fix the attention of the remotest posterity. Under the Old Regime, all was vicious, all was guilty; but could not the amelioration of conditions be perceived even in the substance of vices? A woman only had to be beautiful or amiable; when she possessed these two advantages, she saw a hundred fortunes at her feet. If she did not profit from them, she had a bizarre character or a rare philosophy which made her scorn wealth; then she was deemed to be like a crazy woman; the most indecent made herself respected with gold; commerce in women was a kind of industry in the first class [of society], which, henceforth, will have no more credit. If it still had it, the revolution would be lost, and under the new relationships we would always be corrupted; however, reason can always be deceived [into believing] that any other road to fortune is closed to the woman whom a man buys, like the slave on the African coasts. The difference is great; that is known. The slave is commanded by the master; but if the master gives her liberty without recompense, and at an age when the slave has lost all her charms, what will become of this unfortunate woman? The victim of scorn, even the doors of charity are closed to her; she is poor and old, they say; why did she not know how to make her fortune? Reason finds other examples that are even more touching. A young, inexperienced woman, seduced by a man whom she loves, will abandon her parents to follow him; the ingrate will leave her after a few years, and the older she has become with him, the more inhuman is his inconstancy; if she has children, he will likewise abandon them. If he is rich, he will consider himself excused from sharing his fortune with his noble victims. If some involvement binds him to his duties, he will deny them, trusting that the laws will support him. If he is married, any other obligation loses its rights. Then what laws remain to extirpate vice all the way to its root? The law of dividing wealth and public administration between men and women. It can easily be seen that one who is born into a rich family gains very much from such equal sharing. But the one born into a poor family with merit and virtue—what is her lot? Poverty and opprobrium. If she does not precisely excel in music or painting, she cannot be admitted to any public function when she has all the capacity for it. I do not want to give only a sketch of things; I will go more deeply into this in the new edition of all my political writings, with notes, which I propose to give to the public in a few days.

I take up my text again on the subject of morals. Marriage is the tomb of trust and love. The married woman can with impunity give bastards to her husband, and also give them the wealth which does not belong to them. The woman who is unmarried has only one feeble right; ancient and inhuman laws refuse to her for her children the right to the name and the wealth of their father; no new laws have been made in this matter. If it is considered a paradox and an impossibility on my part to try to give my sex an honorable and just consistency, I leave it to men to attain glory for dealing with this matter; but while we wait, the way can be prepared through national education, the restoration of morals, and conjugal conventions.

Form for a Social Contract Between Man and Woman

We, _____ and _____, moved by our own will, unite ourselves for the duration of our lives, and for the duration of our mutual inclinations, under the following conditions: We intend and wish to make our wealth communal, meanwhile reserving to ourselves the right to divide it in favor of our children and of those toward whom we might have a particular inclination, mutually recognizing that our property belongs directly to our children, from whatever bed they come, and that all of them without distinction have the right to bear the name of the fathers and mothers who have acknowledged them, and we are charged to subscribe to the law which punishes the renunciation of one's own blood. We likewise obligate ourselves, in case of separation, to divide our wealth and to set aside in advance the portion the law indicates for our children, and in the event of a perfect union, the one who dies will divest himself of half his property in his children's favor, and if one dies childless, the survivor will inherit by right, unless the dying person has disposed of half the common property in favor of one whom he judged deserving.

That is approximately the formula for the marriage act I propose for execution. Upon reading this strange document, I see rising up against me the hypocrites, the prudes, the clergy, and the whole infernal sequence. But how it [my proposal] offers to the wise the moral means of achieving the perfection of a happy government! I am going to give in a few words the physical proof of it. The rich, childless Epicurean finds it very good to go to his poor neighbor to augment his family. When there is a law authorizing a poor man's wife to have a rich one adopt their children, the bonds of society will be strengthened and morals will be purer. This law will perhaps save the community's wealth and hold back the disorder which drives so many victims to the almshouses of shame, to a low station, and into degenerate human principles where nature has groaned for so long. May the detractors of wise philosophy then cease to cry out against primitive morals, or may they lose their point in the source of their citations.[1]

Moreover, I would like a law which would assist widows and young girls deceived by the false promises of a man to whom they were attached; I would like, I say, this law to force an inconstant man to hold to his obligations or at least [to pay] an indemnity equal to his wealth. Again, I would like this law to be rigorous against women, at least those who have the effrontery to have recourse to a law which they themselves had violated by their misconduct, if proof of that were given. At the same time, as I showed in *Le Bonheur primitif de l'homme,* in 1788, that prostitutes should be placed in designated quarters. It is not prostitutes who contribute the most to the depravity of morals, it is the women of society. In regenerating the latter, the former are changed. This link of fraternal union will first bring disorder, but in consequence it will produce at the end a perfect harmony.

I offer a foolproof way to elevate the soul of women; it is to join them to all the activities of man; if man persists in finding this way impractical, let him share his fortune with woman, not at his caprice, but by the wisdom of laws. Prejudice falls, morals are purified, and nature regains all her rights. Add to this the marriage of priests and the strengthening of the king on his throne, and the French government cannot fail.

---

[1] Abraham had some very legitimate children by Agar, the servant of his wife.

It would be very necessary to say a few words on the troubles which are said to be caused by the decree in favor of colored men in our islands. There is where nature shudders with horror; there is where reason and humanity have still not touched callous souls; there, especially, is where division and discord stir up their inhabitants. It is not difficult to divine the instigators of these incendiary fermentations; they are even in the midst of the National Assembly; they ignite the fire in Europe which must inflame America. Colonists make a claim to reign as despots over the men whose fathers and brothers they are; and, disowning the rights of nature, they trace the source of [their rule] to the scantiest tint of their blood. These inhuman colonists say: our blood flows in their veins, but we will shed it all if necessary to glut our greed or our blind ambition. It is in these places nearest to nature where the father scorns the son; deaf to the cries of blood, they stifle all its attraction; what can be hoped from the resistance opposed to them? To constrain [blood] violently is to render it terrible; to leave [blood] still enchained is to direct all calamities towards America. A divine hand seems to spread liberty abroad throughout the realms of man; only the law has the right to curb this liberty if it degenerates into license, but it must be equal for all; liberty must hold the National Assembly to its decree dictated by prudence and justice. May it act the same way for the state of France and render her as attentive to new abuses as she was to the ancient ones which each day become more dreadful. My opinion would be to reconcile the executive and legislative power, for it seems to me that the one is everything and the other is nothing—whence comes, unfortunately perhaps, the loss of the French Empire. I think that these two powers, like man and woman, should be united but equal in force and virtue to make a good household. . . .

Speeches of Robespierre

Maximilien Robespierre, a leader of the Paris Jacobin club, served as spokesperson for the Committee of Public Safety before the National Convention during most of the Year II, the year of the Terror. In that capacity, Robespierre introduced legislation and made a number of important policy statements. In these two excerpts, he addresses the principles of revolutionary government, the nature of public virtue, and the relationship between virtue and terror. In the second speech in particular, we hear echoes of Rousseau's Second Discourse (On the Origin of Inequality). Also resonating in this speech are the ominous words penned by Sieyès over five years before:"How easy it would be to dispense with the privileged classes! How difficult to induce them to be citizens!"

Paul Hanson

On Revolutionary Government
December 25, 1793

. . . The theory of revolutionary government is as new as the Revolution that created it. It is as pointless to seek its origins in the books of the political theorists, who failed to foresee this revolution, as in the laws of the tyrant, who are happy enough to abuse their exercise of authority without seeking out its legal justification.

It is the function of government to guide the moral and physical energies of the nation toward the purposes for which it was established.

The object of constitutional government is to preserve the Republic; the object of revolutionary government is to establish it.

Revolution is the war waged by liberty against its enemies; a constitution is that which crowns the edifice of freedom once victory has been won and the nation is at peace.

Reprinted from *Robespierre*, edited by George Rude, (1967), Simon & Schuster, Inc.

The revolutionary government has to summon extraordinary activity to its aid precisely because it is at war. It is subjected to less binding and less uniform regulations, because the circumstances in which it finds itself are tempestuous and shifting, above all because it is compelled to deploy, swiftly and incessantly, new resources to meet new and pressing danger.

The principal concern of constitutional government is civil liberty: that of revolutionary government, public liberty. Under a constitutional government little more is required than to protect the individual against abuses by the state, whereas revolutionary government is obliged to defend the state itself against the factions that assail it from every quarter.

To good citizens revolutionary government owes the full protection of the state; to the enemies of the people it owes only death.

These ideas are in themselves sufficient to explain the origin and the nature of the laws that we term revolutionary. Those who call them arbitrary or tyrannical are foolish or perverse sophists who seek to reconcile white with black and black with white: they prescribe the same system for peace and war, for health and sickness; or rather their only object is to resurrect tyranny and to destroy the fatherland. When they invoke the literal application of constitutional principles, it is only to violate them with impunity. They are cowardly assassins who, in order to strangle the Republic in its infancy without danger to themselves, try to throttle it with vague maxims which they have no intention of observing. . . .

Is a revolutionary government the less just and the less legitimate because it must be more vigorous in its actions and freer in its movements than an ordinary government? No! for it rests on the most sacred of all laws, the safety of the people, and on necessity, which is the most indisputable of all rights.

It also has its rules, all based on justice and on public order. It has nothing in common with anarchy or disorder; on the contrary, its purpose is to repress them and to establish and consolidate the rule of law. It has nothing in common with arbitrary rule; it is public interest that governs it and not the whims of private individuals.

It must adopt the general principles of ordinary government whenever these can be rigorously applied without endangering public liberty. But its force to repress must be commensurate with the audacity or treachery of those who conspire against it. The greater its terrors for the wicked, the greater must be its favors for the good. The more it is compelled by circumstance to act with necessary rigor, the more it must refrain from measures that needlessly interfere with freedom and offend private interests without any advantage to the public.

It must sail between the twin reefs of weakness and temerity, of moderatism and exaggeration: moderatism which is to moderation as impotence is to chastity, and exaggeration whose resemblance to energy is like that of dropsy to good health. . . .

On the Moral and Political Principles of Domestic Policy

. . . What is the end toward which we are aiming? The peaceable enjoyment of liberty and equality; the reign of that eternal justice whose laws have been graven not on marble and stone but in the hearts of all men, even the slave who forgets them and the tyrant who denies them. [Applause.] . . .

We want to substitute, in our land, morality for egotism; probity for honor; principles for customs; ethics for propriety; the rule of reason for the tyranny of fashion; disdain for vice for disdain for misfortune; self-respect for insolence; spiritual grandeur for vanity; love of glory for love of money; good men for good society; merit for intrigue; genius for wit; truth for brilliance; the charm of happiness for the boredom of sensual pleasure; human greatness for the pettiness of the great; a magnanimous, powerful, happy people for an easy, frivolous, and miserable people: that is, all the virtues and all the miracles of the republic for all the vices and all the absurdities of the monarchy. [Applause] . . .

What is the nature of the government that can elect these prodigies? Only that government which is democratic or republican: these two words are synonyms, despite the abuses of common diction; for aristocracy is no more republican than is monarchy. Democracy is not a state in which the whole people, continually assembled, itself rules on all public business, still less is it one in which a hundred thousand fractions of the people decide, by unrelated, hasty, and contradictory measures, on the fate of the entire society; such a government has never existed, and it could exist only to lead the people back to despotism.

Democracy is a state in which the sovereign people, guided by laws which are its own work, itself does all it can do well, and through delegates all it cannot do itself. . . .

Now, what is the fundamental principle of the democratic or popular government—that is, the essential spring which makes it move? It is virtue; I am speaking of the public virtue which effected so many prodigies in Greece and Rome and which ought to produce much more surprising ones in republican France; of that virtue which is nothing other than the love of country and of its laws.

But as the essence of the republic or of democracy is equality, it follows that the love of country necessarily includes the love of equality.

It is also true that this sublime sentiment assumes a preference for the public interest over every particular interest; hence the love of country presupposes or produces all the virtues: for what are they other than that spiritual strength which renders one capable of those sacrifices? And how could the slave of avarice or ambition, for example, sacrifice his idol to his country?

Not only is virtue the soul of democracy; it can exist only in that government. . . .

Republican virtue can be considered in relation to the people and in relation to the government; it is necessary in both. When only the government lacks virtue, there remains a resource in the people's virtue; but when the people itself is corrupted, liberty is already lost. . . .

If the spring of popular government in time of peace is virtue, the springs of popular government in revolution are at once virtue and terror: virtue, without which terror is fatal; terror, without which virtue is powerless. Terror is nothing other than justice, prompt, severe, inflexible; it is therefore an emanation of virtue; it is not so much a special principle as it is a consequence of the general principle of democracy applied to our country's most urgent needs.

NOVALIS

1772–1801

▨ *Novalis was the pseudonym for Friedrich Leopold, Baron von Hardenberg, a Prussian-born poet sometimes called "the prophet of Romanticism." His writing is noted for its dreaminess, lyricism and deep religious mysticism. His major work, the unfinished novel* Heinrich von Otferdingen, *describes the artist's romantic search for the elusive and unattainable "blue flower," which became a symbol for longing among Romantics. In essays such as* Die Christenheit, oder Europe *(published posthumously in 1826), Novalis expresses a romantic nostalgia for the unity and spirituality of medieval Christian Europe.*

DAVID MASON

CHRISTENDOM OR EUROPE

NOVALIS

(WRITTEN 1799; PUB. 1802)

Those were lovely, splendid times, when Europe was a Christian land, when *one* Christendom dwelt in this continent shaped by mankind, and *one* great common interest united the most distant provinces of this vast spiritual kingdom. *One* leader, without great worldly possessions, guided and unified the great political powers. Immediately under him stood a numerous guild, open to all, that carried out his orders and zealously strove to consolidate his benevolent power. Each member of this society was respected everywhere; and if the common people sought his comfort or help, his protection or advice, and in return freely and bountifully supplied his many needs, so likewise the more powerful honored, protected, and

Reprinted from *An Anthology of German Literature of the Romantic Era and the Age of Goethe,* edited and translated by Klaus-Peter Hinze and Leonard M. Trawick, (1993), Edwin Mellen Press.

listened to him; and everyone took care of these chosen men, so wonderfully endowed, as if they were children of Heaven, whose presence and sympathy spread manifold blessings. Childlike faith bound people to their teachings. How cheerfully could every man approach the end of his earthly tasks, when, through these holy men, a sure future was prepared for him; through them, every mistake forgiven; through them, every blemish of life wiped clear and clean! They were the trusty pilots on the great unknown sea, in whose care one could scorn all storms and look confidently to a safe approach and landing in the world that is our true homeland.

The wildest, most voracious impulses shrank in awe and submission before their word. Peace flowed from them. They preached nothing but love for the holy, wonderfully beautiful Lady of Christendom, who with her divine strength was ready to rescue any believer from the most terrible dangers. They told of holy people long dead, who, through faith and constancy to that blessed Mother and her divine, loving Child, withstood the temptations of this earthly life and won glory in Heaven, and now had become powerful and benevolent protectors of their earthly brothers—willing helpers in time of need, intercessors for human frailties, and effective advocates of mankind before the heavenly throne. How happy people used to be, emerging from beautiful services in the dim churches adorned with inspiring works of art, filled with sweet odors, and enlivened with holy, elevating music. Here the consecrated refrains of God-fearing people who lived in earlier times were gratefully preserved in precious shrines, which showed, through splendid wonders and signs, the goodness and power of God, and the mighty beneficence of these happy saints. Just as loving souls will preserve locks of hair or handwriting of their beloved dead to sustain the sweet flame until death reunites them, so, whenever they could, people used to collect with fervent care everything that had belonged to these beloved souls, and a person considered himself lucky to possess, or even touch, such a comforting relic. Every now and then it seemed that heavenly grace would descend particularly upon some unusual picture or grave; to such places people streamed from every region bearing beautiful gifts, and in return gathered heavenly gifts: peace of soul and health of body. This powerful band of peace-making men sought eagerly to make all people share their beautiful faith, and sent representatives to all parts of the world to preach and to make the Kingdom of Heaven the only kingdom on this earth.

Quite properly, the wise head of the church opposed bold secular developments that threatened sacred thought, and dangerous discoveries in the sphere of learning that the times were not ready for. Thus he kept daring thinkers from maintaining publicly that the earth is an insignificant planet, because he knew very well that such a belief would lead people to lose respect not only for their earthly dwelling and homeland, but also for their heavenly home and for the human race, so that they would prefer circumscribed knowledge to infinite belief, and would become used to scorning all great things worthy of wonder, considering them mere dead doctrinal formulations. At his court could be found all the august and brilliant men of Europe. All treasures flowed to him: fallen Jerusalem came into its own—Rome itself was Jerusalem, become the holy seat of God's kingdom on Earth. Princes willingly laid their disputes before the Father of Christendom, their crowns and splendor at his feet; indeed they considered it an honor to live out the evening of their lives as members of that lofty brotherhood, devoted to godly contemplation in the solitude of cloister walls. Just how beneficial this regime was, how appropriate this institution was, to man's inner nature, could be seen by the mighty flowing of the whole range of human powers, the harmonious development of all talents, the extraordinary heights that individual men attained in all the sciences and arts, and the vast commerce, both spiritual and material, that flourished throughout Europe and even to the farthest Indies.

Such were the beautiful qualities of those truly Catholic—or rather, truly Christian—times. Yet mankind was not ready, not sufficiently developed, for this happy state. It was a first love, which, for a great part of the European population, faded in the press of commerce, pushed from man's thoughts by selfish cares, and stripped forever of its attractions—afterward decried as imposture and delusion, condemned in the light of later experience. This great internal division, with the destructive wars that accompanied it, was a striking instance of the damage culture can cause to the spiritual sense, or at least the temporary damage culture can cause at a certain stage. While that immortal sense can never be destroyed, it can be troubled, lamed, crowded out by other senses. A society that remains stable over a long period of time weakens peoples' affections, their belief in their own kind, and accustoms them to turn all their attention and effort exclusively to the attainment of amenities; the arts and means of enjoyment proliferate, and it takes so much time to become familiar with them and expert in them, that the acquisitive person has no time left for quiet composure of his spirit, and careful attention to the inner world. Whenever there is a conflict, immediate interest seems to lie nearer to him, and so the beautiful blossoms of his youth—faith and love—fall and make way for the cruder fruits—facts and possessions. In late autumn, one looks back on springtime as a childish dream, and hopes with naive simplicity that the full granary will last forever. A certain solitude seems necessary for the development of the higher sense, and so too much society will smother many a tender growth of holiness, and frighten away the gods who flee the hurly-burly of social distractions and the transaction of petty affairs. Besides, we are concerned with times and periods, and do these not imply an oscillation, an alternation of opposing tendencies? Do they not imply by their very nature a limited duration, an increase and a decline? But is not a resurrection, a rejuvenation, in a newer, more powerful form, also certainly to be expected of them? Progressive, ever increasing evolution is the stuff of history. Whatever fails to attain perfection now, will attain it in a future attempt or a repeated one. Whatever is once a part of history never disappears: it is renewed in ever richer forms through countless transformations. Christianity, having once appeared in full power and glory, survived as a ruin, a dead letter, in ever increasing weakness and derision, until a new inspiration should once again animate the world. Infinite inertia lay heavy on the guild of the clergy, long accustomed to security. They stagnated in their comfort and the sense of their own importance, while the laity wrested experience and learning from their hands and made great strides in cultural development. Neglecting their true duty—to be first among men in intellect, insight, and culture—they succumbed to low desires, and the meanness and baseness of their way of thinking was the more repugnant because of their dress and vocation. Thus respect and confidence, the cornerstones of this and of every state, gradually crumbled, and, long before the actual Revolution, this guild was ruined and the real power of Rome had silently come to an end. Merely clever (and hence also merely temporary) expedients still held the corpse of the organization together and kept it from too rapid dissolution—a prime example being the abolition of marriage for the clergy, an expedient which, applied analogously to a similar group, the military, would give it a terrific solidarity and notably extend its life. What was more natural than that, sooner or later, an inflammatory mind should preach open rebellion against the despotic dead letter of the moribund organization, and with all the more success because he himself was a member of the guild.

The insurgents called themselves Protestants, for they were solemnly protesting against the usurpation of authority over the conscience by a troublesome and apparently unlawful power. For the time being they took back again, as if it were free, the right they had tacitly given up to examine, determine, and choose their own religion. They also established a number of sound principles, brought about a number of praiseworthy innovations, and did away with a number of bad laws; but they forgot the inevitable consequence of their procedures: they separated the inseparable, divided the indivisible Church, and wantonly tore themselves from the universal Christian community, through which and in which alone true, lasting rebirth was possible. The condition of religious anarchy must be only temporary, because there remains valid and operative a basic need to dedicate a number of people exclusively to this high vocation and to make these people, with respect to its concerns, independent of secular power. The establishment of tribunals and the retention of a kind of clergy did not fulfill this need and was not a satisfactory substitute. Unfortunately the secular princes became involved in this schism, and many used these disputes to strengthen and extend their own territorial power and revenues. They were happy to be relieved of those high external influences, and took the new tribunals under their sovereign protection and guidance. They were zealously concerned with preventing the complete unification of the Protestant churches, and so religion was irreligiously contained within political boundaries; this was where the gradual erosion of religion's international interests had its start. Thus religion lost its great political influence as a power for peace, and its special role as unifying, individualizing principle—as Christendom. Religious peace was settled according to quite erroneous and antireligious principles, and through the continuation of so-called Protestantism something thoroughly contradictory saw the light: a permanent revolutionary regime.

But Protestantism is by no means based exclusively on that one idea; on the contrary, Luther dealt with Christianity rather arbitrarily, mistook its true spirit, and introduced another *letter* and another religion, namely the holy universal validity of the Bible, and in so doing mixed into religious matters another, highly alien secular science—Philology—the debilitating influence of which becomes unmistakable from that time on. A large proportion of Protestants, out of some obscure feeling about this error, elevated him to the rank of an Evangelist and canonized his translation.

This choice was in the highest degree destructive to the religious sense, since nothing deadens its sensitivity so much as the letter. In the past, the situation was such that the letter could never become so pernicious, on account of the pervasiveness, the flexibility, and the rich content of the Catholic faith, as well as the esoteric nature attributed to the Bible, and the sacred power of the councils and the holy pontiff. But now these antidotes were denied and the total popular accessibility of the Bible asserted; and the meager contents, the crude, abstract outline of religion in these books, became all the more markedly oppressive, and made infinitely more difficult the free animation, penetration, and revelation of the Holy Spirit.

Hence the history of Protestantism no longer presents us with splendid manifestations of the supernatural; only its outset glowed with a momentary heavenly fire, and soon afterward it is evident that the religious spirit dried up. The things of this world gained the upper hand; the artistic spirit suffered in sympathy; only occasionally does a real, eternal living spark spring up and a small community of followers assimilate into one body. The spark goes out, and the community drifts apart again and is carried away with the stream. Such were Zinzendorf, Jacob Böhme, and others. The moderates are in the ascendant, and the times are approaching a total deadness of the higher organs, a period of practical unbelief. The Reformation brought Christendom to an end. From then on it did not exist any more. Catholic and Protestant or Reformed stood further from one another in sectarian division than from Mohamedans and heathens. The remaining Catholic states continued to vegetate, not immune to the subtly pernicious influence of the neighboring Protestant states. Modern politics first emerged at this time, and powerful individual states sought to occupy the vacant chair of universal authority, which had been transformed into a throne.

. . .

The Reformation was a sign of its times. It had significance for all of Europe, even though it actually broke out openly only in Germany, where real freedom could be found. The good minds of all the nations had secretly matured, and, in the delusory feeling of their vocation, they inclined all the more boldly against outdated authority. By instinct the intellectual is enemy of the traditional clergy; the two must wage war to the death if they are separate parties, for they are fighting for a single position. This separation became increasingly pronounced, and the intellectuals won all the more ground, as the history of the European people approached the triumph of learning, and knowledge and faith came into decisive opposition to one another. People regarded faith as the origin of the general impasse, and they hoped to remedy it by penetrating knowledge. Everywhere the spirit of religion suffered from the manifold persecutions that had characterized its own actions up until then—that were its personality at that time. The result of the modern way of thinking was called philosophy, which included everything that opposed the old ways, hence in particular every attack on religion. What had begun as a specific hatred of Catholicism gradually turned into hatred of the Bible, of Christianity, and finally of religion itself. Nay, hatred of religion extended quite naturally and inevitably to all objects of enthusiasm; it decried imagination and feeling, morality and art, the future and the past, all as heresies; it grudgingly set man at the top of the hierarchy of nature, and turned the infinite creative music of the cosmos into a monotonous rattling of some monstrous mill, driven by the stream of chance, on which it also floated, an autonomous mill-in-itself, without builder or miller—indeed, a true perpetual motion machine, a self-grinding mill.

One enthusiasm was generously left to the poor human race, and was made the indispensable touchstone of highest culture for everyone concerned: the enthusiasm for this grand, splendid philosophy, and more particularly for its priests and mystagogues. France was so fortunate as to become the womb and seat of this new faith, stuck together out of pure knowledge. However much poetry was decried in this new church, there were still a few poets around who for effect still used the old ornaments and old flashes of illumination, though in doing so they were in danger of kindling the new world system with the old fire. But cleverer members knew how to pour cold water right away on listeners who had grown warm. The members busied themselves tirelessly with cleaning the poetry from nature, earth, the human soul, and the sciences—wiping out every trace of holiness, spoiling with sarcasm the memory of every elevating event and person, and stripping the earth of all its bright ornaments. Light, because of its mathematical tractability and its impudence, became their special favorite: pleased rather by its properties of refraction than by its play of colors, they took its name for their great movement, the Enlightenment. In Germany the movement was carried out even more thoroughly: education was reformed, and there was an attempt to give the old religion a more up-to-date, rational, relevant spirit by carefully scrubbing it free of everything miraculous and mysterious; all scholarship was bent to cut off an escape into the past, as people tried to ennoble history into a domestic and civic portrait of manners and families. God was made into an idle spectator of the great, moving spectacle produced by the scholars, and at the end He was supposed richly to entertain and admire the playwrights and actors. The common folk by actual preference were enlightened and educated in that cultured enthusiasm, and so there appeared a new European guild: that of philanthropists and enlighteners. Too bad that nature remained so wonderful and elusive, so poetic and infinite, despite all efforts to modernize her! If anywhere an old superstition about a higher world and such turned up, then immediately on all sides the alarm was sounded and whenever possible the dangerous spark was reduced to ashes by philosophy and wit; nevertheless *tolerance* was the watchword of the educated, and, especially in France, was synonymous with *philosophy*. This history of modern atheism is highly interesting, and the key to all the monstrous occurrences of modern times. It first began in this century, especially in the latter half, and in a short time has grown to an immense size and diversity; a second Reformation, more comprehensive and appropriate to this situation, was inevitable, and it had to strike first in the country that was most modernized and for want of freedom had lain longest in an asthenic state. The supernatural fire would have long since broken free and thwarted the clever plans of the Enlightenment, had not the latter made use of worldly pressures and influence. But the moment a difference arose between the learned and the rulers—the enemies of religion and all their allies—religion had to step forward again as a third, harmonizing, mediating member—an emergence which every friend of religion now ought to acknowledge and proclaim, if it is not already sufficiently apparent. No person with a mind for history can doubt that the time has come for the resurrection of religion, and that exactly those circumstances which seemed to be against its animation and to threaten the final accomplishment of its demise, have become the most favorable signs of its regeneration. Real anarchy is the element from which religion is born. Out of the annihilation of everything positive it lifts its glorious head as the new founder of the world. Humanity, unbound, rises toward heaven as if spontaneously, and like the original seed of earthly formation, the higher organs move by themselves for the first time out of the undifferentiated mass which holds in solution all human abilities and powers.

The Holy Spirit hovers over the waters, and a heavenly island, dwelling place of the new race of men—vale of eternal life—appears for the first time above the receding waves.

Let the true observer consider calmly and objectively the new revolutionary times. Does not the revolutionary seem to him like Sisyphus? He no sooner reaches the point of equilibrium than the mighty weight rolls down again on the other side. It will never stay up there unless an attraction toward heaven holds it balanced at the top. All your props are too weak, as long as your state keeps its penchant for the earth; but join it by a higher attraction to the heights of heaven, give it a connection with total reality, and then it will spring up for you with unflagging resiliency, and will richly repay all your efforts. I suggest you turn to history: search its instructive fabric for similar periods, and learn to use the magic wand of analogy.

Shall the Revolution remain French, as the Reformation was Lutheran? Shall Protestantism become fixed once more as that freak of nature, a revolutionary establishment? Shall letter replace letter? Do you also seek in the old order, in the old spirit, the germ of its destruction, and imagine you have the key to a better order, a better spirit? Oh, that you were filled with the spirit of spirits and would desist from this foolish effort to recast history and mankind in your own mold! Are they not independent, self-directed, as well as infinitely lovable and prophetic? To study it, to follow it, to learn from it, to keep in step with it, to follow, believing, its promises and signs—these are things that no one thinks of.

In France much was done for religion when it was deprived of its official status and left only the rights of a private householder—to be sure, not like any single person, but in all its countless individual forms. Like a strange, homely orphan it must first reconquer people's hearts and win universal love, before it can be publicly worshipped again and become involved in worldly matters as a source of friendly counsel and mental harmony. Of continuing historical significance is the effort of that great iron mask which, under the name of Robespierre, sought the center and power of the republic in religion; also the coldness with which theophilanthropy, this mysticism of the new Enlightenment, has been accepted; also the new conquests of the Jesuits; also the closer connections with the Orient that have developed with the new political conditions.

Of the other European countries besides Germany, all one can predict is that, with *peace*, a new, higher religious life will begin to pulse within them and will soon swallow up all other worldly interests. In Germany, on the other hand, one can already demonstrate with full certainty evidences of a new world. Germany goes along slowly but surely in advance of the other European countries. While these latter busy themselves with war, speculation, and partisan spirit, the Germans are educating themselves as quickly as possible to be participants in a higher epoch of culture, and in the course of time this progress must give them a great advantage over the others. A great ferment in the arts and sciences is evident. Infinite mental resources are opening up. New, fresh lodes are being tapped. Never has learning been in better hands, or at least aroused greater expectations; the different aspects of things are being traced out, and nothing is left unsifted, unjudged, unanalyzed. Work is going ahead everywhere; writers are becoming more individual and more powerful; every old monument of history, every art, every science is finding advocates, and will be embraced with new love and made fruitful. An unparalleled versatility, a wonderful profundity, a brilliant polish, many-faceted knowledge, and a rich, powerful imagination may be found hither and yon, often in bold combination. Everywhere there seems to be astir a mighty intimation of the inner man's creative will, his boundlessness, his infinite variety, his holy individuality, and his unlimited capability. Waked from the morning dream of helpless childhood, a portion of the race uses its first strength on the serpents that coil about its cradle and try to immobilize its limbs. All these things are still merely indications, disconnected and crude; but they reveal, to the eye attuned to history, a universal individuality, a new history, a new humanity, the sweetest embrace of a loving God and a young church surprised, and the immediate, passionate conception of a new Messiah within its thousand members. Who does not, with sweet shame, feel happily expectant? The newborn will be the image of its father—a new

Golden Age with dark eyes of infinite depth, a prophetic age, wonderworking, miraculously healing, comforting and kindling eternal life—a great age of reconciliation, a Savior who, like a true presiding spirit at home among men, will be believed in, not seen, though visible to the faithful in countless forms, consumed as bread and wine, embraced as a lover, breathed as air, heard as word and song, and received with heavenly delight, with the intensest pain of love, into the inmost depths of the expiring body as death.

Now we stand high enough to cast a friendly smile back on those ages just mentioned, and also to recognize in those incredible follies some remarkable crystalizations of historical material. We will thankfully shake the hands of those scholars and philosophers; for the good of posterity, such errors had to be exhausted and the truly scientific view of things to be validated. Poetry stands brighter and more appealing, like a bejeweled India, as contrasted with the cold, dead Spitsbergen of that closet philosophy. In order that India may lie so warm and splendid in the middle of the globe, a cold, frozen sea, dead cliffs, long night, and fog instead of starry heavens must make the two ends of the earth inhospitable. The deep meaning of mechanics obsessed those anchorites in the desert of reason; the charm of the first insight overwhelmed them, and the past took revenge on them: they sacrificed, in amazing denial, what was holiest and most beautiful in the world to this first self-consciousness, and were the first again by deed to acknowledge and to proclaim the holiness of nature, the infinitude of art, the inevitability of knowledge, the worthiness of this world, and the omnipresence of the truly historical; and in so doing they put an end to a higher, more pervasive, and more dreadful reign of phantoms than they themselves were aware of.

It is first of all through a more exact knowledge of religion that one can best judge that dreadful progeny of religion's sleep, those dreams and deliriums of the faculty of holiness—only then can one learn to appreciate properly the momentousness of that gift. Where no gods are, phantoms rule; and the particular period when European ghosts developed (which rather completely explains the forms they took) is the period of transition from Greek mythology to

Christianity. So come too, you philanthropists and Encyclopedists, into the lodge of peacemakers, and receive the kiss of brotherhood; cast off those gray toils and look with young love at the wondrous splendor of nature, of history, and of humankind!

. . .

Now let us turn to the political spectacle of our time. The old and the new worlds are locked in battle, the defects and bankruptcy of existing political regimes have become apparent in the terrible events. What if here, as in the sciences, closer and more thorough-going connections and contacts among European states were the coming historical goal of war?—if a hitherto slumbering Europe were to bestir itself, if Europe were to awaken again, if a state of states, a political science of knowledge were to confront us! Could it be that hierarchy, that symmetrical basic structure of states, is the principle of federation among states—the intellectual repre-sentation of the political "I"? It is impossible for worldly powers to put themselves in equilibrium: only a third element, at the same time partaking of this world yet transcending it, can resolve the situation. Among the conflicting powers no peace can be concluded; any apparent peace is merely a truce—from the points of view of both political counsels and common opinion, no unification is con-ceivable. Both parties have great, necessary claims and must assert them, driven by the spirits of this world and of humanity. Both are indestructible powers in man's heart: on the one hand, devotion to the past, attachment to historical continuity, love for the monuments of ancestors and the ancient and glorious national family, and the satisfaction of obedience; on the other hand, the delightful feeling of freedom, the limitless expectation of mighty spheres of activity, pleasure in whatever is new and young, easy intercourse with all fel-low citizens, pride in the universal worth of mankind, joy in pri-vate rights and in the possessions of the whole, and the powerful sense of citizenship. Let neither wish to destroy the other; all con-quests mean nothing here, for the innermost capital of every king-dom does not lie behind earthworks and cannot be taken by storm.

Who knows whether we have had enough war? But it will never stop until we grasp the palm branch which only a spiritual power can offer. Blood will stream over Europe until the nations realize their dreadful madness that drives them around in circles, and, struck and softened by sacred music, they approach in all their bright-hued variety the altars of bygone days, there to take up works of peace and, with hot tears upon the smoking battlefield, to celebrate a great love feast, a festival of peace. Only religion can awaken Europe again and give the people security and reinaugurate Christendom in its old role of peacemaker with new magnificence before the eyes of the whole world.

Do nations have all the human qualities—except a heart, man's holy faculty? Will nations not, like men, become friends over the coffins of their loved ones, and forget all their enmity when divine sympathy speaks to them both—and *one* misfortune, *one* grief, *one* feeling fills their eyes with tears? Will not the power of sacrifice and surrender seize them irresistibly, and will they not long to be friends and allies?

Where is that old, beloved belief in the reign of God on earth, in which alone blessedness can be found? Where is that heavenly trust between men, that sweet devotion in the effusions of a divinely inspired spirit, that all-embracing spirit of Christendom?

Christianity has three aspects. One is the creative religious element, the joy of all religion. One, meditation in a broad sense—belief in the efficacy of all things of the earth to be the wine and bread of eternal life. And one, the belief in Christ, his mother, and the saints. Choose which you please. Choose all three, it is all the same—in doing so you become Christians and members of a single, eternal, inexpressibly blessed community.

Applied, living Christianity was the old Catholic faith, the last of these aspects. Its presence everywhere in life, its love of art, its deep humanity, the indissolubility of its marriages, its benevolent sociability, its joy in povery, obedience, and loyalty—all characterize it unmistakably as true religion, and constitute the basic qualities of which it is composed.

It has been purified in the stream of time; in deep, inseparable union with the two other forms of Christianity it will bring felicity to this earth forever.

Its accidental form is for all practical purposes destroyed; the old papacy lies buried and Rome has become a ruin for the second time. Shall not Protestantism finally come to an end and make way for a new, more lasting church?

The other parts of the world await Europe's reconciliation and resurrection, that they may join it and become fellow citizens of the Kingdom of Heaven. Shall we not soon again have a host of truly heavenly spirits in Europe, shall not all who are truly joined in religion long to see heaven on earth, and eagerly raise their voices together in holy song?

Christendom must again become living and effective, and must again create, without considering national boundaries, a visible church, which will take to its bosom the soul thirsty for spiritual life, and which will be a joyful mediator between the old and the new world.

It must again pour out the old cornucopia of blessing over the people. From the holy womb of a venerable European council, Christianity will arise and the course of religious awakening will be carried out according to an all-embracing divine plan. Then no one will protest any more about Christian and secular constraints, for the essence of the church will be true freedom, and all necessary reforms will be carried out under its own guidance as peaceful and orderly civil procedures.

When, oh when? It is not for us to ask. Patience! It will, it must come—the holy time of eternal peace, when the New Jerusalem will be the capital of the world; and until then, be serene and brave amid the dangers of the time, companions of my faith; proclaim with word and deed the divine gospel and remain steadfast in the true, infinite faith, until death.

Adam Smith

Adam Smith was born in Scotland in 1723, was educated at Glasgow and Oxford, and between 1751 and 1763 taught logic and moral philosophy at the University of Glasgow. His enormously influential book Wealth of Nations, published in 1776, pioneered liberal economic theories of labor, markets, wages, and trade. He fiercely criticized mercantilism, the prevailing government economic policy in Europe, proposing instead free trade, free competition, and an economy virtually free of government regulation—subject only to the "invisible hand" of supply and demand.

The passages below, selected from Wealth of Nations, address the advantages of workplace specialization and the division of labor; the "natural" regulation (through supply and demand) of wages, profits, and prices; and the beneficial effects of free markets and free trade.

David Mason

An Inquiry Into the Nature and Causes of the Wealth of Nations

by Adam Smith, L.L.D.

Book I.

Of the causes of improvement in the productive powers of labour, and of the order according to which its produce is naturally distributed among the different ranks of the people.

Reprinted from An Inquiry into the Nature and Causes of the Wealth of Nations, edited by J.R. McCulloch, (1839), Longman & Co.

Chap. I.

Of the Division of Labour.

The greatest improvement in the productive powers of labour, and the greater part of the skill, dexterity, and judgment, with which it is any where directed or applied, seem to have been the effects of the division of labour.

The effects of the division of labour, in the general business of society, will be more easily understood, by considering in what manner it operates in some particular manufactures. It is commonly supposed to be carried furthest in some very trifling ones; not, perhaps, that it really is carried further in them than in others of more importance; but in those trifling manufactures which are destined to supply the small wants of but a small number of people, the whole number of workmen must necessarily be small; and those employed in every different branch of the work can often be collected into the same workhouse, and placed at once under the view of the spectator. In those great manufactures, on the contrary, which are destined to supply the great wants of the great body of the people, every different branch of the work employs so great a number of workmen, that it is impossible to collect them all into the same workhouse. We can seldom see more, at one time, than those employed in one single branch. Though in such manufactures, therefore, the work may really be divided into a much greater number of parts than in those of a more trifling nature, the division is not near so obvious, and has accordingly been much less observed.

To take an example, therefore, from a very trifling manufacture, but one in which the division of labour has been very often taken notice of, the trade of the pin-maker, a workman not educated to this business, (which the division of labour has rendered a distinct trade,) nor acquainted with the use of the machinery employed in it, (to the invention of which the same division of labour has probably given occasion,) could scarce, perhaps, with his utmost industry, make one pin in a day, and certainly could not make twenty. But, in the way in which this business is now carried on, not only the whole work is a peculiar trade, but it is divided into a number of branches, of which the greater part are likewise peculiar trades. One man draws out the wire, another straights it, a third cuts it, a fourth points it, a fifth grinds it at the top for receiving the head: to make the head requires two or three distinct operations: to put it on is a peculiar business, to whiten the pins is another; it is even a trade by itself to put them into the paper; and the important business of making a pin is, in this manner, divided into about eighteen distinct operations, which in some manufactories, are all performed by distinct hands, though in others the same man will sometimes perform two or three of them. I have seen a small manufactory of this kind where ten men only were employed, and where some of them, consequently, performed two or three distinct operations. But though they were very poor, and, therefore, but indifferently accommodated with the necessary machinery, they could, when they exerted themselves, make among them about twelve pounds of pins in a day. There are in a pound upwards of four thousand pins of a middling size. Those ten persons, therefore, could make among them upwards of forty-eight thousand pins in a day. Each person, therefore, making a tenth part of forty-eight thousand pins, might be considered as making four thousand eight hundred pins in a day. But if they had all wrought separately and independently, and without any of them having been educated to this peculiar business, they certainly could not each of them have made twenty, perhaps not one, pin in a day; that is, certainly, not the two hundred and fortieth, perhaps not the four thousand eight hundredth, part of what they are at present capable of performing, in consequence of a proper division and combination of their different operations.

In every other art and manufacture the effects of the division of labour are similar to what they are in this very trifling one; though, in many of them, the labour can neither be so much subdivided, nor reduced to so great a simplicity of operation. The division of labour, however, so far as it can be introduced, occasions, in every art, a proportionable increase of the productive powers of labour. The separation of different trades and employments from one another, seems to have taken place in consequence of this advantage. This separation, too, is generally carried furthest in those countries which enjoy the highest degree of industry and improvement; what is the work of one man in a rude state of society being generally that of several in an improved one. In every improved society, the farmer is generally nothing but a farmer, the manufacture nothing but a manufacturer. The labour too, which is necessary to produce any one complete manufacture is almost always divided among a great number of hands. How many different trades are employed in each branch of the linen and woollen manufactures, from the growers of the flax and the wool to the bleachers and smoothers of the linen, or to the dyers and dressers of the cloth!

. . .

It is the great multiplication of the productions of all the different arts, in consequence of the division of labour, which occasions, in a well-governed society, that universal opulence which extends itself to the lowest ranks of the people. Every workman has a great quantity of his own work to dispose of, beyond what he himself has occasion for; and, every other workman being exactly in the same situation, he is enabled to exchange a great quantity of his own goods for a great quantity, or, what comes to the same thing, for the price of a great quantity of theirs. He supplies them abundantly with what they have occasion for, and they accommodate him as amply with what he has occasion for, and a general plenty diffuses itself through all the different ranks of the society.

. . .

CHAP. VII.

Of the Natural and Market Price of Commodities.[2]

There is in every society or neighbourhood an ordinary or average rate both of wages and profit in every different employment of labour and stock. This rate is naturally regulated, as I shall show hereafter, partly by the general circumstances of the society, their riches or poverty, their advancing, stationary, or declining condition; and partly by the particular nature of each employment.

There is likewise in every society or neighbourhood an ordinary or average rate of rent, which is regulated too, as I shall show hereafter, partly by the general circumstances of the society or neighbourhood in which the land is situated, and partly by the natural or improved fertility of the land.

These ordinary or average rates may be called the natural rates of wages, profit, and rent, at the time and place in which they commonly prevail.

When the price of any commodity is neither more nor less than what is sufficient to pay the rent of the land, the wages of the labour, and the profits of the stock employed in raising, preparing, and bringing it to market according to their natural rates, the commodity is then sold for what may be called its natural price.

The commodity is then sold precisely for what it is worth, or for what it really costs the person who brings it to market; for though in common language what is called the prime cost of any commodity does not comprehend the profit of the person who is to sell it again, yet if he sells it at a price which does not allow him the ordinary rate of profit in his neighbourhood, he is evidently a looser by the trade; since by employing his stock in some other way he might have made that profit. His profit, besides, is his revenue, the proper fund of his subsistence. As, while he is preparing and bringing the goods to market, he advances to his workmen their wages, or their subsistence; so he advances to himself, in the same manner, his own subsistence, which is generally suitable to the profit which he may reasonably expect from the sale of his goods. Unless they yield him this profit, therefore, they do not repay him what they may very properly be said to have really cost him.

Though the price, therefore, which leaves him this profit, is not always the lowest at which a dealer may sometimes sell his goods, it

---

[2] Though Dr. Smith erred in estimating the elements that enter into, and form the natural price of commodities, the principle laid down in this chapter, that their market price is perpetually gravitating towards, and cannot, generally speaking, ever diverge considerably from their natural price, or *cost of production*, is equally true and important. For some farther illustrations of this principle, see *Principles of Political Economy*, 2d ed. pp. 306—314.

---

is the lowest at which he is likely to sell them for any considerable time; at least where there is perfect liberty, or where he may change his trade as often as he pleases.

The actual price at which any commodity is commonly sold is called its market price. It may either be above, or below, or exactly the same with its natural price.

The market price of every particular commodity is regulated by the proportion between the quantity which is actually brought to market, and the demand of those who are willing to pay the natural price of the commodity, or the whole value of the rent, labour, and profit, which must be paid in order to bring it thither. Such people may be called the effectual demanders, and their demand the effectual demand; since it may be sufficient to effectuate the bringing of the commodity to market. It is different from the absolute demand. A very poor man may be said in some sense to have a demand for a coach and six; he might like to have it; but his demand is not an effectual demand, as the commodity can never be brought to market in order to satisfy it.

When the quantity of any commodity which is brought to market falls short of the effectual demand, all those who are willing to pay the whole value of the rent, wages, and profit, which must be paid in order to bring it thither, cannot be supplied with the quantity which they want. Rather than want it altogether, some of them will be willing to give more. A competition will immediately begin among them, and the market price will rise more or less above the natural price, according as either the greatness of the deficiency, or the wealth and wanton luxury of the competitors, happen to animate more or less the eagerness of the competition. Among competitors of equal wealth and luxury the same deficiency will generally occasion a more or less eager competition, according as the acquisition of the commodity happens to be of more or less importance to them. Hence the exorbitant price of the necessaries of life during the blockade of a town or in a famine.

When the quantity brought to market exceeds the effectual demand, it cannot be all sold to those who are willing to pay the whole value of the rent, wages, and profit, which must be paid in order to bring it thither. Some part must be sold to those who are willing to pay less, and the low price which they give for it must reduce the price of the whole. The market price will sink more or less below the natural price, according as the greatness of the excess increases more or less the competition of the sellers, or according as it happens to be more or less important to them to get immediately rid of the commodity. The same excess in the importation of perishable, will occasion a much greater competition than in that of durable commodities; in the importation of oranges, for example, than in that of old iron.

When the quantity brought to market is just sufficient to supply the effectual demand and no more, the market price naturally comes to be either exactly, or as nearly as can be judged of, the same with the natural price. The whole quantity upon hand can be disposed of for this price and cannot be disposed of for more. The competition of the different dealers obliges them all to accept of this price, but does not oblige them to accept of less.

The quantity of every commodity brought to market naturally suits itself to the effectual demand. It is the interest of all those who employ their land, labour, or stock, in bringing any commodity to market, that the quantity never should exceed the effectual demand; and it is the interest of all other people that it never should fall short of that demand.

If at any time it exceeds the effectual demand, some of the component parts of its price must be paid below their natural rate. If it is rent, the interest of the landlords will immediately prompt them to withdraw a part of their land; and if it is wages or profit, the interest of the labourers in the one case, and of their employers in the other, will prompt them to withdraw a part of their labour or stock from this employment. The quantity brought to market will soon be no more than sufficient to supply the effectual demand. All the different parts of its price will rise to their natural rate, and the whole price to its natural price.

If, on the contrary, the quantity brought to market should at any time fall short of the effectual demand, some of the component parts of its price must rise above their natural rate. If it is rent,

the interest of all other landlords will naturally prompt them to prepare more land for the raising of the commodity; if it is wages or
profit, the interest of all other labourers and dealers will soon prompt
them to employ more labour and stock in preparing and bringing
it to market. The quantity brought thither will soon be sufficient to
supply the effectual demand. All the different parts of its price
will soon sink to their natural rate, and the whole price to its
natural price.

The natural price, therefore, is, as it were, the central price, to
which the prices of all commodities are continually gravitating. Different accidents may sometimes keep them suspended a good deal
above it, and sometimes force them down even somewhat below
it. But whatever may be the obstacles which hinder them from settling in this centre of repose and continuance, they are constantly
tending towards it.

The whole quantity of industry annually employed in order to
bring any commodity to market, naturally suits itself in this manner to the effectual demand. It naturally aims at bringing always that
precise quantity thither which may be sufficient to supply, and no
more than supply, that demand.

BOOK IV
CHAP. II.

Of Restraints upon the Importation from Foreign Countries of such Goods as can be produced at home.

By restraining, either by high duties, or by absolute prohibitions, the
importation of such goods from foreign countries as can be produced at home, the monopoly of the home market is more or less
secured to the domestic industry employed in producing them. Thus
the prohibition of importing either live cattle or salt provisions from
foreign countries secures to the graziers of Great Britain the monopoly of the home market for butcher's meat. The high duties upon the
importation of corn, which, in times of moderate plenty, amount to
a prohibition, give a like advantage to the growers of that commodity.

The prohibition of the importation of foreign woollens is equally favourable to the woollen manufactures. The silk manufacture, though altogether employed upon foreign materials, has lately obtained the same advantage. The linen manufacture has not yet obtained it, but is making great strides towards it. Many other sorts of manufacturers have, in the same manner, obtained in Great Britain, either altogether or very nearly, a monopoly against their countrymen. The variety of goods, of which the importation into Great Britain is prohibited, either absolutely or under certain circumstances, greatly exceeds what can easily be suspected by those who are not well acquainted with the laws of the Customs.[1]

That this monopoly of the home market frequently gives great encouragement to that particular species of industry which enjoys it, and frequently turns towards that employment a greater share of both the labour and stock of the society than would otherwise have gone to it, cannot be doubted. But whether it tends either to increase the general industry of the society, or to give it the most advantageous direction, is not perhaps altogether so evident.

The general industry of the society never can exceed what the capital of the society can employ. As the number of workmen that can be kept in employment by any particular person must bear a certain proportion to his capital, so the number of those that can be continually employed by all the members of a great society must

---

[1] In consequence of the more general diffusion of enlightened views upon such subjects, petitions were presented to parliament in 1820, by the principal merchants and manufacturers in favour of a more liberal commercial policy; and some very considerable modifications of the restrictive system were soon after effected under the superintendence of Mr. Huskisson. Comparatively moderate *ad valorem* duties were imposed on many articles that were formerly either entirely prohibited, or loaded with duties equivalent to a prohibition. For example, foreign woollen goods are now admitted on paying an *ad valorem* duty of 15 per cent.; foreign cotton goods on paying 10 per cent.; foreign silk goods on paying 30 per cent., &c. The duty on foreign linens varies from 25 to 40 per cent.; but it is proposed to reduce it. Similar reductions have since been made in the duties on the importation of a vast variety of other commodities. The changes effected in the laws regulating the importation of foreign corn since the publication of the Wealth of Nations, are detailed in the supplemental note on the Corn Laws.

bear a certain proportion to the whole capital of that society, and never can exceed that proportion. No regulation of commerce can increase the quantity of industry in any society beyond what its capital can maintain. It can only divert a part of it into a direction into which it might not otherwise have gone; and it is by no means certain that this artificial direction is likely to be more advantageous to the society that that into which it would have gone of its own accord.

Every individual is continually exerting himself to find out the most advantageous employment for whatever capital he can command. It is his own advantage, indeed, and not that of the society, which he has in view. But the study of his own advantage naturally, or rather necessarily, leads him to prefer that employment which is most advantageous to the society.

First, Every individual endeavours to employ his capital as near home as he can, and consequently as much as he can in the support of domestic industry; provided always that he can thereby obtain the ordinary, or not a great deal less than the ordinary, profits of stock.

Thus, upon equal, or nearly equal, profits, every wholesale merchant naturally prefers the home trade to the foreign trade of consumption, and the foreign trade of consumption to the carrying trade.[2] In the home trade his capital is never so long out of his sight as it frequently is in the foreign trade of consumption. He can know better the character and situation of the persons whom he trusts; and if he should happen to be deceived, he knows better the laws of the country from which he must seek redress.

. . .

Secondly, Every individual who employs his capital in the support of domestic industry, necessarily endeavours so to direct that industry, that its produce may be of the greatest possible value.

The produce of industry is what it adds to the subject or materials upon which it is employed. In proportion as the value of this

---

[2] Upon equal, or nearly equal, gross profits this is the case. But when the nett profits of different businesses are equal, it is immaterial to capitalists whether they invest their stock in the home trade, or the carrying trade, and it is also immaterial to the public.

produce is great or small, so will likewise be the profits of the employer. But it is only for the sake of profit that any man employs a capital in the support of industry; and he will always, therefore, endeavour to employ it in the support of that industry of which the produce is likely to be of the greatest value, or to exchange for the greatest quantity either of money or of other goods.

. . .

By preferring the support of domestic to that of foreign industry, he intends only his own security; and by directing that industry in such a manner as its produce may be of the greatest value, he intends only his own gain, and he is in this, as in many other cases, led by an invisible hand to promote an end which was no part of his intention. Nor is it always the worse for the society that it was no part of it. By pursuing his own interest he frequently promotes that of the society more effectually than when he really intends to promote it. I have never known much good done by those who affected to trade for the public good. It is an affectation, indeed, not very common among merchants, and very few words need be employed in dissuading them from it.

THOMAS ROBERT MALTHUS

1766-1834

▣ *Malthus was born in Surrey, England, studied theology at Cambridge, was ordained in the Church of England, and in 1805 was appointed professor of history and political economy at Haileybury College. The famous "Malthusian doctrine" was propounded in* An Essay on the Principle of Population, *first published in 1798, in which he argues that poverty and distress are unavoidable, because population grows faster than food production. He believed that the misery of the lower classes was their natural punishment, and opposed government relief for the poor as encouraging population growth.*

DAVID MASON

ON THE PRINCIPLE OF POPULATION

THOMAS ROBERT MALTHUS

I think I may fairly make two postulata.

First, That food is necessary to the existence of man.

Secondly, That the passion between the sexes is necessary and will remain nearly in its present state.

These two laws, ever since we have had any knowledge of mankind, appear to have been fixed laws of our nature, and, as we have not hitherto seen any alteration in them, we have no right to conclude that they will ever cease to be what they now are, without an immediate act of power in that Being who first arranged the system of the universe, and for the advantage of his creatures, still executes, according to fixed laws, all its various operations.

I do not know that any writer has supposed that on this earth man will ultimately be able to live without food. But Mr. Godwin

---

Reprinted from *On the Principle of Population,* (1798), Harmondsworth.

has conjectured that the passion between the sexes may in time be extinguished. As, however, he calls this part of his work a deviation into the land of conjecture, I will not dwell longer upon it at present than to say that the best arguments for the perfectibility of man are drawn from a contemplation of the great progress that he had already made from the savage state and the difficulty of saying where he is to stop. But towards the extinction of the passion between the sexes, no progress whatever has hitherto been made. It appears to exist in as much force at present as it did two thousand or four thousand years ago. There are individual exceptions now as there always have been. But, as these exceptions do not appear to increase in number, it would surely be a very unphilosophical mode of arguing to infer, merely from the existence of an exception, that the exception would, in time, become the rule, and the rule the exception.

Assuming then my postulata as granted, I say, that the power of population is indefinitely greater than the power in the earth to produce subsistence for man.

Population, when unchecked, increases in a geometrical ratio. Subsistence increases only in an arithmetical ratio. A slight acquaintance with numbers will shew the immensity of the first power in comparison of the second.

By that law of our nature which makes food necessary to the life of man, the effects of these two unequal powers must be kept equal.

This implies a strong and constantly operating check on population from the difficulty of subsistence. This difficulty must fall somewhere and must necessarily be severely felt by a large portion of mankind. . . .

. . . The germs of existence contained in this spot of earth, with ample food, and ample room to expand in, would fill millions of worlds in the course of a few thousand years. Necessity, that imperious all pervading law of nature, restrains them within the prescribed bounds. The race of plants and the race of animals shrink under this great restrictive law. And the race of man cannot, by any efforts of reason, escape from it. Among plants and animals its effects are waste of seed, sickness, and premature death. Among mankind, misery and vice. The former, misery, is an absolutely necessary consequence of it. Vice is a highly probable consequence, and we therefore see it abundantly prevail, but it ought not, perhaps, to be called an absolutely necessary consequence. The ordeal of virtue is to resist all temptation to evil.

This natural inequality of the two powers of population and of production in the earth, and that great law of our nature which must constantly keep their effects equal, form the great difficulty that to me appears insurmountable in the way to the perfectibility of society. All other arguments are of slight and subordinate consideration in comparison of this. I see no way by which man can escape from the weight of this law which pervades all animated nature. No fancied equality, no agrarian regulations in their utmost extent, could remove the pressure of it even for a single century. And it appears, therefore, to be decisive against the possible existence of a society, all the members of which should live in ease, happiness, and comparative leisure; and feel no anxiety about providing the means of subsistence for themselves and families.

Consequently, if the premises are just, the argument is conclusive against the perfectibility of the mass of mankind.

I have thus sketched the general outline of the argument, but I will examine it more particularly, and I think it will be found that experience, the true source and foundation of all knowledge, invariably confirms its truth.

Working Class Manchester

Friedrich Engels

■ *Engels, the son of a well-to-do German manufacturer, was sent to England in 1842, at the age of twenty-two, to learn business in the office of the Ermen and Engels paper mill in the industrial city of Manchester. He remained in England for nearly two years and while there gathered material for his first book.* The Condition of the Working Class in England in 1844, *which was published in German in 1845. The extract below, from the chapter on "The Great Towns," is taken from the English translation published by the Foreign Languages Publishing House, Moscow, in 1962.*

I now proceed to describe Manchester's worker districts. First of all, there is the Old Town, which lies between the northern boundary of the commercial district and the Irk. Here the streets, even the better ones, are narrow and winding, as Todd Street, Long Millgate, Withy Grove, and Shude Hill, the houses dirty, old, and tumble-down, and the construction of the side streets utterly horrible. Going from the Old Church to Long Millgate, the stroller has at once a row of old-fashioned houses at the right, of which not one has kept its original level; these are remnants of the old premanufacturing Manchester, whose former inhabitants have removed with their descendants into better-built districts, and have left the houses, which were not good enough for them, to a working-class population strongly mixed with Irish blood. Here one is in an almost undisguised workingmen's quarter, for even the shops and beerhouses hardly take the trouble to exhibit a trifling degree of cleanliness. But all this is nothing in comparison with the courts and lanes which lie behind, to which access can be gained only through covered passages, in which no two human beings can pass at the same time. Of the irregular cramming together of dwellings in ways which

Reprinted from *The Condition of the Working Class in England in 1844*, (1892), Swan Sonnenschein & Co.

defy all rational plan, of the tangle in which they are crowded literally one upon the other, it is impossible to convey an idea. And it is not the buildings surviving from the old times of Manchester which are to blame for this; the confusion has only recently reached its height when every scrap of space left by the old way of building has been filled up and patched over until not a foot of land is left to be further occupied.

To confirm my statement I have drawn here a small section of the plan of Manchester—not the worst spot and not one-tenth of the whole Old Town.

This drawing will suffice to characterise the irrational manner in which the entire district was built, particularly the part near the Irk.

The south bank of the Irk is here very steep and between fifteen and thirty feet high. On this declivitous hillside there are planted three rows of houses, of which the lowest rise directly out of the river, while the front walls of the highest stand on the crest of the hill in Long Millgate. Among them are mills on the river, in short, the method of construction is as crowded and disorderly here as in the lower part of Long Millgate. Right and left a multitude of covered passages lead from the main street into numerous courts, and he who turns in thither gets into a filth and disgusting grime, the equal of which is not be found—especially in the courts which lead down to the Irk, and which contain unqualifiedly the most horrible dwellings which I have yet beheld. In one of these courts there stands directly at the entrance, at the end of the covered passage, a privy without a door, so dirty that the inhabitants can pass into and out of the court only by passing through foul pools of stagnant urine and excrement. This is the first court on the Irk above Ducie Bridge—in case any one should care to look into it. Below it on the river there are several tanneries which fill the whole neighborhood with the stench of animal putrefaction. Below Ducie Bridge the only entrance to most of the houses is by means of narrow, dirty stairs and over heaps of refuse and filth. The first court below Ducie Bridge, known as Allen's Court, was in such a state at the time of the cholera that the sanitary police ordered it evacuated, swept and disinfected with chloride of lime. Dr. Kay gives a terrible description of the state of this court at that time.[1] Since then, it seems to have been partially torn away and rebuilt; at least looking down from Ducie Bridge, the passer-by sees several ruined walls and heaps of *débris* with some newer houses. The view from this bridge, mercifully concealed from mortals of small stature by a parapet as high as a man, is characteristic for the whole district. At the bottom flows, or rather stagnates, the Irk, a narrow, coal-black, foul-smelling stream, full of *débris* and refuse, which it deposits on the shallower right bank. In dry weather, a long string of the most disgusting blackish-green slime pools are left standing on this bank, from the depths of which bubbles of miasmatic gas constantly arise and give forth a stench unendurable even on the bridge forty or fifty feet above the surface of the stream. But besides this, the stream itself is checked every few paces by high weirs, behind which slime and refuse accumulate and rot in thick masses. Above the bridge are tanneries, bonemills, and gasworks, from which all drains and refuse find their way into the Irk, which receives further the contents of all the neighbouring sewers and privies. It may be easily imagined, therefore, what sort of residue the stream deposits. Below the bridge you look upon the piles of *débris*, the refuse, filth, and offal from the courts on the steep left bank; here each house is packed close behind its neighbour and a piece of each is visible, all black, smoky, crumbling, ancient, with broken panes and window-frames. The background is furnished by old barrack-like factory buildings. On the lower right bank stands a long row of houses and mills; the second house being a ruin without a roof, piled with *débris;* the third stands so low that the lowest floor is uninhabitable, and therefore without windows or doors. Here the background embraces the pauper burial-ground, the station of the Liverpool and Leeds railway, and, in the rear of this, the Workhouse, the "Poor-Law Bastille" of Manchester, which, like a citadel, looks threateningly down from behind its high walls and parapets on the hilltop, upon the working-people's quarter below.

---

[1] "The Moral and Physical Condition of the Working-Class employed in the Cotton Manufacture in Manchester." By James Ph. Kay, M.D. 2nd Ed. 1832. Dr. Kay confuses the working-class in general with the factory workers; otherwise, an excellent pamphlet. *[Engels]*

Above Ducie Bridge, the left bank grows more flat and the right bank steeper, but the condition of the dwellings on both banks grows worse rather than better. He who turns to the left here from the main street, Long Millgate, is lost; he wanders from one court to another, turns countless corners, passes nothing but narrow, filthy nooks and alleys, until after a few minutes he has lost all clue, and knows not whither to turn. Everywhere half or wholly ruined buildings, some of them actually uninhabited, which means a great deal here; rarely a wooden or stone floor to be seen in the houses, almost uniformly broken, ill-fitting windows and doors, and a state of filth! Everywhere heaps of *débris,* refuse, and offal; standing pools for gutters, and a stench which alone would make it impossible for a human being in any degree civilised to live in such a district. The newly-built extension of the Leeds railway, which crosses the Irk here, has swept away some of these courts and lanes, laying others completely open to view. Immediately under the railway bridge there stands a court, the filth and horrors of which surpass all the others by far, just because it was hitherto so shut off, so secluded that the way to it could not be found without a good deal of trouble. I should never have discovered it myself, without the breaks made by the railway, though I thought I knew this whole region thoroughly. Passing along a rough bank, among stakes and washing-lines, one penetrates into this chaos of small one-storied, one-roomed huts, in most of which there is no artificial floor; kitchen, living and sleeping-room all in one. In such a hole, scarcely five feet long by six broad, I found two beds—and such bedsteads and beds!—which, with a staircase and chimney-place, exactly filled the room. In several others I found absolutely nothing, while the door stood open, and the inhabitants leaned against it. Everywhere before the doors refuse and offal; that any sort of pavement lay underneath could not be seen but only felt, here and there, with the feet. This whole collection of cattle-sheds for human beings was surrounded on two sides by houses and a factory, and on the third by the river, and besides the narrow stair up the bank, a narrow doorway alone led out into another almost equally ill-built, ill-kept labyrinth of dwellings.

Enough! The whole side of the Irk is built in this way, a planless, knotted chaos of houses, more or less on the verge of uninhabitableness, whose unclean interiors fully correspond with their filthy external surroundings. And how could the people be clean with no proper opportunity for satisfying the most natural and ordinary wants? Privies are so rare here that they are either filled up every day, or are too remote for most of the inhabitants to use. How can people wash when they have only the dirty Irk water at hand, while pumps and water pipes can be found in decent parts of the city alone? In truth, it cannot be charged to the account of these helots of modern society if their dwellings are not more clean than the pig sties which are here and there to be seen among them. The landlords are not ashamed to let dwellings like the six or seven cellars on the quay directly below Scotland Bridge, the floors of which stand at least two feet below the low-water level of the Irk that flows not six feet away from them; or like the upper floor of the corner-house on the opposite shore directly above the bridge, where the ground-floor, utterly uninhabitable, stands deprived of all fittings for doors and windows, a case by no means rare in this region, when this open ground-floor is used as a privy by the whole neighbourhood for want of other facilities!

If we leave the Irk and penetrate once more on the opposite side from Long Millgate into the midst of the working-men's dwellings, we shall come into a somewhat newer quarter, which stretches from St. Michael's Church to Withy Grove and Shude Hill. Here there is somewhat better order. In place of the chaos of buildings, we find at least long straight lanes and alleys or courts, built according to a plan and usually square. But if, in the former case, every house was built according to caprice, here each lane and court is so built, without reference to the situation of the adjoining ones. The lanes run now in this direction, now in that, while every two minutes the wanderer gets into a blind alley, or on turning a corner, finds himself back where he started from; certainly no one who has not lived a considerable time in this labyrinth can find his way through it.

If I may use the word at all in speaking of this district, the ventilation of these streets and courts is, in consequence of this confusion, quite as imperfect as in the Irk region; and if this quarter may, nevertheless, be said to have some advantage over that of the Irk, the houses being newer and the streets occasionally having gutters, nearly every house has, on the other hand, a cellar dwelling, which is rarely found in the Irk district, by reason of the greater age and more careless construction of the houses. As for the rest, the filth, *débris,* and offal heaps, and the pools in the streets are common to both quarters, and in the district now under discussion, another feature most injurious to the cleanliness of the inhabitants, is the multitude of pigs walking about in all the alleys, rooting into the offal heaps, or kept imprisoned in small pens. Here, as in most of the working-men's quarters of Manchester, the pork-raisers rent the courts and build pig-pens in them. In almost every court one or even several such pens may be found, into which the inhabitants of the court throw all refuse and offal, whence the swine grow fat; and the atmosphere, confined on all four sides, is utterly corrupted by putrefying animal and vegetable substances. Through this quarter, a broad and measurably decent street has been cut, Millers Street, and the background has been pretty successfully concealed. But if any one should be led by curiosity to pass through one of the numerous passages which lead into the courts, he will find this piggery repeated at every twenty paces.

Such is the Old Town of Manchester, and on re-reading my description, I am forced to admit that instead of being exaggerated, it is far from black enough to convey a true impression of the filth, ruin, and uninhabitableness, the defiance of all considerations of cleanliness, ventilation, and health which characterise the construction of this single district, containing at least twenty to thirty thousand inhabitants. And such a district exists in the heart of the second city of England, the first manufacturing city of the world. If any one wishes to see in how little space a human being can move, how little air—and *such* air!—he can breathe, how little of civilisation he may share and yet live, it is only necessary to travel hither. True, this is the *Old* Town, and the people of Manchester emphasise the fact whenever anyone mentions to them the frightful condition of this Hell upon Earth; but what does that prove? Everything which here arouses horror and indignation is of recent origin, belongs to the *industrial epoch*. The couple of hundred houses, which belong to old Manchester, have been long since abandoned by their original inhabitants; the industrial epoch alone has crammed into them the swarms of workers whom they now shelter; the industrial epoch alone has built up every spot between these old houses to win a covering for the masses whom it has conjured hither from the agricultural districts and from Ireland; the industrial epoch alone enables the owners of these cattlesheds to rent them for high prices to human beings, to plunder the poverty of the workers, to undermine the health of thousands, in order that they *alone,* the owners, may grow rich. In the industrial epoch alone has it become possible that the worker scarcely freed from feudal servitude could be used as mere material, a mere chattel; that he must let himself be crowded into a dwelling too bad for every other, which he for his hard-earned wages buys the right to let go utterly to ruin. This is what manufacture has achieved, and, without these workers and their poverty, this slavery would have been impossible. True, the original construction of this quarter was bad, little good could have been made out of it; but, have the landowners, has the municipality done anything to improve it when rebuilding? On the contrary, wherever a nook or corner was free, a house has been run up; where a superfluous passage remained, it has been built up; the value of land rose with the blossoming out of manufacture, and the more it rose, the more madly was the work of building up carried on, without reference to the health or comfort of the inhabitants, with sole reference to the highest possible profit on the principle that *no hole is so bad but that some poor creature must take it who can pay for nothing better.* However, it is the Old Town, and with this reflection the bourgeoisie is comforted. Let us see, therefore, how much better it is in the New Town.

The New Town, known also as Irish Town, stretches up a hill of clay, beyond the Old Town, between the Irk and St. George's Road. Here all the features of a city are lost. Single rows of houses or groups of streets stand, here and there, like little villages on the naked, not even grassgrown clay soil; the houses, or rather cottages, are in bad order, never repaired, filthy, with damp, unclean, cellar dwellings; the lanes are neither paved nor supplied with sewers, but harbour numerous colonies of swine penned in small sties or yards, or wandering unrestrained through the neighbourhood. The mud in the streets is so deep that there is never a chance, except in the dryest weather, of walking without sinking into it ankle deep at every step. In the vicinity of St. George's Road, the separate groups of buildings approach each other more closely, ending in a continuation of lines, blind alleys, back lanes and courts, which grow more and more crowded and irregular the nearer they approach the heart of the town. True, they are here oftener paved or supplied with paved sidewalks and gutters; but the filth, the bad odor of the houses, and especially of the cellars, remain the same.

EMANCIPATION MANIFESTO
OF ALEXANDER II

■ *Succeeding to the Russian throne in 1855 as Russia was losing the Crimean War, Alexander II moved ahead quickly with basic reforms in Russian society. Of all the Great Reforms, as they were called, none was greater than the emancipation of the serfs from legal bondage to noble landowners. The proclamation of 1861, written for the tsar by Filaret, bishop of Moscow, liberated more than 22 million male "souls" and their dependents.*

PAUL VALLIERE

By the Grace of God We, Alexander II Emperor and Autocrat of All Russia, King of Poland, Grand Duke of Finland, and so forth, make known to all Our faithful subjects:

Called by Divine Providence and by the sacred right of inheritance to the throne of Our Russian ancestors, We vowed in Our heart to respond to the mission which is entrusted to Us and to surround with Our affection and Our Imperial solicitude all Our faithful subjects of every rank and condition, from the soldier who nobly defends the country to the humble artisan who works in industry; from the career official of the state to the plowman who tills the soil.

Examining the condition of classes and professions comprising the state, We became convinced that the present state legislation favors the upper and middle classes, defines their obligations, rights, and privileges, but does not equally favor the serfs, so designated because in part from old laws and in part from custom they have been hereditarily subjected to the authority of landowners, who in turn were obligated to provide for their well-being. Rights of nobles have been hitherto very broad and legally ill defined, because they stem from tradition, custom, and the good will of the noblemen.

Reprinted from the *Complete Collection of the Laws of the Russian Empire* 36, no. 36490 (1893).

In most cases this has led to the establishment of good patriarchal relations based on the sincere, just concern and benevolence on the part of the nobles, and on affectionate submission on the part of the peasants. Because of the decline of the simplicity of morals, because of an increase in the diversity of relations, because of the weakening of the direct paternal attitude of nobles toward the peasants, and because noble rights fell sometimes into the hands of people exclusively concerned with their personal interests, good relations weakened. The way was opened for an arbitrariness burdensome for the peasants and detrimental to their welfare, causing them to be indifferent to the improvement of their own existence.

These facts had already attracted the attention of Our predecessors of glorious memory, and they had adopted measures aimed at improving the conditions of the peasants; but these measures were ineffective, partly because they depended on the free, generous action of nobles, and partly because they affected only some localities, by virtue of special circumstances or as an experiment. Thus Alexander I issued a decree on free agriculturists, and the late Emperor Nicholas, Our beloved father, promulgated one dealing with the serfs. In the Western *gubernias,* inventory regulations determine the peasant land allotments and their obligations. But decrees on free agriculturists and serfs have been carried out on a limited scale only.

We thus became convinced that the problem of improving the condition of serfs was a sacred inheritance bequeathed to Us by Our predecessors, a mission which, in the course of events, Divine Providence has called upon Us to fulfill.

We have begun this task by expressing Our confidence toward the Russian nobility, which has proven on so many occasions its devotion to the Throne, and its readiness to make sacrifices for the welfare of the country.

We have left to the nobles themselves, in accordance with their own wishes, the task of preparing proposals for the new organization of peasant life—proposals that would limit their rights over the peasants, and the realization of which would inflict on them [the nobles] some material losses. Our confidence was justified. Through members of the *gubernia* committees, who had the trust of the nobles' associations, the nobility voluntarily renounced its right to own serfs. These committees, after collecting the necessary data, have formulated proposals on a new arrangement for serfs and their relationship with the nobles.

These proposals were diverse, because of the nature of the problem. They have been compared, collated, systematized, rectified and finalized in the main committee instituted for that purpose; and these new arrangements dealing with the peasants and domestics of the nobility have been examined in the Governing Council.

Having invoked Divine assistance, We have resolved to execute this task.

On the basis of the above mentioned new arrangements, the serfs will receive in time the full rights of free rural inhabitants.

The nobles, while retaining their property rights on all the lands belonging to them, grant the peasants perpetual use of their domicile in return for a specified obligation; and, to assure their livelihood as well as to guarantee fulfillment of their obligations toward the government, [the nobles] grant them a portion of arable land fixed by the said arrangements, as well as other property.

While enjoying these land allotments, the peasants are obliged, in return, to fulfill obligations to the noblemen fixed by the same arrangements. In this state, which is temporary, the peasants are temporarily bound.

At the same time, they are granted the right to purchase their domicile, and, with the consent of the nobles, they may acquire in full ownership the arable lands and other properties which are allotted them for permanent use. Following such acquisition of full ownership of land, the peasants will be freed from their obligations to the nobles for the land thus purchased and will become free peasant landowners.

A special decree dealing with domestics will establish a temporary status for them, adapted to their occupations and their needs. At the end of two years from the day of the promulgation of this decree, they shall receive full freedom and some temporary immunities.

In accordance with the fundamental principles of these arrangements, the future organization of peasants and domestics will be determined, the order of general peasant administration will be established, and the rights given to the peasants and to the domestics will be spelled out in detail, as will the obligations imposed on them toward the government and the nobles.

Although these arrangements, general as well as local, and the special supplementary rules affecting some particular localities, estates of petty nobles, and peasants working in factories and enterprises of the nobles, have been as far as possible adapted to economic necessities and local customs; nevertheless, to preserve the existing order where it presents reciprocal advantages, we leave it to the nobles to reach a friendly understanding with the peasants and to reach agreements on the extent of the land allotment and the obligations stemming from it, observing, at the same time, the established rules to guarantee the inviolability of such agreements.

This new arrangement, because of its complexity, cannot be put into effect immediately, a time of not less than two years is necessary. During this period, to avoid all misunderstanding and to protect public and private interests, the order actually existing on the estates of nobles should be maintained until the new order shall become effective.

Towards that end, We have deemed it advisable:

1. To establish in each *gubernia* a special Office of Peasant Affairs, which will be entrusted with the affairs of the peasant communes established on the estates of the nobility.

2. To appoint in every district justices of the peace to solve all misunderstandings and disputes which may arise from the new arrangement, and to organize from these justices district assemblies.

3. To organize Peace Offices on the estates of the nobles, leaving the village communes as they are, and to open *volost* offices in the large villages and unite small village communes under one *volost* office.

4. To formulate, verify, and confirm in each village commune or estate a charter which would enumerate, on the basis of local conditions, the amount of land alloted to the peasants for permanent use, and the scope of their obligations to the nobleman for the land as well as for other advantages which are granted.

5. To put these charters into practice as they are gradually approved on each estate, and to put them into effect everywhere within two years from the date of publication of this manifesto.

6. Until that time, peasants and domestics must be obedient towards their nobles, and scrupulously fulfill their former obligations.

7. The nobles will continue to keep order on their estates, with the right of jurisdiction and of police, until the organization of *volost* and of *volost* courts.

Aware of the unavoidable difficulties of this reform, We place Our confidence above all in the graciousness of Divine Providence, which watches over Russia.

We also rely upon the zealous devotion of Our nobility, to whom We express Our gratitude and that of the entire country as well, for the unselfish support it has given to the realization of Our designs. Russia will not forget that the nobility, motivated by its respect for the dignity of man and its Christian love of its neighbor, has voluntarily renounced serfdom, and has laid the foundation of a new economic future for the peasants. We also expect that it will continue to express further concern for the realization of the new arrangement in a spirit of peace and benevolence, and that each nobleman will realize, on his estate, the great civic act of the entire group by organizing the lives of his peasants and his domestics on mutually advantageous terms, thereby setting for the rural population a good example of a punctual and conscientious execution of state regulations.

The examples of the generous concern of the nobles for the welfare of peasants, and the gratitude of the latter for that concern, give Us the hope that a mutual understanding will solve most of the difficulties, which in some cases will be inevitable during the application of general rules to the diverse conditions on some estates, and that thereby the transition from the old order to the new will be facilitated, and that in the future mutual confidence will be strengthened, and a good understanding and a unanimous tendency towards the general good will evolve.

To facilitate the realization of these agreements between the nobles and the peasants, by which the latter may acquire in full ownership their domicile and their land, the government will lend assistance, under special regulations, by means of loans or transfer of debts encumbering an estate.

We rely upon the common sense of Our people. When the government advanced the idea of abolishing serfdom, there developed a partial misunderstanding among the unprepared peasants. Some were concerned about freedom and disconcerned about obligations. But, generally, the common sense of the country has not wavered, because it has realized that every individual who enjoys freely the benefits of society owes it in return certain positive obligations; according to Christian law every individual is subject to higher authority (Romans, chap. xiii., 1); everyone must fulfill his obligations, and, above all, pay tribute, dues, respect, and honor (Ibid., chap. xiii., 7). What legally belongs to nobles cannot be taken away from them without adequate compensation, or through their voluntary concession; it would be contrary to all justice to use the land of the nobles without assuming responsibility for it.

And now We confidently expect that the freed serfs, on the eve of a new future which is opening to them, will appreciate and recognize the considerable sacrifices which the nobility has made on their behalf.

They should understand that by acquiring property and greater freedom to dispose of their possessions, they have an obligation to society and to themselves to live up to the letter of the new law by a loyal and judicious use of the rights which are now granted to them. However beneficial a law may be, it cannot make people happy if they do not themselves organize their happiness under protection of the law. Abundance is acquired only through hard work, wise use of strength and resources, strict economy, and above all, through an honest God-fearing life.

The authorities who prepared the new way of life for the peasants and who will be responsible for its inauguration will have to see that this task is accomplished with calmness and regularity, taking the timing into account in order not to divert the attention of cultivators away from their agricultural work. Let them zealously work the soil and harvest its fruits so that they will have a full granary of seeds to return to the soil which will be theirs.

And now, Orthodox people, make the sign of the cross, and join with Us to invoke God's blessing upon your free labor, the sure pledge of your personal well-being and the public prosperity.

Given at St. Petersburg, March 3, the year of Grace 1861, and the seventh of Our reign.

ALEXANDER

THE NEW DEMOCRACY

CONSTANTINE P. POBEDONOSTSEV

The emancipation of the serfs in 1861 profoundly affected all aspects of Russian life. It contributed to the decline of the power of the nobility, discontent among the peasantry, restlessness among the workers, dissatisfaction among the intelligentsia, and increasing reaction among the advocates of autocracy. The principal spokesman of the latter from 1880 to 1905 was Constantine P. Pobedonostsev (1827–1907). A constitutional lawyer by training, Pobedonostsev taught civil law at Moscow University from 1860 to 1865. He left teaching to become first a member of the Senate (Russia's Supreme Court), then a member of the Council of State (a consultative body that advised the tsar in legislative matters), and from 1880 to 1905 he acted as Procurator of the Holy Synod (lay administrator of the Orthodox Church). Since Pobedonostsev was also a tutor in law of Alexander III and Nicholas II, he was, between 1881 and 1905, the most influential member of the government and the prime inspirer of its reactionary policies. [In the following piece, written in the early 1880s, Pobedonostev expresses his criticism of the westernization and liberalization of Russia.]

BASIL DMYTRYSHYN

What is this freedom by which so many minds are agitated, which inspires so many insensate actions, so many wild speeches, which leads the people so often to misfortune? In the democratic sense of the word, freedom is the right of political power, or, to express it otherwise, the right to participate in the government of the State. This universal aspiration for a share in the government has no constant limitations, and seeks no definite issue, but incessantly extends, so that we might apply to it the words of the ancient poet about dropsy: *crescit indulgens sibi*.[1] Forever extending its base, the new

Reprinted from *Imperial Russia: A Source Book,* edited by Basil Dmytryshyn, (1990), Academic International Press.

[1] Horace: "nursed by self-indulgence"

Democracy now aspires to universal suffrage—a fatal error, and one of the most remarkable in the history of mankind. By this means, the political power so passionately demanded by Democracy would be shattered into a number of infinitesimal bits, of which each citizen acquires a single one. What will he do with it, then? How will he employ it? In the result it has undoubtedly been shown that in the attainment of this aim Democracy violates its sacred formula of "Freedom indissolubly joined with Equality." It is shown that this apparently equal distribution of "freedom" among all involves the total destruction of equality. Each vote, representing an inconsiderable fragment of power, by itself signifies nothing; an aggregation of votes alone has a relative value. The result may be likened to the general meetings of shareholders in public companies. By themselves individuals are ineffective, but he who controls a number of these fragmentary forces is master of all power, and directs all decisions and dispositions. We may well ask in what consists the superiority of Democracy. Everywhere the strongest man becomes master of the State; sometimes a fortunate and resolute general, sometimes a monarch or administrator with knowledge, dexterity, a clear plan of action, and a determined will, in a Democracy, the real rulers are the dexterous manipulators of votes, with their place—men, the mechanics who so skillfully operate the hidden springs which move the puppets in the arena of democratic elections. Men of this kind are ever ready with loud speeches lauding equality; in reality, they rule the people as any despot or military dictator might rule it. The extension of the right to participate in elections is regarded as progress and as the conquest of freedom by democratic theorists, who hold that the more numerous the participants in political rights, the greater is the probability that all will employ this right in the interests of the public welfare, and for the increase of the freedom of the people. Experience proves a very different thing. The history of mankind bears witness that the most necessary and fruitful reforms—the most durable measures—emanated from the supreme will of statesmen, or from a minority enlightened by lofty ideas and deep knowledge, and that, on the contrary, the extension of the representative principle is accompanied by an abasement of political ideas and the vulgarization of opinions in the mass of the electors. It shows also that this extension—in great States—was inspired by secret aims to the centralization of power, or led directly to dictatorship. In France, universal suffrage was suppressed with the end of the Terror and was reestablished twice merely to affirm the autocracy of the two Napoleons. In Germany, the establishment of universal suffrage served merely to strengthen the high authority of a famous statesman who had acquired popularity by the success of his policy. What its ultimate consequences will be, Heaven only knows!

The manipulation of votes in the game of Democracy is of the commonest occurrence in most European states, and its falsehood, it would seem, has been exposed to all; yet few dare openly to rebel against it. The unhappy people must bear the burden, while the Press, herald of a supposititious public opinion, stifles the cry of the people with its shibboleth, "Great is Diana of the Ephesians." But to an impartial mind, all this is nothing better than a struggle of parties, and a shuffling with numbers and names. The voters, by themselves inconsiderable unities, acquire a value in the hands of dexterous agents. This value is realised by many means—mainly, by bribery in innumerable forms, from gifts of money and trifling articles, to the distribution of places in the services, the financial departments, and the administration. Little by little, a class of electors has been formed which lives by the sale of votes to one or another of the political organizations. So far has this gone in France, for instance, that serious, intelligent, and industrious citizens in immense numbers abstain from voting, through the difficulty of contending with the cliques of political agents. With bribery go violence and threats, and reigns of terror are organised at elections by the help of which the respective cliques advance their candidates; hence the stormy scenes at electoral demonstrations, in which arms have been used, and the field of battle strewn with the bodies of the killed and wounded.

Organization and bribery—these are the two mighty instruments which are employed with such success for the manipulation of the mass of electors. Such methods are in no way new. Thucydides depicts in vivid colors their employment in the ancient republics of Greece. The history of the Roman Republic presents monstrous examples of corruption as the chief instrument of factions at elections. But in our times a new means has been found of working the masses for political aims, and joining them in adventitious alliances by provoking a fictitious community of views. This is the art of rapid and dexterous generalization of ideas, the composition of phrase and formulas, disseminated with the confidence of burning conviction as the last word of science, as dogmas of politicology, as infallible appreciations of events, of men, and of institutions. At one time it was believed that the faculty of analyzing facts, and deducing general principles, was the privilege of a few enlightened minds and deep thinkers; now it is considered an universal attainment, and, under the name of convictions, the generalities of political science have become a sort of current money, coined by newspapers and rhetoricians. . . .

Selections from the Writings of Charles Darwin

■ *Charles Robert Darwin (1809–1882) was born into an elite and wealthy family. First intending to become a physician, and then a clergyman, after his graduation from Cambridge in 1831 he was hired as the naturalist on the English survey vessel, HMS Beagle. His observations on this trip of geological formations at various coastal sites led him to accept the views of Charles Lyell regarding the gradual formation of the planet over a long period of time (*Principles of Geology, *1830–1833*). Especially influenced by observations of variations among finches he had observed in the Galapagos Islands and examination of the practices of commercial animal breeders in England, he applied Lyell's concept of gradual change to the evolution of species. As to the mechanism of change, he was influenced by the arguments of Thomas Malthus (*Essay on the Principle of Population, *1798) about how competition for available food led to war, famine and disease which acted as a control on human population. By 1838, Darwin had arrived at his basic thesis that species evolve over time through a process of natural selection in which those individuals fitted by natural variation with the best characteristics for survival under the particular conditions in which they find themselves will be selected by nature and pass on their characteristics to subsequent generations. The first publication of this theory (*On the Origin of the Species, *1859) was spurred by the impending publication by a young biologist, Russel Wallace, of a theory of natural selection which he had developed independently of Darwin. Darwin's ideas produced an uproar, with attacks by many scientists and theologians who saw Darwin's ideas as contradicting the Bible. Darwin had himself moved away from his earlier orthodox Christian beliefs. Much of the public advocacy of Darwin's position was done by others (e.g., Thomas Huxley). Darwin, who never had to earn a living, had married in 1839 and lived with his wife and children for most of the rest of his life on a small estate outside of London. He devoted his time to refining and expanding his ideas in a series of published works such as* The Descent of Man *(1871). In this work he turned his attention to the evolution of the human species arguing that the development of certain moral sentiments and intellectual abilities favored group survival, consequently lessening the role of physical (bodily) change as a means*

Reprinted from *The Origin of the Species*, (1859).

of adaptive change. Darwin ventured further in speculating how natural selection at a cultural level had favored the emergence and dominance of some nations (such as the Protestant, northern English) while recognizing that progress was not an inevitable historical process.

MALCOLM CLARK

From THE ORIGIN OF SPECIES

STRUGGLE FOR EXISTENCE

Before entering on the subject of this chapter, I must make a few preliminary remarks, to show how the struggle for existence bears on Natural Selection . . . . Amongst organic beings in a state of nature there is some individual variability; indeed I am not aware that this has ever been disputed. It is immaterial for us whether a multitude of doubtful forms be called species or sub-species or varieties; what rank, for instance, the two or three hundred doubtful forms of British plants are entitled to hold, if the existence of any well-marked varieties be admitted. But the mere existence of individual variability and of some few well-marked varieties, though necessary as the foundation for the work, helps us but little in understanding how species arise in nature. How have all those exquisite adaptations of one part of the organisation to another part, and to the conditions of life, and of one distinct organic being to another being, been perfected? We see these beautiful co-adaptations most plainly in the woodpecker and mistletoe; and only a little less plainly in the humblest parasite which clings to the hairs of a quadruped or feathers of a bird; in the structure of the beetle which dives through the water; in the plumed seed which is wafted by the gentlest breeze; in short, we see beautiful adaptations everywhere and in every part of the organic world.

Reprinted from *The Origin of the Species,* (1859).

Again, it may be asked, how is it that varieties, which I have called incipient species, become ultimately converted into good and distinct species, which in most cases obviously differ from each other far more than do the varieties of the same species? How do those groups of species, which constitute what are called distinct genera, and which differ from each other more than do the species of the same genus, arise? All these results, as we shall more fully see in the next chapter, follow inevitably from the struggle for life. Owing to this struggle for life, any variation, however slight and from whatever cause proceeding, if it be in any degree profitable to an individual of any species, in its infinitely complex relations to other organic beings and to external nature, will tend to the preservation of that individual, and will generally be inherited by its offspring. The offspring, also, will thus have a better chance of surviving, for, of the many individuals of any species which are periodically born, but a small number can survive. I have called this principle, by which each slight variation, if useful, is preserved, by the term of Natural Selection, in order to mark its relation to man's power of selection . . . . Man by selection can certainly produce great results, and can adapt organic beings to his own uses, through the accumulation of slight but useful variations, given to him by the hand of Nature. But Natural Selection, as we shall hereafter see, is a power incessantly ready for action, and is as immeasurably superior to man's feeble efforts, as the works of Nature are to those of Art.

We will now discuss in a little more detail the struggle for existence. In my future work this subject shall be treated, as it well deserves, at much greater length. The elder De Candolle and Lyell have largely and philosophically shown that all organic beings are exposed to severe competition. In regard to plants, no one has treated this subject with more spirit and ability than W. Herbert, Dean of Manchester, evidently the result of his great horticultural knowledge. Nothing is easier than to admit in words the truth of the universal struggle for life, or more difficult—at least I have found it so—than constantly to hear this conclusion in mind. Yet unless it be thoroughly engrained in the mind, I am convinced that the whole economy of nature, with every fact on distribution, rarity,

---

abundance, extinction, and variation, will be dimly seen or quite misunderstood. We behold the face of nature bright with gladness, we often see superabundance of food; we do not see, or we forget, that the birds which are idly singing round us mostly live on insects or seeds, and are thus constantly destroying life, or we forget how largely these songsters, or their eggs, or their nestlings, are destroyed by birds and beasts of prey; we do not always bear in mind, that though food may be now superabundant, it is not so at all seasons of each recurring year.

I should premise that I use the term Struggle for Existence in a large and metaphorical sense, including dependence of one being on another, and including (which is more important) not only the life of the individual, but success in leaving progeny. Two canine animals in a time of dearth, may be truly said to struggle with each other which shall get food and live. But a plant on the edge of a desert is said to struggle for life against the drought, though more properly it should be said to be dependent on the moisture. A plant which annually produces a thousand seeds, of which on an average only one comes to maturity, may be more truly said to struggle with the plants of the same and other kinds which already clothe the ground. The mistletoe is dependent on the apple and a few other trees, but can only in a far-fetched sense be said to struggle with these trees, for if too many of these parasites grow on the same tree, it will languish and die. But several seedling mistletoes, growing close together on the same branch, may more truly be said to struggle with each other. As the mistletoe is disseminated by birds, its existence depends on birds; and it may metaphorically be said to struggle with other fruit-bearing plants, in order to tempt birds to devour and thus disseminate its seeds rather than those of other plants. In these several senses, which pass into each other, I use for convenience sake the general term of struggle for existence.

A struggle for existence inevitably follows from the high rate at which all organic beings tend to increase. Every being, which during its natural lifetime produces several eggs or seeds, must suffer destruction during some period of its life, and during some season or occasional year, otherwise, on the principle of geometrical increase, its numbers would quickly become so inordinately great that no country could support the product. Hence, as more individuals are produced than can possibly survive, there must in every case be a struggle for existence, either one individual with another of the same species, or with the individuals of distinct species, or with the physical conditions of life. It is the doctrine of Malthus applied with manifold force to the whole animal and vegetable kingdoms; for in this case there can be no artificial increase of food, and no prudential restraint from marriage. Although some species may be now increasing, more or less rapidly, in numbers, all cannot do so, for the world would not hold them.

There is no exception to the rule that every organic being naturally increases at so high a rate, that if not destroyed, the earth would soon be covered by the progeny of a single pair. Even slow-breeding man has doubled in twenty-five years, and at this rate, in a few thousand years, there would literally not be standing room for his progeny. Linnaeus has calculated that if an annual plant produced only two seeds—and there is no plant so unproductive as this—and their seedlings next year produced two, and so on, then in twenty years there would be a million plants. The elephant is reckoned to be the slowest breeder of all known animals, and I have taken some pains to estimate its probable minimum rate of natural increase: it will be under the mark to assume that it breeds when thirty years old, and goes on breeding till ninety years old, bringing forth three pairs of young in this interval; if this be so, at the end of the fifth century there would be alive fifteen million elephants, descended from the first pair.

But we have better evidence on this subject than mere theoretical calculations, namely, the numerous recorded cases of the astonishingly rapid increase of various animals in a state of nature, when circumstances have been favourable to them during two or three following seasons. Still more striking is the evidence from our domestic animals of many kinds which have run wild in several parts of the world: if the statements of the rate of increase of slow-breeding cattle and horses in South-America, and latterly in Australia, had not been well authenticated, they would have been quite incredible. So it is with plants: cases could be given of introduced plants which have become common throughout whole islands in a period of less than ten years. Several of the plants now most numerous over the wide plains of La Plata, clothing square leagues of surface almost to the exclusion of all other plants, have been introduced from Europe; and there are plants which now range in India, as I hear from Dr Falconer, from Cape Comorin to the Himalaya, which have been imported from America since its discovery. In such cases, and endless instances could be given, no one supposes that the fertility of these animals or plants has been suddenly and temporarily increased in any sensible degree. The obvious explanation is that the conditions of life have been very favourable, and that there has consequently been less destruction of the old and young, and that nearly all the young have been enabled to breed. In such cases the geometrical ratio of increase, the result of which never fails to be surprising, simply explains the extraordinarily rapid increase and wide diffusion of naturalised productions in their new homes.

. . .

What checks the natural tendency of each species to increase in number is most obscure. Look at the most vigorous species; by as much as it swarms in numbers, by so much will its tendency to increase be still further increased. We know not exactly what the checks are in even one single instance. Nor will this surprise any one who reflects how ignorant we are on this head, even in regard to mankind, so incomparably better known than any other animal . . . . Here I will make only a few remarks, just to recall to the reader's mind some of the chief points. Eggs or very young animals seem generally to suffer most, but this is not invariably the case. With plants there is a vast destruction of seeds, but, from some observations which I have made, I believe that it is the seedlings which suffer most from germinating in ground already thickly stocked with other plants. Seedlings, also, are destroyed in vast numbers by various enemies; for instance, on a piece of ground three feet long and two wide, dug and cleared, and where there could be no choking from other plants, I marked all the seedlings of our native weeds as they came up, and out of the 357 no less than 295 were destroyed, chiefly by slugs and insects. If turf which has long been mown, and the case would be the same with turf closely browsed by quadrupeds, be let to grow, the more vigorous plants gradually kill the less vigorous, though fully grown, plants: thus out of twenty species growing on a little plot of turf (three feet by four) nine species perished from the other species being allowed to grow up freely.

The amount of food for each species of course gives the extreme limit to which each can increase; but very frequently it is not the obtaining food, but the serving as prey to other animals, which determines the average numbers of a species. Thus, there seems to be little doubt that the stock of partridges, grouse, and hares on any large estate depends chiefly on the destruction of vermin. If not one head of game were shot during the next twenty years in England, and, at the same time, if no vermin were destroyed, there would, in all probability, be less game than at present, although hundreds of thousands of game animals are now annually killed. On the other hand, in some cases, as with the elephant and rhinoceros, none are destroyed by beasts of prey: even the tiger in India most rarely dares to attack a young elephant protected by its dam.

Climate plays an important part in determining the average numbers of a species, and periodical seasons of extreme cold or drought, I believe to be the most effective of all checks. I estimated that the winter of 1854–55 destroyed four-fifths of the birds in my own grounds; and this is a tremendous destruction, when we remember that ten per cent is an extraordinarily severe mortality from epidemics with man. The action of climate seems at first sight to be quite independent of the struggle for existence; but in so far as climate chiefly acts in reducing food, it brings on the most severe struggle between the individuals, whether of the same or of distinct species, which subsist on the same kind of food. Even when climate, for instance extreme cold, acts directly, it will be the least vigorous, or those which have got least food through the advancing winter, which will suffer most. When we travel from south to north or from a damp region to a dry, we invariably see some species gradually getting rarer and rarer, and finally disappearing; and the change of climate being conspicuous, we are tempted to attribute the whole effect to its direct action. But this is a very false view: we forget that each species, even where it most abounds, is constantly suffering enormous destruction at some period of its life, from enemies or from competitors for the same place and food; and if these enemies or competitors be in the least degree favoured by any slight change of climate, they will increase in numbers, and, as each area is already fully stocked with inhabitants, the other species will decrease. When we travel southward and see a species decreasing in numbers, we may feel sure that the cause lies quite as much in other species being favoured, as in this one being hurt. So it is when we travel northward, but in a somewhat lesser degree, for the number of species of all kinds, and therefore of competitors, decreases northwards; hence in going northward, or in ascending a mountain, we far oftener meet with stunted forms, due to the *directly* injurious action of climate, than we do in proceeding southwards or in descending a mountain. When we reach the Arctic regions, or snow-capped summits, or absolute deserts, the struggle for life is almost exclusively with the elements.

That climate acts in main part indirectly by favouring other species, we may clearly see in the prodigious number of plants in our gardens which can perfectly well endure our climate, but which never become naturalised, for they cannot compete with our native plants, nor resist destruction by our native animals.

Natural Selection

How will the struggle for existence, discussed too briefly in the last chapter, act in regard to variation? Can the principle of selection, which we have seen is so potent in the hands of man, apply in nature? I think we shall see that it can act most effectually. Let it be borne in mind in what an endless number of strange peculiarities our domestic productions, and, in a lesser degree, those under nature, vary; and how strong the hereditary tendency is. Under domestication, it may be truly said that the whole organisation becomes in some degree plastic. Let it be borne in mind how infinitely complex and close-fitting are the mutual relations of all organic beings to each other and to their physical conditions of life. Can it, then, be thought improbable, seeing that variations useful to man have undoubtedly occurred, that other variations useful in some way to each being in the great and complex battle of life, should sometimes occur in the course of thousands of generations? If such do occur, can we doubt (remembering that many more individuals are born than can possibly survive) that individuals having any advantage, however slight, over others, would have the best chance of surviving and of procreating their kind? On the other hand, we may feel sure that any variation in the least degree injurious would be rigidly destroyed. This preservation of favourable variations and the rejection of injurious variations, I call Natural Selection. Variations neither useful nor injurious would not be attracted by natural selection, and would be left a fluctuating element, as perhaps we see in the species called polymorphic.

We shall best understand the probable course of natural selection by taking the case of a country undergoing some physical change, for instance, of climate. The proportional numbers of its inhabitants would almost immediately undergo a change, and some species might become extinct. We may conclude, from what we have seen of the intimate and complex manner in which the inhabitants of each country are bound together, that any change in the numerical proportions of some of the inhabitants, independently of the change of climate itself, would most seriously affect many of the others. If the country were open on its borders, new forms would certainly immigrate, and this also would seriously disturb the relations of some of the former inhabitants. Let it be remembered how powerful the influence of a single introduced tree or mammal has been shown to be. But in the case of an island, or of a country partly surrounded by barriers, into which new and better adapted forms could not freely enter, we should then have places in the economy of nature which would assuredly be better filled up, if some of the original inhabitants were in some manner modified; for, had the area been open to immigration, these same places would have been seized on by intruders. In such case, every slight modification, which in the course of ages chanced to arise, and which in any way favoured the individuals of any of the species, by better adapting them to their altered conditions, would tend to be preserved; and natural selection would thus have free scope for the work of improvement.

. . .

As man can produce and certainly has produced a great result by his methodical and unconscious means of selection, what may not nature effect? Man can act only on external and visible characters: nature cares nothing for appearances, except in so far as they may be useful to any being. She can act on every internal organ, on every shade of constitutional difference, on the whole machinery of life. Man selects only for his own good; Nature only for that of the being which she tends. Every selected character is fully exercised by her; and the being is placed under well-suited conditions of life. Man keeps the natives of many climates in the same country; he seldom exercises each selected character in some peculiar and fitting manner; he feeds a long and a short beaked pigeon on the same food; he does not exercise a long-backed or long-legged quadruped in any peculiar manner; he exposes sheep with long and short wool to the same climate. He does not allow the most vigorous males to struggle for the females. He does not rigidly destroy all inferior animals, but protects during each varying season, as far as lies in his power, all his productions. He often begins his selection by some half-monstrous form; or at least by some modification prominent enough to catch his eye, or to be plainly useful to him. Under nature, the slightest difference of structure or constitution may well turn the nicely balanced scale in the struggle for life, and so be preserved. How fleeting are the wishes and efforts of man! how short his time! and consequently how poor will his products be, compared with those accumulated by nature during whole geological periods. Can we wonder, then, that nature's productions should be far "truer" in character than man's productions; that they should be infinitely better adapted to the most complex conditions of life, and should plainly bear the stamp of far higher workmanship?

It may be said that natural selection is daily and hourly scrutinising, throughout the world, every variation, even the slightest;

rejecting that which is bad, preserving and adding up all that is good; silently and insensibly working, whenever and wherever opportunity offers, at the improvement of each organic being in relation to its organic and inorganic conditions of life. We see nothing of these slow changes in progress, until the hand of time has marked the long lapses of ages, and then so imperfect is our view into long past geological ages, that we only see that the forms of life are now different from what they formerly were.

Although natural selection can act only through and for the good of each being, yet characters and structures, which we are apt to consider as of very trifling importance, may thus be acted on. When we see leaf-eating insects green, and bark-feeders mottled-grey: the alpine ptarmigan white in winter, the red-grouse the colour of heather, and the black-grouse that of peaty earth, we must believe that these tints are of service to these birds and insects in preserving them from danger. Grouse, if not destroyed at some period of their lives, would increase in countless numbers; they are known to suffer largely from birds of prey; and hawks are guided by eyesight to their prey,—so much so, that on parts of the Continent persons are warned not to keep white pigeons, as being the most liable to destruction. Hence I can see no reason to doubt that natural selection might be most effective in giving the proper colour to each kind of grouse, and in keeping that colour, when once acquired, true and constant. Nor ought we to think that the occasional destruction of an animal of any particular colour would produce little effect: we should remember how essential it is in a flock of white sheep to destroy every lamb with the faintest trace of black. In plants the down on the fruit and the colour of the flesh are considered by botanists as characters of the most trifling importance: yet we hear from an excellent horticulturist, Downing, that in the United States smooth-skinned fruits suffer far more from a beetle, a *Curculio,* than those with down; that purple plums suffer far more from a certain disease than yellow plums; whereas another disease attacks yellow-fleshed peaches far more than those with other coloured flesh. If, with all the aids of art, these slight differences make a great difference in cultivating the several varieties, assuredly, in a state of nature, where the trees would have to struggle with other trees and with a host of enemies, such differences would effectually settle which variety, whether a smooth or downy, a yellow or purple fleshed fruit, should succeed.

Divergence of character. The principle, which I have designated by this term, is of high importance on my theory, and explains, as I believe, several important facts. In the first place, varieties, even strongly-marked ones, though having somewhat of the character of species—as is shown by the hopeless doubts in many cases how to rank them—yet certainly differ from each other far less than do good and distinct species. Nevertheless, according to my view, varieties are species in the process of formation, or are, as I have called them, incipient species. How, then, does the lesser difference between varieties become augmented into the greater difference between species? That this does habitually happen, we must infer from most of the innumerable species throughout nature presenting well-marked differences; whereas varieties, the supposed prototypes and parents of future well-marked species, present slight and ill-defined differences. Mere chance, as we may call it, might cause one variety to differ in some character from its parents, and the offspring of this variety again to differ from its parent in the very same character and in a greater degree; but this alone would never account for so habitual and large an amount of difference as that between varieties of the same species and species of the same genus.

As has always been my practice, let us seek light on this head from our domestic productions. We shall here find something analogous. A fancier is struck by a pigeon having a slightly shorter beak; another fancier is struck by a pigeon having a rather longer beak; and on the acknowledged principle that "fanciers do not and will not admire a medium standard, but like extremes," they both go on (as has actually occurred with tumbler-pigeons) choosing and breeding from birds with longer and longer beaks, or with shorter and shorter beaks. Again, we may suppose that at an early period one man preferred swifter horses; another stronger and more bulky horses. The early differences would be very slight; in the course of time, from the continued selection of swifter horses by some breeders, and of stronger ones by others, the differences would become greater, and would be noted as forming two sub-breeds; finally, after the lapse of centuries, the sub-breeds would become converted into two well-established and distinct breeds. As the differences slowly become greater, the inferior animals with intermediate characters, being neither very swift nor very strong, will have been neglected, and will have tended to disappear. Here, then, we see in man's productions the action of what may be called the principle of divergence, causing differences, at first barely appreciable, steadily to increase, and the breeds to diverge in character both from each other and from their common parent.

But how, it may be asked, can any analogous principle apply in nature? I believe it can and does apply most efficiently, from the simple circumstance that the more diversified the descendants from any one species become in structure, constitution, and habits, by so much will they be better enabled to seize on many and widely diversified places in the polity of nature and so be enabled to increase in numbers.

. . .

The advantage of diversification in the inhabitants of the same region is, in fact, the same as that of the physiological division of labour in the organs of the same individual body—a subject so well elucidated by Milne Edwards. No physiologist doubts that a stomach by being adapted to digest vegetable matter alone, or flesh alone, draws most nutriment from these substances. So in the general economy of any land, the more widely and perfectly the animals and plants are diversified for different habits of life, so will a greater number of individuals be capable of there supporting themselves. A set of animals, with their organisation but little diversified, could hardly compete with a set more perfectly diversified in structure. It may be doubted, for instance, whether the Australian marsupials, which are divided into groups differing but little from each other, and feebly representing, as Mr. Waterhouse and others have remarked, our carnivorous, ruminant, and rodent mammals, could successfully compete with these well-pronounced orders. In the

Australian mammals, we see the process of diversification in an early and incomplete stage of development.

After the foregoing discussion, which ought to have been much amplified, we may, I think, assume that the modified descendants of any one species will succeed by so much the better as they become more diversified in structure, and are thus enabled to encroach on places occupied by other beings. Now let us see how this principle of great benefit being derived from divergence of character, combined with the principles of natural selection and of extinction, will tend to act. The accompanying diagram will aid us in understanding this rather perplexing subject. Let A to L represent the species of a genus large in its own country; these species are supposed to resemble each other in unequal degrees, as is so generally the case in nature, and as is represented in the diagram by the letters standing at unequal distances. I have said a large genus, because we have seen in the second chapter, that on an average more of the species of large genera vary than of small genera; and the varying species of the large genera present a greater number of varieties. We have, also, seen that the species, which are the commonest and the most widely-diffused, vary more than rare species with restricted ranges. Let (A) be a common, widely-diffused, and varying species, belonging to a genus large in its own country. The little fan of diverging dotted lines of unequal lengths proceeding from (A), may represent its varying offspring. The variations are supposed to be extremely slight, but of the most diversified nature; they are not supposed all to appear simultaneously, but often after long intervals of time; nor are they all supposed to endure for equal periods. Only those variations which are in some way profitable will be preserved or naturally selected. And here the importance of the principle of benefit being derived from divergence of character comes in; for this will generally lead to the most different or divergent variations (represented by the outer dotted lines) being preserved and accumulated by natural selection. When a dotted line reaches one of the horizontal lines, and is there marked by a small numbered letter, a sufficient amount of variation is supposed to have been accumulated to have formed a fairly well-marked variety, such as would be thought worthy of record in a systematic work.

The intervals between the horizontal lines in the diagram, may represent each a thousand generations; but it would have been better if each had represented ten thousand generations. After a thousand generations, species (A) is supposed to have produced two fairly well-marked varieties, namely a^1 and m^1. These two varieties will generally continue to be exposed to the same conditions which made their parents variable, and the tendency to variability is in itself hereditary, consequently they will tend to vary, and generally to vary in nearly the same manner as their parents varied. Moreover, these two varieties, being only slightly modified forms, will tend to inherit those advantages which made their common parent (A) more numerous than most of the other inhabitants of the same country; they will likewise partake of those more general advantages which made the genus to which the parent-species belonged, a large genus in its own country. And these circumstances we know to be favourable to the production of new varieties.

If, then, these two varieties be variable, the most divergent of their variations will generally be preserved during the next thousand generations. And after this interval, variety a^1 is supposed in the diagram to have produced variety a^2, which will, owing to the principle of divergence, differ more from (A) than did variety a^1. Variety m^1 is supposed to have produced two varieties, namely m^2 and s^1, differing from each other, and more considerably from their common parent (A). We may continue the process by similar steps for any length of time; some of the varieties, after each thousand generations, producing only a single variety, but in a more and more modified condition, some producing two or three varieties, and some failing to produce any. Thus the varieties or modified descendants proceeding from the common parent (A), will generally go on increasing in number and diverging in character. In the diagram the process is represented up to the ten-thousandth generation, and under a condensed and simplified form up to the fourteen-thousandth generation.

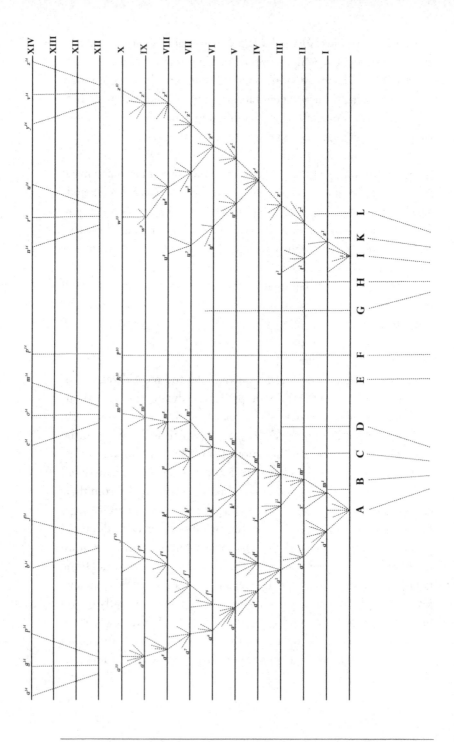

But I must here remark that I do not suppose that the process ever goes on so regularly as is represented in the diagram, though in itself made somewhat irregular. I am far from thinking that the most divergent varieties will invariably prevail and multiply: a medium form may often long endure, and may or may not produce more than one modified descendant; for natural selection will always act according to the nature of the places which are either unoccupied or not perfectly occupied by other beings; and this will depend on infinitely complex relations. But as a general rule, the more diversified in structure the descendants from any one species can be rendered, the more places they will be enabled to seize on, and the more their modified progeny will be increased. In our diagram the line of succession is broken at regular intervals by small numbered letters marking the successive forms which have become sufficiently distinct to be recorded as varieties. But these breaks are imaginary, and might have been inserted anywhere, after intervals long enough to have allowed the accumulation of a considerable amount of divergent variation.

As all the modified descendants from a common and widely diffused species, belonging to a large genus, will tend to partake of the same advantages which made their parent successful in life, they will generally go on multiplying in number as well as diverging in character: this is represented in the diagram by the several divergent branches proceeding from (A). The modified offspring from the later and more highly improved branches in the lines of descent, will, it is probable, often take the place of, and so destroy, the earlier and less improved branches: this is represented in the diagram by some of the lower branches not reaching to the upper horizontal lines. In some cases I do not doubt that the process of modification will be confined to a single line of descent, and the number of the descendants will not be increased; although the amount of divergent modification may have been increased in the successive generations. This case would be represented in the diagram, if all the lines proceeding from (A) were removed, excepting that from a^1 to a^{10}. In the same way, for instance, the English race-horse and English pointer have apparently both gone on slowly diverging in character from their original stocks, without either having given off any fresh branches or races. After ten thousand generations, species (A) is supposed to have produced three forms, a^{10}, f^{10}, and m^{10}, which, from having diverged in character during the successive generations, will have come to differ largely, but perhaps unequally, from each other and from their common parent. If we suppose the amount of change between each horizontal line in our diagram to be excessively small, these three forms may still be only well-marked varieties; or they may have arrived at the doubtful category of sub-species; but we have only to suppose the steps in the process of modification to be more numerous or greater in amount, to convert these three forms into well-defined species: thus the diagram illustrates the steps by which the small differences distinguishing varieties are increased into the larger differences distinguishing species. By continuing the same process for a greater number of generations (as shown in the diagram in a condensed and simplified manner), we get eight species, marked by the letters between a^{14} and m^{14}, all descended from (A). Thus, as I believe, species are multiplied and genera are formed.

. . .

But during the process of modification, represented in the diagram, another of our principles, namely that of extinction, will have played an important part. As in each fully stocked country natural selection necessarily acts by the selected form having some advantage in the struggle for life over other forms, there will be a constant tendency in the improved descendants of any one species to supplant and exterminate in each stage of descent their predecessors and their original parent. For it should be remembered that the competition will generally be most severe between those forms which are most nearly related to each other in habits, constitution, and structure.

Summary of Chapter

If under changing conditions of life organic beings present individual differences in almost every part of their structure, and this cannot be disputed; if there be, owing to their geometrical rate of increase, a severe struggle for life at some age, season,.or year, and this certainly cannot be disputed; then, considering the infinite complexity of the relations of all organic beings to each other and to their conditions of life, causing an infinite diversity in structure, constitution, and habits, to be advantageous to them, it would be a most extraordinary fact if no variations had ever occurred useful to each being's own welfare, in the same manner as so many variations have occurred useful to man. But if variations useful to any organic being ever do occur, assuredly individuals thus characterised will have the best chance of being preserved in the struggle for life; and from the strong principle of inheritance, these will tend to produce offspring similarly characterised. This principle of preservation, or the survival of the fittest, I have called Natural Selection. It leads to the improvement of each creature in relation to its organic and inorganic conditions of life; and consequently, in most cases, to what must be regarded as an advance in organization. Nevertheless, low and simple forms will long endure if well fitted for their simple conditions of life.

Natural selection, on the principle of qualities being inherited at corresponding ages, can modify the egg, seed, or young, as easily as the adult. Amongst many animals, sexual selection will have given its aid to ordinary selection, by assuring to the most vigorous and best adapted males the greatest number of offspring. Sexual selection will also give characters useful to the males alone, in their struggles or rivalry with other males; and these characters will be transmitted to one sex or to both sexes, according to the form of inheritance which prevails.

Whether natural selection has really thus acted in adapting the various forms of life to their several conditions and stations, must be judged by the general tenor and balance of evidence given in the following chapters. But we have already seen how it entails extinction; and how largely extinction has acted in the world's history, geology plainly declares. Natural selection, also leads to divergence of character; for the more organic beings diverge in structure, habits, and constitution, by so much the more can a large number be supported on the area,—of which we see proof by looking to the inhabitants of any small spot, and to the productions naturalised in foreign lands. Therefore, during the modification of the descendants of any one species, and during the incessant struggle of all species to increase in numbers, the more diversified the descendants become, the better will be their chance of success in the battle for life. Thus the small differences distinguishing varieties of the same species, steadily tend to increase, till they equal the greater differences between species of the same genus, or even of distinct genera.

We have seen that it is the common, the widely-diffused and widely-ranging species, belonging to the larger genera within each class, which vary most; and these tend to transmit to their modified offspring that superiority which now makes them dominant in their own countries. Natural selection, as has just been remarked, leads to divergence of character and to much extinction of the less improved and intermediate forms of life. On these principles, the nature of the affinities and the generally well-defined distinctions between the innumerable organic beings in each class throughout the world, may be explained. It is a truly wonderful fact—the wonder of which we are apt to overlook from familiarity—that all animals and all plants throughout all time and space should be related to each other in groups, subordinate to groups, in the manner which we everywhere behold—namely, varieties of the same species most closely related, species of the same genus less closely and unequally related, forming sections and sub-genera, species of distinct genera much less closely related, and genera related in different degrees, forming sub-families, families, orders, sub-classes and classes. The several subordinate groups in any class cannot be ranked in a single file, but seem clustered round points, and these round other points, and so on in almost endless cycles. If species had been independently created, no explanation would have been possible of this kind of classification; but it is explained through inheritance and the complex action of natural selection, entailing extinction and divergence of character, as we have seen illustrated in the diagram.

The affinities of all the beings of the same class have sometimes been represented by a great tree. I believe this simile largely speaks the truth. The green and budding twigs may represent existing species; and those produced during former years may represent the long succession of extinct species. At each period of growth all the growing twigs have tried to branch out on all sides, and to overtop and kill the surrounding twigs and branches, in the same manner as species and groups of species have at all times overmastered other species in the great battle for life. The limbs divided into great branches, and these into lesser and lesser branches, were themselves once, when the tree was young, budding twigs, and this connection of the former and present buds by ramifying branches may well represent the classification of all extinct and living species in groups subordinate to groups. Of the many twigs which flourished when the tree was a mere bush, only two or three, now grown into great branches, yet survive and bear the other branches, so with the species which lived during long-past geological periods, very few have left living and modified descendants. From the first growth of the tree, many a limb and branch has decayed and dropped off; and these fallen branches of various sizes may represent those whole orders, families, and genera which have now no living representatives, and which are known to us only in a fossil state. As we here and there see a thin straggling branch springing from a fork low down in a tree, and which by some chance has been favoured and is still alive on its summit, so we occasionally see an animal like the Ornithorhynchus or Lepidosiren, which in some small degree connects by its affinities two large branches of life, and which has apparently been saved from fatal competition by having inhabited a protected station. As buds give rise by growth to fresh buds, and these, if vigorous, branch out and overtop on all sides many a feebler branch, so by generation I believe it has been with the great Tree of Life, which fills with its dead and broken branches the crust of the earth, and covers the surface with its ever-branching and beautiful ramifications.

RECAPITULATION

I have already recapitulated, as fairly as I could, the opposed difficulties and objections: now let us turn to the special facts and arguments in favour of the theory.

On the view that species are only strongly marked and permanent varieties, and that each species first existed as a variety, we can see why it is that no line of demarcation can be drawn between species, commonly supposed to have been produced by special acts of creation, and varieties which are acknowledged to have been produced by secondary laws. On this same view we can understand how it is that in each region where many species of a genus have been produced, and where they now flourish, these same species should present many varieties; for where the manufactory of species has been active, we might expect, as a general rule, to find it still in action, and this is the case if varieties be incipient species. Moreover, the species of the large genera, which afford the greater number of varieties or incipient species, retain to a certain degree the character of varieties; for they differ from each other by a less amount of difference than do the species of smaller genera. The closely allied species also of the larger genera apparently have restricted ranges, and they are clustered in little groups round other species—in which respects they resemble varieties. These are strange relations on the view of each species having been independently created, but are intelligible if all species first existed as varieties.

As each species tends by its geometrical ratio of reproduction to increase inordinately in number; and as the modified descendants of each species will be enabled to increase by so much the more as they become more diversified in habits and structure, so as to be enabled to seize on many and widely different places in the economy of nature, there will be a constant tendency in natural selection to preserve the most divergent offspring of any one species. Hence during a long-continued course of modification, the slight differences, characteristic of varieties of the same species, tend to be augmented into the greater differences characteristic of species of the same genus. New and improved varieties will inevitably supplant and exterminate the older, less improved and intermediate varieties; and thus species are rendered to a large extent defined and distinct objects. Dominant species belonging to the larger groups tend to give birth to new and dominant forms; so that each large group tends to become still larger, and at the same time more divergent in character. But as all groups cannot thus succeed in increasing in size for the world would not hold them, the more dominant groups beat the less dominant. This tendency in the large groups to go on increasing in size and diverging in character, together with the almost inevitable contingency of much extinction, explains the arrangement of all the forms of life, in groups subordinate to groups, all within a few great classes, which we now see everywhere around us, and which has prevailed throughout all time. This grand fact of the grouping of all organic beings seems to me utterly inexplicable on the theory of creation.

As natural selection acts solely by accumulating slight, successive, favourable variations, it can produce no great or sudden modification; it can act only by very short and slow steps. Hence the canon of *Natura non facit saltum,* which every fresh addition to our knowledge tends to make more strictly correct, is on this theory simply intelligible. We can plainly see why nature is prodigal in variety, though niggard in innovation. But why this should be a law of nature if each species has been independently created, no man can explain.

Many other facts are, as it seems to me, explicable on this theory. How strange it is that a bird, under the form of woodpecker, should have been created to prey on insects on the ground; that upland geese, which never or rarely swim, should have been created with webbed feet; that a thrush should have been created to dive and feed on sub-aquatic insects; and that a petrel should have been created with habits and structure fitting it for the life of an auk or grebe! and so on in endless other cases. But on the view of each species constantly trying to increase in number, with natural selection always ready to adapt the slowly varying descendants of each to any unoccupied or ill-occupied place in nature, these facts cease to be strange, or perhaps might even have been anticipated.

As natural selection acts by competition, it adapts the inhabitants of each country only in relation to the degree of perfection of their associates; so that we need feel no surprise at the inhabitants of any one country, although on the ordinary view supposed to have been specially created and adapted for that country, being beaten and supplanted by the naturalised productions from another land. Nor ought we to marvel if all the contrivances in nature be not, as far as we can judge, absolutely perfect; and if some of them be abhorrent to our ideas of fitness. We need not marvel at the sting of the bee causing the bee's own death; at drones being produced in such vast numbers for one single act, and being then slaughtered by their sterile sisters; at the astonishing waste of pollen by our fir-trees; at the instinctive hatred of the queen bee for her own fertile daughters; at ichneumonidae feeding within the live bodies of caterpillars; and at other such cases. The wonder indeed is, on the theory of natural selection, that more cases of the want of absolute perfection have not been observed.

From THE DESCENT OF MAN

ON THE DEVELOPMENT OF THE INTELLECTUAL AND MORAL FACULTIES DURING PRIMEVAL AND CIVILISED TIMES

The subjects to be discussed in this chapter are of the highest interest, but are treated by me in a most imperfect and fragmentary manner. Mr. Wallace, in an admirable paper before referred to, argues that man after he had partially acquired those intellectual and moral faculties which distinguish him from the lower animals, would have been but little liable to have had his bodily structure modified through natural selection or any other means. For man is enabled through his mental faculties "to keep with an unchanged body in harmony with the changing universe." He has great power of adapting his habits to new conditions of life. He invents weapons, tools and various stratagems, by which he procures food and defends himself. When he migrates into a colder climate he uses clothes, builds sheds, and makes fires; and, by the aid of fire, cooks food otherwise indigestible. He aids his fellow-men in many ways, and anticipates future events. Even at a remote period he practised some subdivision of labour.

The lower animals, on the other hand, must have their bodily structure modified in order to survive under greatly changed conditions. They must be rendered stronger, or acquire more effective teeth or claws, in order to defend themselves from new enemies; or they must be reduced in size so as to escape detection and danger. When they migrate into a colder climate they must become clothed with thicker fur, or have their constitutions altered. If they fail to be thus modified, they will cease to exist.

The case, however, is widely different, as Mr. Wallace has with justice insisted, in relation to the intellectual and moral faculties of man. These faculties are variable; and we have every reason to believe that the variations tend to be inherited. Therefore, if they were

Reprinted from *The Descent of Man,* (1871).

formerly of high importance to primeval man and to his ape-like progenitors, they would have been perfected or advanced through natural selection. Of the high importance of the intellectual faculties there can be no doubt, for man mainly owes to them his predominant position in the world. We can see that, in the rudest state of society, the individuals who were the most sagacious, who invented and used the best weapons or traps, and who were best able to defend themselves, would rear the greatest number of offspring. The tribes which included the largest number of men thus endowed would increase in number and supplant other tribes. Numbers depend primarily on the means of subsistence, and this, depends partly on the physical nature of the country, but in a much higher degree on the arts which are there practised. As a tribe increases and is victorious, it is often still further increased by the absorption of other tribes. The stature and strength of the men of a tribe are likewise of some importance for its success, and these depend in part on the nature and amount of the food which can be obtained. In Europe the men of the Bronze period were supplanted by a more powerful and, judging from their sword-handles, larger-handed race; but their success was probably due in a much higher degree to their superiority in the arts.

All that we know about savages, or may infer from their traditions and from old monuments, the history of which is quite forgotten by the present inhabitants shew that from the remotest times successful tribes have supplanted other tribes. Relics of extinct or forgotten tribes have been discovered throughout the civilized regions of the earth, on the wild plains of America, and on the isolated islands in the Pacific Ocean. At the present day civilised nations are everywhere supplanting barbarous nations, excepting where the climate opposes a deadly barrier; and they succeed mainly, though not exclusively, through their arts, which are the products of the intellect. It is, therefore, highly probable that with mankind the intellectual faculties have been gradually perfected through natural selection; and this conclusion is sufficient for our purpose. Undoubtedly it would be interesting to have traced the development of each separate faculty from the state in which it exists in the lower animals to that in which it exists in man; but neither my ability nor knowledge permit the attempt.

It deserves notice that as soon as the progenitors of man became social (and this probably occurred at a very early period), the advancement of the intellectual faculties will have been aided and modified in an important manner, of which we see only traces in the lower animals, namely, through the principle of imitation, together with reason and experience. Apes are much given to imitation, as are the lowest savages; and the simple fact previously referred to, that after a time no animal can be caught in the same place by the same sort of trap, shews that animals learn by experience, and imitate each others' caution. Now, if some one man in a tribe, more sagacious than the others, invented a new snare or weapon, or other means of attack or defence, the plainest self-interest, without the assistance of much reasoning power, would prompt the other members to imitate him; and all would thus profit. The habitual practice of each new art must likewise in some slight degree strengthen the intellect. If the new invention were an important one, the tribe would increase in number, spread, and supplant other tribes. In a tribe thus rendered more numerous there would always be a rather better chance of the birth of other superior and inventive members. If such men left children to inherit their mental superiority, the chance of the birth of still more ingenious members would be somewhat better, and in a very small tribe decidedly better. Even if they left no children, the tribe would still include their blood-relations; and it has been ascertained by agriculturists that by preserving and breeding from the family of an animal, which when slaughtered was found to be valuable, the desired character has been obtained.

. . .

Natural Selection as affecting Civilised Nations.—In the last and present chapters I have considered the advancement of man from a former semi-human condition to his present state as a barbarian. But some remarks on the agency of natural selection on civilized nations may be here worth adding. This subject has been ably discussed by Mr. W. R. Greg, and previously by Mr. Wallace and Mr. Galton. Most of my remarks are taken from these three authors. With savages, the weak in body or mind are soon eliminated; and those that survive commonly exhibit a vigorous state of health. We civilised men, on the other hand, do our utmost to check the process of elimination; we build asylums for the imbecile, the maimed, and the sick; we institute poor-laws; and our medical men exert their utmost skill to save the life of every one to the last moment. There is reason to believe that vaccination has preserved thousands, who from a weak constitution would formerly have succumbed to small-pox. Thus the weak members of civilised societies propagate their kind. No one who has attended to the breeding of domestic animals will doubt that this must be highly injurious to the race of man; it is surprising how soon a want of care, or care wrongly directed, leads to the degeneration of a domestic race; but excepting in the case of man himself, hardly any one is so ignorant as to allow his worst animals to breed.

The aid which we feel impelled to give to the helpless is mainly an incidental result of the instinct of sympathy, which was originally acquired as part of the social instincts, but subsequently rendered, in the manner previously indicated, more tender and more widely diffused. Nor could we check our sympathy, if so urged by hard reason, without deterioration in the noblest part of our nature. The surgeon may harden himself whilst performing an operation, for he knows that he is acting for the good of his patient; but if we were intentionally to neglect the weak and helpless, it could only be for a contingent benefit, with a certain and great present evil. Hence we must bear without complaining the undoubtedly bad effects of the weak surviving and propagating their kind; but there appears to be at least one check in steady action, namely the weaker and inferior members of society not marrying so freely as the sound; and this check might be indefinitely increased, though this is more to be hoped for than expected, by the weak in body or mind refraining from marriage.

In all civilised countries man accumulates property and bequeaths it to his children. So that the children in the same country do not by any means start fair in the race for success. But this is far from an unmixed evil; for without the accumulation of capital the arts could not progress; and it is chiefly through their power that the civilised races have extended, and are now everywhere extending, their range, so as to take the place of the lower races. Nor does the moderate accumulation of wealth interfere with the process of selection. When a poor man becomes moderately rich, his children enter trades or professions in which there is struggle enough, so that the able in body and mind succeed best. The presence of a body of well-instructed men, who have not to labour for their daily bread, is important to a degree which cannot be over-estimated; as all high intellectual work is carried on by them, and on such work material progress of all kinds mainly depends, not to mention other and higher advantage. No doubt wealth when very great tends to convert men into useless drones, but their number is never large; and some degree of elimination here occurs, for we daily see rich men, who happen to be fools or profligate, squandering away their wealth.

Primogeniture with entailed estates is a more direct evil, though it may formerly have been a great advantage by the creation of a dominant class, and any government is better than anarchy. The eldest sons, though they may be weak in body or mind, generally marry, whilst the younger sons, however superior in these respects, do not so generally marry. Nor can worthless eldest sons with entailed estates squander their wealth. But here, as elsewhere, the relations of civilised life are so complex that some compensatory checks intervene. The men who are rich through primogeniture are able to select generation after generation the more beautiful and charming women; and these must generally be healthy in body and active in mind. The evil consequences, such as they may be, of the continued preservation of the same line of descent, without any selection, are checked by men of rank always wishing to increase their wealth and power; and this they effect by marrying heiresses. But the daughters of parents who have produced single children, are themselves, as Mr. Galton has shewn, apt to be sterile; and thus noble families are continually cut off in the direct line, and their wealth flows into some side channel; but unfortunately this channel is not determined by superiority of any kind.

Although civilisation thus checks in many ways the action of natural selection, it apparently favours, by means of improved food and the freedom from occasional hardships, the better development of the body. This may be inferred from civilised men having been found, wherever compared, to be physically stronger than savages. They appear also to have equal powers of endurance, as has been proved in many adventurous expeditions. Even the great luxury of the rich can be but little detrimental; for the expectation of life of our aristocracy, at all ages and of both sexes, is very little inferior to that of healthy English lives in the lower classes.

We will now look to the intellectual faculties alone. If in each grade of society the members were divided into two equal bodies, the one including the intellectually superior and the other the inferior, there can be little doubt that the former would succeed best in all occupations, and rear a greater number of children. Even in the lowest walks of life, skill and ability must be of some advantage; though in many occupations, owing to the great division of labour, a very small one. Hence in civilised nations there will be some tendency to an increase both in the number and in the standard of the intellectually able. But I do not wish to assert that this tendency may not be more than counterbalanced in other ways, as by the multiplication of the reckless and improvident; but even to such as these, ability must be some advantage.

It has often been objected to views like the foregoing, that the most eminent men who have ever lived have left no offspring to inherit their great intellect. Mr. Galton says, "I regret I am unable to solve the simple question whether, and how far, men and women who are prodigies of genius are infertile. I have, however, shewn that men of eminence are by no means so." Great lawgivers, the founders of beneficent religions, great philosophers and discoverers in science, aid the progress of mankind in a far higher degree by their works than by leaving a numerous progeny. In the case of corporeal structures, it is the selection of the slightly better-endowed and the elimination of the slightly less well-endowed individuals, and not the preservation of strongly-marked and rare anomalies, that leads to the advancement of a species.[1] So it will be with the intellectual faculties, namely from the somewhat more able men in each grade of society succeeding rather better than the less able, and consequently increasing in number, if not otherwise prevented. When in any nation the standard of intellect and the number of intellectual men have increased, we may expect from the law of the deviation from an average, as shown by Mr. Galton, that prodigies of genius will appear somewhat more frequently than before.

In regard to the moral qualities, some elimination of the worst dispositions is always in progress even in the most civilised nation. Malefactors are executed, or imprisoned for long periods, so that they cannot freely transmit their bad qualities. Melancholic and insane persons are confined, or commit suicide. Violent and quarrelsome men often come to a bloody end. Restless men who will not follow any steady occupation—and this relic of barbarism is a great check to civilisation—emigrate to newly-settled countries, where they prove useful pioneers. Intemperance is so highly destructive, that the expectation of life of the intemperate, at the age for instance, of thirty is only 13.8 years; whilst for the rural labourers of England at the same age it is 40.59 years. Profligate women bear few children, and profligate men rarely marry; both suffer from disease. In the breeding of domestic animals, the elimination of those individuals, though few in number, which are in any marked manner inferior, is by no means an unimportant element towards success. This especially holds good with injurious characters which tend to reappear through reversion, such as blackness in sheep; and with mankind some of the worst dispositions, which occasionally without any assignable cause make their appearance in families, may perhaps be reversions to a savage state, from which we are not removed by very many generations. This view seems indeed recognised in the common expression that such men are the black sheep of the family.

With civilised nations, as far as an advanced standard of morality, and an increased number of fairly well-endowed men are concerned, natural selection apparently effects but little; though the

---

[1] "Origin of Species" (fifth edition, 1869), p. 104.

fundamental social instincts were originally thus gained. But I have already said enough, whilst treating of the lower races, on the causes which lead to the advance of morality, namely, the approbation of our fellow-men—the strengthening of our sympathies by habit—example and imitation—reason—experience, and even self-interest—instruction during youth, and religious feelings.

A most important obstacle in civilised countries to an increase in the number of men of a superior class has been strongly urged by Mr. Greg and Mr. Galton, namely, the fact that the very poor and reckless, who are often degraded by vice, almost invariably marry early, whilst the careful and frugal, who are generally otherwise virtuous, marry late in life, so that they may be able to support themselves and their children in comfort. Those who marry early produce within a given period not only a greater number of generations, but, as shewn by Dr. Duncan, they produce many more children. The children, moreover, that are born by mothers during the prime of life are heavier and larger, and therefore probably more vigorous, than those born at other periods. Thus the reckless, degraded, and often vicious members of society, tend to increase at a quicker rate than the provident and generally virtuous members. Or as Mr. Greg puts the case: "The careless, squalid, unaspiring Irishman multiplies like rabbits: the frugal, foreseeing, self-respecting, ambitious Scot, stern in his morality, spiritual in his faith, sagacious and disciplined in his intelligence, passes his best years in struggle and in celibacy, marries late, and leaves few behind him. Given a land originally peopled by a thousand Saxons and a thousand Celts—and in a dozen generations five-sixths of the population would be Celts, but five-sixths of the property, of the power, of the intellect, would belong to the one-sixth of Saxons that remained. In the eternal 'struggle for existence,' it would be the inferior and *less* favoured race that had prevailed—and prevailed by virtue not of its good qualities but of its faults."

There are, however, some checks to this downward tendency. We have seen that the intemperate suffer from a high rate of mortality, and the extremely profligate leave few offspring. The poorest classes crowd into towns, and it has been proved by Dr. Stark from the statistics of ten years in Scotland, that at all ages the death-rate is higher in towns than in rural districts, "and during the first five years of life the town death-rate is almost exactly double that of rural districts." As these returns include both the rich and the poor, no doubt more than twice the number of births would be requisite to keep up the number of the very poor inhabitants in the towns, relatively to those in the country. With women, marriage at too early an age is highly injurious; for it has been found in France that, "twice as many wives under twenty die in the year, as died out of the same number unmarried." The mortality, also, of husbands under twenty is "excessively high," but what the cause of this may be seems doubtful. Lastly, if the men who prudently delay marrying until they can bring up their families in comfort, were to select, as they often do, women in the prime of life, the rate of increase in the better class would be only slightly lessened.

It was established from an enormous body of statistics, taken during 1853, that the unmarried men throughout France, between the ages of twenty and eighty, die in a much larger proportion than the married: for instance, out of every 1000 unmarried men, between the ages of twenty and thirty, 11.3 annually died, whilst of the married, only 6.5 died. A similar law was proved to hold good during the years 1863 and 1864, with the entire population above the age of twenty in Scotland: for instance, out of every 1000 unmarried men, between the ages of twenty and thirty, 14.97 annually died, whilst of the married only 7.24 died, that is less than half. Dr. Stark remarks on this, "Bachelorhood is more destructive to life than the most unwholesome trades, or than residence in an unwholesome house or district where there has never been the most distant attempt at sanitary improvement." He considers that the lessened mortality is the direct result of "marriage, and the more regular domestic habits which attend that state." He admits, however, that the intemperate, profligate, and criminal classes, whose duration of life is low, do not commonly marry; and it must likewise be admitted that men with a weak constitution, ill health, or any great infirmity in body or mind, will often not wish to marry, or will be rejected. Dr. Stark seems to have come to the conclusion that marriage in itself is a main cause of prolonged life, from finding that aged married men still have a considerable advantage in this respect over the unmarried of the same advanced age; but every one must have known instances of men, who with weak health during youth did not marry, and yet have survived to old age, though remaining weak, and therefore always with a lessened chance of life. There is another remarkable circumstance which seems to support Dr. Stark's conclusion, namely, that widows and widowers in France suffer in comparison with the married a very heavy rate of mortality; but Dr. Farr attributes this to the poverty and evil habits consequent on the disruption of the family, and to grief. On the whole we may conclude with Dr. Farr that the lesser mortality of married than of unmarried men, which seems to be a general law, "is mainly due to the constant elimination of imperfect types, and to the skilful selection relating only to the marriage state, and acting on all corporeal, intellectual, and moral qualities. We may, therefore, infer that sound and good men who out of prudence remain for a time unmarried do not suffer a high rate of mortality.

If the various checks specified in the two last paragraphs, and perhaps others as yet unknown, do not prevent the reckless, the vicious and otherwise inferior members of society from increasing at a quicker rate than the better class of men, the nation will retrograde, as has occurred too often in the history of the world. We must remember that progress is no invariable rule. It is most difficult to say why one civilised nation rises, becomes more powerful, and spreads more widely, than another; or why the same nation progresses more at one time than at another. We can only say that it depends on an increase in the actual number of the population, on the number of men endowed with high intellectual and moral faculties, as well as on their standard of excellence. Corporeal structure, except so far as vigour of body leads to vigour of mind, appears to have little influence.

It has been urged by several writers that as high intellectual powers are advantageous to a nation, the old Greeks, who stood some grades higher in intellect than any race that has ever existed, ought to have risen, if the power of natural selection were real, still higher in the scale, increased in number, and stocked the whole of Europe. Here we have the tacit assumption, so often made with respect to corporeal structures, that there is some innate tendency towards continued development in mind and body. But development of all kinds depends on many concurrent favourable circumstances. Natural selection acts only in a tentative manner. Individuals and races may have acquired certain indisputable advantages, and yet have perished from failing in other characters. The Greeks may have retrograded from a want of coherence between the many small states, from the small size of their whole country, from the practice of slavery, or from extreme sensuality; for they did not succumb until "they were enervated and corrupt to the very core." The western nations of Europe, who now so immeasurably surpass their former savage progenitors and stand at the summit of civilisation, owe little or none of their superiority to direct inheritance from the old Greeks; though they owe much to the written works of this wonderful people.

Who can positively say why the Spanish nation, so dominant at one time, has been distanced in the race? The awakening of the nations of Europe from the dark ages is a still more perplexing problem. At this early period, as Mr. Galton has remarked, almost all the men of a gentle nature, those given to meditation or culture of the mind, had no refuge except in the bosom of a Church which demanded celibacy; and this could hardly fail to have had a deteriorating influence on each successive generation. During this same period the Holy Inquisition selected with extreme care the freest and boldest men in order to burn or imprison them. In Spain alone some of the best men—those who doubted and questioned, and without doubting there can be no progress—were eliminated during three centuries at the rate of a thousand a year. The evil which the Catholic Church has thus effected, though no doubt counterbalanced to a certain, perhaps large extent in other ways, is incalculable; nevertheless, Europe has progressed at an unparalleled rate.

The remarkable success of the English as colonists over other European nations, which is well illustrated by comparing the progress of the Canadians of English and French extraction, has been ascribed to their "daring and persistent energy"; but who can say how the English gained their energy? There is apparently much truth in the belief that the wonderful progress of the United States, as well as the character of the people, are the results of natural selection; the more energetic, restless, and courageous men from all parts of Europe have emigrated during the last ten or twelve generations to that great country, and having there succeeded best. Looking to the distant future, I do not think that the Rev. Mr. Zincke takes an exaggerated view when he says: "All other series of events—as that which resulted in the culture of mind in Greece, and that which resulted in the empire of Rome—only appear to have purpose and value when viewed in connection with, or rather as subsidiary to . . . the great stream of Anglo-Saxon emigration to the west." Obscure as is the problem of the advance of civilization, we can at least see that a nation which produced during a lengthened period the greatest number of highly intellectual, energetic, brave, patriotic, and benevolent men, would generally prevail over less favoured nations.

Natural selection follows from the struggle for existence; and this from a rapid rate of increase. It is impossible not bitterly to regret, but whether wisely is another question, the rate at which man tends to increase; for this leads in barbarous tribes to infanticide and many other evils, and in civilised nations to abject poverty, celibacy, and to the late marriages of the prudent. But as man suffers from the same physical evils with the lower animals, he has no right to expect an immunity from the evils consequent on the struggle for existence. Had he not been subjected to natural selection, assuredly he would never have attained to the rank of manhood. When we see in many parts of the world enormous areas of the most fertile land peopled by a few wandering savages, but which are capable of supporting numerous happy homes, it might be argued that the struggle for existence had not been sufficiently severe to force man upwards to his highest standard. Judging from all that we know of man and the lower animals, there has always been sufficient variability in their intellectual and moral faculties, for their steady advancement through natural selection. No doubt such advance demands many favourable concurrent circumstances; but it may well be doubted whether the most favourable would have sufficed, had not the rate of increase been rapid, and the consequent struggle for existence severe to an extreme degree.

Rudyard Kipling

The English short-story writer, novelist, and poet Rudyard Kipling (1865–1936), was born in Bombay, India where his father taught at an art school. He lived in India for the first six years of his life, but at the age of six he was sent to England to be raised by a foster family and was sent to the United Services College. He returned to India at the age of sixteen where he worked for Anglo-Indian newspapers and began to write short stories and poetry. Hailed as the literary heir to Charles Dickens when he returned to England in 1889, he is best known for The Jungle Book *(1894) and* Just So Stories *(1902): he was the first Englishman to receive the Nobel Prize for Literature in 1907. Although many of his works express his enchantment with the Indian subcontinent, he is also remembered for his celebration of British imperialism and heroism in India. His glorification of imperialism gained its peak in the poem "The White Man's Burden," which urged the United States to follow Britain and other European nations in taking on the "burden" of empire in the territories the United States had gained with the treaty that ended the Spanish-American War. Kipling recognized the unpopularity of foreign rule, but considered the "white man's burden" as the duty of Europeans and white Americans to bring order and enlightenment to colonial lands.*

Jon Porter

The White Man's Burden

Take up the White Man's burden—
Send forth the best ye breed—
Go bind your sons to exile
To serve your captives' need;
To wait in heavy harness,
On fluttered folk and wild—
Your new-caught, sullen peoples,
Half-devil and half-child.

Reprinted from the *New York Sun*, February 5, 1899.

Take up the White Man's burden—
In patience to abide,
To veil the threat of terror
And check the show of pride;
By open speech and simple,
An hundred times made plain
To seek another's profit,
And work another's gain.

Take up the White Man's burden—
The savage wars of peace—
Fill full the mouth of Famine
And bid the sickness cease;
And when your goal is nearest
The end for others sought,
Watch sloth and heathen Folly
Bring all your hopes to nought.

Take up the White Man's burden—
No tawdry rule of kings,
But toil of serf and sweeper—
The tale of common things.
The ports ye shall not enter,
The roads ye shall not tread,
Go mark them with your living,
And mark them with your dead.

Take up the White Man's burden—
And reap his old reward:
The blame of those ye better,
The hate of those ye guard—
The cry of hosts ye humour
(Ah, slowly!) toward the light:—
"Why brought he us from bondage,
Our loved Egyptian night?"

Take up the White Man's burden—
Ye dare not stoop to less—
Nor call too loud on Freedom
To cloke your weariness;
By all ye cry or whisper,
By all ye leave or do,
The silent, sullen peoples
Shall weigh your gods and you.

Take up the White Man's burden—
Have done with childish days—
The lightly proferred laurel,
The easy, ungrudged praise.
Comes now, to search your manhood
Through all the thankless years
Cold, edged with dear-bought wisdom,
The judgment of your peers!

VLADIMIR ILYICH LENIN

1870–1924

■ *Lenin was born in theVolga region of Russia, the son of a school inspector named Ulyanov. He was deeply influenced by his brother Alexander, who was executed in 1887 for plotting to kill the tsar. He devoted himself to the study of Marxism and to agitation among workers, and was arrested and exiled in 1895. Living mostly in Europe after 1900, Lenin helped found a Russian Marxist party, the Russian Social Democratic Labor Party. He became the leader of the Bolshevik faction of the RSDLP, which seized power in Russia in November 1917. Lenin was the leader of the new Soviet state until his death in 1924.*

His famous pamphlet What is to Be Done?, *published in 1902, and excerpted below, addressed the dilemma of how to effect a Marxist revolution in Russia, a country with only a small working class.*

DAVID MASON

THE VANGUARD PARTY*

We have seen that the organisation of wide political agitation, and consequently, of all-sided political exposures are an absolutely necessary and *paramount* task of activity, that is, if that activity is to be truly social democratic. We arrived at this conclusion *solely* on the grounds of the pressing needs of the working class for political knowledge and political training. But this ground by itself is too narrow for the presentation of the question, for it ignores the general democratic tasks of social democracy as a whole, and of modern, Russian social democracy in particular. In order to explain the situation more concretely we shall approach the subject from an aspect that is "nearer" to the economist, namely, from the practical aspect. "Every

Reprinted from *Essential Works of Socialism,* edited by Irving Howe, (1970), Bantam Books, a division of Random House, Inc.
* Title supplied by the editor, Irving Howe.

one agrees" that it is necessary to develop the political consciousness of the working class. But the question arises: How is that to be done? What must be done to bring this about? The economic struggle merely brings the workers "up against" questions concerning the attitude of the government toward the working class. Consequently, *however much we may try* to "give to the economic struggle itself a political character," *we shall never be able* to develop the political consciousness of the workers (to the degree of social-democratic consciousness) by confining ourselves to the economic struggle, for *the limits of this task are too narrow. . . .*

The workers can acquire class political consciousness *only from without,* that is, only outside of the economic struggle, outside of the sphere of relations between workers and employers. The sphere from which alone it is possible to obtain this knowledge is the sphere of relationships between *all* classes and the state and the government—the sphere of the interrelations between *all* classes. For that reason, the reply to the question: "What must be done in order that the workers may acquire political knowledge?" cannot be merely the one which, in the majority of cases, the practical workers, especially those who are inclined towards economism, usually content themselves with, i.e., "go among the workers." To bring political knowledge to the workers, the social democrats must *go among all classes of the population,* must despatch units of their army *in all directions.*

We deliberately select this awkward formula, we deliberately express ourselves in a simple, forcible way, not because we desire to indulge in paradoxes, but in order to "stimulate" the economists to take up their tasks which they unpardonably ignore, to make them understand the difference between trade-union and social-democratic politics, which they refuse to understand. Therefore, we beg the reader not to get excited, but to hear us patiently to the end.

Take the type of social-democratic circle that has been most widespread during the past few years, and examine its work. It has "contact with the workers," it issues leaflets—in which abuses in the factories, the government's partiality toward the capitalists, and the tyranny of the police are strongly condemned—and rests content with this. At meetings of workers, there are either no discussions, or they do not extend beyond such subjects. Lectures and discussions, on the history of the revolutionary movement, on questions of the home and foreign policy of our government, on questions of the economic evolution of Russia and of Europe, and the position of the various classes in modern society, etc., are extremely rare. Of systematically acquiring and extending contact with other classes of society, no one even dreams. The ideal leader, as the majority of the members of such circles picture him, is something more in the nature of a trade-union secretary than a socialist political leader. Any trade-union secretary, an English one, for instance, helps the workers to conduct the economic struggle, helps to expose factory abuses, explains the injustice of the laws and of measures which hamper the freedom of strikes and the freedom to picket, to warn all and sundry that a strike is proceeding at a certain factory, explains the partiality of arbitration courts which are in the hands of the bourgeois classes, etc., etc. In a word, every trade-union secretary conducts and helps to conduct "the economic struggle against the employers and the government." It cannot be too strongly insisted that *this is not* enough to constitute social democracy. The social democrat's ideal should not be a trade-union secretary, but *a tribune of the people,* able to react to every manifestation of tyranny and oppression, no matter where it takes place, no matter what stratum or class of the people it affects; he must be able to group all these manifestations into a single picture of police violence and capitalist exploitation; he must be able to take advantage of every petty event in order to explain his socialistic convictions and his social democratic demands *to all,* in order to explain to *all* and every one the world historical significance of the struggle for the emancipation of the proletariat. . . .

I assert: 1) that no movement can be durable without a stable organisation of leaders to maintain continuity; 2) that the more widely the masses are drawn into the struggle and form the basis of the movement, the more necessary is it to have such an organisation and the more stable must it be (for it is much easier then for demagogues to sidetrack the more backward sections of the masses);

3) that the organisation must consist chiefly of persons engaged in revolution as a profession; 4) that in a country with a despotic government, the more we *restrict* the membership of this organisation to persons who are engaged in revolution as a profession and who have been professionally trained in the art of combating the political police, the more difficult will it be to catch the organisation; and 5) the *wider* will be the circle of men and women of the working class or of other classes of society able to join the movement and perform active work in it. . . .

The question in the last analysis, amounts to the question we have considered above, namely, whether it is possible to have a mass *organisation* when the maintenance of strict secrecy is essential. We can never give a mass organisation that degree of secrecy which is essential for the persistent and continuous struggle against the government. But to concentrate all secret functions in the hands of as small a number of professional revolutionists as possible, does not mean that the latter will "do the thinking for all" and that the crowd will not take an active part in the movement. On the contrary, the crowd will advance from its ranks increasing numbers of professional revolutionists, for it will know that it is not enough for a few students and workingmen waging economic war to gather together and form a "committee," but that professional revolutionists must be trained for years; the crowd will "think" not of primitive ways but of training professional revolutionists. The centralisation of the secret functions of the *organisation* does not mean the concentration of all the functions of the *movement*. The active participation of the greatest masses in the dissemination of illegal literature will not diminish because a dozen professional revolutionists concentrate in their hands the secret part of the work; on the contrary, it will *increase tenfold.* Only in this way will the reading of illegal literature, the contribution to illegal literature, and to some extent even the distribution of illegal literature *almost cease to be secret work,* for the police will soon come to realise the folly and futility of setting the whole judicial and administrative machine into motion to intercept every copy of a publication that is being broadcast in thousands. This applies not only to the press, but to every function of the movement, even to demonstrations. The active and widespread participation of the masses will not suffer; on the contrary, it will benefit by the fact that a "dozen" experienced revolutionists, no less professionally trained than the police, will concentrate all the secret side of the work in their hands—prepare leaflets, work out approximate plans, and appoint bodies of leaders for each town district, for each factory district, and for each educational institution (I know that exception will be taken to my "undemocratic" views, but I shall reply to this altogether unintelligent objection later on). The centralisation of the more secret functions in an organisation of revolutionists will not diminish, but rather increase the extent and the quality of the activity of a large number of other organisations intended for wide membership and which, therefore, can be as loose and as public as possible, for example, trade unions, workers' circles for self-education, and the reading of illegal literature, and socialist, and also democratic, circles for *all other sections of the population,* etc., etc. We must have *as large a number as possible* of such organisations having the widest possible variety of functions, but it is absurd and dangerous to *confuse these with organisations of revolutionists,* to erase the line of demarcation between them, to dim still more the already incredibly hazy appreciation by the masses that to "serve" the mass movement we must have people who will devote themselves exclusively to social-democratic activities, and that such people must *train* themselves patiently and steadfastly to be professional revolutionists. . . .

WILFRED OWEN

Wilfred Owen (1893–1918) was teaching in France when the Great War broke out in 1914. He returned to England the next year and enlisted in the Artists' Rifles in October 1915. After training, he was commissioned a second lieutenant and transferred to the Manchester Regiment in France in January 1917, where he began writing poems about his war experience. That summer, Owen was badly injured during the Battle of the Somme when a shell landed just two yards away from him. After spending several days in a bomb crater with the mangled corpse of a fellow officer, Owen was diagnosed as suffering from "neurasthenia," or shell-shock. He was sent back to Britain to recover. In August 1918, Owen was declared fit to return to the Western Front. Awarded the Military Cross for bravery at Amiens, he was killed by machine-gun fire while leading his men across the Sambre Canal on November 4, 1918, a week before the Armistice was signed. News of his death reached his parents on November 11, 1918, the day of the Armistice.

JON PORTER

Dulce et Decorum Est[1]

WILFRED OWEN

Bent double, like old beggars under sacks,
Knock-kneed, coughing like hags, we cursed through sludge,
Till on the haunting flares we turned our backs
And towards our distant rest began to trudge.
Men marched asleep. Many had lost their boots   5

Reprinted from Dulce et Decorum Est, (October 1917–March 1918).
[1] The famous Latin tag [from Horace, Odes 3.2.13] means, of course, It is sweet and fitting to die for one's country. Sweet! And decorous! [Oct. 16, 1917, letter of Owen to his mother].

But limped on, blood-shod. All went lame; all blind;
Drunk with fatigue; deaf even to the hoots
Of tired, outstripped Five-Nines[2] that dropped behind.

Gas! GAS! Quick, boys!—An ecstasy of fumbling,
Fitting the clumsy helmets just in time;   10
But someone still was yelling out and stumbling,
And flound'ring like a man in fire or lime . . .
Dim, through the misty panes[3] and thick green light,
As under a green sea, I saw him drowning.

In all my dreams, before my helpless sight,   15
He plunges at me, guttering, choking, drowning.

If in some smothering dreams you too could pace
Behind the wagon that we flung him in,
And watch the white eyes writhing in his face,
His hanging face, like a devil's sick of sin;   20
If you could hear, at every jolt, the blood
Come gargling from the froth-corrupted lungs,
Obscene as cancer, bitter as the cud
Of vile, incurable sores on innocent tongues,—
My friend,[4] you would not tell with such high zest   25
To children ardent for some desperate glory,
The old Lie: Dulce et decorum est
Pro patria mori.

Oct. 1917–Mar. 1918   1920

---

[2] I.e., 5.9-caliber shells.
[3] Of the gas mask's celluloid window.
[4] Jessie Pope, to whom the poem was originally to have been dedicated, was
the author of numerous prewar children's books as well as *Jessie Pope's War Poems*
(1915).

Siegfried Sassoon

■ *Siegfried Sassoon (1886–1967) studied law and history at Cambridge University but left before taking his degree. He enlisted in the Sussex Yeomanry two days before the British declaration of war, and was eventually commissioned a second lieutenant in the Royal Welch Fusiliers in 1915. He earned the Military Cross— and the nickname "Mad Jack"—in June 1916 for gallantry in battle, after he rescued a wounded soldier from "No Man's Land" under heavy enemy fire.*

While recovering from the wounds he received during the Second Battle of the Scarpe, he sent his pacifist "Statement against the continuation of the War" to his commanding officer, only avoiding a court martial because of the intervention of his friend, the poet Robert Graves, also an officer in the Welch Fusiliers. Sassoon was then sent to Craiglockhart War Hospital near Edinburgh, officially suffering from shell-shock. After four months at Craiglockhart, Sassoon realized that his protest against the war had achieved nothing and applied to return to the front. After three months service in Palestine, his unit was sent back to France where he was again wounded. Sassoon was put on indefinite sick leave until the end of the war.

Jon Porter

Poems of Siegfried Sassoon

"They"

The Bishop tells us: "When the boys come back
They will not be the same; for they'll have fought
In a just cause: they lead the last attack
On Anti-Christ; their comrades' blood has bought
New right to breed an honourable race,   5
They have challenged Death and dared him face to face."

Reprinted from *The Old Huntsman and Other Poems,* (1918).

"We're none of us the same!" the boys reply.
"For George lost both his legs; and Bill's stone blind;
Poor Jim's shot through the lungs and like to die;
And Bert's gone syphilitic: you'll not find   10
A chap who's served that hasn't found *some* change."
And the Bishop said: "The ways of God are strange!"

Oct. 31, 1916   1917

Reconciliation

When you are standing at your hero's grave,
Or near some homeless village where he died,
Remember, through your heart's rekindling pride,
The German soldiers who were loyal and brave.

Men fought like brutes; and hideous things were done;
And you have nourished hatred harsh and blind.
But in that Golgotha perhaps you'll find
The mothers of the men who killed your son.

November 1918

Reprinted from *Picture-Show*, (1920).

Aftermath

Have you forgotten yet? . . .
For the world's events have rumbled on since those gagged days,
Like traffic checked while at the crossing of city-ways:
And the haunted gap in your mind has filled with thoughts that flow
Like clouds in the lit heaven of life; and you're a man reprieved to go,
Taking your peaceful share of Time, with joy to spare.
But the past is just the same—and War's a bloody game . . .
Have you forgotten yet? . . .
Look down, and swear by the slain of the War that you'll never forget.

Do you remember the dark months you held the sector at Mametz—
The nights you watched and wired and dug and piled sandbags
    on parapets?
Do you remember the rats; and the stench
Of corpses rotting in front of the front-line trench—
And dawn coming, dirty-white, and chill with a hopeless rain?
Do you ever stop and ask, "Is it all going to happen again?"

Do you remember that hour of din before the attack—
And the anger, the blind compassion that seized and shook you

As you peered at the doomed and haggard faces of your men?
Do you remember the stretcher-cases lurching back
With dying eyes and lolling heads—those ashen-grey
Masks of the lads who once were keen and kind and gay?

Have you forgotten yet? . . .
Look up, and swear by the green of the spring that you'll never forget.

March 1919

Reprinted from *Modern British Poetry*, (1920).

LIEUTENANT COLONEL JOHN McCRAE, MD

Canadian Army
1872–1918

In Flanders Fields

In Flanders Fields the poppies blow
Between the crosses row on row,
That mark our place; and in the sky
The larks, still bravely singing, fly
Scarce heard amid the guns below.

We are the Dead. Short days ago
We lived, felt dawn, saw sunset glow,
Loved and were loved, and now we lie
In Flanders fields.

Take up our quarrel with the foe:
To you from failing hands we throw
The torch; be yours to hold it high.
If ye break faith with us who die
We shall not sleep, though poppies grow
In Flanders fields.

VÁCLAV HAVEL

b. 1936

🔲 *A prominent playwright and writer, Václav Havel was an important figure in the Charter 77 human rights movement in communist Czechoslovakia. In his extended 1979 essay* The Power of the Powerless, *which is excerpted here, he called on citizens to revolt by "living within the truth" and rejecting the lies and ideology of the government. Ten years later, he helped lead the "Velvet Revolution" that brought down the communist regime. He served as President of the newly democratic Czechoslovakia from 1989–1992 and of the Czech Republic from 1993–2003.*

DAVID MASON

THE POWER OF THE POWERLESS

Václav Havel

1979

The manager of a fruit and vegetable shop places in his window, among the onions and carrots, the slogan: "Workers of the World, Unite!" Why does he do it? What is he trying to communicate to the world? Is he genuinely enthusiastic about the idea of unity among the workers of the world? Is his enthusiasm so great that he feels an irrepressible impulse to acquaint the public with his ideals? Has he really given more than a moment's thought to how such a unification might occur and what it would mean?

I think it can safely be assumed that the overwhelming majority of shopkeepers never think about the slogans they put in their windows, nor do they use them to express their real opinions. That poster was delivered to our greengrocer from the enterprise headquarters along with the onions and carrots. He put them all into

Reprinted from *The Power of the Powerless: Citizens Against the State in Central-Eastern Europe,* edited by John Keane, (1985), M.E. Sharpe, Inc., Publisher.

the window simply because it has been done that way for years, because everyone does it, and because that is the way it has to be. If he were to refuse, there could be trouble. He could be reproached for not having the proper "decoration" in his window; someone might even accuse him of disloyalty. He does it because these things must be done if one is to get along in life. It is one of the thousands of details that guarantee him a relatively tranquil life "in harmony with society," as they say.

Obviously the greengrocer is indifferent to the semantic content of the slogan on exhibit; he does not put the slogan in his window from any personal desire to acquaint the public with the ideal it expresses. This, of course, does not mean that his action has no motive or significance at all or that the slogan communicates nothing to anyone. The slogan is really a *sign,* and as such it contains a subliminal but very definite message. Verbally, it might be expressed this way: "I, the greengrocer XY, live here and I know what I must do. I behave in the manner expected of me. I can be depended upon and am beyond reproach. I am obedient and therefore I have the right to be left in peace." This message, of course, has an addressee: It is directed above, to the greengrocer's superior, and at the same time it is a shield that protects the greengrocer from potential informers. The slogan's real meaning, therefore, is rooted firmly in the greengrocer's existence. It reflects his vital interests. But what are those vital interests?

Let us take note: If the greengrocer had been instructed to display the slogan, "I am afraid and therefore unquestioningly obedient," he would not be nearly as indifferent to its semantics, even though the statement would reflect the truth. The greengrocer would be embarrassed and ashamed to put such an unequivocal statement of his own degradation in the shop window, and quite naturally so, for he is a human being and thus has a sense of his own dignity. To overcome this complication, his expression of loyalty must take the form of a sign which, at least on its textual surface, indicates a level of disinterested conviction. It must allow the greengrocer to say, "What's wrong with the workers of the world uniting?" Thus the sign helps the greengrocer to conceal from himself the low foundations of his obedience, at the same time concealing the low foundations of power. It hides them behind the facade of something high. And that something is *ideology*.

Ideology is a specious way of relating to the world. It offers human beings the illusion of an identity, of dignity, and of morality while making it easier for them to *part* with them. As the repository of something "suprapersonal" and objective, it enables people to deceive their conscience and conceal their true position and their inglorious *modus vivendi,* both from the world and from themselves. It is a very pragmatic, but at the same time an apparently dignified, way of legitimizing what is above, below, and on either side. It is directed toward people and toward God. It is a veil behind which human beings can hide their own "fallen existence," their trivialization, and their adaptation to the status quo. It is an excuse that everyone can use, from the greengrocer, who conceals his fear of losing his job behind an alleged interest in the unification of the workers of the world, to the highest functionary, whose interest in staying in power can be cloaked in phrases about service to the working class. The primary excusatory function of ideology, therefore, is to provide people, both as victims and pillars of the post-totalitarian system, with the illusion that the system is in harmony with the human order and the order of the universe.

The smaller a dictatorship and the less stratified by modernization the society under it, the more directly the will of the dictator can be exercised. In other words, the dictator can employ more or less naked discipline, avoiding the complex processes of relating to the world and of self-justification which ideology involves. But the more complex the mechanisms of power become, the larger and more stratified the society they embrace, and the longer they have operated historically, the more individuals must be connected to them from outside, and the greater the importance attached to the ideological excuse. It acts as a kind of bridge between the regime and the people, across which the regime approaches the people and the people approach the regime. This explains why ideology plays such an important role in the post-totalitarian system: That complex machinery of units, hierarchies, transmission belts, and indirect instruments of manipulation which ensure in countless ways the integrity of the regime, leaving nothing to chance, would be quite simply unthinkable without ideology acting as its all-embracing excuse and as the excuse for each of its parts.

If an entire district town is plastered with slogans that no one reads, it is on the one hand a message from the district secretary to the regional secretary, but it is also something more: a small example of the principle of social *autototality* at work. Part of the essence of the post-totalitarian system is that it draws everyone into its sphere of power, not so they may realize themselves as human beings, but so they may surrender their human identity in favor of the identity of the system, that is, so they may become agents of the system's general automatism and servants of its self-determined goals, so they may participate in the common responsibility for it, so they may be pulled into and ensnared by it, like Faust with Mephistopheles. More than this: so they may create through their involvement a general norm and, thus, bring pressure to bear on their fellow citizens. And further: so they may learn to be comfortable with their involvement, to identify with it as though it were something natural and inevitable and, ultimately, so they may—with no external urging—come to treat any noninvolvement as an abnormality, as arrogance, as an attack on themselves, as a form of dropping out of society. By pulling everyone into its power structure, the post-totalitarian system makes everyone instruments of a mutual totality, the autototality of society.

Everyone, however, is in fact involved and enslaved, not only the greengrocers but also the prime ministers. Differing positions in the hierarchy merely establish differing degrees of involvement: The greengrocer is involved only to a minor extent, but he also has very little power. The prime minister, naturally, has greater power, but in return he is far more deeply involved. Both, however, are unfree, each merely in a somewhat different way. The real accomplice in this involvement, therefore, is not another person, but the system itself.

The fact that human beings have created, and daily create, this self-directed system through which they divest themselves of their innermost identity is not therefore the result of some incomprehensible misunderstanding of history, nor is it history somehow gone off its rails. Neither is it the product of some diabolical higher will which has decided, for reasons unknown, to torment a portion of humanity in this way. It can happen and did happen only because there is obviously in modern humanity a certain tendency toward the creation, or at least the toleration, of such a system. There is obviously something in human beings which responds to this system, something they reflect and accommodate, something within them which paralyzes every effort of their better selves to revolt. Human beings are compelled to live within a lie, but they can be compelled to do so only because they are in fact capable of living in this way.

In highly simplified terms, it could be said that the post-totalitarian system has been built on foundations laid by the historical encounter between dictatorship and the consumer society. Is it not true that the far-reaching adaptability to living a lie and the effortless spread of social autototality have some connection with the general unwillingness of consumption-oriented people to sacrifice some material certainties for the sake of their own spiritual and moral integrity? With their willingness to surrender higher values when faced with the trivializing temptations of modern civilization? With their vulnerability to the attractions of mass indifference? And in the end, is not the grayness and the emptiness of life in the post-totalitarian system only an inflated caricature of modern life in general? And do we not in fact stand (although in the external measures of civilization, we are far behind) as a kind of warning to the West, revealing to it its own latent tendencies?

Let us now imagine that one day something in our greengrocer snaps, and he stops putting up the slogans merely to ingratiate himself. He stops voting in elections he knows are a farce. He begins to say what he really thinks at political meetings. And he even finds the strength in himself to express solidarity with those whom his conscience commands him to support. In this revolt the greengrocer steps out of living within the lie. He rejects the ritual and breaks the rules of the game. He discovers once more his suppressed identity and dignity. He gives his freedom a concrete significance. His revolt is an attempt to *live within the truth.*

The bill is not long in coming. He will be relieved of his post as manager of the shop and transferred to the warehouse. His pay will be reduced. His hopes for a holiday in Bulgaria will evaporate. His children's access to higher education will be threatened. His superiors will harass him, and his fellow workers will wonder about him. Most of those who apply these sanctions, however, will not do so from any authentic inner conviction but simply under pressure from conditions, the same conditions that once pressured the greengrocer to display the official slogans. They will persecute the greengrocer either because it is expected of them, or to demonstrate their loyalty, or simply as part of the general panorama, to which belongs an awareness that this is how situations of this sort are dealt with, that this, in fact, is how things are always done, particularly if one is not to become suspect oneself. The executors, therefore, behave essentially like everyone else, to a greater or lesser degree: as components of the post-totalitarian system, as agents of its automatism, as petty instruments of the social autototality.

Thus the power structure, through the agency of those who carry out the sanctions, those anonymous components of the system, will spew the greengrocer from its mouth. The system, through its alienating presence in people, will punish him for his rebellion. It must do so because the logic of its automatism and self-defense dictates it. The greengrocer has not committed a simple, individual offense, isolated in its own uniqueness, but something incomparably more serious. By breaking the rules of the game, he has disrupted the game as such. He has exposed it as a mere game. He has shattered the world of appearances, the fundamental pillar of the system. He has upset the power structure by tearing apart what holds it together. He has demonstrated that living a lie is living a lie. He has broken throught the exalted facade of the system and exposed the real, base foundations of power. He has said that the emperor is naked. And because the emperor is in fact naked, something extremely dangerous has happened: By his action, the greengrocer has addressed the world. He has enabled everyone to peer behind the curtain. He has shown everyone that it *is* possible to live within the truth. Living within the lie can constitute the system only if it is universal. The principle must embrace and permeate everything. There are no terms whatsoever on which it can coexist with living within the truth, and therefore everyone who steps out of line *denies it in principle and threatens it in its entirety.*

Individuals can be alienated from themselves only because there is *something* in them to alienate. The terrain of this violation is their authentic existence. Living the truth is thus woven directly into the texture of living a lie. It is the repressed alternative, the authentic aim to which living a lie is an inauthentic response. Only against this background does living a lie make any sense: It exists *because* of that background. In its excusatory, chimerical rootedness in the human order, it is a response to nothing other than the human predisposition to truth. Under the orderly surface of the life of lies, therefore, there slumbers the hidden sphere of life in its real aims, of its hidden openness to truth.

The singular, explosive, incalculable political power of living within the truth resides in the fact that living openly within the truth has an ally, invisible to be sure, but omnipresent: this hidden sphere. It is from this sphere that life lived openly in the truth grows; it is to this sphere that it speaks and in it that it finds understanding. This is where the potential for communication exists. But this place is hidden and therefore, from the perspective of power, very dangerous. The complex ferment that takes place within it goes on in semidarkness, and by the time it finally surfaces into the light of day as an assortment of shocking surprises to the system, it is usually too late to cover them up in the usual fashion. Thus they create a situation in which the regime is confounded, invariably causing panic and driving it to react in inappropriate ways.

The profound crisis of human identity brought on by living within a lie, a crisis which in turn makes such a life possible, certainly possesses a moral dimension as well; it appears, among other things, as *a deep moral crisis in society.* A person who has been seduced by the consumer value system, whose identity is dissolved in an amalgam of the accoutrements of mass civilization, and who has no roots in the order of being, no sense of responsibility for anything higher than his or her own personal survival, is a *demoralized* person. The system depends on this demoralization, deepens it, is in fact a projection of it into society.

Living within the truth, as humanity's revolt against an enforced position, is, on the contrary, an attempt to regain control over one's own sense of responsibility. In other words, it is clearly a moral act, not only because one must pay so dearly for it, but principally because it is not self-serving: The risk may bring rewards in the form of a general amelioration in the situation, or it may not. In this regard, as I stated previously, it is an all-or-nothing gamble, and it is difficult to imagine a reasonable person embarking on such a course merely because he or she reckons that sacrifice today will bring rewards tomorrow, be it only in the form of general gratitude. (By the way, the representatives of power invariably come to terms with those who live within the truth by persistently ascribing utilitarian motivations to them—a lust for power or fame or wealth—and thus they try, at least, to implicate them in their own world, the world of general demoralization.)

If living within the truth in the post-totalitarian system becomes the chief breeding ground for independent, alternative political ideas, then all considerations about the nature and future prospects of these ideas must necessarily reflect this moral dimension as a political phenomenon. (And if the revolutionary Marxist belief about morality as a product of the "superstructure" inhibits any of our friends from realizing the full significance of this dimension and, in one way or another, from including it in their view of the world, it is to their own detriment: An anxious fidelity to the postulates of that world view prevents them from properly understanding the mechanisms of their own political influence, thus paradoxically making them precisely what they, as Marxists, so often suspect others of being— victims of "false consciousness.") The very special political significance of morality in the post-totalitarian system is a phenomenon that is at the very least unusual in modern political history, a phenomenon that might well have—as I shall soon attempt to show— far-reaching consequences.

There is no way around it: no matter how beautiful an alternative political model may be, it can no longer speak to the "hidden sphere," inspire people and society, call for real political ferment. The real sphere of potential politics in the post-totalitarian system is elsewhere: in the continuing and cruel tension between the complex demands of that system and the aims of life, that is, the elementary need of human beings to live, to a certain extent at least, in harmony with themselves, that is, to live in a bearable way, not to be humiliated by their superiors and officials, not to be continually watched by the police, to be able to express themselves freely, to find an outlet for their creativity, to enjoy legal security, and so on.

Anything that touches this field concretely, anything that relates to this fundamental, omnipresent, and living tension, will inevitably speak to people. Abstract projects for an ideal political or economic order do not interest them to anything like the same extent—and rightly so—not only because everyone knows how little chance they have of succeeding but also because today people feel that the less political policies are derived from a concrete and human "here and now" and the more they fix their sights on an abstract "some day," the more easily they can degenerate into new forms of human enslavement. People who live in the post-totalitarian system know only too well that the question of whether one or several political parties are in power, and how these parties define and label themselves, is of far less importance than the question of whether or not it is possible to live like a human being.

To shed the burden of traditional political categories and habits and open oneself up fully to the world of human existence and then to draw political conclusions only after having analyzed it: This is not only politically more realistic but at the same time, from the point of view of an "ideal state of affairs," politically more promising as well. A genuine, profound, and lasting change for the better can no longer result from the victory (were such a victory possible) of any particular traditional political conception, which can ultimately be only external, that is, a structural or systemic conception. More than ever before, such a change will have to derive from human existence, from the fundamental reconstitution of the position of people in the world, their relationships to themselves and to each other, and to the universe. If a better economic and political model is to be created, then perhaps more than ever before it must derive from profound existential and moral changes in society. This is not something that can be designed and introduced like a new car. If it is to be more than just a new variation on the old degeneration, it must above all be an expression of life in the process of transforming itself. A better system will not automatically ensure a better life. In fact the opposite is true: Only by creating a better life can a better system be developed.

The point where living within the truth ceases to be a mere negation of living with a lie and becomes articulate in a particular way, is the point at which something is born that might be called "the independent spiritual, social, and political life of society." This independent life is not separated from the rest of life ("dependent life") by some sharply defined line. Both types frequently coexist in the same people. Nevertheless, its most important focus is marked by a relatively high degree of inner emancipation. It sails upon the vast ocean of the manipulated life like little boats, tossed by the waves but always bobbing back as visible messengers of living within the truth, articulating the suppressed aims of life.

What is this independent life of society? The spectrum of its expressions and activities is naturally very wide. It includes everything from self-education and thinking about the world, through free creative activity and its communication to others, to the most varied free, civic attitudes, including instances of independent social self-organization. In short, it is an area in which living within the truth becomes articulate and materializes in a visible way.

And now I may properly be asked the question: What is to be done, then?

My skepticism toward alternative political models and the ability of systemic reforms or changes to redeem us does not, of course, mean that I am skeptical of political thought altogether. Nor does my emphasis on the importance of focusing concern on real human beings disqualify me from considering the possible structural consequences flowing from it. On the contrary, if A was said, then B should be said as well. Nevertheless, I will offer only a few very general remarks.

Above all, any existential revolution should provide hope of a moral reconstitution of society, which means a radical renewal of the relationship of human beings to what I have called the "human order," which no political order can replace. A new experience of being, a renewed rootedness in the universe, a newly grasped sense of "higher responsibility," a newfound inner relationship to other people and to the human community—these factors clearly indicate the direction in which we must go.

MIKHAIL GORBACHEV

b. 1931

▨ *Gorbachev rose through the Communist Party of the Soviet Union to become party leader in 1985. He initiated a series of reforms, including* perestroika *(economic restructuring),* glasnost *(openness), and "new thinking" in foreign policy that included improved relations with the United States, and a relaxing of controls over the Soviet satellite countries in Eastern Europe. These changes contributed to the East European revolutions of 1989 and the eventual collapse of the Soviet Union in 1991. Gorbachev was awarded the Nobel Peace Prize in 1990. The following excerpt is from a speech he gave to the Council of Europe in Strasbourg in July 1989—in the midst of the East European anti-communist revolutions.*

DAVID MASON

From A COMMON EUROPEAN HOME

MIKHAIL GORBACHEV

It is not enough now simply to state that the European states share a common fate and are interdependent. The idea of European unity must be collectively rethought, in a process of creative collaboration among all nations—large, medium, and small.

Is such a formulation of the question realistic? I know that many in the West see the presence of two social systems as the major difficulty. But the difficulty actually lies elsewhere—in the widespread conviction (sometimes even a policy objective) whereby overcoming the split in Europe means "overcoming socialism." But this is a policy of confrontation, if not worse. No European unity will result from such approaches.

Reprinted by permission from *The Current Digest of the Soviet Press* 61, no. 27 (1989).

The fact that European states belong to different social systems is a reality. And recognition of this historical given and respect for the sovereign right of every people to choose a social system at its own discretion constitute the most important prerequisite for a normal European process.

Social and political orders in one or another country have changed in the past and may change in the future. However, this is exclusively the affair of the peoples themselves; it is their choice. Any interference in internal affairs and any attempts to restrict the sovereignty of states—either friends and allies or anyone else—are inadmissible.

Differences between states cannot be eliminated. They are, as I have said on more than one occasion, even beneficial—provided, of course, that the competition between the different types of societies is oriented toward creating better material and spiritual conditions of life for people.

Thanks to restructuring, the U.S.S.R. will be able to be a full-fledged participant in this kind of honest, equitable, and constructive competition. Despite all our current shortcomings and lagging, we are well aware of the strong aspects of our social system that stem from its essential characteristics. And we are sure that we will be able to use them for the benefit of both ourselves and Europe.

It is time to relegate to the archives the postulates of the cold war, when Europe was viewed as an arena of confrontation divided into "spheres of influence" and somebody's "forward defense areas," and as an object of military opposition—a theater of military operations. In today's interdependent world, geopolitical notions born of another epoch are just as useless in real politics as the laws of classical mechanics are in quantum theory.

Meanwhile, it is on the basis of outdated stereotypes that the Soviet Union continues to be suspected of hegemonistic plans and intentions to tear the United States away from Europe. Some people would even like to place the U.S.S.R. outside of Europe from the Atlantic to the Urals, by limiting Europe to the expanse "from Brest to Brest." The U.S.S.R. is allegedly too big for coexistence: Others, it is said, would not feel very comfortable next to it. The realities of today and the prospects for the foreseeable future are obvious: The U.S.S.R. and the United States are a natural part of the European international political structure. And their participation in its evolution is not only justified, but also historically determined. . . .

[Our idea of a common European home] arose from an awareness of the new realities, from an understanding that a linear continuation of the path along which inter-European relations have been developing up to the last quarter of the twentieth century no longer corresponded to these realities.

The idea is connected with our internal economic and political restructuring, for which new relations were needed, above all, in the part of the world to which we, the Soviet Union, belong and with which for centuries we have had more ties than with anyone else.

We also took into consideration the fact that the colossal burden of armaments and the atmosphere of confrontation were not only hindering Europe's normal development but, at the same time, were obstructing—economically, politically, and psychologically—the full-fledged inclusion of our country in the European process and were introducing deforming impulses into our own development.

Those are the motives behind our decision to sharply step up our European policy, which, incidentally, was always of value to us in and of itself.

The philosophy of the concept of a "common European home" rules out the probability of an armed clash and the very possibility of using force or the threat of force, above all, military force—alliance against alliance, within alliances or wherever. To replace the doctrine of deterrence, it offers a doctrine of restraint. This is not just a game of ideas, but the logic of European development dictated by life itself.

Now for the economic content of the common European home. We consider the formation of a vast economic expanse from the Atlantic to the Urals, with a high level of interconnection between its eastern and western parts, to be a realistic prospect, though not an imminent one.

The Soviet Union's transition to a more open economy has fundamental importance in this respect. And not just for us ourselves, for increasing the efficiency of the national economy and satisfying the demands of consumers. It will increase the interdependence of the economies of East and West and, consequently, will have a favorable effect on the whole complex of general European relations.

Similar features in the practical functioning of economic mechanisms, strengthening of ties and economic interest, mutual adaptation, and training of the appropriate specialists—all of these are long-term factors in the course of cooperation, and a pledge of the stability of the European and international process as a whole. . . .

VÁCLAV HAVEL

In the last months of 1989, after huge popular demonstrations in Prague, the communist government of Czechoslovakia resigned, elections were held, and the new legislature chose Havel as the country's new president. Three days after he assumed office, he delivered this address to the nation.

DAVID MASON

NEW YEAR'S DAY SPEECH, 1990

VÁCLAV HAVEL

JANUARY 1, 1990

Dear fellow citizens. For the past 40 years on this day you have heard my predecessors utter different variations on the same theme, about how our country is prospering, how many more billion tons of steel we have produced, how happy we all are, how much we trust our government, and what beautiful prospects lie ahead of us. I do not think you appointed me to this office for me, of all people, to lie to you.

Our country is not prospering. The great creative and spiritual potential of our nation is not being used to its full potential. Whole sectors of industry are producing things in which no one is interested, while the things we need are in short supply.

The state, which calls itself a state of the working people, is humiliating and exploiting the workers. Our outdated economy is squandering energy, of which we are in short supply. A country

Reprinted from *Journal of Democracy* 1, no. 2 (spring 1990), Johns Hopkins University Press.

that could once be proud of the standard of education of its people spends so little on education that today it occupies seventy-second place in the world. We have laid waste and soiled the rivers and the forests that our forefathers bequeathed to us, and we have the worst environment in the whole of Europe today. Adults in our country die earlier than in most other European countries.

Allow me to tell you about a little personal experience of mine. Flying to Bratislava recently, I found time during various meetings to look out of the window. What I saw was the Slovnaft [oil refinery] complex and the Petrzalka suburb immediately beyond it. That view was enough for me to understand that our statesmen and politicians had not even looked—or did not even want to look—out of the windows of their planes. None of the statistics available to me would have enabled me to understand more quickly or more easily the situation we have gotten ourselves into.

But not even all of that is the most important thing. The worst thing is that we are living in a decayed moral environment. We have become morally ill, because we have become accustomed to saying one thing and thinking another. We have learned not to believe in anything, not to have consideration for one another, and only to look after ourselves. Notions such as love, friendship, compassion, humility, and forgiveness have lost their depth and dimension, and for many of us they merely represent some kind of psychological idiosyncrasy, or appear to be some kind of stray relic from times past, something rather comical in the era of computers and space rockets. Few of us managed to cry out that the powerful should not be all-powerful and that the special farms which produce ecologically sound and high-quality foodstuffs for them should send their produce to the schools, children's hostels, and hospitals, since our agriculture is not yet able to offer this to everyone.

The previous regime, armed with its arrogant and intolerant ideology, denigrated man into a production force and nature into a production tool. In this way it attacked their very essence and the relationship between them. It made talented people who were capable of managing their own affairs and making an enterprising living in their own country into cogs in some kind of monstrous, ramshackle, smelly machine whose purpose no one can understand. It can do nothing more than slowly but surely wear itself down, and all the cogs in it.

When I talk about a decayed moral environment, I do not mean merely those gentlemen who eat ecologically pure vegetables and do not look out of their airplane windows. I mean all of us, because all of us have become accustomed to the totalitarian system, accepted it as an unalterable fact, and thereby kept it running. In other words, all of us are responsible, each to a different degree, for keeping the totalitarian machine running. None of us is merely a victim of it, because all of us helped to create it together.

Why do I mention this? It would be very unwise to see the sad legacy of the past 40 years as something alien to us, handed down to us by some distant relatives. On the contrary, we must accept this legacy as something that we have brought upon ourselves. If we can accept this, then we will understand that it is up to all of us to do something about it. We cannot lay all the blame on those who ruled us before, not only because this would not be true, but also because it could detract from the responsibility each of us now faces—the responsibility to act on our own initiative, freely, sensibly, and quickly.

Let us not delude ourselves: not even the best government, the best parliament, or the best president can do much on their own, and it would be profoundly unjust to expect them alone to put everything right. Freedom and democracy, after all, mean that we all have a part to play and bear joint responsibility. If we can realize this, then all the horrors that the new Czechoslovak democracy has inherited will suddenly cease to appear to be terrible. If we can realize this, hope will return to our hearts.

In putting right the general state of affairs, we already have a sound footing on which to build. The recent times, and especially the last six weeks of our peaceful revolution, have shown what an enormous generally humane, moral, and spiritual charge and what high standards of civic maturity lay dormant in our society under the mask of apathy that had been forced upon it. Whenever anyone talking to me began to put categorical labels on our people, I always pointed out that society is a very mysterious creature and that it is never wise to trust only the particular fact that it is presenting to you. I am glad to have been proved right.

Throughout the world, people are surprised that the acquiescent, humiliated, skeptical Czechoslovak people who apparently no longer believed in anything suddenly managed to find the enormous strength in the space of a few weeks to shake off the totalitarian system in a completely decent and peaceful way. We ourselves are also surprised at this, and we ask where do the young people, in particular, who have never known any other system, find the source of their aspirations for truth, freedom of thought, political imagination, civic courage, and civic foresight? How is it that their parents, the generation that was considered lost, also joined in with them? How is it even possible that so many people immediately grasped what had to be done, without needing anyone else's advice or instructions?

I think that this hopeful aspect of our situation today has two main reasons. Above all, man is never merely a product of the world around him, he is always capable of striving for something higher, no matter how systematically this ability is ground down by the world around him. Second, the humanistic and democratic traditions—which are often spoken about in such a hollow way—nonetheless lay dormant somewhere in the subconscious of our nations and national minorities, and were passed on quietly from one generation to the next in order for each of us to discover them within us when the time was right, and to put them into practice.

Of course, for our freedom today we also had to pay a price. Many of our people died in prison in the 1950s; many were executed, thousands of human lives were destroyed, and hundreds of thousands of talented people were driven abroad. Those who defended the honor of our nations in the war were persecuted, as were those who resisted totalitarian government, and those who simply managed to remain true to their own principles and think freely. None of those who paid the price in one way or another for our freedom today should be forgotten. Independent courts should justly assess the appropriate guilt of those responsible, so that the whole truth about our recent past comes out into the open.

Neither should we forget that other nations paid an even higher price for their freedom today, and thus they also paid indirectly for us too. The rivers of blood which flowed in Hungary, Poland, Germany, and recently also in such a horrific way in Romania, as well as the sea of blood shed by the nations of the Soviet Union, should not be forgotten, primarily because all human suffering affects every human being. But more than that, they must not be forgotten because it was these great sacrifices which weaved the tragic backcloth for today's freedom or gradual liberation of the nations of the Soviet bloc, and the backcloth of our newly charged freedom too.

Without the changes in the Soviet Union, Poland, Hungary, and the German Democratic Republic, the developments in our country could hardly have happened, and if they had happened, they surely would not have had such a wonderful peaceful character. The fact that we had favorable international conditions, of course, does not mean that anyone was helping us directly in those weeks. For centuries, in fact, both our nations have risen up by themselves, without relying on any help from more powerful states or big powers.

This, it seems to me, is the great moral stake of the present moment. It contains the hope that in the future we will no longer have to suffer the complex of those who are permanently indebted to someone else. Now it is up to us alone whether this hope comes to fruition, and whether our civic, national, and political self-confidence reawakens in a historically new way.

Self-confidence is not pride. Quite the contrary. Only a man or a nation self-confident in the best sense of the word is capable of listening to the voice of others, accepting them as equal to oneself, forgiving one's enemies, and regretting one's own mistakes. As such people, let us try to introduce self-confidence into the life of our community and as nations into our conduct on the international arena. Only thus shall we regain self-respect and respect for each other, as well as the respect of other nations. Our state should never again be a burden or a poor relation to anyone else. Although we have to take a great many things and learn many things from others, we must do this, after a long period of time, as equal partners who also have something to offer.

Our first president wrote "Jesus and not Caesar." In this he followed up both on Chelcicky and Komensky.[1] This idea has once again been reawakened in us. I dare say that perhaps we even have the possibility of spreading it further, thus introducing a new factor in both European and world politics. Love, desire for understanding, the strength of the spirit and of ideas can radiate forever from our country, if we want this to happen. This radiation can be precisely what we can offer as our very own contribution to world politics.

Masaryk founded his politics on morality. Let us try, in a new time and in a new way, to revive this concept of politics. Let us teach both ourselves and others that politics ought to be a reflection of the aspiration to contribute to the happiness of the community and not of the need to deceive or pillage the community. Let us teach both ourselves and others that politics does not have to be the art of the possible, especially if this means the art of speculating, calculating, intrigues, secret agreements, and pragmatic maneuvering, but that it also can be the art of the impossible, that is the art of making both ourselves and the world better.

We are a small country, but nonetheless we were once the spiritual crossroads of Europe. Is there any reason why we should not be so again? Would this not be another contribution through which we could pay others back for the help we will need from them?

---

[1]Czechoslovakia's first president was Tomás Masaryk (1850–1937). Masaryk was a professor of philosophy in Prague and always took an interest in ethical and national issues, clearing a Jew of a charge of ritual murder, befriending the Slovaks, and inspiring the Croatian secession. The most prominent Czech political figure before World War I, Masaryk agitated for the creation of a Czechoslovak state during the war, and when that event came to pass he became the country's first president. Peter Chelcicky (1390–1460) was the foremost thinker of the Czech reformation movement founded by Jan Hus at the turn of the fifteenth century. His pacifist and utopian teachings gave rise to the Protestant movement called the Bohemian Brethren, the last leader of which was Jan Amos Komensky [John Amos Comenius] (1592–1670). Komensky said, "I love my country and its language and my greatest wish is that it be cultivated." At the same time he felt himself a citizen of Europe and believed in the unity of humankind. Czech patriots consider the moral strength of these men a constituent part of Czech national character.

The home mafia—those who do not look out of their airplane windows and eat specially fed pigs—are still alive, true, and make trouble from time to time, but they are no longer our main enemy, and international mafias are even less of an enemy. Our worst enemy today is our own bad qualities—indifference to public affairs, conceit, ambition, selfishness, the pursuit of personal advancement, and rivalry—and that is the main struggle we are faced with.

I would like to conclude by saying that I want to be a president of action rather than words, a president who not only looks out of the windows of his airplane carefully, but one, above all, who is consistently present among his fellow citizens and listens to them carefully.

Perhaps you are asking what kind of republic I have in mind. My reply is this: a republic that is independent, free, and democratic, with a prospering economy and also socially just—in short a republic of the people that serves the people, and is therefore entitled to hope that the people will serve it too. I have in mind a republic of people with a well-rounded education, because without such people none of our problems—whether human, economic, environmental, social, or political—can be tackled.

One of my most distinguished predecessors began his first speech by quoting Comenius. Allow me to end my first speech with my own paraphrase of that same statement: People, your government has returned to you!

Slavenka Drakulić

Slavenka Drakulić was born in 1946 in Croatia, then a republic within a newly reconstituted and communist Yugoslavia. While Yugoslavia experienced a level of general freedom rarely found in communist regimes, intellectual freedom was still restricted, and the state-managed economy was marked by a scarcity of goods. In addition to this political and economic repression, internal racial and religious strife fomented in the cobbled-together nation as Serbs, Croats, and Muslims sought greater political autonomy and self-direction. The death of long-time communist leader Josip Broz Tito in 1980 weakened Yugoslavia and by 1990 the Croats elected a noncommunist government. Croatia declared its independence in June of 1991.

In How We Survived Communism and Even Laughed, *Drakulić explores the everyday humanity of what it means to live in Eastern Europe under a communist regime, and the changes to daily life brought by the burgeoning democracy of the 1990s. Filtering the effects of Eastern European communism through her own experiences, the essays reprinted here provide an unusually personal narrative that brings into focus the way in which communism impacted a nation of individuals, with particular attention to the female experience.*

Elizabeth A. Barrett

FROM HOW WE SURVIVED COMMUNISM AND EVEN LAUGHED

SLAVENKA DRAKULIĆ

1

YOU CAN'T DRINK YOUR COFFEE ALONE

She is dead. Her grave is covered with ivy and tiny blue forget-me-nots. A candle is burning; her mother must have been here recently. But I haven't been here - not once since the day she was buried, five years ago. It's not that I've forgotten her, just the opposite: I could not face it, her death, the absurdity of it. In August 1985, when she poisoned herself with the gas from the stove in her new apartment, she was thirty-six years old.

I don't know how to tell Tanja's story or even why it should be important. She wasn't a hero; sometimes I think she was a coward. The many fine threads that connected her to life simply unraveled one by one so that she chose death over life. Before she let the gas run, she sealed all the doors and windows with tape and washed the dishes. To this day, I am not sure whether I should resent her for this tidiness in preparing her own death or take it as a last sign of her wish to go on, to live. I see her standing over the kitchen sink, compulsively washing as if it is the most important thing to do at that moment, because it will postpone what is to come soon—the loneliness of death. When she died, it looked like it was one more unhappy love story. It was somehow easier for people not to think too much of it, not to look for the other, less obvious side of it. It was safer to reduce her suicide to a cliché.

Reprinted from *How We Survived Communism and Even Laughed*, (1992), W.W. Norton & Company.

That winter her lover died. He died during open heart surgery, but a surgeon, his friend, said he wouldn't survive anyway; his heart was too weak. 'Worn out,' this is the expression he used. They were both journalists at the same newspaper. He had a wife working at a public library and a teenage daughter, and wouldn't leave them. 'I admire him for his loyalty to his family,' Tanja used to say, and I could not tell whether she really meant it or whether cynicism was her way of dealing with this fact. The summer before his death, she got pregnant. With two divorces behind her and no children, she wanted his child badly. But it so happened that his wife was pregnant at the same time. He stopped seeing Tanja. Devastated, she didn't have the strength to have a baby all by herself and had an abortion. When he heard that she was no longer pregnant, he returned to her. She took him back. A few months later, his wife gave birth to a little girl, whom he adored.

The winter started badly. The gray smoggy air felt as if one was breathing in dirty cotton. She wrote an article that kicked up a lot of dust. It was against nationalizing all privately owned pinball machines on behalf of the state-owned lottery company. 'If today we take away pinballs, because we believe they are doing the work instead of their owners . . . sometime soon we might nationalize privately owned trucks, because they too are working instead of their owners. Or close private hairdressing shops—for what is hand combing or haircutting compared to the work done by one single electric hooded dryer, not to mention curlers, shampoos, conditioners, hair-spray, etc.' She cleverly and humorously compared the case of pinball machines with the case of a Soviet citizen, Vasili Mihailovich Pilipenko, and the polemics in the Soviet press that very summer about whether he could or couldn't keep the horse that he had found and reared. In Byelorussia, the law treated draft animals as an unlawful source of enrichment without work. To a foreigner, this article would look very innocent. What harm can writing about pinball machines do? But we had brought to perfection the social game called 'reading between the lines,' so of course it was understood that her article was not about pinball machines, but about the privatization of the economy. Yugoslavia has passed through different stages of economic reform. One of the stages was privatization, letting small businesses develop by private investment in order to heal the economy. But times were changing, the economic policy was taking a different turn. Read through ideological glasses, her article was clearly political. In fact, her political mistakes were severe. First of all, she took the 'capitalist' orientation of the state seriously, ie, allowing the development of private small business, and she defended it. Then she insulted and ridiculed the judicial system by showing that the parliament in the Socialist Republic of Croatia—as in every one-party state—is only a formality. Her article, naive as it seems today, speaking 'only' about pinball machines, revealed the functioning and hypocrisy of the communist state. She mocked it, and she had to be punished for that.

After a week of 'consultations' (an expression for talks with the party heads about the most recent instructions on editorial policy in newspapers or, in effect, unofficial censorship) the editorial board of her newspaper published a hundred-and-fifty-word boxed statement entitled 'Explanation from the editors'—as far as I remember, perhaps the last of its kind. It was not unusual, though. This practice was a hangover from the past, when editors were directly responsible to the party man, a censor, for articles. But it was also an efficient instrument for settling accounts with the 'enemies of the people,' in other words whoever wrote against (or rather, not according to) a party policy, so editors didn't give up the practice easily. Later on, it served for eliminating 'disobedient' journalists. In Tanja's case, it looked as if the editors were explaining to the public the severe 'error' that had occurred in the newspaper. But everyone knew that it was their token sackcloth and ashes, a declaration written for the party bosses, not for the public: 'The editorial board . . . has considered the opinions expressed in the article. After careful analysis and discussion, the board concluded that publishing the article represents a serious editorial mistake in the professional and political meaning of the word . . . Our newspapers do and will support legislative and other activities stimulating individual and private enterprise, except for those not in accordance with the activity of the Socialist Alliance of Working People and the ideological guidelines of the League of Communists.' However, this was the message they were trying to convey: 'We, the editorial board, admit our mistake in not having had such complete control of our newspaper, that unfortunately, the unwanted ideas appeared. We will make sure it doesn't happen again.'

I can see Tanja, sitting beside her desk on the seventh floor of the glass and aluminum building on Ljubljanska Avenija, reading the fresh newspaper that still smelled of printer's ink, leaving her hands black with it. She read it and read it, thinking, as had many victims before her: *No, this is not possible; this must be some terrible mistake.* Perhaps that was the moment when she finally saw through all the illusions surrounding her. She saw the glass wall of her reality splintering.

What struck her most? Not only the words, but the meaning of the action. The rejection of her as a journalist, as a colleague, as a person. Her editorial board, people she knew, people she had worked with for more than ten years, other party members—because she *was* a member of the Communist Party, she couldn't possibly have been a commentator on the most important daily newspaper without this pedigree—they all renounced her. As soon as the 'explanation' came out, she felt as if she had ceased to exist: 'You know,' she told me, 'my colleagues don't dare to say hello to me any more. I feel as if I'm invisible. Nobody wants to have coffee with me, but you can't drink your coffee alone.' This was it, the sudden invisibility. From then on, she was put 'on ice'—ignored, invisible, nonexistent, a non-journalist, a non-person. She could write and even get her monthly pay, but nothing got into print. The worst was that nobody could tell her how long this situation would last—because nobody could tell how long the system would last.

I don't know when she started to contemplate suicide. Was it after the abortion, when she was alone and badly hurt? Was it after her lover's death in March? And how much did the situation at her job help her to make up her mind? Perhaps it would be wrong to say that she killed herself just because of the psychological pressure she suffered after she wrote that article. But it seems to me that it would also be wrong to say that she died because of her lost lover.

The earth beneath her was crumbling. She couldn't change her job, there was nowhere to go. She was aware that she would suffer the destiny of a dissident. In her life, she couldn't see anything to hold on to.

This was a time of desperate attempts by the Communist Party to maintain communism—or socialism, as we called it—in Yugoslavia. After Tito's death in 1980 there were predictions that the country would fall apart. This was a time of reform of the educational system, of attacks on artistic and intellectual independence (the *Bijela Knjiga,* index of 'unwanted' writers, artists, intellectuals), of political trials . . . It had become obvious that the system of 'self-management' Yugoslavia was so proud of was a ruse, invented to make you believe that you—not the government or the party—are to blame. It was the most perfect system among the one-party states, set up to internalize guilt, blame, failure, or fear, to teach you how you yourself should censor your thoughts and deeds and, at the same time, to make you feel that you had more freedom than anyone in Eastern Europe.

But Tanja was wrong in one thing: she believed it would go on forever like that—the same newspaper, the same faces, the same cold climate of fear and silent accusations, the immobility of the system—forever the same. What communism instilled in us was precisely this immobility, this absence of a future, the absence of a dream, of the possibility of imagining our lives differently. There was hardly a way to say to yourself: This is just temporary, it will pass, it must. On the contrary, we learned to think: This will go on forever, no matter what we do. We can't change it. It looked as if the omnipotent system had mastered time itself. For our generation, it seemed that communism was eternal, that we were sentenced to it and would die before seeing it collapse. We were not revolutionaries trying to destroy it, to bring it down. We were brought up with the idea that it is impossible to modify the system, to change it eventually from within. Still, if only Tanja had waited. One's life is not a waiting room in a provincial train station, where one sits waiting for a train that might never come. Yet a week before she died, she'd cut her hair short. I don't think women do this if they are thinking of dying. She struggled to survive but in the end she lost.

It was the last day of October when I finally visited her grave. The sun was already low and cold, but the yellow and red leaves of a climbing vine like one in my garden on the outside walls of the cemetery made the landscape somehow pleasant, and I didn't resist the thought of sitting down. I didn't try to escape. As I looked at the place where she was buried, I could feel where the memory of her dwelled in me, deep down, under the diaphragm, where I myself had secluded her, squeezing the last remembrance of her, of that summer day in August 1985, and turning it into a tight little ball of pain.

And, as if I was redeemed by this visit to her grave, that hidden memory, the ball in me started melting, and I could see her face, as she sat across from me in my room—I could hear her voice, as if we were both there, now. The day before she died, she had come to tell me something. A farewell, perhaps. I should have guessed by the way she was talking about suicide. But she had talked about it so many times, she had theorized about it as an act of will, an honorable way out in a desperate situation. The flat tone of her voice in the haze of a sleepy summer afternoon, music from somewhere sneaking through the heavy air, sun, heat, it all misled me. We drank beer. As the afternoon passed, she looked more and more as if she were drowning in the armchair, deeper and deeper, and I remember thinking that it was eating up her skinny, fragile body. Suddenly it seemed to me that her hands were trembling, that as she uttered the word 'death', she felt a chill running down her spine. But I was not sure. I blame myself for that.

I heard about her death early in the morning. The telephone rang, there was that voice saying incomprehensible words, words that I was supposed to understand. 'Do you hear me, do you hear me?' The voice repeated the question, meeting a silence on my end of the line. At first, I didn't respond, didn't say anything. Then a scream came. I heard it coming out of my throat, but at the same time I was another person, standing beside me. Looking from a distance at the person holding a telephone and screaming, totally mute, I was without feelings, numb.

Later that day, I went to Tanja's apartment. She had moved in recently, about a month ago, after her parents exchanged their three-room apartment for a smaller one. She had long waited for this to happen and decorated the apartment very carefully, picking out in antique shops by herself every porcelain cup, silver mirror, or vase. Her books were neatly arranged on the shelf, her typewriter open. On the table there was a fresh bunch of daisies. It was as if by tidying her small apartment, she had tried to confront the chaos in her life. On the surface it looked as if she had found the strength to go on. Inside, she just could not go on any more.

There was only one detail that made me cry: a Bible on her bed. It was upside down. I turned it over and took a quick look at the underlined text. It was about life after death. She was not a religious person; in fact, she was an atheist. But in the last moments of her life, nothing else was left to her, and she turned to the Bible. For months afterwards all I could think of was the bunch of fresh daisies and the Bible. I wonder if the people who wrote that 'explanation' ever think about her? Her death was wrong, it was useless, and only today can I see the full absurdity of it. Perhaps communism is collapsing, but what is the price? How many more victims like Tanja will it claim—not big heroes, political prisoners, or dissidents, but people who just couldn't stand it anymore?

Standing at her grave, I simply wish, for her sake, that there is another life after death. I imagine she is sitting there having a coffee with someone. There must be someone up there, because, as she said, you can't drink your coffee alone.

19

How We Survived Communism

Vesna held up the pantyhose to the light, put one hand in for inspection, spread her fingers, and then slowly, looking for a run, pulled the hand out. One leg was good. On the other she discovered a run. 'This pair is no good,' she said, putting it aside and reaching for a new one from the pile in front of her. We were sitting in her kitchen on a bright Sunday morning. I had come across to borrow a vacuum cleaner, as that very morning mine had decided to give up its long, fruitful life. Sitting across from us, her mother reached for the rejected pair. 'But, Vesna, what a shame, these pantyhose are still good to wear around the house. I'll take them to a repair lady to be darned.' Vesna looked at her angrily, then burst out laughing. 'No, you won't,' she said, and turned to me. 'Every time I try to throw away a pair, she tries to "save" it, to repair it, to fill a cushion with it, tie a garbage bag or filter home-made juice—she can find tens of different uses for old stockings or pantyhose. It's like she still lives in the fifties.' Her mother calmly sipped her coffee, shaking her head as if we couldn't understand her however hard we tried. 'I don't live in the fifties, but you never know what might happen. Don't you remember, just a couple of years ago there were no pantyhose to buy. Then you asked me to darn the old, "saved" ones for you. I sewed them with a nylon thread over a light bulb (thank God I saved the old bulbs—I'll never stop regretting a good old wooden mushroom for repairing stockings that I threw away). Besides, to throw it out just because of one run . . . '

I said I didn't know there were any repair ladies left—after stockings had become mass produced, though not cheap. Not in these parts. She said there was one, just one left. She closed her shop, and she works at home now. I could see her at her table with a lamp and a funny little stitching machine. Perhaps it is the same lady on Maksimirska ulica I used to visit once a month with a bag full of stockings to repair. 'Will you wait?' she would ask me, knowing that I had already prepared one pair, with 'just one run,' to take back home. It must have been more than twenty years ago; stockings were rare and expensive items then, and only after many repairs would one throw them away. 'Look now,' Vesna's mother continued, 'what do you know, a civil war might break out any minute: Serbs would fight with Croats, Czechs would fight with Slovaks, Hungarians would fight with Jews. How can you be sure of anything?' 'But, Mother, if this happens, then it will such big trouble that nobody will think about a shortage of pantyhose,' protested Vesna. 'You'd be surprised, my dear, to know that people have to live and survive during wars, too. Besides, how do you think we survived communism?'

Yes—how did we? Certainly not by throwing away useful things. Generally speaking, in any communist country there are not many things to throw away. One could even say that a communist household is almost the perfect example of an ecological unit, except that its ecology has a completely different origin: it doesn't stem from a concern for nature, but from a specific kind of fear for the future. Such an ecological unit—like any other—has two basic principles, collecting and recycling. You recycle, recycle, and recycle, redefining an object (pantyhose, for example) by turning it into something else, giving it one function after another, and you throw it away only when you have made absolutely sure (by experiment, of course) that it can't be used anymore. But in order to recycle properly, ie usefully, you first have to know what to collect. Collecting principles, so to speak, depend greatly on different kinds of experiences in different communist countries, or—better still—on different *degrees* of poverty. But they basically can be divided into several categories: *general objects* (old cloth, shoes, household appliances and furniture, kitchen pots, baskets, brooms, newspapers); *objects that normal people in normal countries usually throw away* (otherwise known as packaging—bottles, jars, cups, cans, stoppers and corks, rubber bands, plastic bags, gift wrappings, cardboard boxes); *foreign objects* (anything from a foreign country, from a pencil or notebook to a dress, from chewing gum to a candy wrapper); and *objects that might disappear* (a very broad and varying category, from flour, coffee, and eggs to detergent, soap, pantyhose, screws, nails, rope, wire, perfumes, notepaper, or books—you simply never know, you never can predict what will be next, which, after all, is the primary reason for collecting). And while I am perfectly aware that poor people in not so poor (Western) countries collect and recycle according maybe to the same principles, people in Eastern Europe were, in the first place, almost all poor enough to have to do it. The other main reason is that they live in a state of constant shortages, never sure what they will find in the shops next day.

I washed the floor in my house with an old pair of man's pants, never realizing how odd a broom dressed in pants looks, until my friend, a foreigner of course, pointed it out to me, laughingly. But, just like Vesna's mother, I thought it was a pity to throw them away, when they could be renamed and reused as a floor mop. Couldn't you buy a rag mop, my friend asked. Yes, but why? My grandma did the same, my mother, too—besides, until the late sixties there were no floor mops to be bought. Long experience proved that genuine cotton underwear has a fantastic ability to absorb dust and wash floors, windows, tiles, and so on, that is why my mother still uses it.

Then I realized that this friend of mind didn't know anything about recycled clothes: reknitted pullovers, old coats turned inside out and made into children's coats, or a new sheet made of two old ones. She wasn't aware that in the 'ecology of poverty,' nothing is wasted—especially clothes. They're not usually given away ('Am I worse than you?'), except to the Gypsies. A person might get offended, since new clothes are proof that you are better off than the others. We don't only use them—that's the second stage—we wear them first as something called 'around-the-house' clothes. An unaccustomed person, coming into the average household, could see the strange yet usual sight of an otherwise respectable, even important person—a university professor, let's say—dressed in striped pyjama trousers, an old pullover eaten by moths or mended with wool of another color, slippers, and a worn-out bathrobe. And because this kind of 'collecting' is a national sport, nobody minds being seen in these absurd rags.

The living conditions kill all privacy—or spread it out to the whole community, if you wish. Apartments are too small, too crowded, or too divided, and either way you are bound to meet other people on your way to the kitchen or the bathroom. Since there is no such thing as a self-sufficient communist household, you depend fatally on your neighbor for all kinds of favors, from borrowing coffee or sugar to washing, cleaning, or cursing politics—or getting your child enrolled in a better school. He or she will inevitably see you in your 'around-the-house' clothes. Perhaps there is a good side to that; people don't have any illusions about each other.

While there is some obvious logic in collecting and recycling old clothes, it's hard to find any logic at all in collecting objects that are meant to be thrown away. That is—if you don't live anywhere near a communist country. For example, why would somebody keep an old shoe box? Once you bring your new shoes home, you simply throw it away. But a nice, strong shoe box can have several purposes. The two most usual were—and are—storing photos and storing old bills. People keep them in the bottom of a closet or at the top of a cupboard in a bedroom. When you ask to see the family pictures, they don't pull out a photo album, but a dusty shoe box. They untie it carefully in front of you, as if that single shoe box holds something very precious, a piece of their lives, something that shouldn't be looked at every day. The reason for the shoe box is a simple one: for a long time there were no albums to buy; then they were very expensive. Besides, it seems that people here don't really have so many photos, and they don't look so often at them or show them around. Shoe boxes are fine for storing bills, too, particularly old ones—very old, in fact, ten, twenty, or more years. Utility bills, rent or credit bills . . . when you are dealing with such a vast and inefficient bureaucracy, you have to be prepared to go back years and years to prove your innocence. A shoe box is almost like a computer, full of neatly stored data necessary to survive in a system that is designed to destroy the individual.

But in every household the absolute priority belongs to collecting glass jars, and I think it is because you can store other objects in them that you collect. Again, what could be more normal than to throw the jar away after eating your pickles or jam—ideally, into a container for recycling. But no—because, living here, you'll soon find that there is another way of recycling it. There's always something that needs to be stored in it. A handful of rusted nails, or number 1 screws (you know that when you look for them in stores, you can never find them), or perhaps buttons or rubber bands (but you have to take those off packages first), or plastic stoppers or corks, old razor blades (you never know when these will disappear from the market), pieces of soap or string (just in case), breadcrumbs, coffee beans, fresh garlic—or maybe even home-made pickles. In bigger jars you can store some food and then keep it on a balcony during winter, like in the refrigerator—a very handy invention. What's more, if a jar gets broken its cap can be turned into an ashtray. With virtually everybody smoking, who has enough ashtrays, anyway?

Most people collect cans, especially big ones—but small ones will do, too. 'It's a shame to throw this away,' my neighbor, an old lady, would say, and she planted red geraniums in dozens of cans she would put on her windows, in halls, on steps, in the bathroom. I think women actually prefer 'gold' to 'silver' cans; they do look nicer on the window sills and balconies, in small yards behind the house, even in the house—wherever you expect to see flowers. You take a can, a nail, and a hammer, turn the can upside down, make a hole with the nail and hammer, and there you are—a new vase, practically out of nothing. Now, that's what I call ecology. A flower can grow in an old washbowl or a pot, most probably sky blue or bright red with white dots. Plants stunted from lack of sunshine in cities look a little bit more lively like that. That is, if such a luxurious use of the old pots is permitted, because they usually end up under the sink, filled with potatoes and onions. Perhaps they see the light once or twice in ten years, when a kitchen or a room is painted (in these parts people still do it themselves) and they serve as a paint pot.

'Even today,' says Vesna, 'I can't get rid of the habit of washing plastic yogurt cups. In the mid-sixties when they started producing them (before that, yogurt was sold in small glass jars that you had to return), I was a school kid and we used them for watercolors. At home, we girls played kitchen with them, or drank out of them, or kept salt and sugar in them. Today, even if I don't use them, I just collect them, God knows why. I guess nowadays collecting doesn't reflect the state of facts as much as the state of our minds. We are hungry for things and afraid of the future—it's deeper than I thought.' Her words made me remember another kind of collecting, another kind of hunger—my hunger as a child for a nice cellophane candy or chocolate wrapper that I could get only from a friend at school whose father lived abroad. I would press them between the pages of a book, and then look at them, at the foreign words like *framboise* or *sucre* or *chocolatier,* still smelling of their extravagant, delicious contents I had never tasted. While 'abroad' (at that time 'abroad' was a category that included everything beyond the border, we made no distinctions) they wrapped each candy in a beautiful paper, the only kind of candy we had was called *505 sa crtom,* and it came in a red metal box, only as a present for New Year's (not Christmas, mind, Christmas didn't exist officially). No wonder, because at that time, in the early fifties, there was only one candy factory, named after the war hero Josip Kras.

Of course we were fascinated with these little wrapping papers—our first contact with something foreign—sensing that there was something still more unknown and desirable out there. Later, we collected foreign tags and stickers of any kind—from candy, beer, cheese, clothing,—then foreign cigarette boxes, beer cans, or Coke bottles that tourists would throw in the sea while waiting for the ferry. The only important thing was that they were foreign. Why? Because everything foreign, from wrapping paper to a beer can, was more beautifully designed and, surrounded by poverty, we were attracted to this other, obviously different world. Much, much later—perhaps too late—we learned that it was all because of consumerism, just to attract buyers. But I don't think it convinced us, because even today we are passionate collectors of foreign objects, as if we are still trying to possess this mythical'abroad' or the imitation of it.

It's a perfectly familiar feeling: I can see my five-year-old self going into the bathroom, reaching for my mother's lipstick, taking my chewing gum out of my mouth, putting some lipstick on it, and mixing the chewing gum until it became pink; then going out and pretending to the girls it was the original 'Bazooka Joe' (even if I tasted it only once in my life, and only one piece), so they would envy me, praying that some of them don't ask me to show the wrapper with the little comic strip (the first comic I had ever seen) inside, with figures talking in clouds in some unknown language from the moon.

My grandma died in the seventies, but before that she spent a couple of months in the hospital. My mother took this opportunity to clean up, at least a little, her cupboards and drawers of 'trash,' as she called it, because my grandma was famous for collecting everything in sight. The contents of the massive old oak cupboard were rather normal. Only old coats (I particularly loved a green one, sewed sometime between the two wars, with a silk label: *Modewerkstatte Franziska Bundschuh*), a balding astrakhan fur stinking of mothballs, several pairs of almost new hand-made shoes, gloves, a pile of sheets, my mother's baby dress from her baptism. Another cupboard was, in fact, a small warehouse or a boat navigating unknown waters. It was full of neatly stored detergent that had turned almost to stone, bottles of rancid oil, several kilos of sugar, flour, and coffee (apparently the household staples), some packages of tea, biscuits, pasta, cans of tomato paste (she loved Italian cooking), beans, and even a kilo or two of salt, in spite of the fact that nobody remembers a shortage of *that*. The food was stored on the lower shelves. On the upper ones was everything else, such as a roll of white tulle, quite a bit of wool in different colors, brand new and repaired pantyhose and stockings (I believe even from before World War II), black and brown hair dye, shampoos, soaps, hand creams, toilet paper, outdated antibiotics, aspirins, insulin (even though nobody in the family is diabetic) and some other pills without labels, absorbent cotton, and about five or six packages of sanitary napkins. Rather than a warehouse, her cupboard looked like a museum of communist shortages.

We were not surprised—not until we opened one of her drawers. That was too much, even for us, collectors ourselves. The drawer was full of plastic bags. Washed, dried, and sorted, then tied into bundles with rubber bands, there were bags in all sizes and colors. Large ones, from foreign department stores or famous shops that we had brought back from our trips to Austria, Germany, Italy, Spain, or Sweden maybe twenty years ago; then smaller ones from shops in Zagreb; then the usual ones, without labels—down to the smallest ones. Like an archeologist, her collection documented the development and use of plastic bags ever since they came into use in this country, with the rise in the standard of living (when they were given out for free) through the economic crisis (when they disappeared) to the present time, when one has to pay extra for them. Friends returning from the USSR, told us that plastic bags are much in demand, especially with labels, because women there carry them as handbags. We didn't, but we washed them, finding new ways to use them, until they ended up in the garbage—as garbage bags, of course.

I think these drawers of my grandma's show not only how we survived communism, but why communism failed: it failed because of distrust, because of a fear for the future. True, people did collect out of poverty, but a very specific kind of poverty, a poverty in which the whole country is deprived, everybody is poor, a poverty when to be poor and deprived is a state of life that hardly ever changes, because it cannot be changed by words, declarations, promises, or threats from politicians. And, what is even more important, collecting was a necessity, because deep down nobody believed in a system that was continuously unable to provide for its citizens' basic needs for forty years or more. While leaders were accumulating words about a bright future, people were accumulating flour and sugar, jars, cups, pantyhose, old bread, corks, rope, nails, plastic bags. If the politicians had only had a chance to peek into our closets, cellars, cupboards, and drawers—looking not for forbidden books or anti-state material—they would have seen the future that was in store for their wonderful plans for communism itself. But they didn't look.

Colonial Nigeria

From THE INTERESTING NARRATIVE OF THE LIFE OF OLAUDAH EQUIANO

▨ Born Olaudah Equiano and given the slave name Gustavus Vassa, Equiano published his Interesting Narrative *in 1789. The text went into nine editions in the next five years and was translated into various European languages.*

Born in the kingdom of Benin in what is now southeastern Nigeria, on the border between the Ibo [Eboe or Igbo] and Edo, Equiano was captured and sold to British slavers at age ten, around 1755. He was in the service of a British naval officer during the Seven Years War; while enslaved he also learned to read and, by his own request, became a Christian. When Equiano challenged his master's right, under British law, to own him, his vengeful master sold him to a captain bound for the New World. Equiano endured slavery in the West Indies and Virginia, and finally managed to save enough money to buy his freedom in 1766. After attaining his freedom, Equiano became a traveller and adventurer: a sailor, a merchant, a plantation overseer on the Mosquito Coast in Central America, a visitor to Europe and the Near East, and even a polar explorer. Equiano was also an important witness, public speaker, and leader in the British abolition movement which, led by Granville Sharp, took off around 1765. He became a Methodist minister and was involved in the missionary movement for the repatriation of British freed slaves in Sierra Leone. In 1792 Equiano married an Englishwoman and was able to leave a considerable estate to his two daughters on his death in 1797.

Equiano's narrative is more than a tale of high adventure—it is at once a "conversion narrative" in the tradition of St. Augustine, an ethnographic source on precolonial Nigeria, and a powerful argument for the abolition of slavery and the recognition of the equality of all human beings.

JAYA MEHTA

Chapter i

I believe it is difficult for those who publish their own memoirs to escape the imputation of vanity; nor is this the only disadvantage under which they labour; it is also their misfortune, that whatever is uncommon is rarely, if ever, believed; and what is obvious we are apt to turn from with disgust, and to charge the writer with impertinence. People generally think those memoirs only worthy to be read or remembered which abound in great or striking events; those, in short, which in a high degree excite either admiration or pity: all others they consign to contempt and oblivion. It is, therefore, I confess, not a little hazardous, in a private and obscure individual, and a stranger too, thus to solicit the indulgent attention of the public; especially when I own I offer here the history of neither a saint, a hero, nor a tyrant. I believe there are a few events in my life which have not happened to many; it is true the incidents of it are numerous; and, did I consider myself an European, I might say my sufferings were great; but, when I compare my lot with that of most of my countrymen[1], I regard myself as a *particular favourite of Heaven,* and acknowledge the mercies of Providence in every occurrence of my life. If, then, the following narrative does not appear sufficiently interesting to engage general attention, let my motive be some excuse for its publication. I am not so foolishly vain as to expect from it either immortality or literary reputation. If it affords any satisfaction to my numerous friends, at whose request it has been written, or in the smallest degree promotes the interest of humanity, the ends for which it was undertaken will be fully attained, and every wish of my heart gratified. Let it therefore be remembered that, in wishing to avoid censure, I do not aspire to praise.

That part of Africa, known by the name of Guinea, to which the trade for slaves is carried on, extends along the coast above 3400 miles, from Senegal to Angola, and includes a variety of kingdoms. Of these the most considerable is the kingdom of Benin, both as to

---

[1] Countrymen: used here to mean those born in the same geographical area, in the widest sense, Africa.

extent and wealth, the richness and cultivation of the soil, the power of its king, and the number and warlike disposition of the inhabitants. It is situated nearly under the line[2] and extends along the coast about 170 miles, but runs back into the interior part of Africa to a distance hitherto I believe unexplored by any traveller; and seems only terminated at length by the empire of Abyssinia[3] near 1500 miles from its beginning. This kingdom is divided into many provinces or districts: in one of the most remote and fertile of which [called Eboe], I was born, in the year 1745, in a charming fruitful vale, named Essaka.[4] The distance of this province from the capital of Benin and the sea coast must be very considerable; for I had never heard of white men or Europeans, nor of the sea; and our subjection to the king of Benin was little more than nominal; for every transaction of the government, as far as my slender observation extended, was conducted by the chiefs or elders of the place. The manners and government of a people who have little commerce with other countries are generally very simple; and the history of what passes in one family or village may serve as a specimen of the whole nation.

My father was one of those elders or chiefs I have spoken of, and was styled Embrenché; a term, as I remember, importing the highest distinction, and signifying in our language a mark of grandeur. This mark is conferred on the person entitled to it, by cutting the skin across at the top of the forehead, and drawing it down to the eye-brows; and, while it is in this situation, applying a warm hand, and rubbing it until it shrinks up into a thick *weal* across the lower part of the forehead. Most of the judges and senators were thus marked; my father had long borne it: I had seen it conferred on one of my brothers, and I was also *destined* to receive it by my parents. Those Embrenché, or chief men, decided disputes and punished crimes; for which purpose they always assembled together.

---

[2] That is, nearly on the equator.
[3] Abyssinia: the ancient name for modern Ethiopia.
[4] Equiano's homeland was that of the present Ibo people of modern Nigeria; scholars' attempts to locate Essaka have been so far unsuccessful.

The proceedings were generally short; and in most cases the law of retaliation prevailed.

I remember a man was brought before my father, and the other judges, for kidnapping a boy; and, although he was the son of a chief or senator, he was condemned to make recompense by a man or woman slave. Adultery, however, was sometimes punished with slavery or death; a punishment which I believe is inflicted on it throughout most of the nations of Africa:[5] so sacred among them is the honour of the marriage bed, and so jealous are they of the fidelity of their wives. Of this I recollect an instance. A woman was convicted before the judges of adultery, and delivered over, as the custom was, to her husband to be punished. Accordingly he determined to put her to death: but it being found, just before her execution, that she had an infant at her breast; and no woman being prevailed on to perform the part of a nurse, she was spared on account of the child. The men, however, do not preserve the same constancy to their wives, which they expect from them; for they indulge in a plurality, though seldom in more than two.

Their mode of marriage is thus—both parties are usually betrothed when young by their parents (though I have known the males to betroth themselves). On this occasion a feast is prepared, and the bride and bridegroom stand up in the midst of all their friends, who are assembled for the purpose, while he declares she is thenceforth to be looked upon as his wife, and that no other person is to pay any addresses to her. This is also immediately proclaimed in the vicinity, on which the bride retires from the assembly. Some time after, she is brought home to her husband, and then another feast is made, to which the relations of both parties are invited: her parents then deliver her to the bridegroom, accompanied with a number of blessings, and at the same time they tie round her waist

---

[5] Equiano's emphasis on the sanctity of marriage and the consequent severe punishment for adultery contrasts sharply with the common pro-slavery assertions of African sexual promiscuity, which, the apologists for slavery claimed, accounted for the low birthrate among slaves that required the constant resupply provided by the slave trade.

a cotton string of the thickness of a goose-quill, which none but married women are permitted to wear: she is now considered as completely his wife; and at this time the dowry is given to the new married pair, which generally consists of portions of land, slaves, and cattle, household goods, and implements of husbandry. These are offered by the friends of both parties; besides which the parents of the bridegroom present gifts to those of the bride, whose property she is looked upon before marriage; but after it she is esteemed the sole property of her husband. The ceremony being now ended, the festival begins, which is celebrated with bonfires, and loud acclamations of joy, accompanied with music and dancing.

We are almost a nation of dancers, musicians, and poets. Thus every great event, such as a triumphant return from battle, or other cause of public rejoicing, is celebrated in public dances, which are accompanied with songs and music suited to the occasion. The assembly is separated into four divisions, which dance either apart or in succession, and each with a character peculiar to itself. The first division contains the married men, who in their dances frequently exhibit feats of arms, and the representation of a battle. To these succeed the married women, who dance in the second division. The young men occupy the third; and the maidens the fourth. Each represents some interesting scene of real life, such as a great achievement, domestic employment, a pathetic story, or some rural sport; and as the subject is generally founded on some recent event, it is therefore ever new. This gives our dances a spirit and variety which I have scarcely seen elsewhere. We have many musical instruments, particularly drums of different kinds, a piece of music which resembles a guitar, and another much like a stickado. These last are chiefly used by betrothed virgins, who play on them on all grand festivals.

As our manners are simple, our luxuries are few. The dress of both sexes is nearly the same. It generally consists of a long piece of calico, or muslin, wrapped loosely round the body, somewhat in the form of a Highland plaid. This is usually dyed blue, which is our favourite colour. It is extracted from a berry, and is brighter and richer than any I have seen in Europe. Besides this, our women of distinction wear golden ornaments, which they dispose with some profusion on their arms and legs. When our women are not employed with the men in tillage, their usual occupation is spinning and weaving cotton, which they afterwards dye, and make into garments. They also manufacture earthen vessels, of which we have many kinds. Among the rest, tobacco pipes, made after the same fashion, and used in the same manner, as those in Turkey.

Our manner of living is entirely plain; for as yet the natives are unacquainted with those refinements in cookery which debauch the taste: bullocks, goats, and poultry supply the greatest part of their food. These constitute likewise the principal wealth of the country, and the chief articles of its commerce. The flesh is usually stewed in a pan. To make it savory, we sometimes use also pepper, and other spices, and we have salt made of wood ashes. Our vegetables are mostly plantains,[6] eadas, yams, beans, and Indian corn. The head of the family usually eats alone; his wives and slaves have also their separate tables. Before we taste food, we always wash our hands: indeed our cleanliness on all occasions is extreme; but on this it is an indispensable ceremony. After washing, libation is made, by pouring out a small portion of the drink on the floor, and tossing a small quantity of the food in a certain place, for the spirits of departed relations, which the natives suppose to preside over their conduct, and guard them from evil. They are totally unacquainted with strong or spiritous liquours; and their principal beverage is palm wine. This is got from a tree of that name, by tapping it at the top, and fastening a large gourd to it; and sometimes one tree will yield three or four gallons in a night. When just drawn it is of a most delicious sweetness; but in a few days it acquires a tartish and more spirituous flavour: though I never saw any one intoxicated by it. The same tree also produces nuts and oil. Our principal luxury is in perfumes; one sort of these is an odoriferous wood of delicious fragrance: the other a kind of earth; a small portion of which thrown into the fire diffuses a most powerful odour. We beat this wood into powder, and mix it with palm-oil; with which both men and women perfume themselves.

---

[6] Plantain: a type of banana that must be cooked before being eaten.

In our buildings we study convenience rather than ornament. Each master of a family has a large square piece of ground, surrounded with a moat or fence, or enclosed with a wall made of red earth tempered, which, when dry, is as hard as brick. Within this are his houses to accommodate his family and slaves; which, if numerous, frequently present the appearance of a village. In the middle stands the principal building, appropriated to the sole use of the master, and consisting of two apartments; in one of which he sits in the day with his family, the other is left apart for the reception of his friends. He has besides these a distinct apartment in which he sleeps, together with his male children. On each side are the apartments of his wives, who have also their separate day and night houses. The habitations of the slaves and their families are distributed throughout the rest of the enclosure. These houses never exceed one story in height; they are always built of wood, or stakes driven into the ground, crossed with wattles, and neatly plastered within, and without. The roof is thatched with reeds. Our dayhouses are left open at the sides; but those in which we sleep are always covered, and plastered in the inside, with a composition mixed with cow-dung, to keep off the different insects which annoy us during the night. The walls and floors also of these are generally covered with mats. Our beds consist of a platform, raised three or four feet from the ground, on which are laid skins, and different parts of a spungy tree called plaintain. Our covering is calico or muslin, the same as our dress. The usual seats are a few logs of wood; but we have benches, which are generally perfumed, to accommodate strangers; these compose the greater part of our household furniture. Houses so constructed and furnished require but little skill to erect them. Every man is a sufficient architect for the purpose. The whole neighbourhood afford their unanimous assistance in building them, and, in return, receive and expect no other recompense than a feast.

As we live in a country where nature is prodigal of her favours, our wants are few and easily supplied; of course we have few manufactures. They consist for the most part of calicoes, earthen ware, ornaments, and instruments of war and husbandry. But these make no part of our commerce, the principal articles of which, as I have

---

observed, are provisions. In such a state money is of little use; however we have some small pieces of coin, if I may call them such. They are made something like an anchor; but I do not remember either their value or denomination. We have also markets, at which I have been frequently with my mother. These are sometimes visited by stout, mahogany-coloured men from the south west of us: we call them *Oye-Eboe,* which term signifies red men living at a distance. They generally bring us firearms, gun-powder, hats, beads, and dried fish. The last we esteemed a great rarity, as our waters were only brooks and springs. These articles they barter with us for odoriferous woods and earth, and our salt of wood-ashes. They always carry slaves through our land; but the strictest account is exacted of their manner of procuring them before they are suffered to pass. Sometimes indeed we sold slaves to them, but they were only prisoners of war, or such among us as had been convicted of kidnapping, or adultery, and some other crimes which we esteemed heinous. This practice of kidnapping induces me to think, that, notwithstanding all our strictness, their principal business among us was to trepan our people. I remember too they carried great sacks along with them, which, not long after, I had an opportunity of fatally seeing applied to that infamous purpose.

Our land is uncommonly rich and fruitful, and produces all kinds of vegetables in great abundance. We have plenty of Indian corn, and vast quantities of cotton and tobacco. Our pineapples grow without culture; they are about the size of the largest sugar-loaf, and finely flavoured. We have also spices of different kinds, particularly pepper; and a variety of delicious fruits which I have never seen in Europe; together with gums of various kinds, and honey in abundance. All our industry is exerted to improve those blessings of nature. Agriculture is our chief employment; and everyone, even the children and women, are engaged in it. Thus we are all habituated to labour from our earliest years. Everyone contributes something to the common stock; and as we are unacquainted with idleness, we have no beggars. The benefits of such a mode of living are obvious. The West-India planters prefer the slaves of Benin or Eboe to those of any other part of Guinea, for their hardiness, intelligence, integrity, and zeal. Those benefits are felt by us in the general healthiness of the people, and in their vigour and activity; I might have added too in their comeliness. Deformity is indeed unknown amongst us, I mean that of shape. Numbers of the natives of Eboe now in London might be brought in support of this assertion; for, in regard to complexion, ideas of beauty are wholly relative. I remember while in Africa to have seen three negro children, who were tawny, and another quite white, who were universally regarded by myself and the natives in general, as far as related to their complexions, as deformed. Our women too were, in my eyes at least, uncommonly graceful, alert, and modest to a degree of bashfulness; nor do I remember to have ever heard of an instance of incontinence amongst them before marriage. They are also remarkably cheerful. Indeed cheerfulness and affability are two of the leading characteristics of our nation.

Our tillage is exercised in a large plain or common, some hours walk from our dwellings, and all the neighbours resort thither in a body. They use no beasts of husbandry; and their only instruments are hoes, axes, shovels, and beaks, or pointed iron to dig with. Sometimes we are visited by locusts, which come in large clouds, so as to darken the air, and destroy our harvest. This however happens rarely, but when it does, a famine is produced by it. I remember an instance or two wherein this happened. This common is oftimes the theatre of war; and therefore when our people go out to till their land, they not only go in a body, but generally take their arms with them, for fear of a surprise; and when they apprehend an invasion they guard the avenues to their dwellings, by driving sticks into the ground, which are so sharp at one end as to pierce the foot, and are generally dipt in poison. From what I can recollect of these battles, they appear to have been irruptions of one little state or district on the other, to obtain prisoners or booty. Perhaps they were incited to this by those traders who brought the European goods I mentioned amongst us. Such mode of obtaining slaves in Africa is common; and I believe more are procured this way, and by kidnapping, than any other. When a trader wants slaves, he applies to a chief for them, and tempts him with his wares. It is not extraordinary, if on this occasion he yields to the temptation with as little firmness, and accepts the price of his fellow creature's liberty with as little reluctance, as the enlightened merchant. Accordingly, he falls on his neighbours, and a desperate battle ensues. If he prevails, and takes prisoners, he gratifies his avarice by selling them; but, if his party be vanquished, and he falls into the hands of the enemy, he is put to death: for, as he has been known to foment their quarrels, it is thought dangerous to let him survive, and no ransom can save him, though all other prisoners may be redeemed. We have firearms, bows and arrows, broad two-edged swords and javelins; we have shields also, which cover a man from head to foot. All are taught the use of the weapons. Even our women are warriors, and march boldly out to fight along with the men. Our whole district is a kind of militia: on a certain signal given, such as the firing of a gun at night, they all rise in arms and rush upon their enemy. It is perhaps something remarkable, that when our people march to the field, a red flag or banner is borne before them.

I was once a witness to a battle in our common. We had been all at work in it one day as usual when our people were suddenly attacked. I climbed a tree at some distance, from which I beheld the fight. There were many women as well as men on both sides; among others my mother was there and armed with a broad sword. After fighting for a considerable time with great fury, and many had been killed, our people obtained the victory, and took their enemy's Chief prisoner. He was carried off in great triumph, and, though he offered a large ransom for his life, he was put to death. A virgin of note among our enemies had been slain in the battle, and her arm was exposed in our market-place, where our trophies were always exhibited. The spoils were divided according to the merit of the warriors. Those prisoners which were not sold or redeemed we kept as slaves: but how different was their condition from that of the slaves in the West-Indies! With us they do no more work than other members of the community, even their master. Their food, clothing, and lodging were nearly the same as theirs, except that they were not permitted to eat with those who were free born and there was scarce any other difference between them, than a superior degree of importance which the head of a family possesses in our state, and that authority which, as such, he exercises over every part of his household. Some of these slaves have even slaves under them, as their own property, and for their own use.

As to religion, the natives believe that there is one Creator of all things, and that he lives in the sun, and is girded round with a belt, that he may never eat or drink; but, according to some, he smokes a pipe, which is our own favourite luxury. They believe he governs events, especially our deaths or captivity; but, as for the doctrine of eternity, I do not remember to have ever heard of it: some however believe in the transmigration of souls in a certain degree. Those spirits, which are not transmigrated, such as our dear friends or relations, they believe always attend them, and guard them from the bad spirits of their foes. For this reason, they always, before eating, as I have observed, put some small portion of the meat, and pour some of their drink, on the ground for them; and they often make oblations of the blood of beasts or fowls at their graves. I was very fond of my mother, and almost constantly with her. When she went to make these oblations at her mother's tomb, which was a kind of small solitary thatched house, I sometimes attended her. There she made her libations, and spent most of the night in cries and lamentations. I have been often extremely terrified on these occasions. The loneliness of the place, the darkness of the night, and the ceremony of libation, naturally awful and gloomy, were heightened by my mother's lamentations; and these, concurring with the doleful cries of birds, by which these places were frequented, gave an inexpressible terror to the scene.

We compute the year from the day on which the sun crosses the line, and, on its setting that evening, there is a general shout throughout the land; at least I can speak from my own knowledge throughout our vicinity. The people at the same time make a great noise with rattles, not unlike the basket rattles used by children here, though much larger, and hold up their hands to heaven for a blessing. It is then the greatest offerings are made; and those children whom our wise men foretell will be fortunate are then presented to different people. I remember many used to come to see me, and

I was carried about to others for that purpose. They have many offerings, particularly at full moons; generally two at harvest, before the fruits are taken out of the ground: and, when any young animals are killed, sometimes they offer up part of them as a sacrifice. These offerings, when made by one of the heads of a family, serve for the whole. I remember we often had them at my father's and my uncle's, and their families have been present. Some of our offerings are eaten with bitter herbs. We had a saying among us to any one of a cross temper, "That if they were to be eaten, they should be eaten with bitter herbs."

We practised circumcision like the Jews, and made offerings and feasts on that occasion in the same manner as they did. Like them also, our children were named from some event, some circumstance, or fancied foreboding at the time of their birth. I was named *Olaudah,* which, in our language, signifies vicissitude, or fortunate also; one favoured, and having a loud voice and well spoken. I remember we never polluted the name of the object of our adoration; on the contrary, it was always mentioned with the greatest reverence; and we were totally unacquainted with swearing, and all those terms of abuse and reproach which find the way so readily and copiously into the languages of more civilized people. The only expressions of that kind I remember were "May you rot, or may you swell, or may a beast take you."

I have before remarked, that the natives of this part of Africa are extremely cleanly. This necessary habit of decency was with us a part of religion, and therefore we had many purifications and washings; indeed almost as many, and used on the same occasions, if my recollection does not fail me, as the Jews. Those that touched the dead at any time were obliged to wash and purify themselves before they could enter a dwelling-house. Every woman too, at certain times, was forbidden to come into a dwelling-house, or touch any person, or any thing we ate. I was so fond of my mother I could not keep from her, or avoid touching her at some of those periods, in consequence of which I was obliged to be kept out with her, in a little house made for that purpose, till offering was made, and then we were purified.

Though we had no places of public worship, we had priests and magicians, or wise men. I do not remember whether they had different offices, or whether they were united in the same persons but they were held in great reverence by the people. They calculated our time, and foretold events, as their name imported, for we called them Ah-affoe-way-cah, which signifies calculators, or yearly men, our year being called Ah-affoe. They wore their beards; and, when they died, they were succeeded by their sons. Most of their implements and things of value were interred along with them. Pipes and tobacco were also put into the grave with the corpse, which was always perfumed and ornamented; and animals were offered in sacrifice to them. None accompanied their funerals but those of the same profession or tribe. These buried them after sunset, and always returned from the grave by a different way from that which they went.

These magicians were also our doctors or physicians. They practised bleeding by cupping, and were very successful in healing wounds and expelling poisons. They had likewise some extraordinary method of discovering jealousy, theft, and poisoning; the success of which no doubt they derived from their unbounded influence over the credulity and superstition of the people. I do not remember what those methods were, except that as to poisoning. I recollect an instance or two, which I hope it will not be deemed impertinent here to insert, as it may serve as a kind of specimen of the rest, and is still used by the negroes in the West Indies. A young woman had been poisoned, but it was not known by whom; the doctors ordered the corpse to be taken up by some persons, and carried to the grave. As soon as the bearers had raised it on their shoulders, they seemed seized with some sudden impulse, and ran to and fro', unable to stop themselves. At last, after having passed through a number of thorns and prickly bushes unhurt, the corpse fell from them close to a house, and defaced it in the fall: and the owner being taken up, he immediately confessed the poisoning.

The natives are extremely cautious about poison. When they buy any eatable the seller kisses it all round before the buyer, to shew him it is not poisoned; and the same is done when any meat or drink

is presented, particularly to a stranger. We have serpents of different kinds, some of which are esteemed ominous when they appear
in our houses, and these we never molest. I remember two of those
ominous snakes, each of which was as thick as the calf of a man's leg,
and in colour resembling a dolphin in the water, crept at different
times into my mother's night-house, where I always lay with her,
and coiled themselves into folds, and each time they crowed like a
cock. I was desired by some of our wise men to touch these, that I
might be interested in the good omens, which I did, for they were
quite harmless, and would tamely suffer themselves to be handled;
and then they were put into a large, open earthen pan, and set on
one side of the highway. Some of our snakes, however, were poisonous: one of them crossed the road one day when I was standing
on it, and passed between my feet, without offering to touch me,
to the great surprise of many who saw it; and these incidents were
accounted by the wise men, and likewise by my mother and the
rest of the people, as remarkable omens in my favour . . . .

These instances, and a great many more which might be
adduced, while they shew how the complexions of the same persons
vary in different climates, it is hoped may tend also to remove the
prejudice that some conceive against the natives of Africa on account
of their colour. Surely the minds of the Spaniards did not change
with their complexions! Are there not causes enough to which the
apparent inferiority of an African may be ascribed, without limiting the goodness of God, and supposing he forbore to stamp understanding on certainly his own image, because "carved in ebony?"
Might it not naturally be ascribed to their situation? When they come
among Europeans, they are ignorant of their language, religion, manners, and customs. Are any pains taken to teach them these? Are they
treated as men? Does not slavery itself depress the mind, and extin-
guish all its fire, and every noble sentiment? But, above all, what
advantages do not a refined people possess over those who are rude
and uncultivated? Let the polished and haughty European recollect
that *his* ancestors were once, like the Africans, uncivilized, and even
barbarous. Did Nature make *them* inferior to their sons? and should
they too have been made slaves? Every rational mind answers, No.

Let such reflections as these melt the pride of their superiority into sympathy for the wants and miseries of their sable brethren, and compel them to acknowledge, that understanding is not confined to feature or colour. If, when they look round the world, they feel exultation, let it be tempered with benevolence to others, and gratitude to God, "who hath made of one blood all nations of men for to dwell on all the face of the earth; and whose wisdom is not our wisdom, neither are our ways his ways."

CHAPTER 2

I hope the reader will not think I have trespassed on his patience in introducing myself to him with some account of the manners and customs of my country. They had been implanted in me with great care, and made an impression on my mind, which time could not erase, and which all the adversity and variety of fortune I have since experienced served only to rivet and record: for, whether the love of one's country be real or imaginary, or a lesson of reason, or an instinct of nature, I still look back with pleasure on the first scenes of my life, though that pleasure has been for the most part mingled with sorrow.

I have already acquainted the reader with the time and place of my birth. My father, besides many slaves, had a numerous family, of which seven lived to grow up, including myself and a sister, who was the only daughter. As I was the youngest of the sons, I became, of course, the greatest favourite with my mother, and was always with her; and she used to take particular pains to form my mind. I was trained up from my earliest years in the arts of agriculture and war: my daily exercise was shooting and throwing javelins; and my mother adorned me with emblems, after the manner of our greatest warriors. In this way I grew up till I was turned the age of eleven, when an end was put to my happiness in the following manner:—Generally, when the grown people in the neighbourhood were gone far in the fields to labour, the children assembled together in some of the neighbours' premises to play; and commonly some of us used to get up a tree to look out for any assailant, or kidnapper, that might come upon us; for they sometimes took those opportunities of our parents' absence, to attack and carry off as many as they could seize. One day, as I was watching at the top of a tree in our yard, I saw one of those people come into the yard of our next neighbour but one, to kidnap, there being many stout young people in it. Immediately, on this, I gave the alarm of the rogue, and he was surrounded by the stoutest of them, who entangled him with cords, so that he could not escape till some of the grown people came and secured him. But, alas! ere long it was my fate to be thus attacked, and to be carried off, when none of the grown people were nigh.

One day, when all our people were gone out to their works as usual, and only I and my dear sister were left to mind the house, two men and a woman got over our walls, and in a moment seized us both; and, without giving us time to cry out, or make resistance, they stopped our mouths, tied our hands, and ran off with us into the nearest wood: and continued to carry us as far as they could, till night came on, when we reached a small house, where the robbers halted for refreshment, and spent the night. We were then unbound, but were unable to take any food; and, being quite overpowered by fatigue and grief, our only relief was some sleep, which allayed our misfortune for a short time. The next morning we left the house, and continued travelling all the day. For a long time we had kept the woods, but at last we came into a road which I believed I knew. I had now some hopes of being delivered;[7] for we had advanced but a little way before I discovered some people at a distance on which I began to cry out for their assistance; but my cries had no other effect than to make them tie me faster, and stop my mouth, and then they put me into a large sack. They also stopped

---

[7] Equiano's use of *deliverance* here to mean only physical salvation, as opposed to its later meaning in the *Narrative* of spiritual salvation, parallels the dual use of the term in spiritual biographies, including fictional ones, like *Robinson Crusoe* (1719), by Daniel Defoe (1660–1731). During the stage of his life before being exposed to Christianity, Equano fails to yet recognize that, from a theological perspective, release from the slavery of sin is far more important than release from bodily bondage.

my sister's mouth, and tied her hands; and in this manner we pro-
ceeded till we were out of the sight of these people. When we went
to rest the following night they offered us some victuals; but we
refused them; and the only comfort we had was in being in one
another's arms all that night, and bathing each other with our tears.
But, alas! we were soon deprived of even the smallest comfort of
weeping together.

The next day proved a day of greater sorrow than I had yet experienced; for my sister and I were then separated, while we lay clasped
in each other's arms. It was in vain that we besought them not to
part us: she was torn from me, and immediately carried away, while
I was left in a state of distraction not to be described. I cried and
grieved continually; and for several days did not eat any thing but
what they forced into my mouth. At length, after many days travelling, during which I had often changed masters, I got into the hands
of a chieftain, in a very pleasant country. This man had two wives
and some children, and, they all used me extremely well, and did
all they could to comfort me; particularly the first wife, who was
something like my mother. Although I was a great many days journey from my father's house, yet these people spoke exactly the same
language with us. This first master of mine, as I may call him, was a
smith, and my principal employment was working his bellows, which
were the same kind as I had seen in my vicinity. They were in some
respects not unlike the stoves here in gentlemen's kitchens; and were
covered over with leather; and in the middle of that leather a stick
was fixed, and a person stood up, and worked it, in the same manner as is done to pump water out of a cask with a hand-pump.
I believe it was gold he worked, for it was of a lovely bright yellow
colour, and was worn by the women on their wrists and ankles.

I was there I suppose about a month, and they at last used to
trust me some little distance from the house. . . .

Soon after this my master's only daughter and child by his first
wife sickened and died, which affected him so much that for some
time he was almost frantic, and really would have killed himself
had he not been watched and prevented. However, in a small time
afterwards he recovered, and I was again sold. I was now carried to

the left of the sun's rising, through many dreary wastes and dismal woods, amidst the hideous roarings of wild beasts. The people I was sold to used to carry me very often, when I was tired, either on their shoulders or on their backs. I saw many convenient well-built sheds along the roads, at proper distances, to accommodate the merchants and travellers, who lay in those buildings along with their wives, who often accompany them; and they always go well armed.

From the time I left my own nation I always found somebody that understood me till I came to the sea coast. The languages of different nations did not totally differ, nor were they so copious as those of the Europeans, particularly the English. They were therefore easily learned; and, while I was journeying thus through Africa, I acquired two or three different tongues. In this manner I had been travelling for a considerable time, when one evening, to my great surprise, whom should I see brought to the house where I was but my dear sister. As soon as she saw me she gave a loud shriek, and ran into my arms—I was quite overpowered; neither of us could speak, but, for a considerable time, clung to each other in mutual embraces, unable to do any thing but weep. Our meeting affected all who saw us; and indeed I must acknowledge, in honour of those sable destroyers of human rights, that I never met with any ill treatment, or saw any offered to their slaves, except tying them, when necessary, to keep them from running away.

When these people knew we were brother and sister they indulged us to be together; and the man, to whom I supposed we belonged, lay with us, he in the middle, while she and I held one another by the hands across his breast all night; and thus for a while we forgot our misfortunes in the joy of being together: but even this small comfort was soon to have an end; for scarcely had the fatal morning appeared, when she was again torn from me for ever! I was now more miserable, if possible, than before. The small relief which her presence gave me from pain was gone, and the wretchedness of my situation was redoubled by my anxiety after her fate, and my apprehensions lest her sufferings should be greater than mine, when I could not be with her to alleviate them. Yes, thou dear partner of all my childish sports! thou sharer of my joys and sorrows! happy should I have ever esteemed myself to encounter every misery for you, and to procure your freedom by the sacrifice of my own. Though you were early forced from my arms, your image has been always rivetted in my heart, from which neither *time nor fortune* have been able to remove it: so that, while the thoughts of your sufferings have damped my prosperity, they have mingled with adversity, and increased its bitterness. To that heaven which protects the weak from the strong, I commit the care of your innocence and virtues, if they have not already received their full reward; and if your youth and delicacy have not long since fallen victims to the violence of the African trader, the pestilential stench of a Guinea ship, the seasoning in the European colonies, or the lash and lust of a brutal and unrelenting overseer.[8]

I did not long remain after my sister. I was again sold, and carried through a number of places, till, after travelling a considerable time, I came to a town called Tinmah, in the most beautiful country I had yet seen in Africa. It was extremely rich, and there were many rivulets which flowed through it; and supplied a large pond in the center of the town, where the people washed. Here I first saw and tasted cocoa nuts, which I thought superior to any nuts I had ever tasted before; and the trees, which were loaded, were also interspersed amongst the houses, which had commodious shades adjoining, and were in the same manner as ours, the insides being neatly plastered and whitewashed. Here I also saw and tasted for the first time sugar-cane.[9] Their money consisted of little white shells,

---

[8]Equiano refers to the four stages of the African slave trade: the original capture by other Africans and transportation to the coast, during which many died from hunger, thirst, and exhaustion; the middle passage across the Atlantic, when disease and despair posed the most lethal threats; the seasoning, or period between arrival in the West Indies and full-time employment on the plantations, when the Africans, were somewhat gradually introduced to the life of forced labor and when they were suddenly introduced to a new and therefore deadly disease environment; and the final stage of enslavement.

[9] Equiano may be sublty reminding his readers of the common abolitionist argument that sugar could be profitably cultivated in Africa by free native labor.

---

the size of the finger nail: they are known in this country by the name of *core*.[10] I was sold here for one hundred and seventy-two of them by a merchant who lived and brought me there.[11]

I had been about two or three days at his house, when a wealthy widow, a neighbour of his, came there one evening, and brought with her an only son, a young gentleman about my own age and size. Here they saw me; and, having taken a fancy to me, I was bought of the merchant, and went home with them. Her house and premises were situated close to one of those rivulets I have mentioned, and were the finest I ever saw in Africa: they were very extensive, and she had a number of slaves to attend her. The next day I was washed and perfumed, and when meal-time came, I was led into the presence of my mistress, and ate and drank before her with her son. This filled me with astonishment: and I could scarce help expressing my surprise that the young gentleman should suffer me, who was bound,[12] to eat with him who was free; and not only so, but that he would not at any time either eat or drink till I had taken first, because I was the eldest, which was agreeable to our custom. Indeed every thing here, and all their treatment of me, made me forget that I was a slave. The language of these people resembled ours so nearly, that we understood each other perfectly. They had also the very same customs as we. There were likewise slaves daily to attend us, while my young master and I, with other boys, sported with our darts and bows and arrows, as I had been used to do at home. In this resemblance to my former happy state I passed about two months, and I now began to think I was to be adopted into the family, and was beginning to be reconciled to my situation, and to forget by degrees my misfortunes, when all at once the delusion vanished; for, without the least previous knowledge, one morning early, while my dear master and companion was still asleep, I was awakened out of my reverie to fresh sorrow, and hurried away even among the uncircumcised.

---

[10] Core: cowry, a shell used as currency in West Africa.
[11] Equiano must mean 172 pounds of cowry shells, because the price of slaves during the the century ranged between 100 and 300 pounds apiece.
[12] Bound: enslaved.

Thus, at the very moment I dreamed of the greatest happiness, I found myself most miserable: and it seemed as if fortune wished to give me this taste of joy only to render the reverse more poignant.[13] The change I now experienced was as painful as it was sudden and unexpected. It was a change indeed from a state of bliss to a scene which is inexpressible by me, as it discovered to me an element I had never before beheld, and till then had no idea of, and wherein such instances of hardship and cruelty continually occurred as I can never reflect on but with horror. . . .

The first object which saluted my eyes when I arrived on the coast was the sea, and a slave-ship, which was then riding at anchor, and waiting for its cargo. These filled me with astonishment, which was soon converted into terror, which I am yet at a loss to describe, nor the then feelings of my mind. When I was carried on board I was immediately handled, and tossed up, to see if I were sound, by some of the crew; and I was now persuaded that I had gotten into a world of bad spirits, and that they were going to kill me. Their complexions too differing so much from ours, their long hair, and the language they spoke, which was very different from any I had ever heard, united to confirm me in this belief. Indeed, such were the horrors of my views and fears at the moment, that, if ten thousand worlds had been my own, I would have freely parted with them all to have exchanged my condition with that of the meanest slave in my own country. When I looked round the ship too, and saw a large furnace of copper boiling, and a multitude of black people of every description chained together, every one of their countenances expressing dejection and sorrow, I no longer doubted of my fate, and, quite overpowered with horror and anguish, I fell motionless on the deck and fainted. When I recovered a little, I found some black people about me, who I believed were some of those who brought me on board, and had been receiving their pay; they talked to me in order to cheer me, but all in vain. I asked them if we were not to be eaten by those white men with horrible looks, red faces,

---

[13] Equiano refers to fortune here because, as a pagan, he still saw life as a matter of chance, rather than as a working out of providential design and order.

and long hair? They told me I was not; and one of the crew brought me a small portion of spirituous liquor in a wine glass; but, being afraid of him, I would not take it out of his hand. One of the blacks therefore took it from him and gave it to me, and I took a little down my palate, which, instead of reviving me, as they thought it would, threw me into the greatest consternation at the strange feeling it produced, having never tasted any such liquor before. Soon after this, the blacks who brought me on board went off and left me abandoned to despair.

I now saw myself deprived of all chance of returning to my native country, or even the least glimpse of hope of gaining the shore, which I now considered as friendly: and I even wished for my former slavery in preference to my present situation, which was filled with horrors of every kind, still heightened by my ignorance of what I was to undergo. I was not long suffered to indulge my grief; I was soon put down under the decks, and there I received such a salutation in my nostrils as I had never experienced in my life; so that with the loathsomeness of the stench, and crying together, I became so sick and low that I was not able to eat, nor had I the least desire to taste any thing. I now wished for the last friend, Death, to relieve me; but soon, to my grief, two of the white men offered me eatables; and, on my refusing to eat, one of them held me fast by the hands, and laid me across, I think, the windlass, and tied my feet, while the other flogged me severely. I had never experienced any thing of this kind before; and although, not being used to the water, I naturally feared that element the first time I saw it; yet, nevertheless, could I have got over the nettings, I would have jumped over the side, but I could not; and, besides, the crew used to watch us very closely who were not chained down to the decks, lest we should leap into the water; and I have seen some of these poor African prisoners most severely cut for attempting to do so, and hourly whipped for not eating. This indeed was often the case with myself.

In a little time after, amongst the poor chained men, I found some of my own nation, which in a small degree gave ease to my mind. I inquired of these what was to be done with us? they gave me to understand we were to be carried to these white people's country to work for them. I then was a little revived, and thought, if it were no worse than working, my situation was not so desperate: but still I feared I should be put to death, the white people looked and acted, as I thought, in so savage a manner; for I had never seen among any people such instances of brutal cruelty. . . .

At last, when the ship we were in had got in all her cargo, they made ready with many fearful noises, and we were all put under deck, so that we could not see how they managed the vessel. But this disappointment was the least of my sorrow. The stench of the hold while we were on the coast was so intolerably loathsome, that it was dangerous to remain there for any time, and some of us had been permitted to stay on the deck for the fresh air; but now that the whole ship's cargo were confined together, it became absolutely pestilential. The closeness of the place, and the heat of the climate, added to the number in the ship, which was so crowded that each had scarcely room to turn himself, almost suffocated us. This produced copious perspirations, so that the air soon became unfit for respiration, from a variety of loathsome smells, and brought on a sickness among the slaves, of which many died, thus falling victims to the improvident avarice, as I may call it, of their purchasers. This wretched situation was again aggravated by the galling of the chains, now become insupportable; and the filth of the necessary tubs, into which the children often fell, and were almost suffocated.[14] The shrieks of the women, and the groans of the dying, rendered the whole a scene of horror almost inconceiveable. Happily perhaps for myself I was soon reduced so low here that it was thought necessary to keep me almost always on deck; and from my extreme youth I was not put in fetters. In this situation I expected every hour to share the fate of my companions, some of whom were almost daily brought upon deck at the point of death, which I began to hope would soon put an end to my miseries. Often did I think many of the inhabitants of the deep much more happy than myself; I envied them the freedom they enjoyed, and as often wished I could change my condition for theirs. Every circumstance I met with served only

---

[14] Necessary tubs: latrines.

---

to render my state more painful, and heighten my apprehensions, and my opinion of the cruelty of the whites.

One day they had taken a number of fishes; and when they had killed and satisfied themselves with as many as they thought fit, to our astonishment who were on the deck, rather than give any of them to us to eat, as we expected, they tossed the remaining fish into the sea again, although we begged and prayed for some as well as we could, but in vain; and some of my countrymen, being pressed by hunger, took an opportunity, when they thought no one saw them, of trying to get a little privately; but they were discovered, and the attempt procured them some very severe floggings.

One day, when we had a smooth sea, and moderate wind, two of my wearied countrymen, who were chained together (I was near them at the time), preferring death to such a life of misery, somehow made through the nettings, and jumped into the sea: immediately another quite dejected fellow, who, on account of his illness, was suffered to be out of irons, also followed their example; and I believe many more would very soon have done the same, if they had not been prevented by the ship's crew, who were instantly alarmed. Those of us that were the most active were, in a moment, put down under the deck; and there was such a noise and confusion amongst the people of the ship as I never heard before, to stop her, and get the boat out to go after the slaves. However, two of the wretches were drowned, but they got the other, and afterwards flogged him unmercifully, for thus attempting to prefer death to slavery. In this manner we continued to undergo more hardships than I can now relate; hardships which are inseparable from this accursed trade.—Many a time we were near suffocation, from the want of fresh air, which we were often without for whole days together. This, and the stench of the necessary tubs, carried off many.

From Through African Doors

Janheinz Jahn

■ *Life history or biography is a valuable tool that we can use to understand the lives of people from other cultures, where individual experience is a reflection of the larger social whole. The story of a young Yoruba woman named Ewumi is no exception. First, historically we can locate her in the center of the colonial period: she was born in 1933 and the narrative which follows brings us to the brink of Nigeria's independence in 1960. Through Ewumi we learn, for example, of the interplay between European and Yoruba religions; the introduction of cash cropping; and the effects of European schooling. In turn, however, these historically-rooted themes provide the backdrop to a larger picture: the daily experiences of girls and women who live in rural village settings of a territory we now call Nigeria. Through Ewumi's story we can explore Yoruba attitudes towards such issues as kinship, child rearing practices, polygynous marriage, pregnancy, and romantic love. As daughter, spouse, mother, co-wife, and market woman, Ewumi's life epitomizes those of other successful Yoruba—and even, more generally, many West African women.*

Lesley Sharp

. . . [A] woman whom I will call Ewumi [was] born twenty-seven years ago in the town of Ede, which may be regarded as fairly typical of Nigeria. It is in Yoruba country, 150 miles from the coast and thus not directly exposed to the commercial influences of the ports. It is not too deep in the bush either, but on the main railway line from Lagos to Kano; and it has a good asphalt road leading to it. It is of medium size, with about 70,000 inhabitants; much of my information on "Ewumi" comes from European friends who live there.

Ewumi, then, was born in 1933. Her father, a respectable citizen of Ede, was like most other citizens a farmer, his land being a day's walk away from the town. He would be away from home for days, planting the yams, hoeing the round hillocks, weeding his land, tying up the beans, harvesting the maize, digging up the yams, and so on. With uncles, cousins and neighbours he marched out into the bush, where amidst much singing and also encouragement from the drummers they would lend each other a hand in tilling their fields. Sometimes, but not often, baby Ewumi was there too, on the back of her mother, who might be helping to hoe, should there ever be a shortage of hands. But Ewumi's mother had her own field between her family's estates, which was usually looked after by her brothers.

In her first years Ewumi seldom saw her father, and he played no part in her life. Only the mother was ever present: Ewumi was strapped to her back, and it was from there that by degrees the girl came to take in her own little world. This included her brother, three years old, and her sister, six years older, who was already helping mother and was sometimes allowed to carry her little sister on her own back. Then there were the grandmother and aunts and their children. Ever since she could think, Ewumi's family provided a solid framework within which she could feel secure; but she was never away from her mother.

Her mother slept near Ewumi. She took Ewumi to market on her back (with the purchases stacked on her head) and to the seasonal dances of town or clan. Ewumi would go to sleep there whenever she felt like it, whether her mother was going out to the fields, sitting at the market or dancing through the night at one of the religious festivals: practically before she could stand, Ewumi learnt the rhythms of the music for these. She sucked at her mother's breasts whenever she wanted, she never had to cry in hunger or lie alone in the dark. "Timetable-feeding is unheard of and self-regulation of the child is the absolute rule," writes Beier. Moreover the child can get as much erotic pleasure from its mother's breast as it likes, as it will be allowed to play with the breast at any time. Weaning too is done most gently and carefully. In some cases, where a child is extremely difficult, it may even be allowed to come to its mother's breast (very occasionally) after the new child is born.

When Ewumi was three, her mother gave birth again, and this time it was a boy. By now Ewumi had grasped something of life, she was weaned and no longer so completely dependent on her mother. But so that she should not feel neglected, she was now treated by her mother with extra tenderness, a cock was sacrificed for her, and she was bathed in the same water as her baby brother to develop feelings of kinship with him. Three years later, when Ewumi was six, her mother had another baby, and now it was the three-year-old brother who was bathed with the baby.

It is no matter of chance that the mother has a child every three years, and there would be great disapproval in her family if things were any different. For as soon as a woman finds herself pregnant, she may not have any more intercourse with her husband until the child is weaned. Most mothers leave their husbands for quite a long time and return to their own mothers, so as to devote themselves wholly to the children. "All this is only possible," Beier remarks, "in a society where men have many wives, because otherwise they would have to remain celibate for stretches of nearly three years."

The three-year rhythm of births has many advantages for the child. In a European family the father may often feel the accidentally-born child as an intruder robbing him of his wife's attention, and conversely the child may feel neglected because of his father, which sometimes leads to an Oedipus complex; whereas here the father does not figure in the small child's existence at all. Moreover the baby's feeding is ensured in a country where the protective bodies contained in the mother's milk are essential defences against a whole series of dangerous diseases; cow's milk would provide no adequate substitute, even if cattle-breeding were possible in these areas infested by the tsetse fly. But there is of course no cow's milk, except for European tinned milk or milk powder, which is both far too expensive and also very hard to obtain, especially in the quantities that would be necessary if the native population were to depart from the three-year rhythm of births. Finally this also stops an elder child feeling too jealous on the birth of the next baby. It is natural for a child of less than two to feel neglected when the new baby arrives; a three-year-old is already more sensible and beginning to discover a world of his own. "All these things may account for the balance and harmony we find in Yoruba children."

While her brother came under his father's care at seven, Ewumi, being a girl, stayed on with her mother, learning housework and having her own household duties, going to fetch water from the well in a calabash, which she had learnt to carry on her head, helping look after her small brother, now four, and minding him when her mother went to market; for her mother had grown older too and did not find it so easy now to have the four-year-old strapped to her hips, as well as the market goods on her head and the baby on her back. Yet Ewumi was by no means alone with her little brother, she was in the midst of her elder sisters and cousins, a whole troop of children going about their games and duties under the surveillance of relatives and neighbours.

She learnt to cook, and wash clothes, to grind pepper, and pound maize and dried yam slices in the mortar. On Sundays she went with her mother and sisters and brothers to the Baptist Mission church, and eagerly joined in the hymns she had learnt there. That did not stop her taking part in the town's old religious festivals, especially in the four-day festival of the new yams in July in honour of the *Orishas* (the gods) and the seven-day festival in honour of the god Shango at the end of the rainy season. Ewumi was an intelligent girl, and the Baptist minister thought she ought to go to the mission school; but since her parents couldn't afford to pay school fees for all the children, they decided to send only the two boys, who might thereby get an office job later on.

Ewumi grew up into a fine girl. At fifteen she was going to market on her own, her wares being matches, razor-blades and cigarettes; and this gave her a chance to talk to and flirt with young men while selling. When her mother had reached marriageable age, *her* parents had long chosen their daughter a mate, who had as little choice in the matter as the girl. Ewumi, however, could herself choose—of course within limits. She was shrewd enough to consider only the young men of whom her clan would approve; it would have been foolish for a young woman to throw away lightheartedly the support she needed from her family when married. Partly with her knowledge and partly without, contacts were made between families: a few young men were tipped off by their relatives to buy razor-blades or cigarettes from her, and between the three or four proposed candidates she could exercise a free choice.

The one she liked best was Dele from the Olabisi family, a merry fellow and a hard-working farmer, who besides the traditional crops grew cocoa on his land—the fashionable new crop from which you were supposed to get rich quick. When both were sure that their families approved the connection, Ewumi received expensive bridal gifts from her suitor, worth the equivalent of about £25. These belonged to her, they were the basic capital for her subsequent trading, and had nothing to do with the bride-price, which at Ede is fixed at £12. Dele found no difficulty in paying this price, for a marriage here is not so much a contract between two individuals as the symbol of two families being joined together. Every member of Dele's family contributed something to the sum needed, and Ewumi's father, who received the bride-price, had to distribute it among all the members of the family.

So the day came when amidst the customary ceremonies and festivities she entered her husband's household. The young couple lived in an annexe, a mud hut with a corrugated-iron roof and room for further expansion. At first she had much to order and arrange before she could settle down in the new clan. Being a true Yoruba woman, she could not let her husband keep her, and with the price of her bridal gifts she bought wares for sale; she set them out on a rough-hewn table outside the hut at a corner of the road, where there would be a lot of people passing. She offered sugar, tinned milk, tinned sardines, soap, matches, kerosene for lamps and refrigerators—all European articles which did not spoil.

When she became pregnant, the marriage had so far fulfilled its purpose, for marriage is not consummated by two people living together but by the begetting of children. Ewumi was proud of her fertility, and as she loved her husband, she brought him her friend Toro, who with Ewumi had for years excelled in the Baptist Church choir, as second wife—after thorough consultation with all the families concerned. Dele's hut got an extension, and Ewumi carried out her duties at the wedding of Dele and Toro, thereby showing herself a true "*iyali*"—mother of the house—as she could now call herself. Having welcomed her husband's guests in the prescribed way, and initiated Toro into her duties, she now returned with all her belongings into her parents' family.

She was now free to concentrate on her business. She got rid of the European wares, which were likely to bring only a small profit, and transferred her activity to the market. She was very good at making *ogi,* a maize-meal dish. Since both her own family and her husband's grew maize, she bought the raw material cheap direct from the producer. She had only to take the maize to the miller to be ground into meal, and then make *ogi* with it. So her profit came from the difference between the retail and wholesale price as well as from the work she put in. These profits were "ploughed back" into wares that would not spoil.

Her confinement was properly celebrated: Dele was proud of Ewumi and buried the after-birth, the ceremony required to make him the legal father, the "owner" of the child. It was a girl, and was given the name of Gbemi after a dead great-grandmother. Ewumi carried her baby daughter on her back, went to the market every day with fresh *ogi,* and increased her prosperity. The only snag was the miller's price for grinding, which was gradually going up.

Communication with her husband and Toro was confined to periodical friendly visits, going to church with them on Sundays, and taking part in the festivals of town and clan. Little Gbemi on her back grew bigger, and when she was beginning to wean her daughter, many a man at the market made her friendly offers—for she was beautiful, had shown she could bear healthy children and had enough milk for them. She was now nineteen.

But she only laughed at her suitors' advances; as soon as Gbemi was weaned, she returned to her husband's house. Toro had still not become pregnant, and Ewumi told her of all sorts of effective "medicines" (charms), recommended prayers and sacrifices to Shango, the *Orisha* embodying reproduction powers, and to

Egungun (the ancestors). As "mother of the house" she organized communal living according to the prevailing custom: for five days she cooked the food for her husband and slept with him; then Toro cooked for him and slept with him for the next five days. Ewumi as "*iyale*" had to welcome guests when they came, but this is the only privilege she had. For a few months the two wives looked after their husband in turn, till Ewumi was sure she was pregnant again and returned once more to her family's farm.

At the market she had long had her fixed place among other women who also sold *ogi*; her two neighbours were old, and their *ogi* was not so good, but their clans saw to it that they also had their turnover. Their children were already grown up, so they no longer needed to earn such large amounts.

When Ewumi was delivered again, it was a boy, and they called him Adebayo. But great as was their joy, it was mixed with anxiety, for Adebayo was rather delicate, and also prone to fits. And when the worried parents brought him to the *Ifa* oracle, it transpired that he was an *abiku,* a spirit-child, who only comes on earth to leave it again soon. Ewumi would have to make all possible efforts to see the child stayed on the earth and did not go back again to his spirit companions. An *abiku* has wonderful dreams, he has visions of his spirit companions and plays wonderful imaginary games with them. And when his time comes, some time between the ages of four and ten, the spirits demand that the child returns to them. However attached he may be to his mother, if he is not strong enough, he must obey them. The mother will then pray that the child be restored to her, and there are women who maintain that they have given birth to the same child seven times. If the child is reborn, it can easily be recognized by a small mark which is scratched on a dead child's face or body; the scar will then appear on the new-born baby in the same place. Many grown-ups show such "identification marks"; in one confirmed case, Beier notes, "the parents expected a certain mark to appear, and described it before the baby was born. The mark appeared as expected, and I saw it myself."

Ewumi would treat Adebayo with the greatest care, would never let him out of her sight, would satisfy his every want, put up with all his moods. If he was called away even so, she could be sure he would be born to her again and again, until one day he would stay alive and with her. But if her care for him never let up for a moment, the *abiku* might even stay with her the first time, and she would be able to have more children than if she had to give birth to the same one several times.

"The *abiku* is often a problem child," says Beier. "Many of those I have known are very temperamental and make great demands on their parents. If a wish is not fulfilled at once, they will threaten to die. The terrified parents will then all too often put up no resistance to the child and suffer its tyranny in the hope that it may be persuaded to live. The *abiku* is nearly always the unusual one, the out-of-the-ordinary child, in many cases it is the exceptionally brilliant child. Therefore the *abiku* is given exceptional treatment. But this does not offend the other children, who are treated much more sternly. Because after all, they know that these are not ordinary children like themselves. Thus Yoruba society has solved the educational problem of how to give the exceptional child the freedom it requires to develop its personality, while at the same time supplying the more rigid discipline which the average child must have to feel secure."

So Ewumi had given birth to a spirit-child, a problem child; but soon other worries were added. The price the miller demanded for grinding the maize had gone up so much that the women who sold *ogi* found their earnings seriously reduced. Ewumi discussed the matter with the other women at the main market, and they all agreed not to accept the price any longer; so Ewumi appealed to the *iyalode,* the woman chief of the town, who looked after the women's interests in their dealings with the men and the king: every town in Yoruba country has such a woman chief.

Ewumi was one of the delegation which conducted negotiations with the millers for the *iyalode.* But millers are men: they were adamant and refused to lower the grinding price. The *iyalode* began to threaten, and after a few days the millers said they were ready to come to terms; yet the negotiations trailed on, and the *iyalode* had the impression that the millers were dragging them out till the *ogi-*

sellers' stores were used up and one or other of them would be forced to have more maize ground and pay the price demanded. Then the *iyalode* called all the *ogi*-sellers out on strike. She sent her messengers—and on the same day all the *ogi*-sellers began to grind their maize by hand. After a week the millers yielded and accepted unconditionally the price fixed by the *iyalode* according to the women's wishes.

The *iyalode* and the *ogi*-sellers would scarcely have heard of such a thing as a trade union. Their strike was no imitation of European methods, no transference of modem European processes into Yoruba life; it was simply the way such conflicts were traditionally settled. As every clan has its chief and every professional group its spokesman, so the women too have their independence and their own organizations, which owe their impact above all to the traditional religious cults. In the Shango cult, which is the most important one at Ede, the high priest is a woman, the *Iya Shango* (Mother of Shango), and it gives her tremendous influence. There are two male secret societies, the *egungun* (ancestors) society, which makes the bond between the living and the dead, and the *oro* society, which has a secret executive power. But the *ogboni* society, which controls both these and is a check on the king's power—it consists of all important tribal chiefs and priests—contains women members as well as men. Unlike Christian social life, that of the Yorubas has never been patriarchal; so the women have long been able to secure special economic monopolies for themselves. Pottery, dyeing, spinning and the batik process are exclusively women's business; no man may practise these trades. At the market women have a monopoly in most of the goods for sale. Men may sell meat and leather goods there, but almost everything else is in the hands of the women: yams and cassava, tomatoes and other vegetables, cola nuts, palm oil, cooked dishes, mats, baskets, skins, necklaces, jewelry, native "medicines," and materials.

Ewumi was now earning well again at the market. Her attention to customers was often distracted, of course, by Adebayo, her spirit-child, but the customers were patient and understanding, for they knew the duties of a mother to an *abiku*. Dele often came to visit her either in the market or in her house, not only to see how Adebayo was going on. He was worried about Toro, who had still not conceived, was unhappy over it and moody, now imploring Ewumi and Dele for new counsels and "medicines," now accusing people of making her barren by witchcraft. Ewumi advised Dele to take a third wife, particularly as she herself had given birth to an *abiku,* did not know if he would stay in this world and how often she might have to bring him into it again. Dele had for some time been toying with the idea, and had already picked out a woman called Efuneye, a blacksmith's second wife, who had already born her husband two healthy children and who sold cola nuts a few market alleys away. Dele had now and then bought cola nuts from her for years, but in the last weeks his need for them seemed to have increased enormously, and Efuneye had shown that she did not object to his wooing—Dele being ten years younger than her husband. So a meeting was arranged between Efuneye and Ewumi, the two women liked each other, and the rest was only a financial matter.

Since Efuneye had lived with her husband for over five years, she had to return only half the bride-price on divorce, and could keep the bridal gifts. Dele readily gave her further bridal gifts, and his family readily found the bride-price. The blacksmith was not exactly pleased, but had to admit that he sometimes beat Efuneye, so that grounds had been given for the divorce. After the usual formalities Efuneye entered Dele's household with her two children, a six-year-old boy and a three-year-old girl.

The coming of a new wife already blessed with children made Toro even more painfully aware of her failure. Her depressions alternated with fits of temper, and Dele's aunts and grandmother had to intervene to see that order was kept in his house. Efuneye, however, was very popular with all, which incensed Toro all the more. Ewumi watched the situation with distress; Efuneye often came and asked her to come home soon, as with two of them there Toro's tempers would be more easily controlled. Dele would have been glad to get rid of Toro, he beat her to give her grounds for divorce, dropped hints to friends about her beauty—she was certainly the most beautiful and also the youngest of his wives—yet no suitor would turn up. Dele had even got his family's permission to do without the return of the bride-price if need be, but Toro wanted to stay, so he just had to put up with her.

The nearer the time came when Ewumi had to wean her problem child, the more worried she became. She went on feeding him longer than usual, which in itself was good for an *abiku*, but because of this child she was afraid of going back into her husband's house. With a directness that was almost unseemly she pointed out to the men who flirted with her at the market that there was a fine shapely girl to be had in Dele's house; but they only laughed, they knew the situation and paid all the more compliments to Ewumi herself. She entreated Dele either to bring Toro somehow to her senses or else get rid of her. But neither the sacrifices to Shango and other *Orishas* nor prayers in the churches seemed to help. Even Toro's mother couldn't cope with her.

Ewumi began to listen more attentively to the friendly things said to her, and in particular she could not help thinking about the advances of a rich elderly merchant. He already had eight wives and a lot of children, all of whom lived together in harmony and comfort; and he offered most attractive bridal gifts.

When Dele learnt that the merchant's hopes were well founded, Ewumi and he had a long discussion. Dele would like to have kept her, but for the sake of her little *abiku* she refused to return into a house of strife. The air the child breathed there was poison, she said: a spirit-child had to have happiness round him and peace; if he saw Toro in one of her rages, he would die. Dele admitted she was right. He loved Ewumi, and she loved him, yet the child's welfare was decisive as ever. "The child is the cornerstone of African society."

She gave him and his family half the bride-money back, neglect on the part of the husband was given as grounds for the divorce, and both wept on parting. The merchant was received formally but very politely by Ewumi's family; his gifts to the bride were in keeping with his wealth, but Ewumi did not seem particularly impressed and kept them with her own savings.

The *iyale* of her new home was an elderly, wise and kindly woman, who took great care over household arrangements and saw to it that the rota of wifely duties did not get out of hand. Some of the wives were already quite old, and only two were suckling children. Ewumi had to prepare her husband's food only five days every month. In such a well-off household there was no lack of assistance or space; she found the peace she had longed for in order to devote herself entirely to her little *abiku*. After she had carried out her wifely duties three times—she had to be passed over at her first turn because of menstruation—it transpired that she was again pregnant. But as she had learnt to appreciate the household's cheerful and harmonious atmosphere, she did not go back to her own family. Adebayo was thriving, and it really seemed as if he meant to stay with her; while Gbemi, now five, romped about with the other children as if they were her brothers and sisters.

With Dele, meanwhile, things were much less peaceful. When Efuneye became pregnant, Toro almost went out of her mind, and the two women came to blows. The relatives had to intervene, and Toro was sternly rebuked, but she only worked everybody up the more with her poisonous talk, and when Dele came home from his fields two days later, he beat her harder than ever. She cried the whole night, but next morning immediately started a new row. Dele's clan conferred, after which a delegation was sent off to Toro's clan, earnestly requesting them to take the misguided creature back. But she would not even listen to the remonstrances of her own relatives, and abused the clan elder so violently that they formally renounced her: the elder said that never in human memory had such a thing occurred in his clan. So Dele had to take her back home again. Divorce is easy for a woman, almost impossible for a man. For morals in Yoruba society, and the rules derived therefrom, are based on a simple but good principle: any arrangement which tends to ensure the production of many children and which guarantees that no women will be left to die as spinsters, is moral in this society. Since nobody now wanted to have Toro, Dele was obliged to go to the last resort.

Having donned his ceremonial robes and taken some money, he seized Toro's hand, pulled her crying out of the house, and went with her into the palace of the king, the Timi of Ede. There he threw himself down before the king, gave him the money, and pointing to Toro said: "Timi, I present her to you." Then he told the king how things had come to this pass. The king could not refuse the present, but had to take her.

A "town king" among the Yorubas has some privileges, of course, in the choice of wives: for instance, if a woman kneels on his carpet by mistake, he may claim her as his wife. But he has more duties than rights, he must marry the crippled and sick girls, all those who normally would have no chance of finding a husband, and must take the women nobody wants.

When she heard what Dele had done, Ewumi did not stay much longer in the merchant's house. She discussed things with Dele and her family, gave the merchant the full bride-money back and all the rich personal gifts, for she had been with him less than a year. In order to marry her again, Dele had to make good half the bride-money which she returned. It was his right to hold it back three months, to make sure of her faithfulness and constancy; but he paid it at once, being sure of his Ewumi.

The celebrations for her re-entry into his house coincided with a farewell party; for Efuneye's eldest son was now seven and returned to his real father, the blacksmith, according to custom. Since both wives, Ewumi and Efuneye, were now pregnant again, they together looked for a third wife for Dele; their choice fell on Ewumi's youngest sister, with whom Ewumi had always got on extremely well.

Since then another three years have passed, Ewumi and Efuneye have had their babies, and their entire offspring, including the "problem child," Adebayo, have stayed alive. Ewumi's sister has also had a baby, but it died soon after it was born—infant mortality is still high. Ewumi and Efuneye have remained close friends, they mind the children alternately and also swap stalls at the market. Efuneye too now sells *ogi,* but Ewumi has spent her savings on hardware: lamps, bicycle-chains, clothes-hangers, alarm-clocks, aluminum pots and buckets. Her youngest brother, a lanky lad of seventeen, still single, who lives with a great-uncle, looks after her stall in the covered market at Onitsha. He is a reliable boy and hands over his profits every month, which she puts back into goods. If her businesses go on flourishing like this, she will soon have her own lorry (as her aunt has), will engage a good driver, and earn still more with haulage deals, which bring in good money. Adebayo will then one day be able to study in Europe.

"SITTING ON A MAN": COLONIALISM AND THE LOST POLITICAL INSTITUTIONS OF IGBO WOMEN

JUDITH VAN ALLEN

🔲 *"Sitting on a Man" has become a classic in both African and gender studies since it shatters the false assumption that colonized people remain passive in the face of injustice. As this essay reveals, Igbo culture was characterized by several institutions which enabled women to exert effective collective social and political pressure, forcing men to reform their behavior.When faced with the threat of unfair policies imposed by the British, Igbo women responded creatively, drawing on tactics used previously only in village settings. As Van Allen shows, it is not the social structural weakness of women in Igbo culture that ensured their protests went unheeded; rather, failure was rooted in the ethnocentric attitudes of their colonizers.*

LESLEY SHARP

In the conventional wisdom, Western influence has "emancipated" African women—through the weakening of kinship bonds and the provision of "free choice" in Christian monogamous marriage, the suppression of "barbarous" practices, the opening of schools, the introduction of modern medicine and hygiene, and, sometimes, of female suffrage.

But Westernization is not an unmixed blessing. The experience of Igbo women under British colonialism shows that Western influence can sometimes weaken or destroy women's traditional autonomy and power without providing modern forms of autonomy of

Reprinted from *Canadian Journal of African Studies* 6, (1972), Canadian Association of African Studies.

power in exchange. Igbo women had a significant role in traditional political life. As individuals, they participated in village meetings with men. But their real political power was based on the solidarity of women, as expressed in their own political institutions—their "meetings" (*mikiri* or *mitiri*), their market networks, their kinship groups, and their right to use strikes, boycotts and force to effect their decisions.

British colonial officers and missionaries, both men and women, generally failed to see the political roles and the political power of Igbo women. The actions of administrators weakened and in some cases destroyed women's bases of strength. Since they did not appreciate women's political institutions, they made no efforts to ensure women's participation in the modern institutions they were trying to foster.

Igbo women haven't taken leadership roles in modern local government, nationalist movements and national government and what roles they *have* played have not been investigated by scholars. The purpose in describing their *traditional* political institutions and source of power is to raise the question of *why* these women have been "invisible" historically, even though they forced the colonial authorities to pay attention to them briefly. We suggest that the dominant view among British Colonial officers and missionaries was that politics was a man's concern. Socialized in Victorian England, they had internalized a set of values and attitudes about what they considered to be the natural and proper role of women that supported this belief. We suggest further that this assumption about men and politics has had a great deal to do with the fact that no one has even asked, "Whatever happened to Igbo women's organizations?" even though all the evidence needed to justify this question has been available for 30 years.

Igbo Tradtional Political Institutions[1]

Political power in Igbo society was *diffuse*. There were no specialized bodies or offices in which legitimate power was vested and no person, regardless of his status or ritual position, had the authority to issue *commands* which others had an obligation to obey. In line with this diffusion of authority, the right to enforce decisions was also diffuse: there was no "state" that held a monopoly of legitimate force, and the use of force to protect one's interests or to see that a group decision was carried out was considered legitimate for individuals and groups. In the simplest terms, the British tried to create specialized political institutions which commanded authority and monopolized force. In doing so they took into account, eventually, Igbo political institutions dominated by men but ignored those of the women. Thus, women were shut out from political power.

---

[1] The Igbo-speaking peoples are heterogeneous and can only be termed a "tribe" on the basis of a common language and a contiguous territory. They were the dominant group in southeastern Nigeria, during the colonial period numbering more than three million according to the 1931 census. The Igbo in Owerri and Calabar Provinces, the two southernmost provinces, were relatively homogeneous politically and it is their political institutions which are discussed here. Studies in depth were done of the Igbo only in the 1930s, but traditional political institutions survived "underneath" the native administration, although weakened more in some areas than in others. There were also many informants who remembered life in the pre-colonial days. The picture of Igbo society drawn here is based on reports by two Englishwomen, Leith-Ross and Green, who had a particular interest in Igbo women; the work of a government anthropological officer, Meek; a brief report by Harris; and the work of educated Igbo describing their own society, Uchendu and Onwuteaka. See M. M. Green, *Igbo Village Affairs* (London: Frank Cass & Co., Ltd., 1947: page citations to paperback edition, New York: Frederick A. Praeger, 1964); J. S. Harris, "The Position of Women in Nigerian Society," *Transactions of the New York Academy of Sciences,* Series II, Vol. 2, No. 5, 1940; Sylvia Leith-Ross, *African Women* (London: Faber and Faber, 1939); C. K. Meek, *Law and Authority in a Nigerian Tribe* (Oxford University Press, 1957, orig. published 1937); J. C. Onwuteaka, "The Aba Riot of 1929 and its Relation to the System of Indirect Rule," *The Nigerian Journal of Economical and Social Studies,* November 1965; Victor C. Uchendu, *The Igbo of Southeast Nigeria,* (New York: Holt, Rinehard and Winston, 1965).

The Igbo lived traditionally in semi-autonomous villages, which consisted of the scattered compounds of 75 or so patri-kinsmen; related villages formed "village-groups" which came together for limited ritual and jural purposes. Villages commonly contained several hundred people; but size varied, and in the more densely populated areas there were "village-groups" with more than 5,000 members.[2] Disputes at all the levels above the compound were settled by group discussion until mutual agreement was reached.[3]

The main Igbo political institution seems to have been the village assembly, a gathering of all adults in the village who chose to attend. Any adult who had something to say on the matter under discussion was entitled to speak—as long as he *or she* had something the others considered worth listening to; as the Igbo say, "a case forbids no one."[4]

Matters dealt with in the village assembly were those of concern to all—either common problems for which collective action was appropriate ("How can we make our markets 'bigger' than the other villages' markets?") or conflicts which threatened the unity of the village.[5]

Decisions agreed upon by the village assembly did not have the force of law in our terms, however. Even after decisions had been reached, social pressure based on consensus and the ability of individuals and groups to enforce decisions in their favour played a major part in giving the force of law to decisions. As Green[6] put it:

> (O)ne had the impression . . . that laws only establish themselves by degrees and then only in so far as they gain general acceptance. A law does not either exist or not exist: rather it goes through a process of establishing itself by common consent or of being shelved by a series of quiet evasions.

---

[2] Daryll Forde and G. I. Jones, *The Ibo- and Ibibio-Speaking Peoples of South-Eastern Nigeria* (London: International African Institute, 1950), p. 39; J. S. Harris, *op. cit.*, p. 141.

[3] Victor C. Uchendu, *op. cit.*, pp. 41–44.

[4] *Ibid.*, p. 41; M. M. Green, *op. cit.*, pp. 78–79.

[5] J. S. Harris, *op. cit.*, pp. 142–43; Victor C. Uchendu, *op. cit.*, pp. 34, 42–43.

[6] M. M. Green, *op. cit.*, p. 137.

Persuasion about the rightness of a particular course of action in terms of tradition was of primary importance in assuring its acceptance and the leaders were people who had the ability to persuade.

The mode of political discourse was that of proverb, parable and metaphor drawn from the body of Igbo tradition.[7] The needed political knowledge was accessible to the average man or woman, since all Igbo were reared with these proverbs and parables. Influential speech was the creative and skillful use of tradition to assure others that a certain course of action was both a wise and right thing to do. The accessibility of this knowledge is indicated by an Igbo proverb: "If you tell a proverb to a fool, he will ask you its meaning."

The leaders of Igbo society were men and women who combined wealth and generosity with "mouth"—the ability to speak well. Age combined with wisdom brought respect but age alone carried little influence. The senior elders who were ritual heads of their lineages were very likely to have considerable influence, but they would not have achieved these positions in the first place if they had not been considered to have good sense and good character.[8] Wealth in itself was no guarantee of influence: a "big man" or "big woman" was not necessarily a wealthy person, but one who had shown skill and generosity in helping other individuals and, especially, the community.[9]

Men owned the most profitable crops such as palm oil, received the bulk of the money from bride wealth, and, if compound heads, presents from the members. Through the patrilineage, they controlled the land, which they could lease to non-kinsmen or to women for a good profit. Men also did most of the long-distance trading

---

[7] The sources for this description are Uchendu and personal conversations with an Igbo born in Umu-Domi village of Onicha clan in Afikpo division who, however, went to mission schools from the age of seven and speaks Union Igbo rather than his village dialect.

[8] Victor C. Uchendu, *op. cit.,* p. 41.

[9] *Ibid.,* p. 34; C. K. Meek, *op. cit.,* p. 111.

which gave higher profit than local and regional trading which was almost entirely in women's hands.[10]

Women were entitled to sell the surplus of their own crops and the palm kernels which were their share of the palm produce. They might also sell prepared foods or the products of special skills, for instance, processed salt, pots and baskets. They pocketed the entire profit, but their relatively lower profit levels kept them disadvantaged relative to the men in acquiring titles and prestige.[11]

For women as well as for men, status was largely achieved, not ascribed. A woman's status was determined more *by her own achievements* than by the achievements of her husband. The resources available to men were greater, however; so that while a woman might rank higher among women than her husband did among men, very few women could acquire the highest titles, a major source of prestige.[12]

At village assemblies men were more likely to speak than were women; women more often spoke only on matters of direct concern to them.[13] Title-holders took leading parts in discussion, and were more likely to take part in "consultation." After a case had been thoroughly discussed, a few men retired in order to come to a decision. A spokesman then announced the decision, which could be accepted or rejected by the assembly.[14]

Apparently no rule forbade women to participate in consultations but they were invited to do so only rarely. The invited women were the older women, for while younger men might have the wealth to acquire the higher titles and thus make up in talent what they lacked in age, younger women could not acquire the needed wealth quickly enough to be eligible.[15]

Women, therefore, came second to men in power and influence. While status and the political influence it could bring were achieved

---

[10] M. M. Green, *op. cit.*, pp. 32–42.

[11] Sylvia Leith-Ross, *op. cit.*, pp. 90–92, 138–39, 143.

[12] C. C. Meek, *op. cit.*, p. 203; Victor C. Udiendu, *op. cit.*, p. 86.

[13] M. M. Green, *op. cit.*, p. 169.

[14] Victor C. Uchendu, *op. cit.*, p. 41.

[15] C. K. Meek, *op. cit.*, p. 203.

and there were no formal limits to women's political power, men through their ascriptive status (members of the patrilineage) acquired wealth which gave them a head start and a life-long advantage over women. The Igbo say that "a child who washes his hands clean deserves to eat with his elders."[16] But at birth some children were given water and some were not.

Women's Political Institutions

Since political authority was diffuse, the settling of disputes, discussions about how to improve the village or its market, or any other problems of general concern were brought up at various gatherings such as funerals, meetings of kinsmen to discuss burial rituals, and the marketplace, gatherings whose ostensible purpose was not political discussion.[17]

The women's base of political power lay in their own gatherings. Since Igbo society was patrilocal and villages were exogamous, adult women resident in a village would almost all be wives, and others were divorced or widowed "daughters of the village" who had returned home to live. Women generally attended age-set gatherings (*ogbo*) in their natal villages, performed various ritual functions, and helped to settle disputes among their "brothers."[18] But the gatherings which performed the major role in self-rule among women and which articulated women's interests as *opposed to* those of men were the village-wide gatherings of all adult women resident in a village which under colonialism came to be called *mikiri* or *mitiri* (from "meeting").[19]

Mikiri were held whenever there was a need.[20] In *mikiri* the same processes of discussion and consultation were used as in the village assembly. There were no official leaders; as in the village women of

---

[16] Victor Uchendu, *op. cit.*, p. 19.
[17] C. K. Meek, *op. cit.*, p. 125; M. M. Green, *op. cit.*, pp. 132–38.
[18] M. M. Green. *op. cit.*, pp. 217–32.
[19] Sylvia Leith-Ross, *op. cit.*, pp. 106–08.
[20] M. M. Green, *op. cit.*, pp. 178–216.

---

wealth and generosity who could speak well took leading roles. Decisions appear often to have been announced informally by wives telling their husbands. If the need arose, spokeswomen—to contact the men, or women in other villages—were chosen through general discussion. If the announcement of decisions and persuasion were not sufficient for their implementation, women could take direct action to enforce their decisions and protect their interests.[21]

Mikiri provided women with a forum in which to develop their political talents among a more egalitarian group than the village assembly. In *mikiri,* women could discuss their particular interests as traders, farmers, wives and mothers. These interests often were opposed to those of the men, and where individually women couldn't compete with men, collectively they could often hold their own.

One of the *mikiri's* most important functions was that of a market association, to promote and regulate the major activity of women: trading. At these discussions prices were set, rules established about market attendance, and fines fixed for those who violated the rules or who didn't contribute to market rituals. Rules were also made which applied to men. For instance, rowdy behavior on the part of young men was forbidden. Husbands and elders were asked to control the young men. If their requests were ignored, the women would handle the matter by launching a boycott or a strike to force the men to police themselves or they might decide to "sit on" the individual offender.[22]

"Sitting on a man" or a woman, boycotts and strikes were the women's main weapons. To "sit on" or "make war on" a man involved gathering at his compound, sometimes late at night, dancing, singing scurrilous songs which detailed the women's grievances against him and often called his manhood into question, banging on his hut with the pestles women used for pounding yams, and perhaps demolishing his hut or plastering it with mud and roughing him up a bit. A man might be sanctioned in this way for mistreating his wife, for violating the women's market rules, or for letting his cows eat the

---

[21] *Ibid.,* p. 180; Sylvia Leith-Ross, *op. cit.,* pp. 106–107.
[22] J. S. Harris, *op. cit.,* pp. 146–47.

women's crops. The women would stay at his hut throughout the day, and late into the night, if necessary, until he repented and promised to mend his ways.[23] Although this could hardly have been a pleasant experience for the offending man, it was considered legitimate and no man would consider intervening.

In tackling men as a group, women used boycotts and strikes. Harris describes a case in which, after repeated requests by the women for the paths to the market to be cleared (a male responsibility), all the women refused to cook for their husbands until the request was carried out.[24] For this boycott to be effective, all women had to cooperate so that men could not go and eat with their brothers. Another time the men of a village decided that the women should stop trading at the more distant markets from which they did not return until late at night because the men feared that the women were having sexual relations with men in those towns. The women, however, refused to comply since opportunity to buy in one market and sell in another was basic to profit-making. Threats of collective retaliation were enough to make the men capitulate.

As farmers, women's interests conflicted with those of the men as owners of much of the larger livestock—cows, pigs, goats and sheep. The men's crop, yams, had a short season and was then dug up and stored, after which the men tended to be careless about keeping their livestock out of the women's crops. Green reports a case in which the women of the village swore an oath that if any woman killed a cow or other domestic animal on her farm the others would stand by her.[25]

A woman could also bring complaints about her husband to the mikiri. If most of the women agreed that the husband was at fault, they would collectively support her. They might send spokeswomen to tell the husband to apologize and to give her a present, and, if he

[23] Ibid., pp. 146–48; M. M. Green, op. cit., pp. 196–97; Sylvia Leith-Ross, op. cit., p. 109.
[24] J. S. Harris, op. cit., pp. 146–147.
[25] M. M. Green, op. cit., pp. 210–11.

was recalcitrant they might "sit on" him. They might also act to protect a right of wives. Harris describes a case of women's solidarity to maintain sexual freedom:

> The men . . . were very angry because their wives were openly having relations with their lovers. The men . . . met and passed a law to the effect that every woman . . . should renounce her lover and present a goat to her husband as a token of repentance. . . . The women held . . . secret meetings and a few mornings later they went to a neighboring [village], leaving all but suckling children behind them. . . . The men endured it for a day and a half and then they went to the women and begged their return . . . [T]he men gave [the women] one goat and apologized informally and formally.[26]

Thus through *mikiri* women acted to force a resolution of their individual and collective grievances.

COLONIAL PENETRATION

Into this system of diffuse authority, fluid and informal leadership, shared rights of enforcement, and a more or less stable balance of male and female power, the British tried to introduce ideas of native administration derived from colonial experience with chiefs and emirs in northern Nigeria. Southern Nigeria was declared a protectorate in 1900 but it was ten years before the conquest was effective. As colonial power was established in what the British perceived as a situation of "ordered anarchy," Igboland was divided into Native Court Areas which violated the autonomy of villages by lumping many unrelated villages into each court area. British District Officers were to preside over the courts but were not always present as there were more courts than officers. The Igbo membership was formed by choosing from each village a "representative" who was given a warrant of office. These Warrant Chiefs also constituted the Native Authority. They were required to see that the orders of the

---

[26] J. S. Harris, *op. cit.*, pp. 146–47.

District Officers were executed in their own villages and were the only link between the colonial power and the people.[27]

It was a violation of Igbo concepts to have one man represent the village in the first place and more of a violation that he should give orders to everyone else. The people obeyed the Warrant Chief when they had to, since British power backed him up. In some places Warrant Chiefs were lineage heads or wealthy men who were already leaders in the village. But in many places they were simply ambitious, opportunistic young men who put themselves forward as friends of the conquerors. Even the relatively less corrupt Warrant Chief was still more than anything else an agent of the British.[28]

The people avoided using Native Courts when they could do so. But Warrant Chiefs could force cases into the Native Courts and could fine people for infractions of rules. By having the ear of the British, the Warrant Chief could himself violate traditions and even British rules and get away with it since his version would be believed.[29]

Women suffered particularly under the arbitrary rule of Warrant Chiefs, who were reported as having taken women to marry without conforming to the customary process which included the woman's right to refuse a particular suitor. They also helped themselves to the women's agricultural produce and to their domestic animals.[30]

Recommendations for reform of the system were made almost from its inception both by junior officers in the field and by senior officers sent out from headquarters to investigate. But no real improvements were made.[31]

---

[27] Daryll Forde, "Justice and Judgment among the Southern Ibo under Colonial Rule" unpublished paper prepared for Interdisciplinary Colloquium in African Studies, University of Califorifia, Los Angeles, pp. 9–13.

[28] *Ibid.*, pp. 9–13; J. C. Anene, *Southern Nigeria in Transition, 1885–1906* (New York: The Cambridge, University Press, 1967), p. 259; C. K. Meek, *op. cit.*, pp. 328–30.

[29] Daryll Forde, *op. cit.*, p. 12.

[30] J. C. Onwuteaka, *op. cit.*, p. 274.

[31] C. K. Meek, *op. cit.*, pp. 329–30; Harry A. Gailey, *The Road to Aba* (New York: New York University Press, 1970), pp. 66–74.

ABA AND THE WOMEN'S WAR

The Native Administration in the years before 1929 took little account of either men's or women's political institutions. In 1929, women in southern Igboland became convinced that they were to be taxed by the British. This fear on top of their resentment of the Warrant Chiefs led to what the British called the Aba Riots and the Igbo Women's War. The rebellion provides perhaps the most striking example of British blindness to the political institutions of Igbo women. The women, "invisible" to the British as they laid their plans, for Native Administration, suddenly became highly visible for a few months, but as soon as they quieted down, they were once again ignored and the reforms made in Native Administration took no account of them politically.[32]

In 1925 Igbo men paid taxes, although during the census count on which the tax was based the British had denied that there was to be any taxation. Taxes were collected without too much trouble. By 1929, the prices for palm products had fallen, however, and the taxes, set at 1925 levels, were an increasingly resented burden.[33] In the midst of this resentment, an overzealous Assistant District Officer in Owerri Province decided to update the census registers by recounting households and household property, which belonged to women. Understandably, the women did not believe his assurances that new taxes were not to be invoked. They sent messages through the market and kinship networks to other villages and called a *mikiri* to decide what to do.

---

[32] Information on the Women's War is derived mainly from Gailey and Perham, who based their descriptions on the reports of the two Commissions of Enquiry, issued as Sessional Papers of the Nigerian Legislative Council, Nos. 12 and 28 of 1930, and the Minutes of Evidence issued with the latter. Gailey also used the early 1930's Intelligence Reports of political officers. Meek and Afigbo also provided quotations from the reports, which were not, unfortunately, available to me in full. See Margery Perman, *Native Administration in Nigeria* (London: Oxford University Press, 1937); Idem, *Lugard: The Years of Adventure, 1858–1898* (London: Collins, 1960); A. E. Afigbo, "Igbo Village Affairs," *Journal of the Historical Society Nigeria*, 4: December 1967.

[33] Harry A. Gailey, *op. cit.*, pp. 94–95; C. K. Meek, *op. cit.*, pp. 330–31.

In the Oloko Native Court area of Owerri Province, the women decided that as long as only men were approached in a compound and asked for information, the women would do nothing. They wanted clear evidence that they were to be taxed before they acted.[34] If any woman was approached, she was to raise the alarm and they would meet to discuss retaliation.

On November 23, the agent of the Oloko Warrant Chief, Okugo, entered a compound and told a married woman, Nwanyeruwa, to count her goats and sheep. She retorted angrily "Was your mother counted?" Thereupon "they closed, seizing each other by the throat."[35] Nwanyeruwa's report to the Oloko women convinced them that they were to be taxed. Messengers were sent to neighboring areas. Women streamed into Oloko from all over Owerri Province. They massed in protest at the district office and after several days of protest meetings succeeded in obtaining written assurances that they were not to be taxed, and in getting Okugo arrested. Subsequently he was tried and convicted of physically assaulting women and of spreading news likely to cause alarm. He was sentenced to two years' imprisonment.[36]

News of this victory spread rapidly through the market *mikiri* network, and women in 16 Native Court areas attempted to get rid of their Warrant Chiefs as well as the Native Administration itself. Tens of thousands of women became involved, generally using the same traditional tactics, though not with the same results as in Oloko. In each Native Court area, the women marched on Native Administration centers and demanded the Warrant Chiefs' caps of office and assurances that they would not be taxed. In some areas the District Officers assured the women to their satisfaction that they were not to be taxed and the women dispersed without further incident. But the British in general stood behind the Warrant Chiefs; at that point they interpreted the women's rebellion as motivated solely

---

[34] Harry A. Gailey, *op. cit.*, pp. 107–08.
[35] Margery Perham, *Native Administration in Nigeria, op. cit.*, p. 207.
[36] Harry A. Gailey, *op. cit.*, pp. 108–13.

by fear of taxation, and Oloko was the only area in which a Warrant Chief had directly provoked the women's fears of taxation by counting their property.

Women in most areas did not get full satisfaction from the British, and, further, some British district officers simply panicked when faced by masses of angry women and acted in ways which made negotiation impossible.

In most of the Native Court areas affected, women took matters into their own hands—they "sat on" Warrant Chiefs and burned Native Court buildings, and, in some cases, released prisoners from jail. Among the buildings burned were those at Aba, a major administrative center from which the British name for the rebellion is derived. Large numbers of police and soldiers, and on one occasion Boy Scouts, were called in to quell the "disturbances." On two occasions, clashes between the women and the troops left more than 50 women dead and 50 wounded from gunfire. The lives taken were those of women only—no men, Igbo or British, were even seriously injured. The cost of property damage—estimated at more than £60,000, was paid for by the Igbo, who were heavily taxed to pay for rebuilding the Native Administration centers.[37]

The rebellion lasted about a month. By late December, "order" was somewhat restored but sporadic disturbances and occupation by government troops continued into 1930. In all, the rebellion extended over an area of six thousand square miles, all of Owerri and Calabar Provinces, containing about two million people.[38]

The British generally saw the rebellion as "irrational" and called it a series of "riots." They discovered that the market network had been used to spread the rumors of taxation, but they did not inquire further into the concerted action of the women, the grassroots leadership, the agreement on demands, or even into the fact that thousands of women showed up at native administration centers dressed

---

[37] S. O. Eskie, "The Aba Riots of 1929," *African Historian*, Vol. 1. No. 3 (1965): 13; J. S. Harris, *op. cit.*, p. 143; Margery Perham, *Native Administration in Nigeria, op. cit.*, pp. 209–12.

[38] Harry A. Gailey, *op. cit.*, p. 137; Margery Perham, *Native Administration in Nigeria, op. cit.*, pp. 209–12.

in the same unusual way: wearing short loincloths, their faces smeared with charcoal or ashes, their heads bound with young ferns, and in their hands carrying sticks wreathed with young palms.[39]

In exonerating the soldiers who fired on the women, a Commission of Enquiry spoke of the "savage passions" of the "mobs," and one military officer told the Commission that "he had never seen crowds in such a state of frenzy." Yet these "frenzied mobs" injured no one seriously, which the British found "surprising."[40]

It is not surprising if the Women's War is seen as the traditional practice of "sitting on a man," only on a larger scale. Decisions were made in *mikiri* to respond to a situation in which women were acutely wronged by the Warrant Chiefs' corruption and by the taxes they believed to be forthcoming. Spokeswomen were chosen to present their demands for the removal of the Warrant Chiefs and women followed their leadership, on several occasions sitting down to wait for negotiations or agreeing to disperse or to turn in Warrant Chiefs' caps.[41] Traditional dress rituals and "weapons" for "sitting on" were used: the head wreathed with young ferns symbolized war, and sticks, bound with ferns or young palms, were used to involve the powers of the female ancestors.[42] The women's behavior also followed traditional patterns: much noise, stamping, preposterous threats and a general raucous atmosphere were all part of the institution of "sitting on a man." Destroying an offender's hut—in this case the Native Court buildings—was clearly within the bounds of this sanctioning process.

The Women's War was coordinated throughout the two provinces by information sent through the market *mikiri* network. Delegates travelled from one area to another and the costs were paid by donations from the women's market profits.[43] Traditional rules were

---

[39] J. S. Harris, *op. cit.*, pp. 147–48; Margery Perham, *Native Administration in Nigeria, op. cit.*, pp. 107ff.; C. K. Meek, *op. cit.*, p. IX.

[40] Margery Perham, *Native Administration in Nigeria, op. cit.*, pp. 212–19.

[41] *Ibid.*, pp. 212ff.

[42] Harris reports a curse sworn by the women on the pestles: "It is I who gave birth to you. It is I who cook for you to eat. This is the pestle I use to pound yams and coco yams for you to eat. May you soon die!" See J. S. Harris, *op. cit.*, pp. 143–45.

---

followed in that the participants were women—only a few men were involved in the demonstrations—and leadership was clearly in the hands of women.

The absence of men from the riots does not indicate lack of support. Men generally approved, and only a few older men criticized the women for not being more respectful toward the government. It is reported that both men and women shared the mistaken belief that the women, having observed certain rituals, would not be fired upon. The men had no illusions of immunity for themselves, having vivid memories of the slaughter of Igbo men during the conquest.[44] Finally the name given the rebellion by the Igbo—the Women's War—indicates that the women saw themselves following their traditional sanctioning methods of "sitting on" or "making war on" a man.

Since the British failed to recognized the Women's War as a collective response to the abrogation of rights, they did not inquire into the kinds of structures the women had that prepared them for such action. They failed to ask, "How do the women make group decisions? How do they choose their leaders?" Since they saw only a "riot," they explained the fact that the women injured no one seriously as "luck," never even contemplating that perhaps the women's actions had traditional limits.

Because the women—and the men—regarded the inquiries as attempts to discover whom to punish, they did not volunteer any information about the women's organizations. But there is at least some question as to whether the British would have understood them if they had. The market network was discovered, but suggested no further lines of inquiry to the British. The majority of District Officers thought that the men organized the women's actions and were secretly directing them. The Bende District Officer and the Secretary of the Southern Province believed that there was a secret "Ogbo Society" which exercised control over women and was responsible

---

[43] Harry A. Gailey, *op. cit.*, p. 112.

[44] Margery Perham, *Native Administration in Nigeria, op. cit.*, 212ff; J. C. Anene, *op. cit.*, pp. 207–24; S. O. Esike, *op. cit., p.* 11; C. K. Meek, *op. cit.*, p. x.

---

for fomenting the rebellion.[45] *The women's demands that they did not want the Native Court to hear cases any longer and that all white men should go to their own country, or, at least, that women should serve on the Native Courts and one be appointed District Officer—demands in line with the power of women in traditional society—were ignored.*[46]

All these responses fell into a pattern: not of purposeful discrimination against women with the intent of keeping them from playing their traditional political roles, but of a prevailing blindness to the possibility that women had *had* a significant role in traditional politics and should participate in the new system of local government. A few political officers were "of the opinion that, if the balance of society is to be kept, the women's organizations should be encouraged alongside those of the men."[47] Some commissioners even recognized "the remarkable character of organization and leadership which some of the women displayed" and recommended that more attention be paid to the political influence of women.[48] But these men were the exception: their views did not prevail. Even in the late 1930's when the investigations of Leith-Ross and Green revealed the decreasing vitality of women's organizations under colonialism, the British still did not include women in the reformed Native Administration. When political officers warned that *young men* were being excluded, however, steps were taken to return their traditional political status.[49]

"Reforms" and Women's Loss of Power

In 1933 reforms were enacted to redress many Igbo grievances against the Native Administration. The number of Native Court Areas was greatly increased and their boundaries arranged to conform roughly to traditional divisions. Warrant Chiefs were replaced by

---

[45] Harry A. Gailey, *op. cit.*, pp. 130ff.
[46] Sylvia Leith-Ross, *op. cit.*, p. 165; Margery Perham, Native Administration in Nigeria, *op. cit.*, pp. 165ff.
[47] Margery Perham, *Native Administration in Nigeria, op. cit.*, p. 246.
[48] A. E. Afigbo, *op. cit.*, p. 187.
[49] C. K. Meek, *op. cit.*, p. 336.

"massed benches"—allowing large numbers of judges to sit at one time. In most cases it was left up to the village to decide whom and how many to send.[50] This benefitted the women by eliminating the corruption of the Warrant Chiefs, and it made their persons and property more secure. But it provided no outlet for collective action, their real base of power.

As in the village assembly, the women could not compete with the men for leadership in the reformed Native Administration because as individuals they lacked the resources of the men.[51] In the various studies done on the Igbo in the 1930's, there is only one report of a woman being sent to the Native Court and her patri-lineage had put up the money for her to take her titles.[52]

Since the reformed Native Administration usually took over many functions of the village assemblies, women's political partici-pation was seriously affected. Discussions on policy no longer included any adult who wished to take part but only members of the native courts. Men who were not members were also excluded, but men's interests and point of view were represented, and, at one time or another, many men had some chance to become members; very few women ever did.[53]

The political participation and power of women had depended on the diffuseness of political power and authority within Igbo soci-ety. In attempting to create specialized political institutions on the Western model with participation on the basis of individual achieve-ment, the British created a system in which there was no place for group solidarity, no place for what thereby became "extra-legal" or

---

[50] Margery Perham, *Native Administration in Nigeria, op. cit.,* pp. 365ff.

[51] C. K. Meek, *op. cit.,* p. 203.

[52] *Ibid.,* pp. 158–159. She was divorced and had to remain unmarried as a condi-tion of her family's paying for her title as they wanted to be sure to get their invest-ment back when future initiates paid their fees to the established members. If she remarried, her husband's family, and not her own, would inherit her property.

[53] Sylvia Leith-Ross, *op. cit.,* pp. 171–72; Lord Hailey, *Native Administration in the British African Territories, Part III, West Africa* (London: H. M. Stationary Office, 1951), pp. 160–65.

---

simply illegal forms of group coercion, and thus very little place for women.

The British reforms undermined and weakened the power of the women by removing many political functions from *mikiri* and from village assemblies. In 1901 the British had declared all jural institutions except the Native Courts illegitimate, but it was only in the years following the 1933 reforms that Native Administration local government became effective enough to make that declaration meaningful. When this happened, the *mikiri* lost vitality,[54] although what has happened to them since has not been reported in detail. The reports that do exist mention the functioning of market women's organizations but only as pressure groups for narrow economic interest[55] and women's participation in Igbo unions as very low in two towns.[56]

The British also weakened women's power by outlawing "self-help"—the use of force by individuals or groups to protect their own interests by punishing wrongdoers. This action—in accord with the idea that only the state may legitimately use force—made "sitting on" anyone illegal, thereby depriving women of one of their best weapons to protect wives from husbands, markets from rowdies, or coco yams from cows.[57]

The British didn't know, of course, that they were banning "sitting on a man"; they were simply banning the "illegitimate" use of force. In theory, this didn't hurt the women, as wife-beaters, rowdies and owners of marauding cows could be taken to court. But courts were expensive, and the men who sat in them were likely to have different views from the women's on wife-beating, market "fun" and men's cows. By interfering with the traditional balance of power, the British effectively eliminated the women's ability to protect their

---

[54] Sylvia Leith-Ross, *op. cit.*, pp. 110, 163, 214.

[55] Henry L. Bretton, "Political Influence in Southern Nigeria," in Herbert J. Spiro (ed.), *Africa: The Primacy of Politics* (New York: Random House, 1966), p. 61.

[56] Audrey C. Smock, *Ibo Politics: The Role of Ethnic Unions in Eastern Nigeria* (Cambridge: The Harvard University Press, 1971), pp. 65,137.

[57] Sylvia Leith-Ross, *op. cit.*, p. 109.

---

own interests and made them dependent upon men for protection against men.

Since the British did not understand this, they did nothing to help women develop new ways of protecting their interests within the political system. (What the women *did* do to try to protect their interests in this situation should be a fruitful subject for study.) What women did *not* do was to participate to any significant extent in local government or, much later, in national government, and a large part of the responsibility must rest on the British, who removed legitimacy from women's traditional political institutions and did nothing to help women move into modern political institutions.

MISSIONARY INFLUENCE

The effect of the colonial administration was reinforced by the missionaries and mission schools. Christian missions were established in Igboland in the late 19th century. They had few converts at first, but their influence by the 1930's was considered significant, generally among the young.[58] A majority of Igbo eventually "became Christians"—they had to profess Christianity in order to attend mission schools, and education was highly valued. But regardless of how nominal their membership was, they had to obey the rules to remain in good standing, and one rule was to avoid "pagan" rituals. Women were discouraged from attending *mikiri* where traditional rituals were performed or money collected for the rituals, which in effect meant all *mikiri*.[59]

---

[58] *Ibid.,* pp. 109–18; C. K. Meek, *op. cit.,* p. xv. Maxwell states that by 1925 there were 26 mission stations and 63 missionaries (twelve of them missionary wives) in Igboland. The earliest station was established in 1857, but all but three were founded after 1900. Fifteen mission stations and 30 missionaries were among Igbo in Owerri and Calabar Provinces. See J. Lowry Maxwell, *Nigeria:The Land, the People and Christian Progress* (London: World Dominion Press, 1926), pp. 150–52.

[59] Sylvia Leith-Ross, *op. cit.,* p. 110; J. F. Ade Ajayi, *Christian Missions in Nigeria, 1841–1891:The Making of a New Elite* (Evanston, Ill.: The Northwestern University Press, 1965), pp. 108–09.

Probably more significant, since *mikiri* were in the process of losing some of their political functions anyway, was mission education. English and Western education came to be seen as increasingly necessary for political leadership—needed to deal with the British and their law—and women had less access to this new knowledge than men. Boys were more often sent to school, for a variety of reasons generally related to their favored position in the patrilineage.[60] But even when girls did go, they tended not to receive the same type of education. In mission schools, and increasingly in special "training homes" which dispensed with most academic courses, the girls were taught European domestic skills and the Bible, often in the vernacular. The missionaries' avowed purpose in educating girls was to train them to be Christian wives and mothers, not for jobs or for citizenship.[61] Missionaries were not necessarily against women's participation in politics—clergy in England, as in America, could be found supporting women's suffrage. But in Africa their concern was the church, and for the church they needed Christian families. Therefore, Christian wives and mothers, not female political leaders, was the missions' aim. As Mary Slessor, the influential Calabar missionary, said: "God-like motherhood is the finest sphere for women, and the way to the redemption of the world."[62]

---

[60] Sylvia Leith-Ross, *op. cit.*, pp. 133, 196–97, 316.

[61] *Ibid.*, pp. 189–90. According to Leith-Ross, in the "girls' training homes . . . the scholastic education given was limited, in some of the smaller homes opened at a later date almost negligible, but the domestic training and the general civilizing effect were good." Evidence of these views among missionaries can be found in J. F. Ade Ajayi, *op. cit.*, pp. 67, 142–44; G. T. Basden, *Edith Sarner of the Niger* (London: Seeley, Service and Co., Ltd., 1927), pp. 13, 16, 33, 55, 77, 86; Josephine C. Bulifant, *Forty Years in the African Bush* (Grand Rapids, Mich.: Zondervan Publishing House, 1950), pp. 163 and *passim;* W. P. Livingstone, *Mary Slessor of Calabar* (New York: George H. Doran Co., n.d.), pp. iii–vi; J. Lowry Maswell, *op. cit.*, pp. 55, 118.

[62] W. P. Livingstone, *op. cit.*, p. 328.

Victorianism and Women's Invisibility

The missionaries' beliefs about woman's natural and proper role being that of a Christian helpmate, and the administration's refusal to take the Igbo women seriously when they demanded political participation, are understandable in light of the colonialists having been socialized in a society dominated by Victorian values. It was during Queen Victoria's reign that the woman's-place-is-in-the-home ideology hardened into its most recent highly rigid form.[63] Although attacked by feminists, it remained the dominant mode of thought through that part of the colonial period discussed here; and it is, in fact, far from dead today, when a woman's primary identity is most often seen as that of wife and mother even when she works 40 hours a week outside the home.[64]

We are concerned here primarily with the Victorian view of women and politics which produced the expectation that men would be active in politics, but women would not. The ideal of Victorian womanhood-attainable, of course, by only the middle class, but widely believed in throughout society-was of a sensitive, morally superior being who was the hearthside guardian of Christian virtues and sentiments absent in the outside world. Her mind was not strong enough for the appropriately masculine subjects: science, business, and politics.[65] A woman who showed talent in these areas did not challenge any ideas about typical women: the exceptional woman simply "had the brain of a man," as Sir George Goldie said of Mary Kingsley.[66]

A thorough investigation of the diaries, journals, reports, and letters of colonial officers and missionaries would be needed to prove that most of them held these Victorian values. But preliminary reading of biographies, autobiographies, journals and "reminiscences," and the evidence of their own statements about Igbo women at the

---

[63] Page Smith, *Daughters of the Promised Land* (Boston: Little, Brown and Co. 1970).
[64] Eva Figes, *Patriarchal Attitudes* (New York: Stein and Day, 1970); Ruth E. Hartley, "Children's Concepts of Male and Female Roles", *Merrill-Palmer Quarterly*, January 1960.

time of the Women's War, strongly suggest the plausibility of the hypothesis that they were deflected from any attempt to discover and protect Igbo women's political role by their assumption that politics isn't a proper, normal place for women.[65]

When Igbo women with their Women's War forced the colonial administrators to recognize their presence, their brief "visibility" was insufficient to shake these assumptions. Their behavior was simply seen as aberrant. When they returned to "normal," they were once again invisible. Although there was a feminist movement in England during that time, it had not successfully challenged basic ideas about women nor made the absence of women from public life seem to be a problem which required remedy. The movement had not succeeded in creating a "feminist" consciousness in any but a few "deviants," and such a consciousness is far from widespread today;

---

[65] Walter E. Houghton, *The Victorian Frame of Mind, 1830–1870* (New Haven: The Yale University Press, 1957), pp. 349–53. Numerous studies of Victorian and post-Victorian ideas about women and politics describe these patterns. In addition to Houghton, Smith and Stenton, see, for example, Kirsten Amundsen, *The Silenced Majority* (Prentice-Hall, 1970); and Harriet Taylor Mill, *Essays on Sex Equality* (University of Chicago Press, 1970); Martha Vicinus (ed.), *Suffer and Be Still: Women in the Victorian Age* (Indiana University Press, 1972); Cecil Woodham-Smith, *Florence Nightingale, 1820–1910* (McGraw-Hill, 1951). It was not until 1929 that all English women could vote; women over 30 who met restrictive property qualifications got the vote in 1918.

[66] Stephen Gwynn, *The Life of Mary Kingsley* (London: Macmillan and Co., Ltd., 1932), p. 252. Mary Kingley, along with other elite female "exceptions" like Flora Shaw Lugard and Pargery, all of whom influenced African colonial policy, held the same values as men, at least in regard to women's roles. They did not expect ordinary women to have political power any more than the men did, and they showed no particular concern for African women.

[67] See, for non-missionary examples, J. C. Anene, *op. cit.*, pp. 222–34; W. R. Crocker, *Nigeria: a Critique of British Colonial Administration* (London: George Allen and Unwin, Ltd., 1936); C. K. Meek, *op. cit.*; Mary H. Kingsley, *Travels in West Africa* (London: Macmillan and Co., Ltd., 1897); Idem, *West African Studies* (London: Macmillan and Co;, Ltd., 1899); Margery Perham, *op. cit.*; A. H. St. John Wood, "Nigeria: Fifty Years of Political Development among the Ibos," in Raymond Apthorpe (ed.), *From Tribal Rule to Modern Government* (Lusaka, Northern Rhodesia: Rhodes-Livingstone Institute for Social Research, 1960).

---

for to have a "feminist" consciousness means that one *notices* the "invisibility" of women.

Understanding the assumptions about women's roles prevalent in Victorian society—and still common today—helps to explain how the introduction of supposedly modern political structures and values could reduce rather than expand the political lives of Igbo women. As long as politics is presumed to be a male realm, no one wonders where the women went. The loss of Igbo women's political institutions—in life and in print—shows the need for more Western scholars to develop enough of a feminist consciousness to start wondering.

Hausa Dilemma Tales

🔳 *The traditional dilemma tales belong to the Hausa of Northern Nigeria. Instrumental in the ethical upbringing of the youth, the stories are part of the oral culture, and they illustrate how Islam as well as older traditions inform ethical conduct among the Hausa. Typically told during evening gatherings, each tale develops a complicated human situation and ends with an irresolute dilemma for both the protagonist and the young listeners. In "Who Should He Kill?" for instance, a son is asked to kill either his natural father or his adoptive father. The purpose of the dilemma tales is not so much to "teach" correct ethical behavior as it is to engage youngsters in a lively discussion about ethical values among themselves so that they seek and understand the right and the wrong through collective reasoning. More specifically, the tales demonstrate two crucial aspects of ethical decision-making: that it takes place in a public context, and that understanding the subtle difficulties of a human situation is, at the least, as important as passing judgment on its ethical correctness.*

Aron Aji

Who Should He Kill?

There was once a man who did no other job but digging out pesky ground squirrels. Taking his son to work with him one day, he said, "You stop up the back entrances, and I'll dig." But when the father set about digging in the ground squirrel's hole, the ground squirrel came out where the son was, and made off. Then the father hit his son and with the handle of his hoe and knocked him senseless.

A little later in the evening, up came an Arab taking a stroll, and he saw the son of the squirrel digger, who was just coming to his senses. Now this Arab had never had any children, so he picked up the boy and took him home. His nose was dirty and full of ants, and the Arab wiped them away and had him bathed in hot water. When the boy recovered completely, the Arab dressed him in a black and white gown, embroidered trousers, and a heavily indigoed gown, as well, with a turban twenty cubits long and twenty strips wide.

Now in this area, the rich merchants' sons used to ride and compete at the racetrack. The Arab brought out a saddle ornamented in gold and silver, with brass stirrups from Tripoli, and all the other trappings for a horse. Then he told the boy to mount up, and said to him, "When you get to the track, whatever you see the other riders do—you do it, too!" So the boy joined the rich merchants' sons and went along with them. Some great arguments arose among the people over whose son he was, but no one knew the truth.

When the merchants' sons got home, each one said to his father, "There's an Arab who has a son who has more finery than we have." And their fathers answered, "No, it's not really his son. That's false." But they added, "All the same, we will test him. Tomorrow when you go riding with him, let each one give away his horse and equipment before he comes home. Then we'll see! For generosity is the way to demonstrate true wealth."

So the sons went out the next day, and afterwards they gave away their horses. And watching carefully, the Arab's boy, too, gave away his horse.

After this, the merchants gave their sons other horses, each worth a million cowries, and told them, "When you go riding, before you come home, cut down your horses!" And the Arab's boy was given a horse worth ten million. When they had had their gallop, each one took his sword and cut down his horse. Then the Arab's boy, without even troubling to take the saddle off, cut down his horse and went off home. And they said, "Did you see? He cut down his horse," and again, "Well! The Arab's boy didn't even take off the horse's equipment; he left it there." Then people said, "So it seems he is his son after all!"

Time passed and the Muslim festival was at hand. In the morning, the usual mounted procession took place, and in all the town, there wasn't a youth whose horse was fitted out to touch the Arab's. And as they were coming back from the mosque, they passed among the common people who had come from the country into the town for prayers.

Well, it happened that the squirrel digger, the real father of the boy, had come to town for the festival and had joined the crowd. When he saw his son, he exclaimed, "Hey! Get down from that horse—you know it's not your own father's, you rascal! Look at your brothers there—one of them has killed nine ground squirrels, one of them ten, and you—here are you in dissipation and idleness!" And the Arab said to him, "Please, please keep it to yourself! Here—take your son!"

And in the evening, the Arab chose two horses and saddled them up, picked out two gowns, a black one and a white one, and gave them to the boy's father. And the Arab gave him twenty thousand cowry shells and provisions for the journey. Then all three mounted up and rode out.

They left the town and came into the bush. Suddenly, the Arab produced a sword and gave it to the boy, saying, "Now! Either me or your father—cut down one of us!"

Well that's the question—the Arab, who had given him so many things? Or his own father, who had struck him unconscious because of the ground squirrel? Which should he kill?

An Eye for an Eye?

The son of a chief once heard tell of the beautiful daughter of another chief and set off to visit her. And as he traveled, he met a young fellow. He said, "Young man, I'd like you to come with me, for I'm off to seek a wife." "Oh, no," said the other, "for I have a father who has nothing, neither gown nor trousers nor loincloth; and this leather loincloth that you see me wearing is all that we have between us, my father and I. If my father is going out from our hole in the baobab tree, then he takes it and puts it on; and I do the same when I'm going out." "Where is your father?" asked the chief's son. "Over there, in the hole in the baobab tree." And the chief's son asked to be taken to him.

And off they went. When the boy got to the hole in the baobab tree, he said "Daddy, look! I was out walking, I met the son of a chief who said he wanted me to go with him to seek a wife. But I answered that I must come and tell you first and hear whatever you had to say about it." "By all means go along with him," answered his father. And the chief's son said, "Take the leather loincloth off and give it to your father." And the chief's son had a traveling bag opened and a gown taken out, and trousers, and a turban, and a cap, and a sword, and sword sling, and all these together were given to the other. And he had him shaved and bathed, too.

And so they took the road and traveled till they reached the other town. When word was brought to the chief's daughter that she had visitors, they were taken to lodgings. She had food prepared for them—three rams were slaughtered, and chickens, too.

Soon the chief's daughter rose and came to them. But when she got there, her heart went out to the servant of the chief's son, he whose father lived in the hole of the tree. And she spoke and said that he was the one she loved. "No, no!" he said, "I wouldn't dare. See, here's my master." "No," she answered, "You're the one I love." But again he protested that he and his father had nothing, but lived in a hole in baobab tree, and added, "Even the clothes that I'm wearing were given me by the chief's son here." "Oh," she replied, "is that all?"

She sent home to her father's compound, asking for two carrying bags, one with a gown, and one with trousers; and she sent for a turban, as well. All her wishes were conveyed to her father, who got together everything she had asked for, and handed it over to her. Then she said, "Take those things off, and return them to him. Take these and put them on." "Very well," he answered, and did as she had said. He collected the chief's son's clothes, and returned them to him.

So the chief's son set off home alone, leaving the son of the man with the leather loincloth. For the chief's daughter had decided it was he that she loved. Then she went and told her father, saying, "Father, today I want to be married." "Very well," he said, and so they were married.

Time passed and her father died. His large estate was duly divided and she inherited it all as he had no sons or other daughters. Her mother left the chief's compound and had a separate compound built for herself. Then the girl said to her husband, "Where is your father? Let someone go and fetch him, and let him and my mother be married." And he answered, "He's back there in the hole in the baobab tree."

They went and fetched him, and when they returned, the marriage duly took place and so they lived for some time.

But after a while there came a time when the elder couple had a quarrel and the father of the girl's husband knocked his wife down, striking out one of her eyes. The girl then said, angrily, "Your father has quarreled with my mother and knocked her eye out. If you value our marriage, you'll go and put out one of your father's eyes. If you don't, take your leather loincloth, and you and your father can go back to your hole in the baobab tree. But if you do, then let our marriage continue." Well, here was a nice problem! He had been quite destitute. If he put out his own father's eye, he might continue to live with his wife; but if he didn't, then he must go back with his father to the hole in the baobab tree, whence they had come!

The Devil Comes between Them

A youth once saw a maiden and told her that he loved her; she saw him and told him the same. So the young fellow went and picked up his sleeping mat, took the girl by the hand, and went off with her into the bush. There the boy spread out the mat and invited the girl to sit. The two sat and chatted. *Iblis* the devil came by that way, seized the boy, killed him, and then cut off his head. The girl could do nothing but sit on the mat and lament.

Meanwhile both mothers and both fathers were searching for their son and daughter. An old woman told them where they should look for them. Thanking her, they went quickly off down the road, where, the boy's parents found their son killed, with his head taken off. At this, they began to lament, as well.

Suddenly, up came *Iblis* again. He made a river of fire, and a river of water, and a river of black-hooded cobras, and in this last he placed a land monitor. Then he went up to the group—the girl's mother and her father, and the boy's mother and his father, and the girl herself—and said to them, "Would you like me to help you recover your son and bring him back to life?" "Of course!" they answered. "Very well," he said, "You, the boy's mother, must go into the river of fire, and then into the river of water, and then into the river of cobras, where you must seize the land monitor and bring it out." But the boy's mother answered, "No! I'm not going into a river of fire to be burnt up, nor am I going into the river of cobras, to be thoroughly bitten." *Iblis* said, "Had you gone and captured the land monitor, I'd have helped you with your son."

Whereupon the girl said, "Is that so? If that land monitor is captured and brought here, will the boy come to life?" "Yes," said *Iblis*. Up jumped the girl and swam across the river of fire. Then she plunged into the river of water and swam till she was through it. Then into the river of cobras, where pushing aside the slithering snakes, she seized the land monitor. Back she came through the rivers, and handed the lizard to *Iblis*.

Then, said *Iblis*, "So! So you've got the land monitor for me?" And the boy came to life and stood up. Then *Iblis* spoke again, saying, "Now, if this land monitor is slaughtered, the boy's mother will die, but if it isn't slaughtered, the girl's mother will die."

Well then—is the boy going to slaughter the land monitor, so that his own mother dies or will he spare it, so that the girl's mother dies? Which of the two will he choose do you think?

A Spirited Contending

There were once two young men who were courting the same girl, and each man had two spears. One day, on their way home with her, they passed through the bush, and a lion waylaid them. The girl fell down saying that her stomach was paining her. The lion leapt at them, and the first youth threw his spear, but the lion dodged and the spear fell to the ground. The youth threw his second spear also, and that, too, fell to the ground.

In his turn, the other young fellow, stepped forward and he, too, threw a spear, but like the rest it just fell to the ground. Then he threw his second spear, but again he missed the lion. So all their spears were used up and still the beast hadn't been hit.

Then one of the two youths said to the other, "Hurry, and run home. In my mother's hut, at the head of the bed, you'll find some spears. Bring them, and some water in a calabash, and some potash, too." At once, the boy ran off to do these things.

Meanwhile, the other young fellow leapt at the lion, and after a struggle, threw him, and taking his knife cut his throat. Then he lifted the lion into a squatting position, and the girl came over and lay down beside the lion. The youth got behind the mane and hid.

Soon the one who had left returned with the spears, the water, and the potash, but he couldn't find the other youth and the girl. A little further on, he bumped into the lion crouching there, with the girl lying in front of him, but he didn't recognize her. He said to himself, "So that was the trick was it? The two went off and ran away, and left the lion to kill someone else's child! Well, then, I can't let the lion live to do that again." And tossing away his spears and his little calabash of water and the potash, he threw himself at the lion. He grappled with it, and the lion, of course, fell right over. The girl and the other boy got up laughing.

Well then—which of the two, the boy who killed the lion, or the other boy who went and fetched the spears and the little calabash of water and the potash—which of the two of them showed greater spirit?